Praise
Juval L

"I attended both the Architect's Master Class and the Project Design Master Class. Before these two classes I had almost lost all hope of ever being able to figure out why the efforts of my team were never leading to a successful end, and I was struggling to find a working solution to stop the insane death march we were on. The Master Classes opened my eyes to a world where software development is elevated to the level of all other engineering disciplines and is conducted in a professional, predictable, and reliable manner, resulting in high-quality working software developed on time and within budget. The knowledge gained is priceless! From revealing how to create a solid and sound architecture, which withstands ever-changing user requirements, to the intricate details on how to plan and guide the project to a successful end—all this was presented with expertise and professionalism that are hard to match. Considering that every bit of distilled truth Juval shared with us in class is acquired, tested, and proven in real life, it transforms this learning experience into a powerful body of knowledge that is an absolute necessity for anyone who aspires to be a Software Architect."

—*Rossen Totev, software architect/project lead*

"The Project Design Master Class is a career-changing event. Having come from an environment where deadlines and budgets are almost pathologically abused, having the opportunity to learn from Juval was a godsend. Piece by piece he provided the parts and the appropriate tools for properly designing a project. The result is that costs and timelines are kept in check in the dynamic and even chaotic environment of modern software development. Juval says that you are going to engage in asymmetric warfare against overdue and over cost, and you walk away truly feeling that you have a gun to take to a knife fight. There is no magic—only the application of basic engineering and manufacturing tenets to software—but you will go back to your office feeling like a wizard."

—*Matt Robold, software development manager, West Covina Service Group*

"Fantastic experience. Changed my way of thinking on how to approach software development. I always knew some of what I was thinking was right with regard to design and coding. I never could express it in words but now I have them. It not only affects my way of thinking about software design but also other types of design."

—*Lee Messick, lead architect*

"The software project I work on was plagued with breakneck deadlines for years. Trying to understand software development methodologies and proper process felt like an energy drain because I had to battle management's unwillingness to change, on top of meeting the unreasonable demands of my clients. I was fighting a war on two fronts and felt hopeless. I felt like a rōnin. The Master Class provided a rush of clarity I never knew existed. It taught the exact knowledge that I was searching for. I learned profound techniques that transformed my understanding of how software projects operate. I now have the tools to efficiently and effectively navigate my project in a torrent of never-ending requirement changes. In a world of chaos this class brought order. I am forever grateful to IDesign. My life will never be the same."

—*Aaron Friedman, software architect*

"Life changing. I feel like a tuned piano after collecting dust for a couple of decades."

—*Jordan Jan, CTO/architect*

"The course was amazing. Easily this was the most intense but rewarding week of my professional life."

—*Stoil Pankov, software architect*

"Learning from Juval Löwy has changed my life. I went from being just a developer to being a true software architect, applying engineering principals from other disciplines to design not just software, but also my career."

—*Kory Torgersen, software architect*

"The Architect Master Class is a life lesson on skills and design—which I took twice. It was so transformational the first time I attended that I wished I had taken this class decades back, when I started my career. Even taking it for the second time has only gotten me to 25% because the ideas are so profound. The required brain rewiring and unlearning is really painful, but I needed to come back again with more of my colleagues. Finally, every day that goes by I reflect back on what Juval said in the classes and use that to help my teams implementing even the small things so that we can all eventually call ourselves Professional Engineers. (P.S. I took 100 pages of notes second time around!)"

—*Jaysu Jeyachandran, software development manager, Nielsen*

"If you are frustrated, lacking energy, and demotivated after seeing and experiencing many failed attempts of our industry, the class is a boost of rejuvenation. It takes you to the next level of professional maturity and also gives you the hope and confidence that you can apply things properly. You will leave the Project Design Master Class with a new mindset and enough priceless tools that will give you no excuse to ever fail a software project. You get to practice, you get your hands dirty, you get insight, and experience. Yes, you CAN be accurate when it is time to provide your stakeholders with the cost, the time, and the risk of a project. Now, just don't wait for a company to send you to this class. If you are serious about your career, you should hurry to take this or any IDesign Master Classes. It is the best self-investment you can make. Thank the entire great team of IDesign for their continuous efforts in helping the software industry become a solid engineering discipline."

—*Lucian Marian, software architect, Mirabel*

"As someone in their late twenties, relatively early in their career, I can honestly say that this course has changed my life and the way I view my career path. I honestly expect this to be one of the most pivotal points of my life."

—*Alex Karpowich, software architect*

"I wanted to thank you for a (professional) life-changing week. Usually I can't sit at class more than 50% of the time—it is boring and they don't teach me anything I couldn't teach myself or already know. In the Architect's Master Class I sat for nine hours a day and couldn't get enough of it: I learned what my responsibilities are as an architect (I thought the architect is only the software designer), the engineering aspect of software, the importance of delivering not only on time but also on budget and on quality, not to wait to 'grow' to be an architect but to manage my career, and how to quantify and measure what I previously considered as hunches. I have much more insight from this week and many pieces are now in place. I can't wait to attend the next Master Class."

—*Itai Zolberg, software architect*

RIGHTING SOFTWARE

RIGHTING SOFTWARE

A METHOD FOR SYSTEM
AND PROJECT DESIGN

Juval Löwy

✦Addison-Wesley

Boston • Columbus • New York • San Francisco • Amsterdam • Cape Town
Dubai • London • Madrid • Milan • Munich • Paris • Montreal • Toronto • Delhi • Mexico City
São Paulo • Sydney • Hong Kong • Seoul • Singapore • Taipei • Tokyo

Library of Congress Control Number: 2019950124

ISBN-13: 978-0-13-652403-8
ISBN-10: 0-13-652403-6

1 2019

To My Father, Thomas Charles (Tommy) Löwy

CONTENTS

PREFACE

Hardly anyone gets into software development because they were forced into it. Many literally fall in love with programming and decide to pursue it for a living. And yet there is a vast gap between what most hoped their career would be like and the dark, depressing reality of software development. The software industry as a whole is in a deep crisis. What makes the crisis so acute is that it is multi-dimensional; every aspect of software development is broken:

- **Cost.** There is weak correlation between the budget set for a project and what it will actually cost to develop the system. Many organizations do not even try to address the cost issue, perhaps because they simply do not know how, or perhaps because doing so will force them to recognize they cannot afford the system. Even if the cost of the first version of a new system is justified, often the cost across the life of the system is much higher than what it should have been due to poor design and an inability to accommodate changes. Over time, maintenance costs become so prohibitive that companies routinely decide to wipe the slate clean, only to end up shortly thereafter with an equally or even more expensive mess as a new system. No other industry opts for a clean slate on a regular basis simply because doing so does not make economic sense. Airlines maintain jumbo jets for decades, and a house can be a century old.

- **Schedule.** Deadlines are often just arbitrary and unenforceable constructs because they have little to do with the time it takes to actually develop the system. For most developers, deadlines are these useless things whooshing by as they plow ahead. If the development team does meet the deadline, everyone is surprised because the expectation is always for them to fail. This, too, is a direct result of a poor system design that causes changes and new work to ripple through the system and invalidate previously completed work. Moreover, it is the result of a very inefficient development process that ignores both the dependencies between activities and the fastest, safest way of building the system. Not only is the time to market for the whole system exceedingly long, but the time for a single feature may be just as inflated. It is bad enough when the project slips its schedule; it is even worse when the slip was hidden from management and customers since no one had any idea what the true status of the project was.

- **Requirements.** Developers often end up solving the wrong problems. There is a perpetual communication failure between the end customers or their internal intermediaries (such as marketing) and the development team. Most developers also fail to accommodate their failure to capture the requirements. Even when requirements are perfectly communicated, they will likely change over time. This change invalidates the design and unravels everything the team tried to build.

- **Staffing.** Even modest software systems are so complex that they have exceeded the capacity of the human brain to make sense of them. The internal and external complexity is a direct result of poor system architecture, which in turn leads to convoluted systems that are very difficult to maintain, extend, or reuse.

- **Maintenance.** Most software systems are not maintained by the same people who developed them. The new staff does not understand how the system operates, and as a result they constantly introduce new problems as they try to solve old ones. This quickly drives up the cost of maintenance and the time to market, and leads to clean-slate efforts or canceled projects.

- **Quality.** Perhaps nothing is as broken with software systems as quality. Software has bugs, and the word "software" is itself synonymous with "bugs." Developers cannot conceive of defect-free software systems. Fixing defects often increases the defect count, as does adding features, or just plain maintenance. Poor quality is a direct result of a system architecture that does not lend itself to being testable, understandable, or maintainable. Just as important, most projects do not account for essential quality-control activities and fail to allocate enough time for every activity to be completed in an impeccable manner.

Decades ago, the industry started developing software to solve the world's problems. Today, software development itself is a world-class problem. The problems of software development frequently manifest themselves in nontechnical ways such as a high-stress working environment, high turnover rate, burnout, lack of trust, low self-esteem, and even physical illness.

None of the problems in software development is new.[1] Indeed, some people have spent their entire careers in software development without seeing software done right even once. This leads them to believe that it simply cannot be done, and they are dismissive of any attempt to address these issues because "that's just the way things are." They may even fight those who are trying to improve software development. They have already concluded that this goal is impossible, so anyone who is trying to get better results is trying to do the impossible, which insults their intellect.

My own track record is a counterexample demonstrating that it is possible to successfully develop software systems. Every project for which I was responsible shipped on schedule, on budget, and with zero defects. I continued this record after founding IDesign, where we have helped customers again and again deliver on their commitments.

This consistent, repeatable track record of success was no accident. My training and schooling were in systems engineering, of both physical systems and software systems, and it was easy to recognize the similarities across the two worlds. Applying practical principles to software design, ideas that are common-sense in other engineering fields made sense in software systems, too. It never occurred to me not to treat software development as engineering or to develop a system without a design or without a plan. I saw no need to compromise on my conviction, or to give in to expediencies because doing the right things just worked, and the appalling consequences of not doing so were plain to see. I was fortunate to have great mentors, to be at the right place at the right time to see what worked and what did not, to have the opportunity to participate early on in large critical efforts, and to be part of cultures of excellence.

In recent years, I have noticed that the industry's problems are getting worse. More and more software projects fail. These failures are getting more expensive in both time and money, and even completed projects tend to stray further afield from their original commitments. The crisis is worsening not just because the systems are getting bigger or because of the cloud, aggressive deadlines, or higher rate of change. I suspect the real reason is that the knowledge of how to design and develop software systems is slowly fading from within the development ranks. Once, most teams had a veteran who mentored the young and handed down the tribal knowledge. Nowadays these mentors have moved on or are retiring. In their absence, the rank and file is left with access to infinite information but zero knowledge.

---

1. Edsger W. Dijkstra, "The Humble Programmer: ACM Turing Lecture," *Communications of the ACM* 15, no. 10 (October 1972): 859–866.

I wish there was just one thing you could do to fix the software crisis such as using a process, a development methodology, a tool, or a technology. Unfortunately, to fix a multidimensional problem, you need a multidimensional solution. In this book I offer a unified remedy: righting software.

In the abstract, all I suggest is to design and develop software systems using engineering principles. The good news is that there is no need to reinvent the wheel. Other engineering disciplines are quite successful, so the software industry can borrow their key universal design ideas and adapt them to software. You will see in this book a set of first principles in software engineering, as well as a comprehensive set of tools and techniques that apply to software systems and projects. To succeed, you have to assume an engineering perspective. Ensuring that the software system is maintainable, extensible, reusable, affordable, and feasible in terms of time and risk are all engineering aspects, not technical aspects. These engineering aspects are traced directly to the design of the system and the project. Since the term **software engineer** largely refers to a software developer, the term **software architect** has emerged to describe the person in the team who owns all the design aspects of the project. Accordingly, I refer to the reader as a software architect.

The ideas in this book are not the only things you will need to get right, but they certainly are a good start because they treat the root cause of the problems mentioned earlier. That root cause is poor design, be it of the software system itself or of the project used to build that system. You will see that it is quite possible to deliver software on schedule and on budget and to design systems that meet every conceivable requirement. The results are also systems that are easy to maintain, extend, and reuse. I hope that by practicing these ideas you will right not just your system but your career and rekindle your passion for software development.

How This Book Is Organized

The book demonstrates a structured engineering approach to system and project design. The methodology has two parts, reflected by the structure of this book: system design (commonly known as architecture) and project design. Both parts complement each other and are required for success. The appendices provide some supplemental content to the main discussion.

In most technical books, each chapter addresses a single topic and discusses it in depth. This makes the book easier to write, but that is typically not how people learn. In contrast, in this book, the teaching is analogous to a spiral. In both parts of the book, each chapter reiterates ideas from the previous chapters, going deeper or developing ideas using additional insight across multiple aspects. This mimics the natural learning process. Each chapter relies on those that preceded it, so you should read the chapters in order. Both parts of the book include a detailed case study that demonstrates the ideas as well as additional aspects. At the same time, to keep the iterations concise, as a general rule I usually avoid repeating myself, so even key points are discussed once.

Here is a brief summary of the chapters and appendices:

Chapter 1, *The Method*

Chapter 1 introduces this key idea: To succeed, you must design both the system and the project to build it. Both designs are essential for eventual success. You cannot design the project without the architecture, and it is pointless to design a system that you cannot build.

PART I: SYSTEM DESIGN

Chapter 2, *Decomposition*

Chapter 2 is dedicated to decomposing the system into the components that make up its architecture. Most people decompose systems in the worst possible way, so the chapter starts with explaining what not to do. Once that is established, you will see how to correctly decompose the system, and learn a set of simple analysis tools and observations that help in that process.

Chapter 3, *Structure*

Chapter 3 improves on the ideas of Chapter 2 by introducing structure. You will see how to capture requirements, how to layer your architecture, the taxonomy of the components of the architecture, their interrelationships, specific classification guidelines, and some related issues such as subsystems design.

Chapter 4, *Composition*

Chapter 4 shows how to assemble the system components into a valid composition that addresses the requirements. This short chapter contains several of the book's key design principles, and it leverages the previous two chapters into a powerful mental tool you will use in every system.

Chapter 5, *System Design Example*

Chapter 5 is an extensive case study that demonstrates the system design ideas discussed so far. This final iteration of the system design spiral presents an actual system, aligns the system design with the business, and shows how to produce the architecture and validate it.

PART II: PROJECT DESIGN

Chapter 6, *Motivation*

Since most people have never even heard of—let alone practiced—project design, this chapter introduces the concept and provides the motivation for engaging in project design. This is iteration zero of the project design spiral.

Chapter 7, *Project Design Overview*

Chapter 7 provides a broad overview of how to design a project. It starts by defining success in software development, and then presents the key concepts of educated decisions, project staffing, project network, critical path, scheduling, and cost. The chapter covers most of the ideas and techniques used in subsequent chapters, and it ends with an important discussion of roles and responsibilities.

Chapter 8, *Network and Float*

Chapter 8 dives into the project network and its use as a design tool. You will see how to model the project as a network diagram, learn the key concept of float, understand how to use floats in staffing and scheduling, and recognize how floats relate to risk.

Chapter 9, *Time and Cost*

Chapter 9 defines the possible tradeoffs between time and cost in any project and prescribes ways to accelerate any project by working cleaning and correctly. Beyond that, you will learn the key concepts of compression, the time–cost curve, and the elements of cost.

Chapter 10, *Risk*

Chapter 10 presents the missing element in most projects: quantified risk. You will see how to measure and map risk to the time and cost concepts from the previous chapter, and how to calculate risk based on the network. Risk is often the best way of evaluating options and is a first-class planning tool.

Chapter 11, *Project Design in Action*

Chapter 11 puts all the concepts of the previous chapters into use via a systematic walkthrough of the steps involved in designing a project. While it has the makings of an example, the objective is to demonstrate the thought process used when designing a project, as well as how to prepare for review by business decision makers.

Chapter 12, *Advanced Techniques*

Following the spiral model of learning, this chapter offers advanced techniques and concepts. These techniques are useful in projects with all levels of complexity, from the simple to the most challenging. These advanced techniques complement the previous chapters and each other, and you will often use them in combination.

Chapter 13, *Project Design Example*

Chapter 13 is the project design example corresponding to the system design example of Chapter 5. It, too, is a case study demonstrating the end-to-end process of designing a project. The focus in this chapter is on the case study and less about the techniques.

Chapter 14, *Concluding Thoughts*

This final chapter takes a step back from the technical aspects of design and offers a collection of guidelines, tips, perspectives, and development process ideas. It starts by answering the important question of when to design a project, and it ends with the effect project design has on quality.

APPENDICES

Appendix A, *Project Tracking*

Appendix A shows you how to track the project's progress with regard to the plan and how to take corrective actions when needed. Project tracking is more about project management than it is about project design, but it is crucial in assuring you meet your commitments once the work starts.

Appendix B, *Service Contract Design*

The architecture itself is broad and coarse, and you have to design the details of each of its components. The most important of these details is the service contract. Appendix B points you toward the correct way of designing service contracts. In addition, the discussion of modularity, size, and cost resonates very well with most chapters in this book.

Appendix C, *Design Standard*

Appendix C is a consolidated list of the key directives, guidelines, and dos and don'ts mentioned throughout this book. The standard is terse and is all about the "what," not the "why." The rationale behind the standard is found in the rest of the book.

SOME ASSUMPTIONS ABOUT THE READER

While this book targets software architects, it has a much broader audience. I assume that you, the reader, are an architect or senior software professional, a project manager, or someone who wears multiple hats. That said, aspiring developers wanting to grow their skill set will benefit greatly from the book. Regardless of your current position, this book will open doors for you through the rest of your career. You may not be an accomplished architect when you first pick up this book, but you will be among the top in the world once you have read it and have mastered the methodology.

The techniques and ideas for the book apply regardless of programming language (such as C++, Java, C#, and Python), platform (such as Windows, Linux, mobile, on-premise, and cloud), and project size (from the smallest to the largest projects). They also cross all industries (from healthcare to defense), all business models, and company sizes (from the startup to the large corporation).

The most important assumption I have made about the reader is that you care about what you do, at a deep level, and the current failures and waste distresses you. You want to do better but lack guidance or are confused by bad practices.

WHAT YOU NEED TO USE THIS BOOK

The only prerequisite for this book is an open mind. Past failures and frustration are a plus.

CONVENTIONS USED IN THIS BOOK

The book uses the following typographic conventions:

Bold
Used for defining terms and concepts.

Directive
Used for first principles, design rules, or key guidance and advice.

Reserved Words
Used for when referring to reserved words of the methodology.

> **Note**   This text style indicates a general note.

> **Caution**   This text style indicates a warning or caution.

ADDITIONAL ONLINE RESOURCES

The web page for this book provides sample files, addenda, and errata. You can access this page at the following address:

http://www.rightingsoftware.org

You will find the example files and related supporting material in this book under the "Download Support Files" link.

For additional information about this book, go to

informit.com/title/9780136524038.

You can also contact the author at this address:

http://www.idesign.net

REGISTER YOUR PRODUCT

Register your copy of *Righting Software* on the InformIT site for convenient access to updates and/or corrections as they become available. To start the registration process, go to informit.com/register and log in or create an account. Enter the product ISBN (9780136524038) and click Submit. Look on the Registered Products tab for an Access Bonus Content link next to this product, and follow that link to access any available bonus materials. If you would like to be notified of exclusive offers on new editions and updates, please check the box to receive email from us.

ACKNOWLEDGMENTS

Let me start by thanking the two who urged me to write the book, each in their own unique way: Gad Meir and Jarkko Kemppainen.

Thanks go to the development editor and sounding board, Dave Killian: Any more editing and I would have to list you as a co-author. Next, thanks to Beth Siron for reviewing the raw manuscript. The following people contributed their time by reviewing the draft: Chad Michel, Doug Durham, George Stevens, Josh Loyd, Riccardo Bennett-Lovsey, and Steve Land.

Finally, I am grateful to my wife, Dana, who keeps inspiring me to write and makes it possible for me to take the time away from the family; and to my parents, who imparted to me the love for engineering.

ABOUT THE AUTHOR

Juval Löwy, founder of IDesign, is a master software architect specializing in system and project design. He has helped countless companies around the world deliver quality software on schedule and on budget. Recognized by Microsoft as one of the world's top experts and industry leaders, he participated in internal strategic design reviews for C#, WCF, and related technologies, and was named a "Software Legend." He has published several best-sellers and numerous articles on almost every aspect of modern software development. Löwy speaks frequently at major international software development conferences and conducts Master Classes around the world, teaching thousands of professionals the skills required of modern software architects and how to take an active role as design, process, and technology leaders.

For the beginner architect, there are many options.

For the master architect, there are but a few.

1

THE METHOD

The Zen of Architects[1] simply states that for the beginner architect, there are many options of doing pretty much anything. For the master architect, however, there are only a few good options, and typically only one.

Beginner architects are often perplexed by the plethora of patterns, ideas, methodologies, and possibilities for designing their software system. The software industry is bursting at the seams with ideas and people eager to learn and improve themselves, including you who are reading this book. However, since there are so few correct ways of doing any given design task, you might as well focus only on those and ignore the noise. Master software architects know to do just that; as if by supernatural inspiration, they immediately zoom in and yield the correct design solution.

The Zen of Architects applies not just to the system design but also to the project that builds it. Yes, there are countless ways of structuring the project and assigning work to the team members, but are they all equally safe, fast, cheap, useful, effective, and efficient? The master architect also designs the project to build the system and even helps management decide if they can afford the project in the first place.

True mastery of any subject is a journey. With very few exceptions, no one is a born expert. My own career is a case in point. I started as a junior architect almost 30 years ago when the term *architect* was not commonly used within software organizations. Moving on first as a project architect then as a division architect, by the late 1990s I was the chief software architect of a Fortune 100 company in Silicon Valley. In 2000, I founded IDesign as a company solely dedicated to software design. At IDesign, we have since designed hundreds of systems and projects. While each engagement had its own specific architecture and project plan, I observed that no matter the customer, the project, the system, the technology, or the developers, my design recommendations were, in the abstract, the same.

---

1. https://en.wikipedia.org/wiki/Zen_Mind,_Beginner's_Mind

I therefore asked myself a simple question: Do you really have to be a master software architect with decades of experience designing systems and dozens of projects under your belt to know the right thing to do? Or can you structure it somehow so that anyone with a clear understanding of the underlying methodology can produce a decent system and project design?

The answer to the second question is a resounding affirmative. I call the result *The Method*, and it is the subject of this book. Having applied *The Method* across a multitude of projects, having taught and mentored a few thousand architects the world over, I can attest that, when applied properly, it works. I am not discounting here the value of having a good attitude, technical skills, and analytical capabilities. These are necessary ingredients for success regardless of the methodology you use. Sadly, these ingredients are insufficient; I often see projects fail despite having people with all these great qualities and attributes. However, when combined with *The Method*, these ingredients give you a fighting chance. By grounding your design on sound engineering principles, you will learn to steer clear of the misguided practices and false intuition that are the prevailing wisdom.

WHAT IS THE METHOD?

The Method is a simple and effective analysis and design technique. You can express *The Method* as a formula:

$$\textit{The Method} = \text{System Design} + \text{Project Design}$$

With system design, *The Method* lays out a way of breaking down a big system into small modular components. *The Method* offers guidelines for the structure, role, and semantics of the components and how these components should interact. The result is the architecture of the system.

With project design, *The Method* helps you provide management with several options for building the system. Each option is some combination of schedule, cost, and risk. Each option also serves as the system assembly instructions, and it sets up the project for execution and tracking.

Project design is the second part of the book and is far more important for success than system design. Even a mediocre system design can succeed if the project has adequate time and resources and if the risk is acceptable. However, even a world-class system design will fail if the project has inadequate time or resources to build the system or if the project is too risky. Project design is also more intricate than system design and, as such, requires additional tools, ideas, and techniques.

Because it combines system and project design, *The Method* is actually a design process. Over the years, the software industry has given great attention to the development process but has devoted little attention to the design process. This book aims at filling this gap.

DESIGN VALIDATION

Design validation is critical because an organization should not risk having a team start developing against an inadequate architecture or developing a system the organization cannot afford to build. *The Method* supports and enables this critical task, allowing the architect to assert with reasonable confidence that the proposed design is adequate; that is, the design fulfills two key objectives. First, the design must address the customer requirements. Second, the design must address the organization or the team capabilities and constraints.

Once the coding starts, changing the architecture is often unacceptable due to the cost and schedule implications. In practice, this means that without system design validation, there is risk of locking in, at best, an imperfect architecture and, at worst, a monstrosity. The organization will have to try to live with the resulting system for the next few years and several versions until the next big rewrite. A poorly designed software system may seriously damage the business, depriving it of the ability to respond to business opportunities, and may even financially ruin it with escalating software maintenance costs.

Early validation of the design is imperative. For example, discovering three years after the work started that a particular idea or the whole architecture was wrong is intellectually interesting but of no practical value. Ideally, one week into the project, you must know if the architecture is going to hold water (or not). Anything longer runs the risk of commencing development with a questionable architecture. The following chapters describe precisely how to validate a system design.

Note that I am referring here to the system design, the architecture, not the detailed design of the system. Detailed design produces for each component in the architecture the key implementation artifacts, such as interfaces, class hierarchies, and data contracts. Detailed design takes longer to produce, can be done during the project execution, and may change as the system is constructed or evolved.

Similarly, you must validate your project design. Running out of time or running over budget (or both) mid-project is simply unacceptable. Failing to meet your commitments will limit your career. You must proactively validate your project design to ensure that the team at hand can deliver the project.

In addition to providing the architecture and project plans, the objective of *The Method* is to remove design as a risk to the project. No project should fail because the architecture was too complex for developers to build and maintain. *The Method* discovers the architecture efficiently and effectively and does so in a short period of time. The same benefit applies to project design. No project should fail because it did not have enough time or resources from the start. This book shows you how to accurately calculate the project duration and costs and how to drive educated decisions.

TIME CRUNCH

Using *The Method*, you can produce an entire system design in mere days, typically in three to five days, with project design taking similar time. Given the lofty goals of the effort, namely, producing the system architecture and the project plans for a new system, the duration may look too short. Typical business systems get the option of a new design only every few years. Why not spend 10 days on the architecture? Measured against a system lifetime of years, five additional days are not even a rounding error. However, adding design time often does not improve the result and can even be detrimental.

Most work environments have horrendously inefficient time management, mostly due to human nature. A time crunch forces you (and the others involved) to focus, to prioritize, and to produce the design. You should go through *The Method* quickly and decisively.

In general, design is not time-consuming (as opposed to implementation). Building architects charge hourly and often work only a week or two at most designing a house. Constructing a house from the architect's design might take an agonizing two to three years of working with contractors, and yet the architect did not take long to produce the architecture.

The time crunch also helps avoid design gold plating. Parkinson's law[2] states that work always expands to fill the allotted time. Given 10 days to complete a design that could be completed in five days, the architect will likely work on the design for 10 days. The architect will use the extra time to design frivolous aspects that add nothing but complexity, disproportionally increasing the cost of implementation and maintenance for years to come. Limiting the design time forces you to produce a good-enough design.

---

2. Cyril N. Parkinson, "Parkinson's Law," *The Economist* (November 19, 1955).

ELIMINATING ANALYSIS-PARALYSIS

Analysis-paralysis is a predicament that occurs when someone (or a group) who is otherwise capable, clever, and even hardworking (as are most software architects) is stuck in a seemingly endless cycle of analysis, design, new revelations, and back to more analysis. The person or group is effectively paralyzed and precluded from producing any productive outcome.

Design Decisions Tree

The main reason for the paralysis is being unaware of the design decision tree for both the system and the project. The design decision tree is a general concept that applies to all design tasks, not just in software engineering. The design of any complex entity is a collection of many smaller design decisions, arranged hierarchically in a tree-like structure. Each branching in the tree represents a possible design option that leads to additional, finer design decisions. The leaves of the tree represent complete design solutions for the requirements. Each leaf is a consistent, distinct, and valid solution, different in some ways from all other leaves.

When the person or group in charge of producing the design is unaware of the correct decision tree, they start at some place other than the root of the tree. Invariably, at some point, a downstream design decision will invalidate a prior decision; all decisions made in between these two points will be invalid. Designing this way is akin to performing a bubble sort of the design decision tree. Since bubble sort roughly involves as many operations as the square of the number of elements involved, the penalty is severe. A simple software system requiring some 20 system and project design decisions potentially has 400 design iterations if you do not follow the decision tree. Going through so many meetings (even if you spread it over time) is paralysis. Being given the time to perform even 40 iterations is unlikely. When the system and project design effort is out of time, development will commence with the system and the project in an immature state. This defers discoveries that invalidate the design decisions to an even worse point in the future when time, effort, and artifacts already are associated with the incorrect choices. In essence, you have maximized the cost of the incorrect design decision.

Software System Design Decision Tree

As it turns out, most software business systems have a lot in common, and at least the outline of the decision tree is not only common but also uniform across such systems. The leaves are naturally different.

The Method provides the decision tree of a typical business system both for the system design and for the project design. Only after you have designed the system is there any point in designing the project to build that system. Each of these design efforts, both the system and the project, has its own subtree of design decisions. *The Method* guides you through it, starting at the root, avoiding rework and reevaluation of prior decisions.

One of the most valuable techniques in pruning the decision tree is the application of constraints. As pointed by Dr. Fredrick Brooks,[3] contrary to common wisdom or intuition, the worst design problem is a clean canvas. Without constraints, the design should be easy, right? Wrong. The clean canvas should terrify every architect. There are infinite ways of getting it wrong or going against unstated constraints. The more constraints there are, the easier the design task is. The less leeway allowed, the more obvious and clear the design. In a totally constrained system, there is nothing to design: it is what it is. Since there are always constraints (whether explicit or implicit), by following the design decision tree, *The Method* places increasing constraints on the system and the project, to the point that the design converges and resolves quickly.

COMMUNICATION

An important advantage of *The Method* is in communicating design ideas. Once participants are familiar with the structure of the architecture and the design semantics, *The Method* enables sharing design ideas and precisely conveying what the design requires. You can communicate the thought process behind the design to the team. You should share the tradeoffs and insights that guided you in the architecture, documenting in an unambiguous way the operational assumptions and the resulting design decisions.

This level of clarity and transparency in design intent is critical for architecture survival. A good design is one that was well conceived, survived through development, and ended up as working bits on customer machines. You must be able to communicate the design to the developers and ensure that they value the intent and the concepts behind the design. You must enforce the design by using reviews, inspection, and mentoring. *The Method* excels at this type of communication because of the combination of well-defined service semantics and structure.

Rest assured that if the developers who are tasked with building the system do not understand and value the design, they will butcher it. No amount of design or code

---

3. Frederick P. Brooks Jr., *The Design of Design: Essays from a Computer Scientist* (Upper Saddle River, NJ: Addison-Wesley, 2010).

review can ever fix that butchery. The purpose of reviews should be to catch the unintended deviation from the architecture as early as possible.

The same holds true when it is time to communicate the project plan to project managers, managers, or other stakeholders. Clear, unambiguous, comparable options are key to educated decisions. When people make the wrong decisions, it is often because they do not understand the project and have the wrong mental model for how projects behave. By producing the correct models for the project across time, cost, and risk, the architect can enable the right decision. *The Method* provides the right vocabulary and metrics for communicating with decision makers in a simple and concise way. Once managers are exposed to the possibilities of project design, they will become its greatest advocates and insist on working that way. No amount of passionate arguments can accomplish what a simple set of charts and numbers can. Moreover, project design is important not only at the beginning of the project. As the work commences, you can use the tools of project design to communicate to management the effect and viability of changes. Appendix A discusses project tracking and managing changes.

Besides communicating the design to developers and managers, *The Method* allows the architect to accurately and easily communicate the design to other architects. The insights you gain from review and criticism in this manner are invaluable.

WHAT THE METHOD IS NOT

Brooks wrote in 1987, "There is no silver bullet."[4] Certainly, *The Method* is not one. Using *The Method* does not guarantee success and may make matters worse if used in isolation from anything else in the project or just for the sake of using it.

The Method does not take away the architect's creativity and effort in producing the right architecture. The architect is still responsible for distilling the required behavior of the system. The architect is still liable for getting the architecture wrong or for failing to communicate the design to developers or for failing to lead the development effort until delivery without compromising the architecture, all in the face of mounting pressure. Furthermore, as illustrated in the second part of this book, the architect must produce a viable project design, stemming out of the architecture. The architect must calibrate the project to the available resources, to

---

4. Frederick P. Brooks Jr., "No Silver Bullet: Essence and Accidents of Software Engineering," *Computer* 20, no. 4 (April 1987).

what the resources can produce, to the risks involved, and to the deadline. Going through the motions of project design for their own sake is pointless. The architect must eliminate any bias and produce the correct set of planning assumption and resulting calculations.

The Method provides a good starting point for system and project design, along with a list of the things to avoid. However, *The Method* works only as long as you do it truthfully while devoting the time and mental energy to gather the required information. You must fundamentally care about the design process and what it produces.

Part I

SYSTEM DESIGN

2

DECOMPOSITION

Software architecture is the high-level design and structure of the software system. While designing the system is quick and inexpensive compared with building the system, it is critical to get the architecture right. Once the system is built, if the architecture is defective, wrong, or just inadequate for your needs, it is extremely expensive to maintain or extend the system.

The essence of the architecture of any system is the breakdown of the concept of the system as a whole into its comprising components, be it a car, a house, a laptop, or a software system. A good architecture also prescribes how these components interact at run-time. The act of identifying the constituent components of a system is called **system decomposition**.

The correct decomposition is critical. A wrong decomposition means wrong architecture, which in turn inflicts a horrendous pain in the future, often leading to a complete rewrite of the system.

In years past, these building blocks were C++ objects and later COM, Java, or .NET components. In a modern system and in this book, services (as in service-orientation) are the most granular unit of the architecture. However, the technology used to implement the components and their details (such as interfaces, operations, and class hierarchies) are detailed design aspects, not system decomposition. In fact, such details can change without ever affecting the decomposition and therefore the architecture.

Unfortunately, the majority, if not the vast majority, of all software systems are not designed correctly and arguably are designed in the worst possible way. The design flaws are a direct result of the incorrect decomposition of the systems. This chapter therefore starts by explaining why the common ways of decomposition are flawed to the core and then discusses the rationale behind *The Method*'s decomposition approach. You will also see some powerful and helpful techniques to leverage when designing the system.

AVOID FUNCTIONAL DECOMPOSITION

Functional decomposition decomposes a system into its building blocks based on the functionality of the system. For example, if the system needs to perform a set of operations, such as invoicing, billing, and shipping, you end up with the `Invoicing` service, the `Billing` service, and the `Shipping` service.

PROBLEMS WITH FUNCTIONAL DECOMPOSITION

The problems with functional decomposition are many and acute. At the very least, functional decomposition couples services to the requirements because the services are a reflection of the requirements. Any change in the required functionality imposes a change on the functional services. Such changes are inevitable over time and impose a painful future change to your system by requiring a new decomposition after the fact to reflect the new requirements. In addition to costly changes to the system, functional decomposition precludes reuse and leads to overly complex systems and clients.

Precluding Reuse

Consider a simple functionally decomposed system that uses three services A, B, and C, which are called in the order of A then B then C. Because functional decomposition is also decomposition based on time (call A and then call B), it effectively precludes individual reuse of services. Suppose another system also needs a B service (such as `Billing`). Built into the fabric of B is the notion that it was called after an A and before a C service (such as first `Invoicing`, and only then `Billing` against an invoice, and finally `Shipping`). Any attempt to lift the B service from the first system and drop it in the second system will fail because, in the second system, no one is doing A before it and C after it. When you lift the B service, the A and the C services are hanging off it. B is not an independent reusable service at all—A, B, and C are a clique of tightly coupled services.

Too Many or Too Big

One way of performing functional decomposition is to have as many services as there are variations of the functionalities. This decomposition leads to an explosion of services, since a decently sized system may have hundreds of functionalities. Not only do you have too many services, but these services often duplicate a lot of the common functionality, each customized to their case. The explosion of services inflicts a disproportional cost in integration and testing and increases overall complexity.

Another functional decomposition approach is to lump all possible ways of performing the operations into mega services. This leads to bloating in the size of the services, making them overly complex and impossible to maintain. Such god monoliths become ugly dumping grounds for all related variations of the original functionality, with intricate relationships inside and between the services.

Functional decomposition, therefore, tends to make services either too big and too few or too small and too many. You often see both afflictions side by side in the same system.

> **Note**   Appendix B, devoted to service contract design, further discusses the dire consequences of too many or too big services and the effect on the project.

Clients Bloat and Coupling

Functional decomposition often leads to flattening of the system hierarchy. Since each service or building block is devoted to a specific functionality, someone must combine these discrete functionalities into a required behavior. That someone is often the client. When the client is the one orchestrating the services, the system becomes a flat two-tier system: clients and services, and any notion of additional layering is gone. Suppose your system needs to perform three operations (or functionalities): A, B and C, in that order. As illustrated in Figure 2-1, the client must stitch the services together.

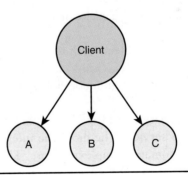

Figure 2-1 Bloated client orchestrating functionality

By bloating the client with the orchestration logic, you pollute the client code with the business logic of the system. The client is no longer just about invoking operations on the system or presenting information to users. The client is now intimately aware of all internal services, how to call them, how to handle their errors, how to compensate for the failure of B after the success of A, and so on. Calling the services is almost always synchronous because the client proceeds along the expected sequence of A then B then C, and it is difficult otherwise to ensure the order of the calls while remaining responsive to the outside world. Furthermore, the client is now coupled to the required functionality. Any change in the operations, such as calling B' instead of B, forces the client to reflect that change. The hallmark of a bad design is when any change to the system affects the client. Ideally, the client and services should be able to evolve independently. Decades ago, software engineers discovered that it was a bad idea to include business logic with the client. Yet, when designed as in Figure 2-1, you are forced to pollute the client with the business logic of sequencing, ordering, error compensation, and duration of the calls. Ultimately, the client is no longer the client—it has become the system.

What if there are multiple clients (e.g., rich clients, web pages, mobile devices), each trying to invoke the same sequence of functional services? You are destined to duplicate that logic across the clients, making maintenance of all those clients wasteful and expensive. As the functionality changes, you now are forced to keep up with that change across multiple clients, since all of them will be affected. Often, once that is the case, developers try to avoid any changes to the functionality of the services because of the cascading effect it will have on the clients. With the multiplicity of clients, each with its own version of the sequencing tailored to its needs, it becomes even more challenging to change or interchange services, thus precluding reuse of the same behavior across the clients. Effectively, you end up maintaining multiple complex systems, trying to keep them all in sync. Ultimately, this leads to both stifling of innovation and increased time to market when the changes are forced through development and production.

As an example of the problems with functional decomposition discussed thus far, consider Figure 2-2. It is the visualization of cyclomatic complexity analysis of a system I reviewed. The design methodology used was functional decomposition.

Cyclomatic complexity measures the number of independent paths through the code of a class or service. The more the internals are convoluted and coupled, the higher the cyclomatic complexity score. The tool used to generate Figure 2-2 measured and rated the various classes in the system. In the visualization, the more complex the class is, the larger and darker it is in color. At first glance, you see three very large and very complex classes. How easy would it be to maintain MainForm? Is this just a form, a UI element, a clean conduit from the user to the system, or is it the system? Observe the complexity required to set up MainForm in the size and shade of FormSetup. Not to be outdone, Resources is very complex, since it is very complex to change the resources used in MainForm.

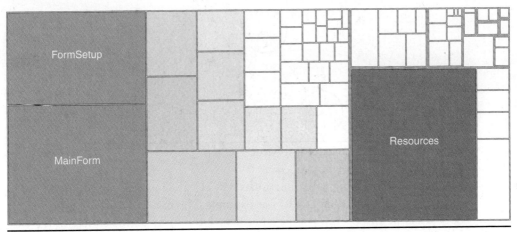

Figure 2-2 Complexity analysis of a functional design

Ideally, Resources should have been trivial, comprising simple lists of images and strings. The rest of the system is made up of dozens of small, simple classes, each devoted to a particular functionality. The smaller classes are literally in the shadow of the three massive ones. However, while each of the small classes may be trivial, the sheer number of the smaller classes is a complexity issue all on its own, involving intricate integration across that many classes. The result is both too many components and too big components as well as a bloated client.

Multiple Points of Entry

Another problem with the decomposition of Figure 2-1 is that it requires multiple points of entry to the system. The client (or clients) needs to enter the system in three places: once for the A, then for the B, then for the C service. This means there are multiple places to worry about authentication, authorization, scalability, instance management, transaction propagation, identities, hosting, and so on. When you need to change the way you perform any one of these aspects, you will need to change it in multiple places across services and clients. Over time, these multiple changes make adding new and different clients very expensive.

Services Bloating and Coupling

As an alternative to sequencing the functional services as in Figure 2-1, you can opt for what, on the face of it, appears as a lesser evil by having the functional services call each other, as shown in Figure 2-3.

The advantage of doing so is that you get to keep the clients simple and even asynchronous: the clients issue the call to the A service. The A service then calls B, and B calls C.

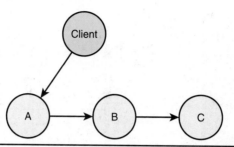

Figure 2-3 Chaining functional services

The problem now is that the functional services are coupled to each other and to the order of the functional calls. For example, you can call the `Billing` service only after the `Invoicing` service but before the `Shipping` service. In the case of Figure 2-3, built into the A service is the knowledge that it needs to call the B service. The B service can be called only after the A service and before the C service. A change in the required ordering of the calls is likely to affect all services up and down the chain because their implementation will have to change to reflect the new required order.

But Figure 2-3 does not reveal the full picture. The B service of Figure 2-3 is drastically different from that of Figure 2-1. The original B service performed only the B functionality. The B service in Figure 2-3 must be aware of the C service, and the B contract must contain the parameters that will be required by the C service to perform its functionality. These details were the responsibility of the client in Figure 2-1. The problem is compounded by the A service, which must now accommodate in its service contract the parameters required for calling the B and the C services for them to perform their respective business functionality. Any change to the B and C functionality is reflected in a change to the implementation of the A service, which is now coupled to them. This kind of bloating and coupling is depicted in Figure 2-4.

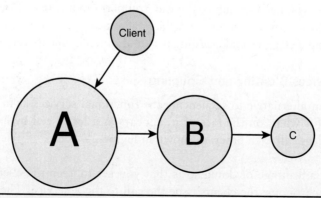

Figure 2-4 Chaining functionality leads to bloated services.

Sadly, even Figure 2-4 does not tell the whole truth. Suppose the A service performed the A functionality successfully and then proceeded to calling the B service to perform the B functionality. The B service, however, encountered an error and failed to execute properly. If A called B synchronously, then A must be intimately aware of the internal logic and state of B in order to recover its error. This means the B functionality must also reside in the A service. If A called B asynchronously, then the B service must now somehow reach back to the A service and undo the A functionality or contain the rollback of A within itself. In other words, the A functionality also resides in the B service. This creates tight coupling between the B service and the A service and bloats the B service with the need to compensate for the success of the A service. This situation is shown in Figure 2-5.

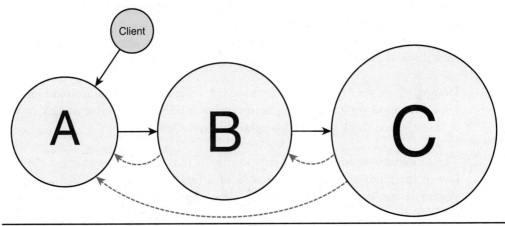

Figure 2-5 Additional bloating and coupling due to compensation

The issue is compounded in the C service. What if both the A and B functionalities succeeded and completed, but the C service failed to perform its business function? The C service must reach back to both the B and the A services to undo their operations. This creates far more bloating in the C service and couples it to the A and B services. Given the coupling and bloating in Figure 2-5, what will it take to replace the B service with a B' service that performs the functionality differently than B? What will be the adverse effects on the A and C services? Again, what degree of reuse exists in Figure 2-5 when the functionality in the services is asked for in other contexts, such as calling the B service after the D service and before the E service? Are A, B, and C three distinct services or just one fused mess?

REFLECTING ON FUNCTIONAL DECOMPOSITION

Functional decomposition holds an almost irresistible allure. It looks like a simple and clear way of designing the system, requiring you to simply list the required functionalities and then create a component in your architecture for each. Functional decomposition (and its kin, the domain decomposition discussed later) is how most systems are designed. Most people choose functional decomposition naturally, and it is likely what your computer science professor showed you in school. The prevalence of functional decomposition in poorly designed systems makes a near-perfect indicator of something to avoid. At all costs, you must resist the temptations of functional decomposition.

Nature of the Universe (TANSTAAFL)

You can prove that functional decomposition is precluded from ever working without using a single software engineering argument. The proof has to do with the very nature of the universe, specifically, the first law of thermodynamics. Stripping away the math, the first law of thermodynamics simply states that you cannot add value without sweating. A colloquial way of saying the same is: "There ain't no such thing as a free lunch."

Design, by its very nature, is a high-added-value activity. You are reading this book instead of yet another programming book because you value design, or put differently, you think design adds value, or even a lot of value.

The problem with functional decomposition is that it endeavors to cheat the first law of thermodynamics. The outcome of a functional decomposition, namely, system design, should be a high-added-value activity. However, functional decomposition is easy and straightforward: given a set of requirements that call for performing the A, B, and C functionalities, you decompose into the A, B, and C services. "No sweat!" you say. "Functional decomposition is so easy that a tool could do it." However, precisely because it is a fast, easy, mechanistic, and straightforward design, it also manifests a contradiction to the first law of thermodynamics. Since you cannot add value without effort, the very attributes that make functional decomposition so appealing are those that preclude functional decomposition from adding value.

The Anti-Design Effort

It will be an uphill struggle to convince colleagues and managers to do anything other than functional decomposition. "We have always done it that way," they will say. There are two ways to counter that argument. The first is replying, "And how many times have we met the deadline or the budget to which we committed? What were our quality and complexity like? How easy was it to maintain the system?"

The second is to perform an anti-design effort. Inform the team that you are conducting a design contest for the next-generation system. Split the team into halves, each in a separate conference room. Ask the first half to produce the best design for the system. Ask the second half to produce the worst possible design: a design that will maximize your inability to extend and maintain the system, a design that will disallow reuse, and so on. Let them work on it for one afternoon and then bring them together. When you compare the results, you will usually see they have produced the same design. The labels on the components may differ, but the essence of the design will be the same. Only now confess that they were not working on the same problem and discuss the implications. Perhaps a different approach is called for this time.

Example: Functional House

The fact you should never design using functional decomposition is a universal observation that has nothing to do with software systems. Consider building a house functionally, as if it were a software system. You start by listing all the required functionalities of the house, such as cooking, playing, resting, sleeping, and so on. You then create an actual component in the architecture for each functionality, as shown in Figure 2-6.

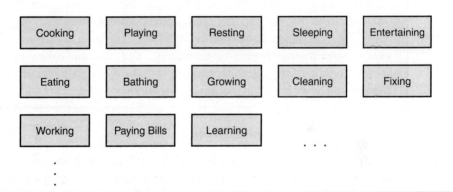

Figure 2-6 Functional decomposition of a house

While Figure 2-6 is already preposterous, the true insanity becomes evident only when it is time to build this house. You start with a clean plot of land and build cooking. Just cooking. You take a microwave oven out of its box and put it aside. Pour a small concrete pad, build a wood frame on the pad, cover it with countertop, and place the microwave on it. Build a small pantry for the microwave and hammer a tiny roof over it, connect just the microwave to the power grid. "We have cooking!" you announce to the boss and customers.

But is cooking really done? Can cooking ever be done this way? Where are you serving the meal, storing the leftovers, or disposing of trash? What about cooking over the gas stove? What will it take to duplicate this feat for cooking over the stove? What degree of reuse can you have between the two separate ways of expressing the functionality of cooking? Can you extend any one of them easily? What about cooking with a microwave somewhere else? What does it take to relocate the microwave? All of this mess is not even the beginning because it all depends on the type of cooking you perform. You need to build separate cooking functionality, perhaps, if cooking involves multiple appliances and differs by context—for example, if you are cooking breakfast, lunch, dinner, dessert, or snacks. You end up with either explosion of minute cooking services, each dedicated to a specific scenario that must be known in advance, or you end up with massive cooking service that has it all. Will you ever build a house like that? If not, why design and build a software system that way?

WHEN TO USE FUNCTIONAL DECOMPOSITION

The derision in these pages does not mean functional decomposition is a bad idea. Functional decomposition has a place—it is a decent requirements discovery technique. It helps architects (or product managers) discover hidden or implied areas of functionality. Starting at the top, even with vague functional requirements, you can drive functional decomposition to a very fine level, uncovering requirements and their relationship, arranging the requirements in a tree-like manner, and identifying redundancies or mutually exclusive functionalities. Extending functional decomposition into a design, however, is deadly. There should never be direct mapping between the requirements and the design.

AVOID DOMAIN DECOMPOSITION

The house design in Figure 2-6 is obviously absurd. In your house, you likely do the cooking in the kitchen, so an alternative decomposition of the house is shown in Figure 2-7. This form of decomposition is called **domain decomposition**: decomposing a system into building blocks based on the business domains, such as sales, engineering, accounting, and shipping. Sadly, domain decomposition such as Figure 2-7 shows is even worse than the functional decomposition of Figure 2-6. The reason domain decomposition does not work is that it is still functional decomposition in disguise: Kitchen is where you do the cooking, Bedroom is where you do the sleeping, Garage is where you do the parking, and so on.

In fact, every one of the functional areas of Figure 2-6 can be mapped to domains in Figure 2-7, which presents severe problems. While each bedroom may be unique, you must duplicate the functionality of sleeping in all of them. Further duplication occurs when sleeping in front of the TV in the living room or when entertaining guests in the kitchen (as almost all house parties end up in the kitchen).

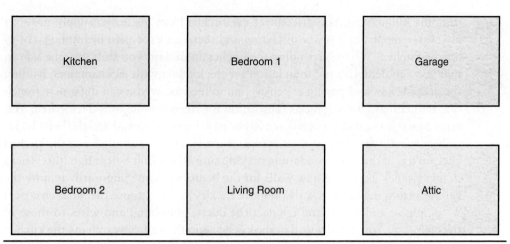

Figure 2-7 Domain decomposition of a house

Each domain often devolves into an ugly grab bag of functionality, increasing the internal complexity of the domain. The increased inner complexity causes you to avoid the pain of cross-domain connectivity, and communication across domains is typically reduced to simple state changes (CRUD-like) rather than actions triggering required behavior execution involving all domains. Composing more complex behaviors across domains is very difficult. Some functionalities are simply impossible in such domain decompositions. For example, in the house in Figure 2-7, where would you perform cooking that cannot take place in the kitchen (e.g., a barbecue)?

Building a Domain House

As with the pure functional approach, the real problems with domain decomposition become evident during construction. Imagine building a house along the decomposition of Figure 2-7. You start with a clean plot of land. You dig a trench for the foundation for the kitchen, pour concrete for the foundation (just for the kitchen), and add bolts in the concrete. You then erect the kitchen walls (all have to be exterior walls); bolt them to the foundation; run electrical wires and plumbing in the walls; connect the kitchen to the water, power, and gas supplies; connect the kitchen to the sewer discharge; add heating and cooling ducts and vents; connect the kitchen to a furnace; add water, power, and gas meters; build a roof over the kitchen; screw drywall on the inside; hang cabinets; coat the outside walls (all walls) with stucco; and paint it. You announce to the customer that the `Kitchen` is done and that milestone 1.0 is met.

Then you move on to the bedroom. You first bust the stucco off the kitchen walls to expose the bolts connecting the walls to the foundation and unbolt the kitchen from the foundation. You disconnect the kitchen from the power supply, gas supply, water supply, and sewer discharge and then use expensive hydraulic jacks to lift the kitchen. While suspending the kitchen in midair, you shift it to the side so that you can demolish the foundation for the kitchen with jackhammers, hauling the debris away and paying expensive dump fees. Now you can dig a new trench that will contain a continuous foundation for the bedroom and the kitchen. You pour concrete into the trenches to cast the new foundation and add the bolts hopefully at exactly the same spots as before. Next, you very carefully lower the kitchen back on top of the new foundation, making sure all the bolt holes align (this is next to impossible). You erect new walls for the bedroom. You temporarily remove the cabinets from the kitchen walls; remove the drywall to expose the inner electrical wires, pipes, and ducts; and connect the ducts, plumbing, and wires to those of the bedroom. You add drywall in the kitchen and the bedroom, rehang the kitchen cabinets, and add closets in the bedroom. You knock down any remaining stucco from the walls of the kitchen so that you can apply continuous, crack-free stucco on the outside walls. You must convert several of the previous outside walls of the kitchen to internal walls now, with implications on stucco, insulation, paint, and so on. You remove the roof of the kitchen and build a new continuous roof over the bedroom and the kitchen. You announce to the customer that milestone 2.0 is met, and `Bedroom 1` is done.

The fact that you had to rebuild the kitchen is not disclosed. The fact that building the kitchen the second time around was much more expensive and riskier than the first time is also undisclosed. What will it take to add another bedroom to this house? How many times will you end up building and demolishing the kitchen? How many times can you actually rebuild the kitchen before it crumbles into a shifting pile of useless debris? Was the kitchen really done when you announced it so? Rework penalties aside, what degree of reuse is there between the various parts of the house? How much more expensive is building a house this way? Why would it make sense to build a software system this way?

FAULTY MOTIVATION

The motivation for functional or domain decomposition is that the business or the customer wants its feature as soon as possible. The problem is that you can never deploy a single feature in isolation. There is no business value in `Billing` independent from `Invoicing` and `Shipping`.

The situation is even worse when legacy systems are involved. Rarely do developers get the privilege of a completely new, green-field system. Most likely there is an existing, decaying system that was designed functionally whose inflexibility and maintenance costs justify the new system.

Suppose your business has three functionalities A, B, and C, running in a legacy system. When building a new system to replace the old, you decide to build and, more important, deploy the A functionality first to satisfy the customers and managers who wish to see value early and often. The problem is that the business has no use for just A on its own. The business needs B and C as well. Performing A in the new system and B and C in the old system will not work, because the old system does not know about the new system and cannot execute just B and C. Doing A in both the old system and the new system adds no value and even has negative value due to the repeated work, so users are likely to revolt. The only solution is to somehow reconcile the old and the new systems. The reconciliation typically far eclipses in complexity the challenge of the original underlying business problem, so developers end up solving a far more complex problem. To use the house analogy again, what would it be like to live in a cramped old house while building a new house on the other side of town according to Figure 2-6 or Figure 2-7? Suppose you are building just cooking or the kitchen in the new house while continuing to live in the old house. Every time you are hungry, you have to drive to the new house and come back. You would not accept it with your house, so you should not inflict this kind of abuse on your customers.

TESTABILITY AND DESIGN

A crucial flaw of both functional and domain decomposition has to do with testing. With such designs, the level of coupling and complexity is so high that the only kind of testing developers can do is unit testing. However, that does not make unit testing important, and it is merely another example of the streetlight effect[1] (i.e., searching for something where it is easiest to look).

The sad reality is that unit testing is borderline useless. While unit testing is an essential part of testing, it cannot really test a system. Consider a jumbo jet that has numerous internal components (pumps, actuators, servos, gears, turbines, etc.). Now suppose all components have independently passed unit testing perfectly, but that is the only testing that took place before the components were assembled into an aircraft. Would you dare board that airplane? The reason unit testing is so marginal is that in any complex system, the defects are not going to be in any of the units but rather are the result of the interactions between the units. This is why you instinctively know that, while each component in the jumbo jet example works, the aggregate could be horribly wrong. Worse, even if the complex system is at a perfect state of impeccable quality, changing a single, unit-tested component could break some other unit(s) relying on an old behavior. You must

1. https://en.wikipedia.org/wiki/Streetlight_effect

repeat testing of all units when changing a single unit. Even then it would be meaningless because the change to one of the components could affect some interaction between other components or a subsystem, which no unit testing could discover. The only way to verify change is full regression testing of the system, its subsystems, its components and interactions, and finally its units. If, as a result of your change, other units need to change, the effect on regression testing is nonlinear. The inefficacy of unit testing is not a new observation and has been demonstrated across thousands of well-measured systems.

In theory, you could perform regression testing even on a functionally decomposed system. In practice, the complexity of that task would set the bar very high. The sheer number of the functional components would make testing all the interactions impractical. The very large services would be internally so complex that no one could effectively devise a comprehensive strategy that tests all code paths through such services. With functional decomposition, most developers give up and perform just simple unit testing. Therefore, by precluding regression testing, functional decomposition makes the entire system untestable, and untestable systems are always rife with defects.

PHYSICAL VERSUS SOFTWARE SYSTEMS

In this book, I resort to using examples from the physical world (such as houses) to demonstrate universal design principles. A common sentiment in the software industry is that you cannot extrapolate from the design of such physical entities to software, that software design and construction are somehow exempt from the design or process limitations of physical systems, or that software is too different from physical systems. After all, in software you can paint a house first and then build the walls to fit the paint. In software you do not have cost-of-goods such as beams and bricks.

I find that not only can the industry borrow from the physical world experience and best practices; it must do so. Contrary to intuition, software requires design even more than physical systems do. The reason is simple: complexity. The complexity of physical systems such as typical houses is capped by physical constraints. You cannot have a poorly designed house with hundreds of interconnecting corridors and rooms. The walls will either weigh too much, have too many openings, be too thin, have doors too small, or cost too much to assemble. You cannot use too much building materials because the house will implode, or you will not have the cash flow to buy them or a place to store the extra material on-site.

Without such natural physical restraints, complexity in software systems can get quickly out of control. The only way to rein in that complexity is to apply good engineering methods, of which design and process are paramount. Well-designed software systems are very much like physical entities and are built very much the same way. They are like well-designed machines.

Functional or domain decomposition makes no sense when designing and building either a house or a software system. All complex entities (physical or not) share the same abstract attributes, from the design decision tree to the project critical path of execution. All composite systems should be designed to be safe, maintainable, reusable, extensible, and of high quality. This is true for a house, a machine part, or a software system. These are practical engineering attributes, and the only way to obtain and maintain them is to use universal engineering practices.

That said, there is a fundamental difference between a physical system and a software system: visibility. Anyone who tries to build a house as in Figure 2-6 or Figure 2-7 will be fired on the spot. Such a person is clearly insane, and the horrendous waste of building material, time, and money as well as the risk of injuries would be plain for everyone to see. The problem with software systems is that while there is enormous waste, that waste is hidden. In software, dust and debris are replaced by wasted career prospects, energy, and youth. Yet no one ever sees or cares about this hidden waste, and the insanity is not only permitted but encouraged, as if the inmates have taken over the asylum. Correct design allows you to break free and restore control by eliminating the concealed waste. This is even more the case with project design, as the second part of this book shows.

EXAMPLE: FUNCTIONAL TRADING SYSTEM

Instead of a house, consider the following simplified requirements for a stock trading system for a financial company:

- The system should enable in-house traders to:
  - Buy and sell stocks
  - Schedule trades
  - Issue reports
  - Analyze the trades

- The users of the system utilize a browser to connect to the system and manage connected sessions, completing a form and submitting the request.
- After a trade, report, or analysis request, the system sends an email to the users confirming their request or containing the results.
- The data should be stored in a local database.

A straightforward functional decomposition would yield the design of Figure 2-8.

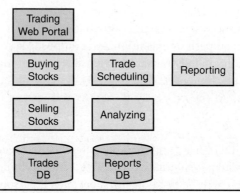

Figure 2-8 Functional trading system

Each of the functional requirements is expressed in a respective component of the architecture. Figure 2-8 represents a common design to which many novice software developers would gravitate without hesitation.

Problems with the Functional Trading System

The flaws of such a system design are many. It is very likely the client in the present system is the one that orchestrates `Buying Stocks`, `Selling Stocks`, and `Trade Scheduling`; issues a report with `Reporting`; and so on. Suppose the user wants to fund purchasing of a certain number of stocks by selling other stocks. This means two orders: first sell and then buy. But what should the client do if by the time these two transactions take place, the price of the stocks sold has dropped or the price of the bought stocks has risen so that the selling cannot fulfill the buying? Should the client buy just as many as possible? Should it perhaps sell more stocks than intended? Should it dip into the cash account behind the trading account to supplement the order? Should it abort the whole thing? Should it ask for user assistance? The exact resolution is immaterial for this discussion. Whatever the resolution, it requires business logic, which now resides in the client.

What will it take to change the client from a web portal to a mobile device? Would that not mean duplicating the business logic into the mobile device? It is likely that little of the business logic and the effort invested in developing it for the web client can be salvaged and reused in the mobile client because it is embedded in the web portal. Over time, the developers will end up maintaining several versions of the business logic in multiple clients.

Per the requirements, `Buying Stocks`, `Selling Stocks`, `Trade Scheduling`, `Reporting`, and `Analyzing` all respond to the user with an email listing their activities. What if the users prefer to receive a text message (or a paper letter) instead of an email? You will have to change the implementation of `Buying Stocks`, `Selling Stocks`, `Trade Scheduling`, `Reporting`, and `Analyzing` activities from an email to a text message.

Per the design decision, the data is stored in a database, and `Buying Stocks`, `Selling Stocks`, `Trade Scheduling`, `Reporting`, and `Analyzing` all access that database. Now suppose you decide to move the data storage from the local database to a cloud-based solution. At the very least, this will force you to change the data-access code in `Buying Stocks`, `Selling Stocks`, `Trade Scheduling`, `Reporting`, and `Analyzing` to go from a local database to a cloud offering. The way you structure, access, and consume the data has to change across all components.

What if the client wishes to interact with the system asynchronously, issuing a few trades and collecting the results later? You built the components with the notion of a connected, synchronous client that orchestrates the components. You will likely need to rewrite `Buying Stocks`, `Selling Stocks`, `Trade Scheduling`, `Reporting`, and `Analyzing` activities to orchestrate each other, along the lines of Figure 2-5.

Often, financial portfolios are comprised of multiple financial instruments besides stocks, such as currencies, bonds, commodities, and even options and futures on those instruments. What if the users of the system wish to start trading currencies or commodities instead of stocks? What if the users demand a single application, rather than several applications, to manage all of their portfolios? `Buying Stocks`, `Selling Stocks`, and `Trade Scheduling` are all about stocks and cannot handle currencies or bonds, requiring you to add additional components (like Figure 2-6). Similarly, `Reporting` and `Analyzing` need a major rewrite to accommodate reporting and analysis of trades other than stocks. The client needs a rewrite to accommodate the new trade items.

Even without branching to commodities, what if you must localize the application to foreign markets? At the very least, the client will need a serious makeover to accommodate language localization, but the real effect is going to be the system components again. Foreign markets are going to have different trading rules, regulations, and compliance requirements, drastically affecting what the system is allowed to do and how it is to go about trading. This will mean much rework to `Buying Stocks`, `Selling Stocks`, `Trade Scheduling`, `Reporting`, and `Analyzing` whenever entering a new locale. You are going to end up with either bloated god services that can trade in any market or a version of the system for each deployment locale.

Finally, all components presently connect to some stock ticker feed that provides them with the latest stock values. What is required to switch to a new feed provider or to incorporate multiple feeds? At the very least, `Buying Stocks`, `Selling Stocks`, `Trade Scheduling`, `Reporting`, and `Analyzing` will require work to move to a new feed, connect to it, handle its errors, pay for its service, and so on. There are also no guarantees that the new feed uses the same data format as the old one. All components require some conversion and transformation work as well.

VOLATILITY-BASED DECOMPOSITION

The Method's design directive is:

Decompose based on volatility.

Volatility-based decomposition identifies areas of potential change and encapsulates those into services or system building blocks. You then implement the required behavior as the interaction between the encapsulated areas of volatility.

The motivation for volatility-based decomposition is simplicity itself: any change is encapsulated, containing the effect on the system.

When you use volatility-based decomposition, you start thinking of your system as a series of vaults, as in Figure 2-9.

Any change is potentially very dangerous, like a hand grenade with the pin pulled out. Yet, with volatility-based decomposition, you open the door of the appropriate vault, toss the grenade inside, and close the door. Whatever was inside the vault may be destroyed completely, but there is no shrapnel flying everywhere, destroying everything in its path. You have contained the change.

With functional decomposition, your building blocks represent areas of functionality, not volatility. As a result, when a change happens, by the very definition

Change

Figure 2-9 Encapsulated areas of volatility (Images: media500/Shutterstock; pikepicture/Shutterstock)

of the decomposition, it affects multiple (if not most) of the components in your architecture. Functional decomposition therefore tends to maximize the effect of the change. Since most software systems are designed functionally, change is often painful and expensive, and the system is likely to resonate with the change. Changes made in one area of functionality trigger other changes and so on. Accommodating change is the real reason you must avoid functional decomposition.

All the other problems with functional decomposition pale when compared with the poor ability and high cost of handling change. With functional decomposition, a change is like swallowing a live hand grenade.

What you choose to encapsulate can be functional in nature, but hardly ever is it domain-functional, meaning it has no meaning for the business. For example, the electricity that powers a house is indeed an area of functionality but is also an important area to encapsulate for two reasons. The first reason is that power in a house is highly volatile: power can be AC or DC; 110 volts or 220 volts; single phase or three phases; 50 hertz or 60 hertz; produced by solar panels on the roof, a generator in the backyard, or plain grid connectivity; delivered on wires with different gauges; and on and on. All that volatility is encapsulated behind a receptacle. When it is time to consume power, all the user sees is an opaque receptacle, encapsulating the power volatility. This decouples the power-consuming appliances from the power volatility, increasing reuse, safety, and extensibility while reducing overall complexity. It makes using power in one house indistinguishable from using it in another, highlighting the second reason it is valid to identify power as something to encapsulate in the house. While powering a house is an area of functionality, in general, the use of power is not specific to the domain of the house (the family living in the house, their relationships, their wellbeing, property, etc.).

What would it be like to live in a house where the power volatility was not encapsulated? Whenever you wanted to consume power, you would have to first expose the wires, measure the frequency with an oscilloscope, and certify the voltage with a voltmeter. While you could use power that way, it is far easier to rely on the encapsulation of that volatility behind the receptacle, allowing you instead to add value by integrating power into your tasks or routine.

DECOMPOSITION, MAINTENANCE, AND DEVELOPMENT

As explained previously, functional decomposition drastically increases the system's complexity. Functional decomposition also makes maintenance a nightmare. Not only is the code in such systems complex, changes are spread across multiple services. This makes maintaining the code labor intensive, error prone, and very time-consuming. Generally, the more complex the code, the lower its quality, and low quality makes maintenance even more challenging. You must contend with high complexity and avoid introducing new defects while resolving old ones. In a functionally decomposed system, it is common for new changes to result in new defects due to the confluence of low quality and complexity. Extending the functional system often requires effort disproportionally expensive with respect to the benefit to the customer.

Even before maintenance ever starts, when the system is under development, functional decomposition harbors danger. Requirements will change throughout development (as they invariably do), and the cost of each change is huge, affecting multiple areas, forcing considerable rework, and ultimately endangering the deadline.

Systems designed with volatility-based decomposition present a stark contrast in their ability to respond to change. Since changes are contained in each module, there is at least a hope for easy maintenance with no side effects outside the module boundary. With lower complexity and easier maintenance, quality is much improved. You have a chance at reuse if something is encapsulated the same way in another system. You can extend the system by adding more areas of encapsulated volatility or integrate existing areas of volatility in a different way. Encapsulating volatility means far better resiliency to feature creep during development and a chance of meeting the schedule, since changes will be contained.

UNIVERSAL PRINCIPLE

The merits of volatility-based decomposition are not specific to software systems. They are universal principles of good design, from commerce to business interactions to biology to physical systems and great software. Universal principles, by their very nature, apply to software too (else they would not be universal). For example, consider your own body. A functional decomposition of your own body would have components for every task you are required to do, from driving to programming to presenting, yet your body does not have any such components. You accomplish a task such as programming by integrating areas of volatility. For example, your heart provides an important service for your system: pumping blood. Pumping blood has enormous volatility to it: high blood pressure and low pressure, salinity, viscosity, pulse rate, activity level (sitting or running), with and without adrenaline, different blood types, healthy and sick, and so on. Yet all that volatility is encapsulated behind the service called the heart. Would you be able to program if you had to care about the volatility involved in pumping blood?

> **Note**   Given near-infinite time and energy while operating at practically 0% efficiency, nature has converged on volatility-based decomposition. However, the human world has more constrained resources. Humans do have the advantage of tried-and-tested engineering principles, creative intellect, and the ability to transfer knowledge that help us avoid the inevitable dead ends that trial-and-error produces. Volatility-based decomposition is the ultimate culmination of human engineering building upon the principles of nature.

You can also integrate into your implementation external areas of encapsulated volatility. Consider your computer, which is different from literally any other computer in the world, yet all that volatility is encapsulated. As long as the computer can send a signal to the screen, you do not care what happens behind the graphic port. You perform the task of programming by integrating encapsulated areas of volatility, some internal, some external. You can reuse the same areas of volatility (such as the heart) while performing other functionalities such as driving a car or presenting your work to customers. There is simply no other way of designing and building a viable system.

Decomposing based on volatility is the essence of system design. All well-designed systems, software and physical systems alike, encapsulate their volatility inside the system's building blocks.

VOLATILITY-BASED DECOMPOSITION AND TESTING

Volatility-based decomposition lends well to regression testing. The reduction in the number of components, the reduction in the size of components, and the simplification of the interactions between components all drastically reduce the complexity of the system. This makes it feasible to write regression testing that tests the system end to end, tests each subsystem individually, and eventually tests independent components. Since volatility-based decomposition contains the changes inside the building blocks of the system, once the inevitable changes do happen, they do not disrupt the regression testing in place. You can test the effect of a change in a component in isolation from the rest of the system without interfering with the inter-components and inter-subsystems testing.

SHOULDERS OF GIANTS: DAVID PARNAS

In 1972, David Parnas (an early pioneer of software engineering) published a seminal paper called "On the Criteria to Be Used in Decomposing Systems into Modules."[a] This short, five-page paper contains most elements of modern software engineering, including encapsulation, information hiding, cohesion, modules, and loose coupling. Most notably, Parnas identified in that paper the need to look for change as the key criteria for decomposition as opposed to functionality. While the specifics of that paper are quite archaic, it was the very first time anyone in the software industry asked the pertinent questions about what it takes to make software systems maintainable, reusable, and extensible. As such, this paper represents the genesis of modern software engineering. Parnas spent the next 40 years trying to introduce proven classic engineering practices to software development.

a. *Communications of the ACM* 15, no. 12 (1972): 1053–1058.

THE VOLATILITY CHALLENGE

The ideas and motivations behind volatility-based decomposition are simple, practical, and consistent with reality and common sense. The main challenges in performing a volatility-based decomposition have to do with time, communication, and perception. You will find that volatility is often not self-evident. No customer or product manager at the onset of a project will ever present you the requirements for the system the following way: "This could change, we will change that one later, and we will never change those." The outside world (be it customers, management, or marketing) always presents you with requirements in terms of functionality: "The system should do this and that." Even you, reading these pages, are likely struggling to wrap your head around this concept as you to try to identify the areas of volatility in your current system. Consequently, volatility-based decomposition takes longer compared with functional decomposition.

Note that volatility-based decomposition does not mean you should ignore the requirements. You must analyze the requirements to recognize the areas of volatility. Arguably, the whole purpose of requirements analysis is to identify the areas of volatility, and this analysis requires effort and sweat. This is actually great news because now you are given a chance to comply with the first law of thermodynamics. Sadly, merely sweating on the problem does not mean a thing. The first law of thermodynamics does not state that if you sweat on something, you will add value. Adding value is much more difficult. This book provides you with powerful mental tools for design and analysis, including structure, guidelines, and a sound engineering methodology. These tools give you a fighting chance in your quest to add value. You still must practice and fight.

The 2% Problem

With every knowledge-intensive subject, it takes time to become proficient and effective and even more to excel at it. This is true in areas as varied as kitchen plumbing, internal medicine, and software architecture. In life, you often choose not to pursue certain areas of expertise because the time and cost required to master them would dwarf the time and cost required to utilize an expert. For example, precluding any chronic health problem, a working-age person is sick for about a week a year. A week a year of downtime due to illness is roughly 2% of the working year. So, when you are sick, do you open up medicine books and start reading, or do you go and see a doctor? At only 2% of your time, the frequency is low enough (and the specialty bar high enough) that there is little sense in doing anything other than going to the doctor. It is not worth your while to become as good as a doctor. If, however, you were sick 80% of the time, you might spend a considerable portion of your time educating yourself about your condition, possible complications, treatments, and options, often to the point of sparring with your doctor. Your innate propensity for anatomy and medicine has not changed; only your degree of investment has (hopefully, you will never have to be really good at medicine).

Similarly, when your kitchen sink is clogged somewhere behind the garbage disposal and the dishwasher, do you go to the hardware store, purchase a P-trap, an S-trap, various adapters, three different types of wrenches, various O-rings and other accessories, or do you call a plumber? It is the 2% problem again: it is not worth your while learning how to fix that sink if it is clogged less than 2% of the time. The moral is that when you spend 2% of your time on any complex task, you will never be any good at it.

With software system architecture, architects get to decompose a complete system into modules only on major revolutions of the cycle. Such events happen, on average, every few years. All other designs in the interim between clean slates are at best incremental and at worse detrimental to the existing systems. How much time will the manager allow the architect to invest in architecture for the next project? One week? Two weeks? Three weeks?? Six weeks??? The exact answer is irrelevant. On one hand, you have cycles measured in years and, on the other, activities measured in weeks. The week-to-year ratio is roughly 1:50, or 2% again. Architects have learned the hard way that they need to hone their skills getting ready for that 2% window. Now consider the architect's manager. If the architect spends 2% of the time architecting the system, what percentage of the time does that architect's manager spend managing said architect? The answer is probably a small fraction of that time. Therefore, the manager is never going to be good at managing architects at that critical phase. The manager is constantly going to exclaim, "I don't understand why this is taking so long! Why can't we just do A, B, C?"

Gaining the time to do decomposition correctly will likely be as much of a challenge as doing the decomposition, if not more so. However, the difficulty of a task should not preclude it from being done. Precisely because it is difficult, it must be done. You will see later on in this book several techniques for gaining the time.

The Dunning-Kruger Effect

In 1999, David Dunning and Justin Kruger published their research[2] demonstrating conclusively that people unskilled in a domain tend to look down on it, thinking it is less complex, risky, or demanding than it truly is. This cognitive bias has nothing to do with intelligence or expertise in other domains. If you are unskilled in something, you never assume it is more complex than it is, you assume it is less!

When the manager is throwing hands in the air saying, "I don't understand why this is taking so long," the manager really does not understand why you cannot just do the A, then B, and then C. Do not be upset. You should expect this behavior and resolve it correctly by educating your manager and peers who, by their own admission, do not understand.

---

2. Justin Kruger and David Dunning, "Unskilled and Unaware of It: How Difficulties in Recognizing One's Own Incompetence Lead to Inflated Self-Assessments," *Journal of Personality and Social Psychology* 77, no. 6 (1999): 1121–1134.

Fighting Insanity

Albert Einstein is attributed with saying that doing things the same way but expecting better results is the definition of insanity. Since the manager typically expects you to do better than last time, you must point out the insanity of pursuing functional decomposition yet again and explain the merits of volatility-based decomposition. In the end, even if you fail to convince a single person, you should not simply follow orders and dig the project into an early grave. You must still decompose based on volatility. Your professional integrity (and ultimately your sanity and long-term peace of mind) is at stake.

IDENTIFYING VOLATILITY

The rest of this chapter provides you with a set of tools to use when you go searching for and identifying areas of volatility. While these techniques are valuable and effective in their own right, they are somewhat loose. The next chapter introduces structure and constraints that allow for quicker and repeatable identification of areas of volatility. However, that discussion merely fine-tunes and specializes the ideas in this section.

VOLATILE VERSUS VARIABLE

A key question many novices struggle with is the difference between things that change and things that are volatile. Not everything that is variable is also volatile. You resort to encapsulating a volatility at the system design level only when it is open-ended and, unless encapsulated in a component of the architecture, would be very expensive to contain. Variability, on the other hand, describes those aspects that you can easily handle in your code using conditional logic. When searching for volatility, you should be on the lookout for the kind of changes or risks that would have ripple effects across the system. Changes must not invalidate the architecture.

AXES OF VOLATILITY

Finding areas of volatility is a process of discovery that takes place during requirements analysis and interviews with the project stakeholders.

There is a simple technique I call **axes of volatility**. This technique examines the ways the system is used by customers. **Customer** in this context refers to a consumer of the system, which could be a single user or a whole other business entity.

In any business, there are only two ways your system could face change: the first axis is at the same customer over time. Even if presently the system is perfectly aligned with a particular customer's needs, over time, that customer's business context will change. Even the use of the system by the customer will often change the requirements against which it was written in the first place.[3] Over time, the customer's requirements and expectation of the system will change.

The second way change could come is at the same time across customers. If you could freeze time and examine your customer base, are all your customers now using the system in exactly the same way? What are some of them doing that is different from the others? Do you have to accommodate such differences? All such changes define the second axis of volatility.

When searching for potential volatility in interviews, you will find it very helpful to phrase the questions in terms of the axes of volatility (same customer over time, all customers at the same point in time). Framing the questions in this way helps you identify the volatilities. If something does not map to the axes of volatility, you should not encapsulate it at all, and there should be no building block in your system to which it is mapped. Creating such a block would likely indicate functional decomposition.

Design Factoring

Often, the act of looking for areas of volatility using the axes of volatility is an iterative process interleaved with the factoring of the design itself. Consider, for example, the progression of design iterations in Figure 2-10.

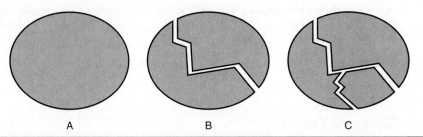

     A   B   C

Figure 2-10 Design iterations along axes of volatility

---

3. The tendency of a solution to change the requirements against which it was developed was first observed by the 19th-century English economist William Jevons with regard to coal production, and it is referred to since as the *Jevons paradox*. Other manifestations are the increase in paper consumption with the digital office and the worsening traffic congestion following an increase in road capacity.

Your first take of the proposed architecture might look like diagram A—one big thing, one single component. Ask yourself, Could you use the same component, as is, with a particular customer, forever? If the answer is no, then why? Often, it is because you know that customer will, over time, want to change a specific thing. In that case, you must encapsulate that thing, yielding diagram B. Ask yourself now, Could you use diagram B across all customers now? If the answer is no, then identify the thing that the customers want to do differently, encapsulate it, and produce diagram C. You keep factoring the design that way until all possible points on the axes of volatility are encapsulated.

Independence of the Axes

Almost always, the axes should be independent. Something that changes for one customer over time should not change as much across all customers at the same point in time, and vice versa. If areas of change cannot be isolated to one of the axes, it often indicates a functional decomposition in disguise.

Example: Volatility-Based Decomposition of a House

You can use the axes of volatility to encapsulate the volatility of a house. Start by looking at your own house and observe how it changes over time. For example, consider furniture. Over time, you may rearrange the furniture in the living room and occasionally add new pieces or replace old ones. The conclusion is that furniture in a house is volatile. Next consider appliances. Over time, you may switch to energy-efficient appliances. You likely have already replaced the old CRT with flat plasma screen and that with a large, wafer-thin OLED TV. This is a strong indication that at your house, appliances are volatile. How about the occupants of the house? Is that aspect static? Do you ever have guests come over? Can the house be empty of people? The occupants of the house are volatile. What about appearance? Do you ever paint the house, change the draperies or landscaping? The appearance of a house is volatile. The house is likely connected to some utilities, from Internet to power and security. Previously, I pointed out the power volatility in a house, but what about Internet? In years past, you may have used dial-up for Internet, then moved to DSL, then cable, and now fiber optics or a satellite connection. While these options are drastically different, you would not want to change the way you send emails based on the type of connectivity. You should encapsulate the volatilities of all utilities. Figure 2-11 shows this possible decomposition along the first axis of volatility (same customer over time).

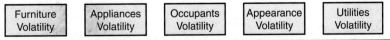

Figure 2-11 Same house over time

Now, even at the same point in time, is your house the same as every other house? Other houses have a different structure, so the structure of the house is volatile. Even if you were to copy and paste your house to another city, would it be the same house?[4] The answer is clearly negative. The house will have different neighbors and be subjected to different city regulations, building codes, and taxes. Figure 2-12 shows this possible decomposition along the second axis of volatility (different customers at the same point in time).

Structure Volatility	Neighbors Volatility	City Volatility

Figure 2-12 **At the same time across houses**

Note the independence of the axis. The city where you live over time does change its regulations, but the changes come at a slow pace. Similarly, the likelihood of new neighbors is fairly low as long as you live in the same house but is a certainty if you compare your house to another at the same point in time. The assignment of a volatility to one of the axes is therefore not an absolute exclusion but more one of disproportional probability.

Note also that the `Neighbors Volatility` component can deal with volatility of neighbors at the same house over time as easily as it can do that across different houses at the same point in time. Assigning the component to an axis helps to discover the volatility in the first place; the volatility is just more apparent across different houses at the same point in time.

Finally, in sharp contrast to the decompositions of Figure 2-6 and Figure 2-7, in Figure 2-11 and Figure 2-12 there is no component in the decomposition for cooking or kitchen. In a volatility-based decomposition, the required behavior is accomplished by an interaction between the various encapsulated areas of volatility. Cooking dinner may be the product of an interaction between the occupants, the appliances, the structure, and the utilities. Since something still needs to manage that interaction, the design is not complete. The axes of volatility are a great starting point, but it is not the only tool to bring to bear on the problem.

SOLUTIONS MASQUERADING AS REQUIREMENTS

Consider again the functional requirement for the house to support the cooking feature. Such requirements are quite common in requirements specs, and many

---

4. The ancient Greeks grappled with this question in Theseus's paradox (https://en.wikipedia.org/wiki/Ship_of_Theseus).

developers will simply map that to a `Cooking` component in their architecture. Cooking, however, is not a requirement (even though it was in the requirement spec). Cooking is a possible solution for the requirement of feeding the people in the house. You can satisfy the feeding requirement by ordering pizza or taking the family out for dinner.

It is exceedingly common for customers to provide solutions masquerading as requirements. With functional decomposition, once you deploy the system with only `Cooking`, the customer will ask for the pizza option, resulting in either another component in your system or bloating of another component. The "going out to dinner" requirement will soon follow, leading to a never-ending cycle of features going around and around the real requirement. With volatility-based decomposition, during requirements analysis, you should identify the volatility in feeding the occupants and provide for it. The volatility of feeding is encapsulated within the `Feeding`, component and as the feeding options change, your design does not.

However, while feeding is a better requirement than cooking, it is still a solution masquerading as a requirement. What if in the interest of diet, the people in the house should go to bed hungry tonight? A feeding requirement and diet requirement might be mutually exclusive. You can do either one, but not both. Mutually exclusive requirements are also quite common.

The real requirement for any house is to take care of the well-being of the occupants, not just their caloric intake. The house should not be too cold or too warm or too humid or too dry. While the customers may only discuss cooking and never discuss temperature control, you should recognize the real volatility, well-being, and encapsulate that in the `Wellbeing` component of your architecture.

Since most requirements specifications are chock-full of solutions masquerading as requirements, functional decomposition absolutely maximizes your pain. You will forever be chasing the ever-evolving solutions, never recognizing the true underlying requirements.

The fact that requirements specifications have all those solutions masquerading as requirements is actually a blessing in disguise because you can generalize the example of cooking in the house into a bona fide analysis technique for discovering areas of volatility. Start by pointing out the solutions masquerading as requirements, and ask if there are other possible solutions? If so, then what were the real requirements and the underlying volatility? Once you identify the volatility, you must determine if the need to address that volatility is a true requirement or is still a solution masquerading as a requirement. Once you have finished scrubbing away all the solutions, what you are left with are likely great candidates for volatility-based decomposition.

VOLATILITIES LIST

Prior to decomposing a system and creating an architecture, you should simply compile a list of the candidate areas of volatility as a natural part of requirements gathering and analysis. You should approach the list with an open mind. Ask what could change along the axes of volatility. Identify solutions masquerading as requirements, and apply the additional techniques described later in this chapter. The list is a powerful instrument for keeping track of your observations and organizing your thoughts. Do not commit yet to the actual design. All you are doing is maintaining a list. Note that while the design of the system should not take more than a few days, identifying the correct areas of volatility may take considerably longer.

EXAMPLE: VOLATILITY-BASED TRADING SYSTEM

Using the previous requirements for the stock trading system, you should start by preparing a list of possible areas of volatility, capturing also the rationale behind each:

- **User volatility.** The traders serve end customers on whose portfolios they operate. The end customers are also likely interested in the current state of their funds. While they could write the trader a letter or call, a more appropriate means would be for the end customers to log into the system to see the current balance and the ongoing trades. Even though the requirements never stated anything about end customer access (the requirements were for professional traders), you should contemplate such access. While the end customers may not be able to trade, they should be able to see the status of their accounts. There could also be system administrators. There is volatility in the type of user.

- **Client application volatility.** Volatility in users often manifests in volatility in the type of client application and technology. A simple web page may suffice for external end customers looking up their balance. However, professional traders will prefer a multi-monitor, rich desktop application with market trends, account details, market tickers, newsfeed, spreadsheet projection, and proprietary data. Other users may want to review the trades on mobile devices of various types.

- **Security volatility.** Volatility in users implies volatility in how the users authenticate themselves against the system. The number of in-house traders could be small, from a few dozens to a few hundred. The system, however, could have millions of end customers. The in-house traders could rely on domain accounts for authentication, but this is a poor choice for the millions of customers accessing information through the Internet. For Internet users, perhaps a simple user name and password will do, or maybe some sophisticated federated security single sign-on option is needed. Similar volatility exists with authorization options. Security is volatile.

- **Notification volatility.** The requirements specify that the system is to send an email after every request. However, what if the email bounces? Should the system fall back to a paper letter? How about a text message or a fax instead of an email? The requirement to send an email is a solution masquerading as a requirement. The real requirement is to notify the users, but the notification transport is volatile. There is also volatility in who receives the notification: a single user or a broadcast to several users receiving the same notification and over whichever transport. Perhaps the end customer prefers an email while the end customer's tax lawyer prefers a documented paper statement. There is also volatility in who publishes the notification in the first place.

- **Storage volatility.** The requirements specify the use of a local database. However, over time, more and more systems migrate to the cloud. There is nothing inherent in stock trading that precludes benefiting from the cost and economy of scale of the cloud. The requirement to use a local database is actually another solution masquerading as a requirement. A better requirement is data persistence, which accommodates the volatility in the persistence options. However, the majority of users are end customers, and those users actually perform read-only requests. This implies the system will benefit greatly from the use of an in-memory cache. Furthermore, some cloud offerings utilize a distributed in-memory hash table that offers the same resiliency as traditional file-based durable storage. Requiring data persistence would exclude these last two options because data persistence is still a solution masquerading as a requirement. The real requirement is simply that the system must not lose the data, or that the system is required to store the data. How that is accomplished is an implementation detail, with a great deal of volatility, from a local database to a remote in-memory cache in the cloud.

- **Connection and synchronization volatility.** The current requirements call for a connected, synchronous, lock-step manner of completing a web form and submitting it in-order. This implies that the traders can do only one request at a time. However, the more trades the traders execute, the more money they make. If the requests are independent, why not issue them asynchronously? If the requests are deferred in time (trades in the future), why not queue up the calls to the system to reduce the load? When performing asynchronous calls (including queued calls), the requests can execute out of order. Connectivity and synchronicity are volatile.

- **Duration and device volatility.** Some users will complete a trade in one short session. However, traders earn their keep and maximize their income when they perform complicated trades that distribute and hedge risk, involving multiple stocks and sectors, domestic or foreign markets, and so on. Constructing such a trade can be time-consuming, lasting anywhere from several hours to several days. Such a long-running interaction will likely span multiple system sessions and possibly multiple physical devices. There is volatility in the duration of the interaction, which in turn triggers volatility in the devices and connections involved.

- **Trade item volatility.** As discussed previously, over time, the end customers may want to trade not just stocks but also commodities, bonds, currencies, and maybe even future contracts. The trade item itself is volatile.

- **Workflow volatility.** If the trade item is volatile, processing of the steps involved in the trade will be volatile too. Buying and selling stocks, scheduling their orders, and so on are very different from selling commodities, bonds, or currencies. The workflow of the trade is therefore volatile. Similarly, the workflow of trade analysis is volatile.

- **Locale and regulations volatility.** Over time, the system may be deployed into different locales. Volatility in the locale has drastic implications on the trading rules, UI localization, the listing of trade items, taxation, and regulatory compliance. The locale and the regulations that apply therein are volatile.

- **Market feed volatility.** The source of market data could change over time. Various feeds have a different format, cost, update rate, communication protocols, and so on. Different feeds may show slightly different value for the same stock at the same point in time. The feeds can be external (e.g., Bloomberg or Reuters) or internal (e.g., simulated market data for testing, diagnostics, or trading algorithms research). The market feed is volatile.

A Key Observation

The preceding list is by no means an exhaustive list of all the things that could change in a stock trading system. Its objective is to point out what could change and the mindset you need to adopt when searching for volatility. Some of the volatile areas may be out of scope for the project. They may be ruled out by domain experts as improbable or may relate too much to the nature of the business (such as branching out of stocks into currencies or foreign markets). My experience, however, is that it is vital to call out the areas of volatility and map them in your decomposition as early as possible. Designating a component in the architecture costs you next to nothing. Later, you must decide whether or not to allocate the effort to designing and constructing it. However, at least now you are aware how to handle that eventuality.

System Decomposition

Once you have settled on the areas of volatility, you need to encapsulate them in components of the architecture. One such possible decomposition is depicted in Figure 2-13.

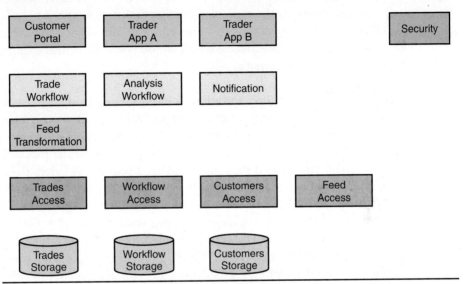

Figure 2-13 Volatility-based decomposition of a trading system

The transition from the list of volatile areas to components of the architecture is hardly ever one to one. Sometimes a single component can encapsulate more than one area of volatility. Some areas of volatility may not be mapped directly to a component but rather to an operational concept such as queuing or publishing an event. At other times, the volatility of an area may be encapsulated in a third-party service.

With design, always start with the simple and easy decisions. Those decisions constrain the system, making subsequent decisions easier. In this example, some mapping is easy to do. The volatility in the data storage is encapsulated behind data access components, which do not betray where the storage is and what technology is used to access it. Note in Figure 2-13 the key abstraction of referring to the storage as `Storage` and not as `Database`. While the implementation (according to the requirements) is a local database, there is nothing in the architecture that precludes other options, such as the raw file system, a cache, or the cloud. If a change to the storage takes place, it is encapsulated in the respective access component (such as the `Trades Access`) and does not affect the other components, including any other access component. This enables you to change the storage with minimal consequences.

The volatility in notifying the clients is encapsulated in the `Notification` component. This component knows how to notify each client and which clients subscribe to which event. For simple scenarios, you can manage sufficiently with a general-purpose events publishing and subscription service (**Pub/Sub**) instead of a custom `Notification` component. However, in this case, there are likely some business rules on the type of transport and nature of the broadcast. The `Notification` component may still use some Pub/Sub service underneath it, but that is an internal implementation detail whose volatility is also encapsulated in the `Notification` component.

The volatility in the trading workflow is encapsulated in the `Trade Workflow` component. That component encapsulates the volatility of what is being traded (stocks or currencies), the specific steps involved in buying or selling a trade item, the required customization for local markets, the details for the required reports, and so on. Note that even if the trade items are fixed (not volatile), the workflow of trading stocks can change, justifying the use of `Trade Workflow` to encapsulate the volatility. The design also relies on the operational concept of storing the workflows (this should be implemented using some third-party workflow tool). `Trade Workflow` retrieves the appropriate workflow instance for each session, operates on it, and stores it back in the `Workflow Storage`. This concept helps encapsulate several volatilities. First, different trade items can now have distinct trading workflows. Second, different locales can have different workflows. Third, this enables supporting long-running workflows spanning multiple devices and sessions. The system does not care if two calls are seconds apart or days apart. In each case, the system loads the workflow instance to process the next step. The design treats connected, single-session trades exactly the same as a long-running distributed trade. Symmetry and consistency are good qualities in system architecture. Note also that the workflow storage access is encapsulated in the same fashion as the trades storage access.

You can use the same pattern for the stock trading workflow and the analysis workflows. The dedicated `Analysis Workflow` component encapsulated the volatility in the analysis workflows, and it can use the same `Workflow Storage`.

The volatility of accessing the market feed is encapsulated in the `Feed Access`. This component encapsulates how to access the feed and whether the feed itself is internal or external. The volatility in the format or even value of the various market data coming from the different feeds is encapsulated in the `Feed Transformation` component. Both of these components decouple the other components from the feeds by providing a uniform interface and format regardless of the origin of the data.

The `Security` component encapsulates the volatility of the possible ways of authenticating and authorizing the users. Internally, it may look up credentials from a local storage or interact with some distributed provider.

The clients of the system can be the trading application (`Trader App A`) or a mobile app (`Trader App B`). The end customers can use their own website (`Customer Portal`). Each client application also encapsulates the details and the best way of rendering the information on the target device.

> **Note** The previous discussion performed a somewhat loose mapping of areas of volatility to architecture. The next chapter introduces structure and guidelines, making the process much more deterministic.

RESIST THE SIREN SONG

Note in Figure 2-13 the absence of a dedicated reporting component. For demonstration purposes, reporting was not listed as a volatile area (from the business perspective). Therefore, there is nothing to encapsulate with a component. Adding such a component manifests functional decomposition. However, if functional decomposition is all you have ever done, you will likely hear an irresistible siren song calling you to add a reporting block. Just because you always have had a reporting block, or even because you have an existing reporting block, does not mean you need a reporting block.

In Homer's *Odyssey*, a story that is more than 2500 years old, Odysseus sails home via the Straights of the Sirens. The Sirens are beautiful winged fairy-like creatures who have the voices of angels. They sing a song that no man can resist. The sailors jump to their arms, and the Sirens drown the men under the waves and eat them. Before encountering the deadly allure of the Sirens' songs, Odysseus (you, the architect) is advised to plug with beeswax the ears of his sailors (the rank and file software developers) and tie them to the oars. The sailors' job is to row (write code), and they are not even at liberty to listen to the Sirens. Odysseus himself, on the other hand, as the leader, does not have the luxury of plugging his ears (e.g., maybe you do need that reporting block). Odysseus ties himself to the mast of the ship so that he cannot succumb to the Sirens even if he wanted to do so (see Figure 2-14, depicting the scene on a period vase). You are Odysseus, and volatility-based decomposition is your mast. Resist the siren song of your previous bad habits.

Figure 2-14 Tied to the mast (Image: Werner Forman Archive/Shutterstock)

VOLATILITY AND THE BUSINESS

While you must encapsulate the volatile areas, not everything that could change should be encapsulated. Put differently, things that could change are not necessarily volatile. A classic example is the nature of the business, and you should not attempt to encapsulate the nature of the business. With almost all business applications, the applications exist to serve some need of the business or its customers. However, the nature of the business, and by extension, each application, tends to be fairly constant. A company that has been in a business for a long time will likely stay in that business. For example, Federal Express has been, is, and will be in the shipment and delivery business. While in theory it is possible for Federal Express to branch into healthcare, such a potential change is not something you should encapsulate.

During system decomposition, you must identify both the areas of volatility to encapsulate and those not to encapsulate (e.g., the nature of the business). Sometimes, you will have initial difficulty in telling these apart. There are two simple indicators if something that could change is indeed part of the nature of the business. The first indicator is that the possible change is rare. Yes, it could happen, but the likelihood of it happening is very low. The second indicator is that any attempt to encapsulate the change can only be done poorly. No practical amount of investment in time or effort will properly encapsulate the aspect in a way of which you can be proud.

For example, consider designing a simple residential house on a plot of land. At some point in the future, the homeowner may decide to extend the home into a 50-story skyscraper. Encapsulating that possible change in your house design produces a very different design than that of your typical residential house design. Instead of a shallow form-poured foundation, the house foundation must include dozens of friction pylons, driven down to maybe hundreds of feet to support the weight of the building. This will allow the foundation to support both a single family residential and a skyscraper. Next, the power panel must be able to distribute thousands of amps and likely requires the house to have its own transformer. While the water company can bring water to the house, you must devote a room for a large water pump that can push the water up 50 floors. The sewer line must be able to handle 50 floors of inhabitants. You will have to do all that tremendous investment for a single-family home.

When you are finished, the foundation will encapsulate the change to the weight of the building, the power panel will encapsulate the demands of both a single home and 50 stories, and so on. However, the two indicators are now violated. First, how many homeowners in your city annually do convert their home to a skyscraper? How common is that? In a large metropolitan area with a million homes, it may happen once every few years, making the change very rare, once in a million if that. Second, do you really have the funds (allocated initially for a single home) to properly execute all these encapsulations? A single pylon may cost more than the single-family building. Any attempt to encapsulate the future transition to a skyscraper will be done poorly and will be neither useful nor cost-effective.

Converting the single-family home to a 50-story building is a change to the nature of the business. No longer is the building in the business of housing a family. Now it is in the business of being a hotel or an office building. When a land developer purchases that plot of land for the purpose of such conversion, the developer usually chooses to raze the building, dig out the old foundation, and start afresh. A change to the nature of the business permits you to kill the old system and start from scratch. It is important to note that the context of the nature of the business is somewhat fractal. The context can be the business of the company, the business of a department or a division in a company, or even the business added value of a specific application. All these represent things that you should not encapsulate.

Speculative Design

Speculative design is a variation on trying to encapsulate the nature of the business. Once you subscribe to the principle of volatility-based decomposition, you will start seeing possible volatilities everywhere and can easily overdo it. When taken to the extreme, you run the risk of trying to encapsulate anything and everywhere. Your design will have numerous building blocks, a clear sign of a bad design.

Consider for example the item in Figure 2-15.

Figure 2-15 Speculative design (Image: Gercen/Shutterstock)

The item is a pair of SCUBA-ready lady's high heels. While a lady adorned in a fine evening gown could entertain her guests at the party wearing these, how likely is it that she will excuse herself, proceed immediately to the porch, draw on SCUBA gear, and dive into the reef? Are these shoes as elegant as conventional high heels? Are these as effective as regular flippers when it comes to swimming or stepping on sharp coral? While the use of the items in Figure 2-15 is possible, it is extremely unlikely. In addition, everything they try to provide is done very poorly because of the attempt to encapsulate a change to the nature of the shoe, from a fashion accessory to a diving accessory, something you should never attempt. If you try this, you have fallen into the speculative design trap. Most such designs are simply frivolous speculation on a future change to your system (i.e., a change to the nature of the business).

DESIGN FOR YOUR COMPETITORS

Another useful technique for identifying volatilities is to try to design a system for your competitor (or another division in your company). For example, suppose you are the lead architect for Federal Express's next-generation system. Your main competitor is UPS. Both Federal Express and UPS ship packages. Both collect funds, schedule pickup and delivery, track packages, insure content, and manage trucks and airplane fleets. Ask yourself the following question: Can Federal Express use the software system UPS is using? Can UPS use the system Federal Express wants to build? If the likely answer is no, start listing all the barriers for such a reuse or extensibility. While both companies perform in the abstract the same service, the way they conduct their business is different. For example, Federal Express may plan shipment routes one way, while UPS may plan them another. In that case, shipment planning is probably volatile because if there are two ways of doing something, there may be many more. You must encapsulate the shipment planning and designate a component in your architecture for that purpose. If Federal Express starts planning shipments the same as UPS at some future time, the change is now contained in a single component, making the change easy and affecting only the implementation of that component, not the decomposition. You have future-proofed your system.

The opposite case is also true. If you and your competitor (and even better, all competitors) do some activity or sequence the same way, and there is no chance of your system doing it any other way, then there is no need to allocate a component in the architecture for that activity. To do so would create a functional decomposition. When you encounter something your competitors do identically, more likely than not, it represents the nature of the business, and as discussed previously, you should not encapsulate it.

VOLATILITY AND LONGEVITY

Volatility is intimately related to longevity. The longer the company or the application has been doing something the same way, the higher the likelihood the company will keep doing it the same way. Put differently, the longer things do not change, the longer they have until they do change or are replaced. You must put forward a design that accommodates such changes, even if at first glance such changes are independent of the current requirements.

You can even guesstimate how long it will be until such a change is likely to take place using a simple heuristic: the ability of the organization (or the customer or the market) to instigate or absorb a change is more or less constant because it is tied to the nature of the business. For example, a hospital IT department is more conservative and has less tolerance for change than a nascent blockchain startup. Thus, the more frequently things change, the more likely they will change in the future, but at the same rate. For example, if every 2 years the company changes its payroll system, it is likely the company will change the payroll system within the next 2 years. If the system you design needs to interface with the payroll system and the horizon for using your system is longer than 2 years, then you must encapsulate the volatility in the payroll system and plan to contain the expected change. You must take into account the effect of a payroll system change even if the change was never given to you as an explicit requirement. You should strive to encapsulate changes that occur within the life of the system. If that projected lifespan is 5 to 7 years, a good starting point is identifying all the things that have changed in the application domain over the past 7 years. It is likely similar changes will occur within a similar timespan.

You should examine this way the longevity of all involved systems and subsystems with which your design interacts. For example, if the enterprise resource planning (ERP) system changes every 10 years, the last ERP change was 8 years ago, and the horizon for your new system is 5 years, then it is a good bet the ERP will change during the life of your system.

THE IMPORTANCE OF PRACTICING

If you only spend 2% of the time on anything, you will never be any good at it, regardless of your built-in intellect or methodology used. An amazing level of hubris is required to believe that once every few years someone can approach a whiteboard, draw a few lines, and nail the architecture. The basic expectation of professionals, be they doctors, pilots, welders or lawyers, is that they master their craft by training for it. You would not wish to be the passenger aboard a plane where the pilot has only a handful of flying hours. You would not wish to be the first patient of a doctor. Commercial airline pilots spend years (plural) in simulators and are trained through hundreds of flights by veteran pilots. Doctors dissect countless cadavers before they can touch the first patient, and even then, they are closely supervised.

Identifying areas of volatility is an acquired skill. Hardly any software architect is initially trained in volatility-based decomposition, and the vast majority of systems and projects use functional decomposition (with abysmal results). The best way of going about mastering volatility-based decomposition is to practice. This is the only way to address the 2% problem. Here are several ways you can start:

• Practice on an everyday software system with which you are familiar, such as your typical insurance company, a mobile app, a bank, or an online store.

• Examine your own past projects. In hindsight, you already know what the pain points were. Was that architecture of that past project done functionally? What things did change? What were the ripple effects of those changes? If you had encapsulated that volatility, would you have been able to deal with that change better?

- Look at your current project. It may not be too late to save it: Is it designed functionally? Can you list the areas of volatility and propose a superior architecture?

- Look at non-software systems such as a bicycle, a laptop, a house, and identify in those the areas of volatility.

Then do it again and do it some more. Practice and practice. After you have analyzed three to five systems, you should get the general technique. Sadly, learning to identify areas of volatility is not something you get to master by watching others. You cannot learn to ride a bicycle from a book. You have to mount a bicycle (and fall) a few times. The same is true with volatility-based decomposition. It is, however, preferable to fall during practice than to experiment on live subjects.

3

STRUCTURE

The previous chapter discussed the universal design principle of volatility-based decomposition. This principle governs the design of all practical systems—from houses, to laptops, to jumbo planes, to your own body. To survive and thrive, they all encapsulate the volatility of their constituent components. Software architects only have to design software systems. Fortunately, these systems share common areas of volatility. Over the years I have found these common areas of volatility within hundreds of systems. Furthermore, there are typical interactions, constraints, and run-time relationships between these common areas of volatility. If you recognize these, you can produce correct system architecture quickly, efficiently, and effectively.

Given this observation, *The Method* provides a template for the areas of volatility, guidelines for the interaction, and recommends operational patterns. By doing so, *The Method* goes beyond mere decomposition. Being able to furnish such general guidelines and structure across most software systems may sound far-fetched. You may wonder how these kinds of broad strokes could possibly apply across the diversity of software systems. The reason is that good architectures allow use in different contexts. For example, a mouse and an elephant are vastly different, yet they use identical architecture. The detailed designs of the mouse and the elephant, however, are very different. Similarly, *The Method* can provide you with the system architecture, but not its detailed design.

This chapter is all about *The Method*'s way of structuring a system, the advantages this brings, and its implications on the architecture. You will see classification of services based on their semantics and the associated guidelines, as well as how to layer your design. In addition, having clear, consistent nomenclature for components in your architecture and their relationship brings two other advantages. First, it provides a good starting point. You will still have to sweat over it, but at least you start at a reasonable point. Second, it improves communication because you can now convey your design intent to other architects or developers. Even communicating with yourself in this way is very valuable, as it helps to clarify your own thoughts.

USE CASES AND REQUIREMENTS

Before diving into architecture, consider requirements. Most projects, if they even bother to capture the requirements, use functional requirements. Functional requirements simply state the required functionality, such as "The system should do A." This is actually a poor way of specifying requirements, because it leaves the system's implementation of the A functionality open for interpretation. In fact, functional requirements allow for multiple opportunities for misinterpretations to arise between the customers and marketing, between marketing and engineering, and even between developers. This kind of ambiguity tends to persist until you have already spent considerable effort on developing and deploying the system, at which point rectifying it is the most expensive.

Requirements should capture the required behavior rather than the required functionality. You should specify how the system is required to operate as opposed to what it should do, which is arguably the essence of requirements gathering. As with most other things, this does take additional work and effort (something that people in general try to avoid), so getting requirements into this form will be an uphill struggle.

REQUIRED BEHAVIORS

A **use case** is an expression of required behavior—that is, how the system is required to go about accomplishing some work and adding value to the business. As such, a use case is a particular sequence of activities in the system. Use cases tend to be verbose and descriptive. They can describe end-user interactions with the system, or the system's interactions with other systems, or back-end processing. This ability is important because in any well-designed system, even one of modest size and complexity, the users interact with or observe just a small part of the system, which represents the tip of the iceberg. The bulk of the system remains below the waterline, and you should produce use cases for it as well.

You can capture use cases either textually or graphically. Textual use cases are easy to produce, which is a distinct advantage. Unfortunately, using text for use cases is an inferior way of describing use cases because the use cases may be too complex to capture with high fidelity in text. The real problem with textual use cases is that hardly anyone bothers to read even simple text, and for a good reason. Reading is an artificial activity for the human brain, because the brain is not wired to easily absorb and process complex ideas via text. Mankind has been reading for 5000 years—not long enough for the brain to catch up, evolutionarily speaking (thank you for making the effort with this book, though).

The best way of capturing a use case is graphically, with a diagram (Figure 3-1). Humans perform image processing astonishingly quickly, because almost half the human brain is a massive video processing unit. Diagrams allow you to take advantage of this processor to communicate ideas to your audience.

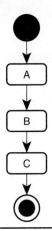

Figure 3-1 A use case diagram

Graphical use cases, however, can be very labor-intensive to produce, especially in large numbers. Many use cases may be simple enough to understand without a diagram. For example, the use case diagram in Figure 3-1 can be represented in text equally well. My rule of thumb: The presence of a nested "if" tells you that you should to draw the use case. No reader can parse a sentence containing a nested "if." Instead, readers will likely continually reread the use case or, more likely, pick up a pen and paper and try to visualize the use case themselves. By doing so, readers are interpreting the behavior—which also raises the possibility of misinterpretation. When readers are scribbling on the side of your textual use case, you know you should have provided the visualization in the first place. Diagrams also allow readers to easily follow a larger number of nested "if"s in a complex use case.

Activity Diagrams

The Method prefers activity diagrams[1] for graphical representation of use cases, primarily because activity diagrams can capture time-critical aspects of behavior, something that flowcharts and other diagrams are incapable of doing. You cannot represent parallel execution, blocking, or waiting for some event to take place in a flowchart. Activity diagrams, by contrast, incorporate a notion of concurrency.

---

1. https://en.wikipedia.org/wiki/Activity_diagram

For example, in Figure 3-2, you intuitively see the handling of parallel execution as a response to the event without even seeing a notation guide for the diagram. Note also how easy it is to follow the nested condition.

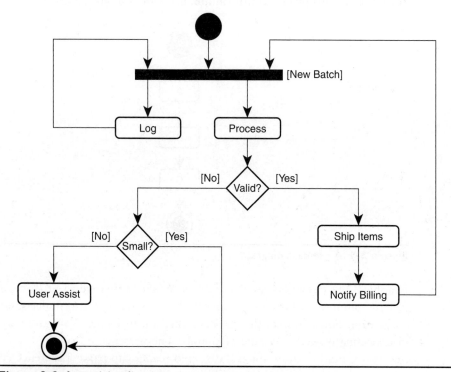

Figure 3-2 An activity diagram

> **Caution**   Do not confuse activity diagrams with use case diagrams. Use case diagrams[a] are user-centric and should have been called user case diagrams. Use case diagrams also do not include a notion of time or sequence.
>
> a. https://en.wikipedia.org/wiki/Use_case_diagram

LAYERED APPROACH

Software systems are typically designed in layers, and *The Method* relies heavily on layers. Layers allow you to layer encapsulation. Each layer encapsulates its own volatilities from the layers above and the volatilities in the layers below. Services inside the layers encapsulate volatility from each other, as shown in Figure 3-3.

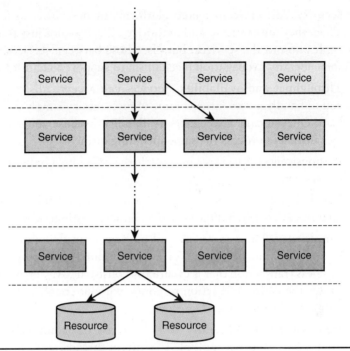

Figure 3-3 Services and layers

Even simple systems should be designed in layers to gain the benefit of encapsulation. In theory, the more layers, the better the encapsulation. Practical systems will have only a handful of layers, terminating with a layer of actual physical resources such as a data storage or a message queue.

USING SERVICES

The preferred way of crossing layers is by calling services. While you certainly can benefit from the structure of *The Method* and volatility-based decomposition even with regular classes, relying on services provides distinct advantages. Which technology and platform you use to implement your services is a secondary concern. When you do use services (as long as the technology you chose allows), you immediately gain the following benefits:

• **Scalability.** Services can be instantiated in a variety of ways, including on a per-call basis. This allows for a very large number of clients without placing a proportional load on the back-end resources, as you need only as many service instances as there are calls in progress.

- **Security.** All service-oriented platforms treat security as a first-class aspect. Thus, they authenticate and authorize all calls—not just those from the client application to the services, but also those between services. You can even use some identity propagation mechanism to support a chain-of-trust pattern.

- **Throughput and availability.** Services can accept calls over queues, allowing you to handle a very large volume of messages by simply queuing up the excess load. Queued calls also enable availability, because you can have multiple service instances process the same incoming queue.

- **Responsiveness.** Services can throttle the calls into a buffer to avoid maxing out the system.

- **Reliability.** Clients and services can use some reliable messaging protocol to guarantee delivery, handle network connectivity issues, and even order the calls.

- **Consistency.** The services can all participate in the same unit of work, either in a transaction (when supported by the infrastructure) or in a coordinated business transaction that is eventually consistent. Any error along the call chain causes the entire interaction to abort, without coupling the services along the nature of the error and the recovery logic.

- **Synchronization.** The calls to the service can be automatically synchronized even if the clients use multiple concurrent threads.

TYPICAL LAYERS

The Method calls for four layers in the system architecture. These layers conform to some classic software engineering practices. However, using volatility to drive the decomposition inside these layers may be new to you. Figure 3-4 depicts the typical layers in *The Method*.

THE CLIENT LAYER

The top layer in architecture is the **client layer**, also known as the **presentation layer**. I find the term "presentation" to be somewhat misleading. "Presentation" implies some information is being presented to human users, as if that is all that is expected from the top layer. The elements in the client layer may very well be end-user applications, but they can also be other systems interacting with your system. This is an important distinction: By calling this the client layer, you equalize all possible clients, treating them in the same way. All *Clients* (whether end-user applications or other systems) use the same entry points to the system (an important aspect of any good design) and are subject to the same access security, data types, and other interfacing requirements. This, in turn, promotes reuse and extensibility and allows for easier maintenance, as a fix at one entry point affects all *Clients* the same way.

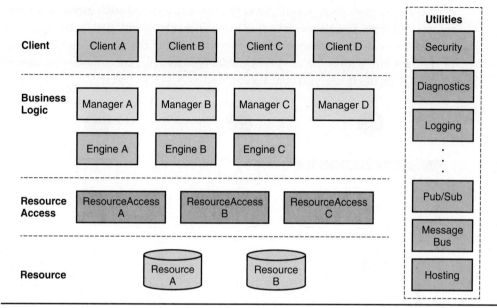

Figure 3-4 Typical layers in The Method

Having the *Clients* consume services caters to better separation of presentation from business logic. Most service-oriented technologies are very strict about the types of data they allow over the endpoints. This limits the ability to couple the *Clients* to the services, treats all *Clients* uniformly, and makes adding different types of *Clients*, at least in theory, easier to accomplish.

The client layer also encapsulates the potential volatility in *Clients*. Your system now and in the future across the axes of volatility may have different *Clients* such as desktop applications, web portals, mobile apps, holograms and augmented reality, APIs, administration applications, and so on. The various *Client* applications will use different technologies, be deployed differently, have their own versions and life cycles, and may be developed by different teams. Indeed, the client layer is often the most volatile part of a typical software system. However, all of that volatility is encapsulated in the various blocks of the client layer, and changes in one component do not affect another *Client* component.

THE BUSINESS LOGIC LAYER

The **business logic layer** encapsulates the volatility in the system's business logic. This layer implements the system's required behavior, which, as mentioned previously, is best expressed in use cases. If the use cases were static, there would be no need for a business logic layer. Use cases, however, are volatile, across both customers and time. Since a use case contains a sequence of activities in the system, a particular use case can change in only two ways: Either the sequence itself changes or the activities within the use case change. For example, consider the use case in Figure 3-1 versus the use cases in Figure 3-5.

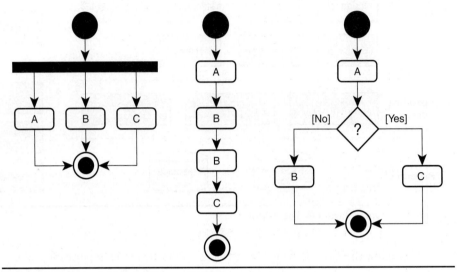

Figure 3-5 Sequence volatility

All four use cases in Figures 3-1 and 3-5 use the same activities A, B, and C, but each sequence is unique. The key observation here is that the sequence or the orchestration of the workflow can change independently from the activities.

Now consider the two activity diagrams in Figure 3-6. Both call for exactly the same sequence, but they use different activities. The activities can change independently from the sequence.

Both the sequence and the activities are volatile, and in *The Method* these volatilities are encapsulated in specific components called *Managers* and *Engines*. *Manager* components encapsulate the volatility in the sequence, whereas **Engine** components encapsulate the volatility in the activity. In Chapter 2, in the stock trading decomposition example, the Trade Workflow component (see Figure 2-13) is a *Manager*, while the Feed Transformation component is an *Engine*.

Since use cases are often related, *Managers* tend to encapsulate a family of logically related use cases, such as those in a particular subsystem. For example, with the stock trading system of Chapter 2, Analysis Workflow is a separate *Manager*

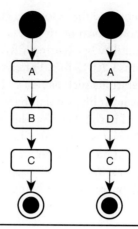

Figure 3-6 Activity volatility

from `Trade Workflow`, and each *Manager* has its own related set of use cases to execute. *Engines* have more restricted scope and encapsulate business rules and activities.

Since you can have great volatility in the sequence without any volatility in the activities of the sequence (see Figure 3-5), *Managers* may use zero or more *Engines*. *Engines* may be shared between *Managers* because you could perform an activity in one use case on behalf of one *Manager* and then perform the same activity for another *Manager* in a separate use case. You should design *Engines* with reuse in mind. However, if two *Managers* use two different *Engines* to perform the same activity, you either have functional decomposition on your hands or you have missed some activity volatility. You will see more on *Managers* and *Engines* later in this chapter.

THE RESOURCEACCESS LAYER

The aptly named **resource access layer** encapsulates the volatility in accessing a resource, and the components in this layer are called ***ResourceAccess***. For example, if the resource is a database, literally dozens of methods are available for accessing a database, and no single method is superior to all other methods in every respect. Over time, you may want to change the way you access the database, so that change or the volatility involved should be encapsulated. Note that you should not simply encapsulate the volatility in accessing the resource; that is, you must also encapsulate the volatility in the resource itself, such as a local database versus a cloud-based database, or in-memory storage versus durable storage. Resource changes invariably change *ResourceAccess* as well.

While the motivation behind the resource access layer is readily evident and many systems incorporate some form of an access layer, most such layers end up exposing the underlying volatility by creating a *ResourceAccess* contract that resembles I/O operations or that is CRUD-like. For example, if your *ResourceAccess* service contract contains operations such as `Select()`, `Insert()`, and `Delete()`, the underlying resource is most likely a database. If you later change the database to a distributed cloud-based hash table, that database-access-like contract will become useless, and a new contract is required. Changing the contract affects every *Engine* and *Manager* that has used the *ResourceAccess* component. Similarly, you must avoid operations such as `Open()`, `Close()`, `Seek()`, `Read()`, and `Write()` that betray the underlying resource as being a file. A well-designed *ResourceAccess* component exposes in its contract the atomic business verbs around a resource.

Use Atomic Business Verbs

The *Manager* services in the system execute some sequence of business activities. These activities, in turn, often comprise an even more granular set of activities. However, at some point you will have such low-level activities that they cannot be expressed by any other activity in the system. *The Method* refers to these indivisible activities as **atomic business verbs**. For example, in a bank, a classic use case would be to transfer money between two accounts. The transfer is done by crediting one account and debiting another. In a bank, credit and debit are atomic operations from the business's perspective. Note that an atomic business verb may require several steps from the system perspective to implement. The atomicity is geared toward the business, not the system.

Atomic business verbs are practically immutable because they relate strongly to the nature of the business, which, as discussed in Chapter 2, hardly ever changes. For example, since the time of the Medici, banks have performed credit and debit operations. Internally, the *ResourceAccess* service should convert these verbs from its contract into CRUDs or I/O against the resources. By exposing only the stable atomic business verbs, when the *ResourceAccess* service changes, only the internals of the access component change, rather than the whole system atop it.

ResourceAccess Reuse

ResourceAccess services can be shared between *Managers* and *Engines*. You should explicitly design *ResourceAccess* components with this reuse in mind. If two *Managers* or two *Engines* cannot use the same *ResourceAccess* service when accessing the same resource or have some need for specific access, perhaps you did not encapsulate some access volatility or did not isolate the atomic business verbs correctly.

THE RESOURCE LAYER

The **resource layer** contains the actual physical **Resources** on which the system relies, such as a database, file system, a cache, or a message queue. In *The Method*, the *Resource* can be internal to the system or outside the system. Often, the *Resource* is a whole system in its own right, but to your system it appears as just a *Resource*.

UTILITIES BAR

The **utilities** vertical bar on the right side of Figure 3-4 contains **Utility** services. These services are some form of common infrastructure that nearly all systems require to operate. *Utilities* may include `Security`, `Logging`, `Diagnostics`, `Instrumentation`, `Pub/Sub`, `Message Bus`, `Hosting`, and more. You will see later in this chapter that *Utilities* require different rules compared with the other components.

CLASSIFICATION GUIDELINES

As is true for every good idea, *The Method* can be abused. Without practice and critical thinking, it is possible to use *The Method* taxonomy in name only and still produce a functional decomposition. You can mitigate this risk to a great extent by adhering to the simple guidelines provided in this section.

Another use for leveraging guidelines is initiating design. At the beginning of nearly every design effort, most people are stumped, unsure where to even start. It is very helpful to be armed with some key observations that can both initiate and validate a budding design effort.

WHAT'S IN A NAME

Service names as well as diagrams are important in communicating your design to others. Descriptive names are so important within the business and resource access layers that *The Method* recommends the following conventions for naming them:

- Names of services must be two-part compound words written in Pascal case.
- The suffix of the name is always the service's type—for example, `Manager`, `Engine`, or `Access` (for *ResourceAccess*).
- The prefix varies with the type of service.
  - For *Managers*, the prefix should be a noun associated with the encapsulated volatility in the use cases.

- For *Engines*, the prefix should be a noun describing the encapsulated activity.
- For *ResourceAccess*, the prefix should be a noun associated with the *Resource*, such as data that the service provides to the consuming use cases.

• Gerunds (a gerund is a noun created by tacking "ing" onto a verb) should be used as a prefix only in with *Engines*. The use of gerunds elsewhere in the business or access layers usually signals functional decomposition.

• Atomic business verbs should not be used in a prefix for a service name. These verbs should be confined to operation names in contracts interfacing with the resource access layer.

As examples, in a bank design, `AccountManager` and `AccountAccess` are acceptable service names. However, the names `BillingManager` and `BillingAccess` smell of functional decomposition because the gerund prefixes convey a concept of "doing" rather than of an orchestration or access volatility. `CalculatingEngine` is a good candidate name because *Engines* "do" things such as aggregate, adapt, strategize, validate, rate, calculate, transform, generate, regulate, translate, locate, and search. The name `AccountEngine`, by contrast, is devoid of any indicator of the activity volatility and again carries a strong smell of functional or domain decomposition.

THE FOUR QUESTIONS

The layers of services and resources in the architecture loosely correspond to the four English questions of "who," "what," "how," and "where." "Who" interacts with the system is in the *Clients*, "what" is required of the system is in *Managers*, "how" the system performs business activities is in *Engines*, "how" the system accesses *Resources* is in *ResourceAccess*, and "where" the system state is in *Resources* (see Figure 3-7).

The four questions loosely correspond to the layers because volatility trumps everything. For example, if there is little or no volatility in the "how," the *Managers* can perform both "what" and "how."

Asking and answering the four questions is useful at both ends of the design effort, for initiation and for validation. If all you have is a clean slate and no clear idea where to start, you can initiate the design effort by answering the four questions. Make a list of all the "who" and put them in one bin as candidates for *Clients*. Make a list of all the "what" and put them in another bin as candidates for *Managers*, and so on. The result will not be perfect—for example, all "what" components will not necessarily coalesce into individual *Managers*—but it is a start.

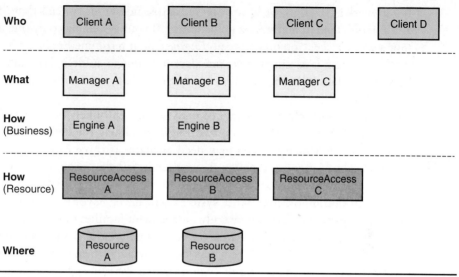

Figure 3-7 Questions and layers

Once you complete your design, take a step back and examine the design. Are all your *Clients* "who," with no trace of "what" in them? Are all the *Managers* "what," without a smidgen of "who" and "where" in them? Again, the mapping of questions to layers will not be perfect. In some cases, you could have crossover between questions. However, if you are convinced the encapsulation of the volatility is justified, there is no reason to doubt that choice further. If you are unconvinced, the questions could indicate a red flag and a decomposition to investigate.

The four questions tie in nicely with the previous guideline on naming the services. If the *Manager* prefixes describe the encapsulated volatilities, it is more natural to talk about them in terms of "what" as opposed to the verb-like "how." If the *Engine* prefixes are gerunds describing the encapsulated activities, it is more natural to talk about them in terms of "how" as opposed to "what" or "where." For similar reasons, *ResourceAccess* encapsulates "how" to access the *Resources* that lie behind it.

MANAGERS-TO-ENGINES RATIO

Most designs end up with fewer *Engines* than you might initially imagine. First, for an *Engine* to exist, there must be some fundamental operational volatility that you should encapsulate—that is, an unknown number of ways of doing something. Such volatilities are uncommon. If your design contains a large number of *Engines*, you may have inadvertently done a functional decomposition.

In our work at IDesign, we have observed across numerous systems that *Managers* and *Engines* tend to maintain a golden ratio. If your system has only one *Manager* (not a god service), you may have no *Engines*, or at most one *Engine*. Think about it: If the system is so simple that one decent *Manager* suffices, how likely is it to have high volatility in the activities but not that many types of use cases?

Generally, if your system has two *Managers*, you will likely need one *Engine*. If your system has three *Managers*, two *Engines* is likely the best number. If your system has five *Managers*, you may need as many as three *Engines*. If your system has eight *Managers*, then you have already failed to produce a good design: The large number of *Managers* strongly indicates you have done a functional or domain decomposition. Most systems will never have that many *Managers* because they will not have many truly independent families of use cases with their own volatility. In addition, a *Manager* can support more than one family of use cases, often expressed as different service contracts, or facets of the service. This can further reduce the number of *Managers* in a system.

KEY OBSERVATIONS

Armed with the recommendations of *The Method*, you can make some sweeping observations about the qualities you expect to see in a well-designed system. Deviating from these observations may indicate a lingering functional decomposition or at least an unripe decomposition in which you have encapsulated few of the glaring volatilities but have missed others.

> **Note**   Clear terminology for the various pieces of the architecture enables this type of communication of observations and recommendations.

Volatility Decreases Top-Down

In a well-designed system, volatility should decrease top-down across the layers. *Clients* are very volatile. Some customers may want the *Clients* this way, other customers would want the *Clients* that way, and others may want the same thing but on a different device. This naturally high level of volatility has nothing to do with the required behavior of the underlying system. *Managers* do change, but not as much as their *Clients*. *Managers* change when the use cases—the required behavior of the system—change. *Engines* are less volatile than *Managers*. For an *Engine* to change, your business must change the way it is performing some activity, which is more uncommon than changing the sequencing of activities. *ResourceAccess* services are even less volatile than *Engines*. How often do you change the way you access a *Resource* or, for that matter, change the *Resource*?

You can change activities and their sequence without ever changing the mapping of the atomic business verbs to *Resources*. *Resources* are the least volatile components, changing at a glacial pace compared with the rest of the system.

A design in which the volatility decreases down the layers is extremely valuable. The components in the lower layers have more items that depend on them. If the components you depend upon the most are also the most volatile, your system will implode.

Reuse Increases Top-Down

Reuse, unlike volatility, should increase going down the layers. *Clients* are hardly ever reusable. A *Client* application is typically developed for a particular type of platform and market and cannot be reused. For example, the code in a web portal cannot easily be reused in a desktop application, and the desktop application cannot be reused in a mobile device. *Managers* are reusable because you can use the same *Manager* and use cases from multiple *Clients*. *Engines* are even more reusable than *Managers* because the same *Engine* could be called by multiple *Managers*, in different use cases, to perform the same activity. *ResourceAccess* components are very reusable because they can be called by *Engines* and *Managers*. The *Resources* are the most reusable element in any well-designed systems. The ability to reuse existing *Resources* in a new design is often a key factor in business approval of a new system's implementation.

Almost-Expendable *Managers*

Managers can fall into one of three categories: expensive, expendable, and almost expendable. You can distinguish the category to which a *Manager* belongs by the way you respond when you are asked to change it. If your response is to fight the change, to fear its cost, to argue against the change, and so forth, then the *Manager* was clearly expensive and not expendable. An expensive *Manager* indicates that the *Manager* is too big, likely due to functional decomposition. If your response to the change request is just to shrug it off, thinking little of it, the *Manager* is pass-through and expendable. Expendable *Managers* are always a design flaw and a distortion of the architecture. They often exist only to satisfy the design guidelines without any real need for encapsulating use case volatility.

If, however, your response to the proposed *Manager* change is contemplative, causing you to think through the specific ways of adapting the *Manager* to the change in the use case (perhaps even quickly estimating the amount of work required), the *Manager* is almost expendable. If the *Manager* merely orchestrates the *Engines* and the *ResourceAccess*, encapsulating the sequence volatility, you have a great *Manager* service, albeit an almost expendable one. A well-designed *Manager* service should be almost expendable.

SUBSYSTEMS AND SERVICES

The *Managers*, *Engines*, and *ResourceAccess* are all services on their own right. A cohesive interaction between the *Manager*, *Engines*, and *ResourceAccess* may constitute a single logical service to external consumers. You can view such a set of interacting services as a logical subsystem. You group these together as a **vertical slice** of your system (Figure 3-8), where each vertical slice implements a corresponding set of use cases.

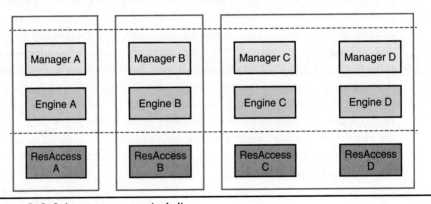

Figure 3-8 Subsystems as vertical slices

Avoid over-partitioning your system into subsystems. Most systems should have only a handful of subsystems. Likewise, you should limit the number of *Managers* per subsystem to three. This also allows you to somewhat increase the total number of *Managers* in the system across all subsystems.

INCREMENTAL CONSTRUCTION

If the system is relatively simple and small, the business value of the system—that is, the execution of the use cases—will likely require all components of the architecture. For such systems, there is no sense in releasing, say, just the *Engines* or the *ResourceAccess* components.

With a large system, it could be that certain subsystems (such as the vertical slices of Figure 3-8) can stand alone and provide direct business value. Such systems will be more expensive to build and take longer to complete. In such cases it makes sense to develop and deliver the system in stages, one slice at a time, as opposed to providing a single release at the end of the project. Moreover, the customer will be able to provide early feedback to the developers on the incremental releases as opposed to only the complete system at the end.

With both small and large systems, the right approach to construction is another universal principle:

Design iteratively, build incrementally.

This principle is true regardless of domain and industry. For example, suppose you wish to build your house on a plot of land you have purchased. Even the best architect will not be able to produce the design for your house in a single session. There will be some back-and-forth as you define the problem and discuss constraints such as funds, occupants, style, time, and risk. You will start with some rough cuts to the blueprints, refine them, evaluate the implications, and examine alternatives. After several of these iterations, the design will converge. When it is time to build the house, will you do that iteratively, too? Will you start with a two-person tent, grow it out to a four-person tent, then to a small shed, then to a small house, and finally to a bigger house? It would be insane to even contemplate such an approach. Instead, you are likely to dig and cast the foundation, then erect the walls to the first floor, then connect utilities to the structure, then add the second floor, and finally add the roof. In short, you build a simple house incrementally. There is no value for the prospective homeowner in having just the foundations or the roof. That is, the house—like an incrementally built simple software system—has no real value until complete. However, if the building has multiple floors (or multiple wings), it may be possible to build it incrementally and deliver intermediate value. Your design may allow you to complete one floor at a time (or one wing at a time), similar to the "one slice at a time" approach to a large software system.

Another example is assembling cars. While the car company may have had a team of designers designing a car across multiple iterations, when it is time to build the car, the manufacturing process does not start with a skateboard, grow that to a scooter, then a bicycle, then a motorcycle, and finally a car. Instead, a car is built incrementally. First, the workers weld a chassis together, then they bolt on the engine block, and then they add the seats, the skin, and the tires. They paint the car, add the dashboard, and finally install the upholstery.

There are two reasons why you can build only incrementally, and not iteratively. First, building iteratively is horrendously wasteful and difficult (turning a motorcycle into a car is much more difficult than just building a car). Second, and much more importantly, the intermediate iterations do not have any business value. If the customer wants a car to take the kids to school, what would the customer do with a motorcycle and why should the customer pay for it?

Building incrementally also allows you to accommodate constraints on your time and budget. If you design a four-story dream house but you can afford only a single-floor house, you have two options. The first option is still build a four-story house with a single-floor budget by using plywood for all walls, sheet plastic for windows, buckets for a bathroom, dirt for floors, and a thatched roof. The second option is to properly build just the first floor of the four-story house. When you accumulate additional funds, you can then construct the second and third floors. A decade later, when you finally complete the building, that construction still matches the original architecture.

The ability to build incrementally over time, within the confines of the architecture, is predicated on the architecture remaining constant and true. With functional decomposition, you face ever-shifting piles of debris. It is fair to assume that those who know only functional decomposition are condemned to iterative construction. With volatility-based decomposition, you have a chance of getting it right.

Extensibility

The vertical slices of the system also enable you to accommodate extensibility. The correct way of extending any system is not by opening it up and hammering on existing components. If you have designed correctly for extensibility, you can mostly leave existing things alone and extend the system as a whole. Continuing the house analogy, if you want to add a second floor to a single-story house at some point in the future, then the first floor must have been designed to carry the additional load, the plumbing must have been done in a way that could be extended to the second floor, and so on. Adding a second floor by destroying the first floor and then building new first and second floors is called rework, not extensibility. The design of a *Method*-based system is geared toward extensibility: Just add more of these slices or subsystems.

ABOUT MICROSERVICES

I am credited as one of the pioneers of microservices. As early as 2006, in my speaking and writing I called for building systems in which every class was a service.[2,3] This requires the use of a technology that can support such granular

---

2. https://wikipedia.org/wiki/Microservices#History
3. Juval Löwy, *Programming WCF Services*, 1st ed. (O'Reilly Media, 2007), 543–553.

use of services. I extended Windows Communication Foundation (WCF) at the time to do just that, taking every class and treating it as a service while maintaining the conventional programming model of classes.[4] I never called these services "microservices." Then, as now, I did not think the microservices concept existed. There are no microservices—only services. For example, the water pump in my car provides a critical service to my car, and that pump is only 8 inches long. The water pump that the local water company uses to push water to my town provides the town with a very valuable service, but it is 8 feet long. The existence of a larger pump does not suddenly transform the pump in my car into a micropump: It is still just a pump. Services are services regardless of their size. To understand the origin of the artificial concept of microservices, you have to reflect on the history of service-orientation.

History and Concerns

At the dawn of service-orientation, in the early 2000s, many organizations simply exposed their system as a whole as a service. The resulting monstrous monolith was impossible to maintain and extend due to its complexity. Some 10 years of agony later, the industry recognized the error of this approach and started calling for more granular use of services, which it dubbed microservices. In common usage, **microservices** correspond to domains or subsystems—that is, to the slices (red boxes) of Figure 3-8. There are three problems with this idea as practiced today.

The first problem is the implied constraint on the number of services. If smaller services are better than larger services, why stop at the subsystem level? The subsystem is still too big as the most granular service unit. Why not have the building blocks of the subsystem be services? You should push the benefits of services as far down the architecture as possible. In a *Method* subsystem, the *Manager, Engine,* and *ResourceAccess* components within a subsystem must be services as well.

> **Note**   Appendix B discusses the issue of service granularity. The appendix explains why having few large services (corresponding to subsystems) is a poor design.

The second problem is the widespread use of functional decomposition in microservice design by the industry at large. This factor alone will doom every nascent microservices effort. Those attempting to construct microservices will have to contend with the complexity of both functional decomposition and service-orientation

---

4. Löwy, *Programming WCF Services*, 1st ed., pp. 48–51; Juval Löwy, *Programming WCF Services*, 3rd ed. (O'Reilly Media, 2010), 74–75.

without gaining any of the benefits of the modularity of the services. This double punch may be more than what most projects can handle. Indeed, I fear that microservices will be the biggest failure in the history of software. Maintainable, reusable, extensible services are possible—just not in this way.

The third problem relates to communication protocols. Although the choice of communication protocols has more to do with detailed design than with architecture, the effect of the choice is worth a passing comment here. The vast majority of microservice stacks (as of this writing) use REST/WebAPI and HTTP to communicate with the services. Most technology vendors and consultants endorse this practice across the board (perhaps because it makes their life easier if everyone uses the lowest common denominator). These protocols, however, were designed for publicly facing services, as the gateway to systems. As a general principle, in any well-designed system you should never use the same communication mechanism both internally and externally.

For example, my laptop has a drive that provides it with a very important service: storage. The laptop also consumes a service offered by the network router for all DNS requests, and an SMTP server that offers email service. For the external services, the laptop uses TCP/IP; for the internal services like the drive, it uses SATA. The laptop utilizes multiple such specialized internal protocols to perform its essential functions.

Another example is the human body. Your liver provides you with a very important service: metabolism. Your body also provides a valuable service to your customers and organization, and you use a natural language (English) to communicate with them. However, you do not speak English to communicate with your liver. Instead, you use nerves and hormones.

The protocol used for external services is typically low bandwidth, slow, expensive, and error prone. Such attributes indicate a high degree of decoupling. Unreliable HTTP may be perfect for external services, but this protocol should be avoided between internal services where the communication and the services must be impeccable.

Using the wrong protocol between services can be fatal. It is not the end of the world if you cannot talk with your boss or have a misunderstanding with a customer, but you will die if you cannot communicate correctly or at all with your liver.

Similar level-of-service issues exist with specialization and efficiency. Using HTTP between internal services is akin to using English to control your body's internal services. Even if the words were perfectly heard and understood, English lacks the adaptability, performance, and vocabulary required for describing the internal services' interactions.

Internal services such as *Engines* and *ResourceAccess* should rely on fast, reliable, high-performance communication channels. These include TCP/IP, named pipes, IPC, Domain Sockets, Service Fabric remoting, custom in-memory interception chains, message queues, and so on.

OPEN AND CLOSED ARCHITECTURES

Any layered architecture can have one of two possible operational models: open or closed. This section contrasts the two alternatives. From this discussion, you can glean some additional design guidelines in the context of the classification of services.

OPEN ARCHITECTURE

In an **open architecture**, any component can call any other component regardless of the layer in which the components reside. Components can call up, sideways, and down as much as you like. Open architectures offer the ultimate flexibility. However, an open architecture achieves that flexibility by sacrificing encapsulation and introducing a significant amount of coupling.

For example, imagine in Figure 3-4 that the *Engines* directly call the *Resources*. While such a call is technically possible, when you wish to switch *Resources* or merely change the way you access a *Resource*, suddenly all your *Engines* must change. How about the *Clients* calling *ResourceAccess* services directly? While that is not as bad as calling the *Resources* themselves, all the business logic must migrate to the *Clients*. Any change to the business logic would then force reworking the *Clients*.

Calling up a layer is also inadvisable. In Figure 3-4, what if a *Manager* called a *Client* to update some control in the UI? Now as the UI changes, the *Manager* must respond to that change, too. You have imported the volatility of the *Clients* to the *Managers*.

Calling sideways (intra-layer) also creates an inordinate amount of coupling. Imagine Manager A calling Manager B in Figure 3-4. In this case, Manager B is just an activity inside a use case executed by Manager A. *Managers* are supposed to encapsulate a set of independent use cases. Are the use cases of Manager B now independent of those of Manager A? Any change to Manager B's way of doing the activity will break Manager A, calling to mind the issues of Figure 2-5. Calling sideways in this way is almost always the result of functional decomposition at the *Managers* level.

How about Engine A calling Engine B? Was Engine B a separate volatile activity from Engine A? Again, functional decomposition is likely behind the need to chain the *Engines* calls.

When using open architecture, there is hardly any benefit of having architectural layers in the first place. In general, in software engineering, trading encapsulation for flexibility is a bad trade.

CLOSED ARCHITECTURE

In a **closed architecture**, you strive to maximize the benefits of the layers by disallowing calling up between layers and sideways within layers. Disallowing calling down between layers would maximize the decoupling between the layers but produce a useless design. A closed architecture opens a chink in the layers, allowing components in one layer to call those in the adjacent lower layer. The components within a layer are of service to the components in the layer immediately above them, but they encapsulate whatever happens underneath. Closed architecture promotes decoupling by trading flexibility for encapsulation. In general, that is a better trade than the other way around.

SEMI-CLOSED/SEMI-OPEN ARCHITECTURE

It is easy to point out the clear problems with open architectures—of allowing calling up, down, or sideways. However, are all three sins equally bad? The worst of them is calling up: That not only creates cross-layer coupling, but also imports the volatility of a higher layer to the lower layers. The second worst offender is calling sideways because such calls couple components inside the layer. The closed architecture allows calling one layer below, but what about calling multiple layers down? A **semi-closed/semi-open architecture** allows calling more than one layer down. This, again, is a trade of encapsulation for flexibility and performance and, in general, is a trade to avoid.

Notably, the use of semi-closed/semi-open architecture is justified in two classic cases. This first case occurs when you design some key piece of infrastructure, and you must squeeze every ounce of performance from it. In such a case, transitioning down multiple layers may adversely affect performance. For example, consider the Open Systems Interconnection (OSI) model of seven layers for network communication.[5] When vendors implement this model in their TCP stack, they cannot afford the performance penalty incurred by seven layers for every call, and they sensibly choose a semi-closed/semi-open architecture for the stack. The second case occurs within a codebase that hardly ever changes. The loss in encapsulation and the additional coupling in such a codebase is immaterial because you will not have to maintain the code much, if at all. Again, a network stack implementation is a good example for code that hardly ever changes.

Semi-closed/semi-open architectures do have their place. Nevertheless, most systems do not have the level of performance required to justify such designs, and their codebase is never that immutable.

RELAXING THE RULES

For real-life business systems, the best choice is always a closed architecture. The discussion in the previous sections of the open and semi-open options should discourage you from any other choice.

While closed architecture systems are the most decoupled and the most encapsulated, they are also the least flexible. This inflexibility could lead to Byzantine-like levels of complexity due to the indirections and intermediacy, and rigid design is inadvisable. *The Method* relaxes the rules of closed architecture to reduce complexity and overhead without compromising encapsulation or decoupling.

Calling *Utilities*

In a closed architecture, *Utilities* pose a challenge. Consider Logging, a service used for recording run-time events. If you classify Logging as a *Resource*, then the *ResourceAccess* can use it, but the *Managers* cannot. If you place Logging at the same level as the *Managers*, only the *Clients* can log. The same goes for Security or Diagnostics—services that almost all other components require. In short, there is no good location for *Utilities* among the layers of a closed architecture. *The Method* places *Utilities* in a vertical bar on the side of the layers (see Figure 3-4). This bar cuts across all layers, allowing any component in the architecture to use any *Utility*.

You may see attempts by some developers to abuse the utilities bar by christening as a *Utility* any component they wish to short-circuit across all layers. Not all

---

5. https://en.wikipedia.org/wiki/OSI_model

components can reside in the utilities bar. To qualify as a *Utility*, the component must pass a simple litmus test: Can the component plausibly be used in any other system, such as a smart cappuccino machine? For example, a smart cappuccino machine could use a `Security` service to see if the user can drink coffee. Similarly, the cappuccino machine may want to log how much coffee the office workers drink, have diagnostics, and be able to use the `Pub/Sub` service to publish an event notifying that it is running low on coffee. Each of these needs justifies encapsulation in a *Utility* service. In contrast, you will be hard-pressed to explain why a cappuccino machine has a mortgage interest calculating service as a *Utility*.

Calling *ResourceAccess* by Business Logic

This next guideline may be implied, but it is important enough to state explicitly. Because they are in the same layer, both *Managers* and *Engines* can call *ResourceAccess* services without violating the closed architecture (see Figure 3-4). Allowing *Managers* to call *ResourceAccess* is also implied from the section defining *Managers* and *Engines*. A *Manager* that uses no *Engines* must be able to access the underlying *Resources*.

Managers Calling *Engines*

Managers can directly call *Engines*. The separation between *Managers* and *Engines* is almost at the detailed design level. *Engines* are really just an expression of the Strategy design pattern[6] used to implement the activities within the *Managers'* workflows. Therefore, *Manager*-to-*Engine* calls are not truly sideways calls, as is the case with *Manager*-to-*Manager* calls. Alternatively, you can think of *Engines* as residing in a different or orthogonal plane to the *Managers*.

Queued *Manager-to-Manager*

While *Managers* should not call directly sideways to other *Managers*, a *Manager* can queue a call to another *Manager*. There are actually two explanations—a technical one and a semantic one—why this does not violate the closed architecture principle.

The technical explanation involves the very mechanics of a queued call. When a client calls a queued service, the client interacts with a proxy to the service, which then deposits the message into a message queue for the service. A queue listener entity monitors the queue, detects the new message, picks it off the queue, and

---

6. Erich Gamma, Richard Helm, Ralph Johnson, and John Vlissides, *Design Patterns: Elements of Reusable Object-Oriented Software* (Addison-Wesley, 1994).

calls the service. Using *The Method* structure, when a *Manager* queues a call to another *Manager*, the proxy is a *ResourceAccess* to the underlying *Resource*, the queue; that is, the call actually goes down, not sideways. The queue listener is effectively another *Client* in the system, and it is also calling downward to the receiving *Manager*. No sideways call actually takes place.

The semantic explanation involves the nature of use cases. Business systems quite commonly have one use case that triggers a latent, much-deferred execution of another use case. For example, imagine a system in which a *Manager* executing a use case must save some system state for analysis at the end of the month. Without interrupting its flow, the *Manager* could queue the analysis request to another *Manager*. The second *Manager* could dequeue at the month's end and perform its analysis workflow. The two use cases are independent and decoupled on the timeline.

Opening the Architecture

Even with the best set of guidelines, time and again you will find developers trying to open the architecture by calling sideways, calling up, or committing some other violation of a closed architecture. Do not brush these transgressions aside or demand blind compliance with the guidelines. Nearly always, the discovery of such a transgression indicates some underlying need that made developers violate the guidelines. You must address that need correctly, in a way that complies with the closed architecture principle. For example, suppose that during design or code review, you discover one *Manager* directly calling another *Manager*. The developer may attempt to justify the sideways call by pointing out some requirement for another use case to execute in response to the original use case. It is very unlikely, however, that the response of the second *Manager* must occur immediately. Queuing the inter-*Manager* call would both be a better design and avoid the sideways call.

In another review, suppose you detect a *Manager* calling up to a *Client*—a gross violation of the closed architecture principle. As justification, the developer points to a requirement to notify the *Client* when something happens. While a valid requirement, calling up is not an acceptable resolution. Over time, other *Clients* could need the notification, or other *Managers* might need to notify the *Client*. What you have unearthed is volatility in who notifies and volatility in who receives that event. You should encapsulate that volatility by using a Pub/Sub service from the utilities bar. The *Manager* can, of course, call that *Utility*. In the future, adding other subscribing *Clients* or publishing *Managers* is a trivial task and would have no undesired repercussions in the system.

DESIGN "DON'TS"

With the definitions in place for both the services and the layers, it is also possible to compile a list of things to avoid—the design "don'ts." Some of the items on the list may appear obvious to you after the previous sections, yet I have seen them often enough to conclude they were not obvious after all. The main reason people go against a "don't" guideline is that they have created a functional decomposition and have managed to convince themselves that it is not functional.

If you do one of the things on this list, you will likely live to regret it. Treat any violation of these rules as a red flag and investigate further to see what you are missing:

- *Clients* do not call multiple *Managers* in the same use case. Doing so implies that the *Managers* are tightly coupled and no longer represent separate families of use cases, or separate subsystems, or separate slices. Chained *Manager* calls from the *Client* indicate functional decomposition, requiring the *Client* to stitch the underlying functionalities together (see Figure 2-1). *Clients* can call multiple *Managers* but not in the same use case; for example, a *Client* can call Manager A to perform use case 1 and then call Manager B to perform use case 2.

- *Clients* do not call *Engines*. The only entry points to the business layer are the *Managers*. The *Managers* represent the system, and the *Engines* are really an internal layer implementation detail. If the *Clients* call the *Engines*, use case sequencing and associated volatility are forced to migrate to the *Clients*, polluting them with business logic. Calls from *Clients* to *Engines* are the hallmark of a functional decomposition.

- *Managers* do not queue calls to more than one *Manager* in the same use case. If there are two *Managers* receiving a queued call, why not a third? Why not all of them? The need to have two (or more) *Managers* respond to a queued call is a strong indication that more *Managers* (and maybe all of them) would need to respond, so you should use a Pub/Sub *Utility* service instead.

- *Engines* do not receive queued calls. *Engines* are utilitarian and exist to execute a volatile activity for a *Manager*. They have no independent meaning on their own. A queued call, by definition, executes independently from anything else in the system. Performing just the activity of an *Engine*, disconnected from any use case or other activities, does not make any business sense.

- *ResourceAccess* services do not receive queued calls. Very similar to the *Engines* guideline, *ResourceAccess* services exist to service a *Manager* or an *Engine* and have no meaning on their own. Accessing a *Resource* independently from anything else in the system does not make any business sense.

- *Clients* do not publish events. Events represent changes to the state of the system about which *Clients* (or *Managers*) may want to know. A *Client* has no need to notify itself (or other *Clients*). In addition, knowledge of the internals of the system is often required to detect the need to publish an event—knowledge that the *Clients* should not have. However, with a functional decomposition, the *Client* is the system and needs to publish the event.

- *Engines* do not publish events. Publishing an event requires noticing and responding to a change in the system and is typically a step in a use case executed by the *Manager*. An *Engine* performing an activity has no way of knowing much about the context of the activity or the state of the use case.

- *ResourceAccess* services do not publish events. *ResourceAccess* services have no way of knowing the significance of the state of the *Resource* to the system. Any such knowledge or responding behavior should reside in *Managers*.

- *Resources* do not publish events. The need for the *Resource* to publish events is often the result of a tightly coupled functional decomposition. Similar to the case for *ResourceAccess*, business logic of this kind should reside in *Managers*. As a *Manager* modifies the state of the system, the *Manager* should also publish the appropriate events.

- *Engines*, *ResourceAccess*, and *Resources* do not subscribe to events. Processing an event is almost always the start of some use case, so it must be done in a *Client* or a *Manager*. The *Client* may inform a user about the event, and the *Manager* may execute some back-end behavior.

- *Engines* never call each other. Not only do such calls violate the closed architecture principle, but they also do not make sense in a volatility-based decomposition. The *Engine* should have already encapsulated everything to do with that activity. Any *Engine*-to-*Engine* calls indicate functional decomposition.

- *ResourceAccess* services never call each other. If *ResourceAccess* services encapsulate the volatility of an atomic business verb, one atomic verb cannot require another. This is similar to the rule that *Engines* should not call each other. Note that a 1:1 mapping between *ResourceAccess* and *Resources* (every *Resource* has its own *ResourceAccess*) is not required. Often two or more *Resources* logically must be joined together to implement some atomic business verbs. A single *ResourceAccess* service should perform the join rather than inter-*ResourceAccess* services calls.

Strive for Symmetry

Another universal design rule is that all good architectures are symmetric. Consider your own body. You do not have a third hand sticking up on your right side because evolutionary pressures were omnidirectional, enforcing symmetry. Evolutionary pressures apply to software systems as well, forcing the systems to respond to the changing environment or become extinct. The quest for symmetry, however, is only at the architecture level, not in detailed design. Certainly, your internal organs are not symmetric because such symmetry offered no evolutionary advantage to your ancestors (i.e., the system dies when you expose its internals).

The symmetry in software systems manifests in repeated call patterns across use cases. You should expect symmetry, and its absence is a cause for concern. For example, suppose a *Manager* implements four use cases, three of which publish an event with the Pub/Sub service and the fourth of which does not. That break of symmetry is a design smell. Why is the fourth case different? What are you missing or overdoing? Is that *Manager* a real *Manager*, or is it a functionally decomposed component without volatility? Symmetry can also be broken by the presence of something, not just by its absence. For example, if a *Manager* implements four use cases, of which only one ends up with a queued call to another *Manager*, that asymmetry is also a smell. Symmetry is so fundamental for good design that you should generally see the same call patterns across *Managers*.

4

COMPOSITION

Your software system's reason for being is to service the business by addressing its customers' requirements and needs. The previous two chapters discussed how to decompose the system into its components to create its architecture. The decomposition into components is inherently a static layout of the system, like a blueprint. During execution, the system is dynamic, and the various components interact with each other. But how do you know the **composition** of these components at runtime adequately satisfies all the requirements? Validating your design has to do with requirements analysis, system design, and your added value as the architect. Design validation and composition, as you will see, are intimately related. You can and must be able to produce a viable design and validate it in a repeatable manner.

This chapter provides you with the tools to verify that the system not only addresses the current requirements but also can withstand future changes to the requirements. That objective requires first recognizing the nature of requirements and change, and how both relate to system design. This recognition, in turn, yields a fundamental observation about system design along with practical recommendations for producing a valid design.

REQUIREMENTS AND CHANGES

Requirements change. Accept it—that's what requirements do.

Requirement change is fantastic. If requirements were static, none of us would have a job: Someone, somewhere, would have developed some adequate version of the system in the past, and that system would have been in service ever since. The more requirements change, the better off everyone among the technical ranks will be. The world is heavily dependent on software, yet there are still so few developers and architects and so many of everyone else. The more the requirements change, the higher the demand for software professional services will be, and since the supply of software professionals is limited, the higher their compensation and benefits will be.

RESENTING CHANGE

As wonderful as changes to requirements are, many in the industry have spent their entire career resenting such changes. The reason is simple: Most developers and architects design their system against the requirements. In fact, they go to great lengths to transcribe the requirements to components of the architecture. They strive to maximize the affinity between the requirements and the system design. However, when the requirements change, their design also must change. In any system, a change to the design is very painful, often destructive, and always expensive. Since nobody likes pain (even when it is self-inflicted, as in this case), people have learned to resent changes to requirements, literally resenting the hand that feeds them.

DESIGN PRIME DIRECTIVE

The solution for this dissonance of resenting the changes is so simple that it has eluded almost everyone for their entire career:

Never design against the requirements.

This simple directive goes contrary to what most have been taught and have practiced, even though it should have been plainly evident for all to see. Any attempt at designing against the requirements will always guarantee pain. Since pain is bad, there should be no excuse for doing something that is so ill advised. People may even be fully aware that their design process cannot work and has never worked, but lacking alternatives they resort to the one option they know—to design against the requirements.

> **Note** The perils of designing against the requirements are not limited to software systems. Chapter 2 discussed the maddening experience of building a house while designing against the required functionality.

Futility of Requirements

As discussed in Chapter 3, the correct way of capturing the requirements is in the form of use cases: the required set of behaviors of the system. A decent-sized system has dozens of these use cases, and large systems may have hundreds. At the same time, no one in the history of software has ever had the time to correctly spec-out hundreds of use cases at the beginning of the project.

Suppose that on day 1 of a new project you are given a folder with 300 use cases. Can you trust that this collection is correct and complete? Would you be surprised to learn that the real number was actually 330 use cases and that you are missing a few use cases? If you are given 300 use cases, will you be shocked to learn that the real number was actually 200 because the requirements spec contains many duplicates? In this case, if you design against the requirements, will you not be doing at least 50% more work? Is it impossible for you to receive a set of use cases in which some of the use cases are mutually exclusive? How about the risk of having defective use cases that compel you to implement the wrong behavior?

Even if by some miracle someone did take the considerable time needed to correctly capture all 300 use cases in activity diagrams, to confirm there are no missing use cases, to reconcile the mutually exclusive use cases, and to consolidate the duplicate use cases, that effort will be of little value because requirements will change. Over time you will have new requirements, some existing requirements will be removed, and other requirements will just change in place. In short, any attempt of gathering the complete set of requirements and designing against them is an exercise in futility.

COMPOSABLE DESIGN

Before prescribing the correct way of satisfying the requirements, you have to set the bar correctly for satisfying the requirements. The goal of any system design is to be able to satisfy all use cases. The word *all* in the previous sentence really means all: present and future, known and unknown use cases. This expectation is where the bar is set. Nothing less will do. If you fail to pass that bar, then at some point in the future, when the requirements change, your design will have to change. The hallmark of a bad design is that when the requirements change, the design has to change as well.

CORE USE CASES

In any given system, not all use cases are distinct and unique. Most of the use cases are variations of other user cases. The main required behavior has numerous permutations—for example, the normal case, the incomplete case, the case for a specific customer in a particular locale, the error case, and so on. There are only two types of use cases: core use cases and all other use cases. The **core use cases** represent the essence of the business of the system. As discussed in Chapter 2, the nature of the business hardly ever changes, and the same goes for the core use cases. The regular, non-core use cases will, of course, change at great rate across and between customers of the business. While your customers can and likely will have their own customization and interpretation of the regular use cases, all customers share the core use cases.

While the system may have hundreds of use cases, the saving grace is that the system will have only a handful of core use cases. In our practice at IDesign, we commonly see systems with surprisingly few core use cases. Most systems have as few as two or three core use cases, and the number seldom exceeds six. Reflect on your system at the office or on a recent project with which you were involved and count in your head the number of truly distinct use cases the system is required to handle. You will find that this number is small, very small. Alternatively, bring up a single-page marketing brochure for the system and count the number of bullets. You will likely have no more than three bullets.

Finding the Core Use Cases

The core use cases will hardly ever be presented explicitly in the requirements document, as refined as that document may be. Their small number does not mean the core use cases are easy to find, nor does the small number make it simple to agree with others on what is a core use case versus a regular use case. A core use case will almost always be some kind of an abstraction of other use cases, and it may even require a new term or name to differentiate it from the rest. Even when you are given a requirements spec that turns out to have many missing use cases, such a flawed document will contain the core use cases because they are the essence of the business. In addition, while you should not design against the requirements, that does not mean you should ignore the requirements. The whole point of requirements analysis is to recognize the core use cases (and the areas of volatility). It is up to you as the architect (along with the requirements owner) to identify the core use cases, often via some iterative process.

THE ARCHITECT'S MISSION

Your mission as an architect is to identify the smallest set of components that you can put together to satisfy all the core use cases. Since all the other use cases are merely variations of the core use cases, the regular use cases simply represent a different interaction between the components, not a different decomposition. Now when the requirements change, your design does not.

> **Note** This observation is about the decomposition into components, not the implementation of code inside the components. For example, when using *The Method*, the code integrating the components mostly resides in *Managers*. The integration code likely will change as a response to the change in the requirements. Such change is not an architectural change; it is an implementation change. Furthermore, the degree of this kind of implementation changes in response to changes in the requirements is independent from the merit of the design.

I call this approach **composable design**. A composable design does not aim to satisfy any use case in particular.

You do not target any use case in particular not just because the use cases you were given were incomplete, faulty, and full of holes and contradictions, but because they will change. Even if the existing use case will not change, over time you will have new use cases added and others removed.

A simple example is the design of the human body. *Homo sapiens* appeared on the plains of Africa more than 200,000 years ago, when the requirements at the time did not include being a software architect. How can you possibly fulfill the requirements for a software architect today while using the body of a hunter-gatherer? The answer is that while you are using the same components as a prehistoric man, you are integrating them in different ways. The single core use case has not changed with time: survive.

Architecture Validation

Since the goal of any system is to satisfy the requirements, composable design enables something else: design validation. Once you can produce an interaction between your services for each core use case, you have produced a **valid design**. There is no need to know the unknown or to predict the future. Your design can now handle any use case, because all use cases manifest themselves only as different interactions between the same building blocks. Stop yearning for some mythical project where one day someone will give you all the requirements complete and properly documented. There is no point in wasting inordinate amount of time up front trying to nail down the requirements in minute detail. You can easily design valid systems even with grossly impaired requirements.

The act of validating the design can be as straightforward as producing simple diagrams demonstrating the interactions between the components of the architecture that support the use cases. Figure 4-1 is, in *The Method*'s parlance, a **call chain** diagram.

A call chain demonstrates the interaction between components required to satisfy a particular use case. You can literally superimpose the call chain onto the layered architecture diagram. The components in the diagram are connected by arrows indicating the direction and type of the call between components—a solid black arrow for synchronous (request/response) calls, and a dashed gray arrow for a queued call. Call chain diagrams are specializations of a dependency graph and as such are quite useful during project design (as discussed in the second half of this book).

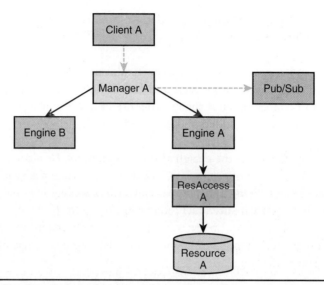

Figure 4-1 Simple call chain demonstrating support of a core use case

Call chain diagrams are a simple and quick way of examining a use case and demonstrating how the design supports it. The downside of call chain diagrams is that they have no notion of call order, they have no way of capturing the duration of the calls, and they get confusing when multiple parties make multiple calls to the same type of components. In many cases, the interaction between the components may be simple, so you do not need to show order, duration, or multiple calls. For these cases, you may decide that a call chain diagram is good enough for the validation purpose. Also, call chains are often easier for nontechnical audiences to understand.

A **sequence diagram** in *The Method*'s parlance is similar to a UML sequence diagram.[1] However, it includes notational differences to assure common meanings between diagram types. Lifelines are colored according to the architectural layers, and the arrow styles are the same as in call chain diagrams. Figure 4-2 is a sequence diagram equivalent to Figure 4-1.

In a sequence diagram, each participating component in the use case has a vertical bar representing its lifeline. The vertical bars correspond to some work or activity that the component performs. Time flows from top to bottom of the diagram, and the length of the bars indicates the relative duration of the component's use. A single component may participate multiple times in the same use case, and you

---

1. https://en.wikipedia.org/wiki/Sequence_diagram

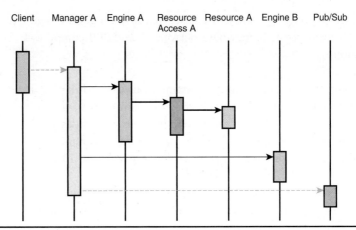

Figure 4-2 Demonstrating support for a core use case with a sequence diagram

can even have different lifelines for different instances of the same component. The horizontal arrows (solid black for synchronous and dashed gray for queued) indicate calls between components.

Sequence diagrams take longer to produce due to the additional level of details they offer, but they are often the right tool to demonstrate a complex use case, especially for technical audience. In addition, sequence diagrams are extremely useful in subsequent detailed design for helping to define interfaces, methods, and even parameters. If you are going to produce them for the detailed design, you might as well produce them first for design validation, albeit with fewer details (e.g., omit operations and messages for now).

Smallest Set

Remember: Your mission as the architect is to identify not just a set of components that you can put together to satisfy all the core use case, but the *smallest* set of components. Why smallest? And what does smallest even mean?

In general, you should produce an architecture that minimizes, rather than maximizes, the amount of work involved in detailed design and implementation. Less is more when it comes to architecture. That said, a natural constraint exists on the number of components in any architecture. For example, suppose you are given a requirements spec with 300 use cases. On the one hand, a single-component architecture satisfying these requirements constitutes the ultimate smallest number of components, but such a monolith is a horrible design due to its internal complexity (see Appendix B for an in-depth discussion of the effect of service size on cost). On the other hand, if you create an architecture consisting of 300 components, each corresponding to a single use case, that is not a good design either, due to the high integration cost. Somewhere between 1 and 300 components is the good enough number.

When there is uncertainty in estimation, using orders of magnitude can be very helpful. For example, in a system with 300 use cases, what is the order of magnitude of the number of components required for a valid design? Is it 1, 10, 100, or 1000 components? Regardless of the specifics of the system, you know intuitively that 1, 100, and 1000 are wrong answers, leaving you with 10 as an order of magnitude.

The smallest set of services required in a typical software system contains 10 services in order of magnitude (e.g., sets of both 12 and 20 are on the order of 10). This particular order of magnitude is another universal design concept. How many internal components does your body have, as an order of magnitude? Your car? Your laptop? For each, the answer is about 10 because of combinatorics. If the system supports the required behaviors by combining the 10 or so components, a staggering number of such combinations becomes possible even without allowing repetition of participating components or partial sets. As a result, even a small number of valid internal components can support an astronomical number of possible use cases.

Going back to well-designed software systems, the components of the system encapsulate areas of volatility. Using *The Method*, even in a large system you are commonly looking at two to five *Managers*, two to three *Engines*, three to eight *ResourceAccess* and *Resources*, and a half-dozen *Utilities*. The total number of building blocks will be a dozen or two at the most. With anything larger than this number, you will have to break up the system into logically related subsets (subsystems) that are more manageable in size. Once you cannot think of a smaller set of building blocks, you have found your best design. It does not matter that a better architect could have come up with an even smaller set of components, because that other architect is not designing your system. Every design effort always has a point of diminishing return, and your smallest set is your point.

> **Note**   You cannot validate architectures that have a single component or hundreds of components. A single large component by definition does everything, and a component per use case also supports all use cases.

Duration of Design Effort

You may spend weeks or months trying to identify the core use cases and the areas of volatility. However, that is not design—that is requirements gathering and requirements analysis, which may be very time-consuming indeed. Once you have settled on the core use cases and the areas of volatility, how long will it take you to produce a valid design using *The Method*? You can use orders of magnitude here as well: Is it more like an hour? A day? A week? A month? A year? I expect most readers of this book to pick a day or a week, and with practice you can bring the time down to a few hours. Design is not time-consuming if you know what you are doing.

THERE IS NO FEATURE

Putting together the observations of this chapter along with the previous two chapters reveals this fundamental system design rule:

Features are always and everywhere aspects of integration, not implementation.

This is a universal design rule which governs the design and implementation of all systems. As mentioned in Chapter 2, the very nature of the word "universal" includes software systems.

The process of building automobiles is a simple demonstration of this rule. Your car has a crucial feature: It must transport you from location A to location B. If you were to observe how a car is manufactured, when would you see this feature? The feature emerges once you have integrated the chassis with the engine block, the gear box, the seats, the dashboard, a driver, a road, insurance, and fuel. Integrating all of these yields the feature.

What is even more impressive with this rule is that it is a fractal. For example, I am typing the manuscript for this book right now on a laptop, which provides me with a very important feature: word processing. But is there any box in the architecture of the laptop called `Word Processing`? The laptop provides the feature of word processing by integrating the keyboard, the screen, the hard drive, the bus, the CPU, and the memory. Each of these components provides a feature, too: The CPU provides computation, and the hard drive provides storage. Yet if you examine the feature of storage, is there a single block in the drive's design called `Storage`? The hard drive provides the storage feature by integrating internal components such as memory, the internal data bus, media, cables, ports, power regulators, and small screws that hold everything together. The screws themselves provide a very important feature: fastening. But how does a screw provide fastening? The screw performs the fastening by integrating the head of the screw, the thread, and its stem. The integration of these provides the fastening feature. You can keep drilling down this way all the way to the quarks, and you will never see a feature.

Read the design rule just given a second time. If you still find it hard to accept, you have been plugged into a matrix that is telling you to write code that implements a feature. Doing so goes against the way the universe is actually put together. There is no ~~spoon~~feature.

HANDLING CHANGE

Your software system must respond to changes in the requirements. Most software systems are implemented using functional decomposition, which maximizes the effects of the change. If the design has been based on features, the change, by definition, is never in one place. Instead, it is spread across multiple components and aspects of the system. With functional decomposition, change is expensive and painful so people do their best to avoid the pain by deferring the change. They will add the change request to the next semi-annual release because they prefer to take future pain over present pain. They may even fight the change outright by explaining to the customer that the requested change is a bad idea.

Unfortunately, fighting the change is tantamount to killing the system. Live systems are systems that customers use, and dead systems are systems that customers do not use (even if they still pay for them). When developers tell customers that the change will be part of a future release, what do they expect the customers to do in the subsequent six months until the developers roll out the requested change? The customers do not want the feature six months in the future—they need the feature now. Consequently, the customers will have to work around the system by using the legacy system, or some external medium, or a competing product. Since fighting the change results in pushing customers away from using the system, fighting the change is killing the system. Part and parcel of responding to the change is responding *quickly*, even if that aspect was never explicitly stated.

CONTAINING THE CHANGE

The trick to addressing change is not to fight it, postpone it, or punt it altogether. The trick is containing its effects. Consider a system designed using volatility-based decomposition and the structure guidelines of Chapter 3. A change to a requirement is actually a change to the required behavior of the system—specifically, a change to a use case. In *The Method*, some *Manager* implements the workflow executing the use case. The *Manager* may be gravely affected by a change. Perhaps you even need to discard the whole implementation of that *Manager* and create a new one in its place. However, the underlying components that the *Manager* integrates are not affected by the change to the required behavior.

Recall from Chapter 3 that the *Manager* should be almost expendable. This enables you to absorb the cost of the change, to contain it. Furthermore, the bulk of the effort in any system typically goes into the services that the *Manager* uses:

- Implementing *Engines* is expensive. Each *Engine* represents business activities vital to the system's workflows and encapsulates the associated volatility and complexity.

- Implementing a *ResourceAccess* is nontrivial, and not just because of the cost of writing the *ResourceAccess* code. Identifying the atomic business verbs, translating them into the access methodologies for some *Resource*, and exposing them as a *Resource*-neutral interface also takes a significant effort.

- Designing and implementing *Resources* that are scalable, reliable, highly performant, and very reusable is time- and effort-consuming. These tasks may include designing data contracts, schemas, cache access policies, partitioning, replication, connection management, timeouts, lock management, indexing, normalization, message formats, transactions, delivery failures, poison messages, and much more.

- Implementing *Utilities* always requires top skills, and the result must be trustworthy. *Utilities* are the backbone of your system. World-class security, diagnostics, logging, message processing, instrumentation, and hosting do not happen accidentally.

- Designing a superior user experience or a convenient and reusable API for *Clients* is time and labor intensive. The *Clients* also have to interface and integrate with the *Managers*.

When a change happens to the *Manager*, you get to salvage and reuse all the effort that went into the *Clients*, the *Engines*, the *ResourceAccess*, the *Resources*, and the *Utilities*. By reintegrating these services in the *Manager*, you have contained the change and can quickly and efficiently respond to changes. Is that not the essence of agility?

5

SYSTEM DESIGN EXAMPLE

The previous three chapters presented the universal design principles for system design. However, most people learn best by example. Therefore, this chapter demonstrates the application of concepts from prior chapters with a comprehensive example: a case study. The case study describes the design of a new system called TradeMe, a replacement for a legacy system. The case study is derived directly from an actual system that IDesign designed for one of its customers, albeit with the specific business details scrubbed and obfuscated. The essence of the system remains unchanged, from the business case to the decomposition: I have not glossed over issues or tried to beautify the situation. As mentioned in Chapter 1, design should not be time-consuming. In this case, the design was completed in less than a week by a two-person design team consisting of a seasoned IDesign architect and an apprentice.

The goal of this case study is to show the thought process and the deductions used to produce the design. These are often difficult to learn on your own, but are more easily understood by watching somebody else do it while reasoning about what is taking place. This chapter starts with an overview of the customer and the system, then presents the requirements in the form of several use cases. The identification of the areas of volatility and the architecture relies on *The Method* structure.

> **Caution** You should not use this example dogmatically as a template. Every system is different, having its own constraints and requiring its own design considerations and tradeoffs. As an architect, you add value when you devise the correct design for the system at hand. This requires practice and critical thinking. In this chapter, you should focus on the rationale for the design decisions, and use this example to start off your practice, as discussed in Chapter 2.

SYSTEM OVERVIEW

TradeMe is a system for matching tradesmen to contractors and projects. Tradesmen may be plumbers, electricians, carpenters, welders, surveyors, painters, telephone network technicians, gardeners, and solar panel installers, among others. They all work independently and are self-employed. Each tradesman has a skill level, and some, such as electricians, are certified by regulators to do certain tasks. The payment rate for the tradesman varies based on various factors such as discipline (welders are paid more than carpenters), skill level, years of experience, project type, location, and even weather. Other factors affecting their work include regulatory compliance issues (such as minimum wage or employment taxes), risk premium (such as exterior work on skyscrapers or with high voltage), certification of tradesmen's qualifications for certain kinds of task (such as welding girders or power grid tie-in), reporting requirements, and more.

The contractors are general contractors, and they need tradesmen on an ad hoc basis, from as little as a day to as long as a few weeks. Contractors often have a base crew of generalists whom they employ outside the system on a full-time basis, using TradeMe for the specialized work. On the same project, different tradesmen are needed for different periods of time (one for a day, another for a week) at different times. Tradesmen can come and go on a single project.

The TradeMe system allows tradesmen to sign up, list their skills, their general geographic area of availability, and the rate they expect. It also allows contractors to sign up, list their projects, the required trades and skills, the location of the projects, the rates they are willing to pay, the duration of engagement, and other attributes of the project. Contractors can even request (but not insist upon) specific tradesmen with whom they would like to work.

Other than the factors already mentioned, the rate the contractor is willing to pay depends on supply and demand. When a project is idle, the contractor will increase the price. When the tradesman is idle, the tradesman will lower the price. Similar consideration is given to the duration or requested commitment. The ideal project for a tradesman often pays a high rate and has a short duration. Once the tradesmen have committed to a project, they have to stay for the amount of time to which they committed. Contractors may offer more pay with longer commitments. In general, the system lets market forces set the rate and find equilibrium.

The projects are construction projects for buildings. The system may also be useful in newly emerging markets, such as oil fields or marine yards.

TradeMe allows the tradesmen and the contractors to find one another. The system processes the requests and dispatches the required tradesmen to the work sites. It also keeps track of the hours and wages, and the rest of the reporting to the authorities, saving both contractors and tradesmen the hassle of handling these tasks themselves.

The system isolates tradesmen from contractors. It collects funds from the contractors and pays the tradesmen. Contractors cannot bypass the system and hire the tradesmen directly because the tradesmen have exclusivity with the system.

The TradeMe system aims to find the best rate for the tradesmen and the most availability for the contractors. It makes money on the small spread between the ask rate and the bid rate. Another source of income is the membership fee that both tradesmen and contractors pay. The fee is collected annually but that could change. Consequently, both tradesmen and contractors are called members in the system.

Presently, nine call centers handle the majority of the assignments. Each call center is specific to a particular locale, regulations, building codes, standards, and labor laws. The call centers are staffed with account representatives called reps. The reps today rely on experience to optimize the scheduling across all projects and available tradesmen. Some call centers operate as their own business, whereas others are operated by the same business.

There is also at least one competing application geared more toward finding the cheapest tradesmen, and some contractors prefer that system. Contractors opting for tradesmen based on price as opposed to availability could be a growing trend.

LEGACY SYSTEM

The legacy system, which is deployed in European call centers, has full-time users who rely on a two-tier desktop application connected to a database. Both tradesmen and contractors call in, with the reps entering the details and even performing the matching in real time. Some rudimentary web portals for managing membership bypass the legacy system and work with the database directly. The various subsystems are isolated and very inefficient, requiring a lot of human intervention at almost every step. Users are required to employ as many as five different applications to accomplish their tasks. These applications are independent, and the integration is done by hand. The client applications are chock-full of business logic, and the lack of separation between UI and business logic prevents updating the applications to modern user experience.

Each subsystem even has its own repository, and the users have to reconcile them to make sense of it all. This process is error prone and imposes expensive training and onboarding time for new users.

The legacy system is vulnerable, and its haphazard approach to security exposes it to many possible attack vectors. The legacy system was never designed with security in mind. For that matter, it was never designed at all, but rather grew organically.

The legacy simply cannot accommodate several new features and desirable capabilities:

- Mobile device support
- Higher degree of automation of the workflow
- Some connectivity to other systems
- Migration to the cloud
- Fraud detection
- Quality of work surveys, including incorporating the tradesman's safety record in the rate and skill level
- Entering new markets (such as deployment at marine yards)

Both the business and users are frustrated with the legacy system's inability to keep up with the times, and there is a never-ending stream of desired value-added features. One such feature, continuing education, turned out to be a must-have, so it was cobbled on top of the legacy system. The legacy system assigns tradesmen to certification classes and government-required tests and tracks the tradesmen's progress. Although external education centers provide training and register the certifications, the users have to manually connect them with the legacy system. While unrelated to the core system aspects, tradesmen are really keen on this feature, as is the business, because the certification feature helps prevent tradesmen from moving to the competitors.

The legacy system is having trouble complying with new legislation across locales. Dealing with any change is very difficult, and the system is highly specific for its current business context. Since the company cannot afford to support a unique version of the system per locale, it created an incentive to dumb down the system to the lowest common denominator across locales. This further increases the burden on the users in terms of their manual workflows, which decreases efficiency, increases training time and costs, and causes loss of business opportunities.

Overall, the system has some 220 reps across all locations. Neither scalability nor throughput poses a problem. However, responsiveness is an issue, although this may just be a side effect of the legacy system.

NEW SYSTEM

Given the issues of the poorly designed legacy, the company's management is interested in designing a new system correctly. The new system should automate the work as much as possible. Ideally, the company would like to have a single, small call center that is used as a backup for an automated process. This call center would use a single system across all locales. While the system is deployed in Europe, there are requests to deploy the system in the United Kingdom[1] and even Canada (i.e., outside the European Union). Another driver for investing in the new system is that the competitors have much more flexible, efficient systems, with superior user experience.

While contractors could staff a project using multiple sources of tradesmen, including competing products, integration with competing products and project optimizations in general are beyond the scope of the system: The company is not in the business of optimization or integration. Expanding the marketplace to include other trades such as IT or nursing is also out of scope. Adding these markets would redefine the nature of the business, and the company's forte is matching tradesmen to construction projects, not general staffing.

THE COMPANY

The company views itself as a tradesmen broker, not as a software organization. Software is not its business. In the past the company did not acknowledge what it would really take to develop great software. The company did not devote adequate effort to process or development practices. The company's attempts to build a replacement system in the past all failed. What the company does have is plenty of financial resources—the legacy application is very profitable. The bitter lessons of the past have convinced management to turn a new page and adopt a sound approach for software development.

---

1. While this design effort took place prior to Brexit (the departure of the United Kingdom from the EU), Brexit is a classic example of a massive change that was unanticipated at the time, yet the new system accommodated it seamlessly.

Use Cases

There were no existing requirements documents for either the old system or the new system. The customer was able to provide Figures 5-1 to 5-8, depicting some use cases. These may or may not be core use cases; they are simply the required behaviors of the system. To a large extent, the use cases reflected what the legacy system was supposedly doing. Since the design team was looking for core use cases, they ignored low-level use cases such as entering financial details, collecting fees from contractors, and distributing payments to tradesmen. Some use cases, such as continuing education, were not even specified. Moreover, there was clearly room for additional use cases complementing the use cases provided by the company.

> **Note**   As discussed in Chapter 4, you rarely will receive a perfect set of use cases (TradeMe was no exception), and even a decent list of use cases is hard to come by. One of the main objectives of this chapter is to demonstrate how to produce a valid design even under such uncertainty.

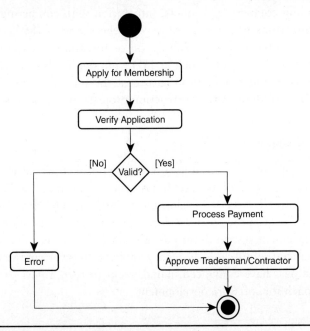

Figure 5-1 Add Tradesman or Contractor use case

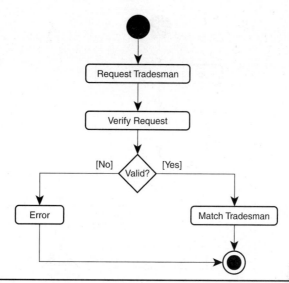

Figure 5-2 Request Tradesman or Contractor use case

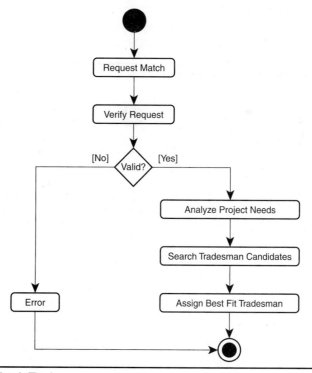

Figure 5-3 Match Tradesman use case

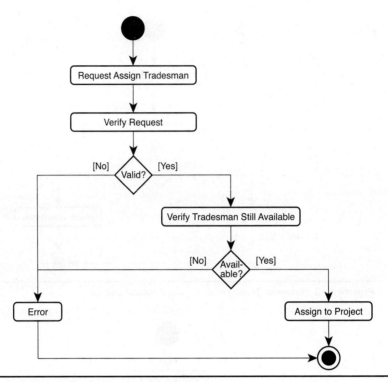

Figure 5-4 Assign Tradesman use case

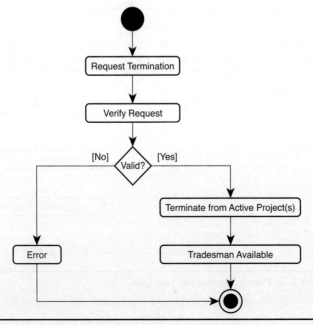

Figure 5-5 Terminate Tradesman use case

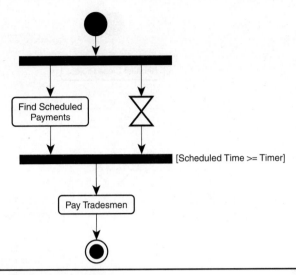

Figure 5-6 Pay Tradesman use case

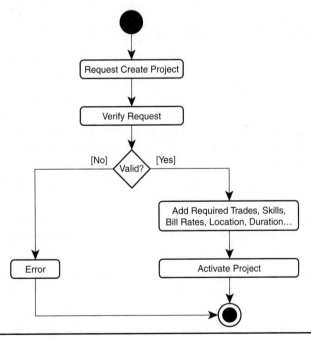

Figure 5-7 Create Project use case

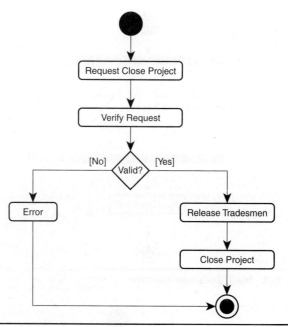

Figure 5-8 Close Project use case

Core Use Case

Most of the company-provided use cases did not look like core use cases, but rather appeared to be just a list of simple functionalities. Recall that a core use case represents the essence of the business. The essence of the system is not to add a tradesman or contractor, to create a project, or to pay a tradesman. All of these tasks may be done in any number of ways; they add little business value and do not differentiate the system from the competition. Instead, the system's raison d'être is given in the opening one-sentence definition: "TradeMe is a system for matching tradesmen to contractors and projects." The only use case with any semblance to that point was the Match Tradesman use case (Figure 5-3).

> **Note** Even though for design validation you need to support just the core use cases, that does not mean you should ignore the other use cases— far from it. A great way of demonstrating the versatility of your design is to show how easy it will be to support all the other use cases and anything else the business might require of the system.

Simplifying the Use Cases

Customers rarely ever present the requirements in a useful format, let alone in a way that is conducive to good design. You must always transform, clarify, and consolidate the raw data. Early in the design process you may even recognize areas of interaction that will later make mapping the areas to subsystems or layers much more natural. For example, with TradeMe, there were at least three types of roles across all the use cases: the users, the market, and the members. The users can be back-office data entry reps or system administrators. Perhaps only an administrator can terminate a tradesman, but that information was absent from Figure 5-5.

It is useful to show the flow of control between roles, organizations, and other responsible entities, using "swim lanes" in your activity diagrams. For example, Figure 5-9 provides an alternative way of expressing the Terminate Tradesman use case from Figure 5-5.

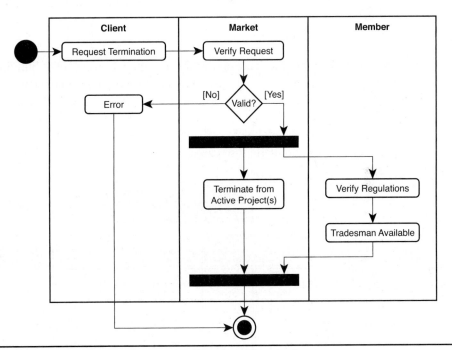

Figure 5-9 Subdividing the activity diagram with swim lanes

You transform the raw use case by subdividing the activity diagram into areas of interactions. This also helps clarify the required behavior of the system by adding decision boxes or synchronization bars as required. You will see how to use the swim lanes technique later on in this chapter to both initiate and validate the design.

THE ANTI-DESIGN EFFORT

Chapter 2 mentioned an anti-design effort as an effective technique to sway people from functional decomposition by deliberately trying to design the worst possible system. While a good anti-design effort produces a valid design because it supports the use cases, it offers no encapsulation and demonstrates tight coupling. Such a design often feels natural to others (i.e., they would have produced something similar). Odds are that the anti-design will be some flavor of functional decomposition.

THE MONOLITH

One simple anti-design example is a god service—an ugly dumping ground of all the functionalities in the requirements, all implemented in one place. While this design is so common it even has a name (the Monolith), by now most people have learned the hard way not to design this way.

GRANULAR BUILDING BLOCKS

Figure 5-10 shows another take on the anti-design: a massive set of building blocks. Literally every activity in the use cases has a corresponding component in the architecture. There is no encapsulation of either the database access or the database itself.

With so many fine-grained blocks, the *Clients* become responsible for implementing the business logic of the use cases, as shown in Figure 5-11. Contaminating

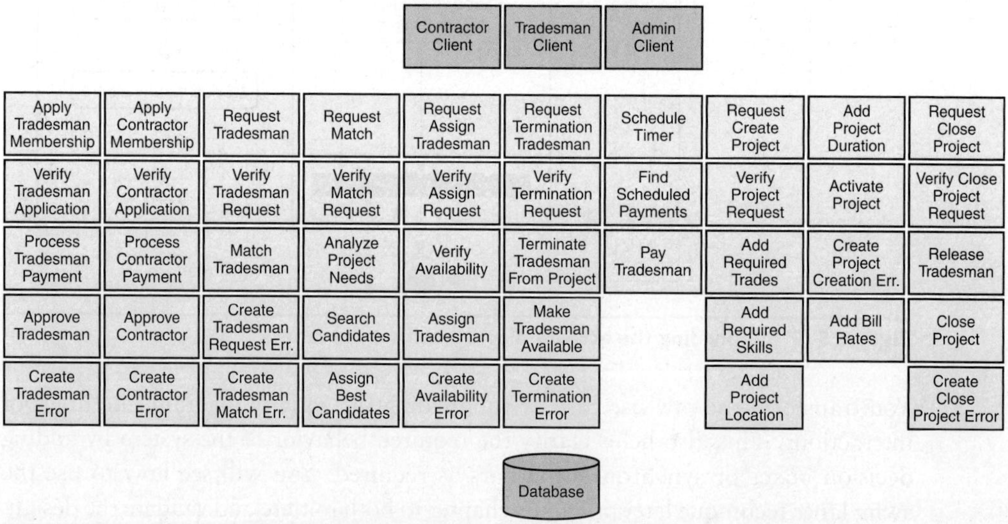

Figure 5-10 Services explosion anti-design

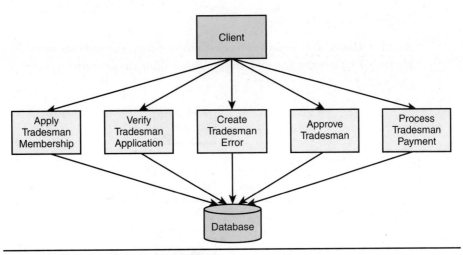

Figure 5-11 Polluted and inflated Client

the *Client*'s code with business logic results in a bloated *Client* in which the entire system migrates to the *Client*, as shown in Figure 2-1.

Alternatively, you can have the services call each other, as shown in Figure 5-12. However, chaining the highly functional services together in this way creates coupling between them, as depicted in Figure 2-5. Note also in Figure 5-12 the open architecture issues of calling up and sideways.

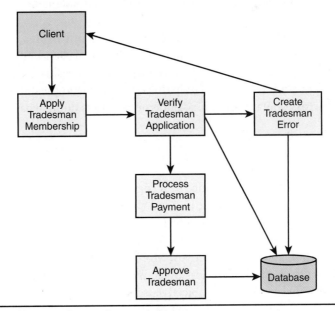

Figure 5-12 Chaining the services anti-design

DOMAIN DECOMPOSITION

Another classic anti-design is to decompose along the domain lines, as shown in Figure 5-13. Here the system is decomposed along the domain lines of Tradesman, Contractor, and Project.

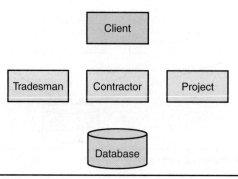

Figure 5-13 Domain decomposition anti-design

Even with a relatively simple system such as TradeMe, there are nearly limitless additional possibilities for domain decomposition, such as Accounts, Administration, Analytics, Approval, Assignment, Certificates, Contracts, Currency, Disputes, Finance, Fulfillment, Legislation, Payroll, Reports, Requisition, Staffing, Subscription, and so on. Who is to say that Project is a better candidate for a domain than Accounts? And which criteria should be used to make that judgment?

Besides having the many drawbacks discussed in Chapter 2, domain decomposition makes it nearly impossible to validate the design by demonstrating support of the use cases. For example, a request for a tradesman will appear on both the Project and Tradesman domain services. Due to the duplication of functionalities across domain lines, it is ambiguous who is doing what and when.

BUSINESS ALIGNMENT

It is of the utmost importance to recognize that the architecture does not exist for its own sake. The architecture (and the system) must serve the business. Serving the business is the guiding light for any design effort. As such, you must ensure that the architecture is aligned with the vision that the business has for its future and with the business objectives. Moreover, you must have complete bidirectional traceability from the business objectives to the architecture. You must be able to easily point out how each objective is supported in some way by the architecture, and how each aspect of the architecture is derived from some objectives of the business. The alternatives are pointless designs and orphaned business needs.

As discussed in the previous chapters, the architect producing the design has to first recognize the areas of volatility and then encapsulate these areas in system components, operational concepts, and infrastructure. The integration of the components is what supports the required behaviors, and the way the integration takes place is what realizes the business objectives. For example, if a key objective is extensibility and flexibility, then integrating the components over a message bus is a good solution (more on this point later). Conversely, if the key objective is performance and simplicity, introducing a message bus contributes too much complexity.

The rest of this chapter provides a detailed walkthrough of the steps that transform the business needs into a design for TradeMe. These steps start with capturing the system vision and the business objectives, which then drive the design decisions.

THE VISION

Seldom will everyone in any environment share the same vision as to what the system should do. Some may have no vision at all. Others may have a different vision than the rest or a vision that serves only their narrow interests. Some may misinterpret the business goals. The company behind TradeMe was stymied by a myriad of additional issues resulting from its failure to keep up with the changing market. These issues were reflected in the existing systems, in the company's structure, and in the way software development was set up. The new system had to tackle all the issues head-on rather than in a piecemeal fashion, because solving just some of them was insufficient for success.

The first order of business is to get all stakeholders to agree on a common vision. The vision must drive everything, from architecture to commitments. Everything that you do later has to serve that vision and be justified by it. Of course, this cuts both ways—which is why it is a good idea to start with the vision. If something does not serve the vision, then it often has to do with politics and other secondary or tertiary concerns. This provides you with an excellent way of repelling irrelevant demands that do not support the agreed-upon vision. In the case of TradeMe, the design team distilled the vision to a single sentence:

A platform for building applications to support the TradeMe marketplace.

A good vision is both terse and explicit. You should read it like a legal statement.

Note that the vision for TradeMe was to build a platform on which to build the applications. This kind of platform mindset addressed the diversity and extensibility the business craved and may be applicable in systems you design.

THE BUSINESS OBJECTIVES

After agreeing on the vision (and only then), you can itemize the vision to specific objectives. You should reject all objectives that do not serve the vision; you should include all objectives that are essential to support the vision. These two types are usually easy to pick out. When you list objectives, you should adopt a business perspective. You must not allow the engineering or marketing people to own the conversation, or to include technology objectives or specific requirements. The design team extracted the following objectives from the TradeMe system overview:

1. **Unify the repositories and applications.** The legacy system had entirely too many inefficiencies, requiring a lot of human intervention to keep the system up to date and running.

2. **Quick turnaround for new requirements.** The legacy turnaround time for features was abysmal. The new platform had to allow very fast, frequent customization, often tailored just for a specific skill, time of the week, project type, and any combination of these. Ideally, much of this quick turnaround should be automated, from coding to deployment.

3. **Support a high degree of customization across countries and markets.** Localization was an incredible pain point because of differences in regulations, legislations, cultures, and languages.

4. **Supports full business visibility and accountability.** Fraud detection, audit trails, and monitoring were nonexistent in the legacy system.

5. **Forward looking on technology and regulations.** Instead of being in perpetual reactive mode, the system must anticipate change. The company envisioned that this was how TradeMe would defeat the competitors.

6. **Integrate well with external systems.** Although somewhat related to the previous objective, the objective here is to enable a high degree of automation over previously laborious manual processes.

7. **Streamline security.** The system must be properly secured, and literally every component must be designed with security in mind. To meet the security objective, the development team must introduce security activities such as security audits into the software life cycle and support it in the architecture.

> **Note**   Development cost was not an objective for this system. While no one likes wasting money, the business pain was in the items listed here, and the company could afford even an expensive solution that addressed the objectives.

MISSION STATEMENT

It may come as a surprise, but articulating the vision (what the business will receive) and the objectives (why the business wants the vision) is often insufficient. People are usually too mired in the details and cannot connect the dots. Thus, you should also specify a mission statement (how you will do it). The TradeMe Mission Statement was:

Design and build a collection of software components that the development team can assemble into applications and features.

This mission statement deliberately does not identify developing features as the mission. The mission is not to build features—the mission is to build components. It now becomes much easier to justify volatility-based decomposition that serves the mission statement because all the dots are connected:

Vision → Objectives → Mission Statement → Architecture

In fact, you have just compelled the business to instruct you to design the right architecture. This is a reversal of the typical dynamics, in which the architect pleads with management to avoid functional decomposition. It is a lot easier to drive the correct architecture through the business by aligning the architecture with the business's vision, its objectives, and the mission statement. Once you have them agree on the vision, the objectives, and then the mission statement, you have them on your side. If you want the business people to support your architecture effort, you must demonstrate how the architecture serves the business.

THE ARCHITECTURE

Misunderstanding and confusion are endemic with software development and often lead to conflict or unmet expectations. Marketing may use different terms than engineering for the same thing or—even worse—may use the same term but mean a different thing. Such ambiguities may go undetected for years. Before you dive into the act of system design, ensure everyone is on the same page by compiling a short glossary of domain terminology.

TRADEME GLOSSARY

A good way of starting a glossary is to answer the four classic questions of "who," "what," "how," and "where." You answer the questions by examining the system overview, the use cases, and customer interview notes, if you have any. For TradeMe, the answers to the four questions were as follows:

- **Who**
  - Tradesmen
  - Contractors
  - TradeMe reps
  - Education centers
  - Background processes (i.e., scheduler for payment)
- **What**
  - Membership of tradesmen and contractors
  - Marketplace of construction projects
  - Certificates and training for continuing education
- **How**
  - Searching
  - Complying with regulations
  - Accessing resources
- **Where**
  - Local database
  - Cloud
  - Other systems

Recall from Chapter 3 that you often can map the answers to the four questions to layers, if not to components of the architecture itself.

The list of the "what" is of particularly interest because it hints strongly at possible subsystems or the swim lanes mentioned previously. You can use the swim lanes and the answers to seed and initiate your decomposition effort as you look for areas of volatility. This does not preclude having additional subsystems or imply that these will necessarily be all the subsystems needed—you always decompose based on volatility, and if a "what" is not volatile, then it will not merit a component in the architecture. At this point all it provides is a nice starting point to reason about your design.

TradeMe Areas of Volatility

The essence of the decomposition is in identifying the areas of volatility as outlined in the previous chapters. The following list highlights a few of the candidate volatilities for TradeMe and the factors the design team considered:

- **Tradesman.** Is this an area of volatility in the system? It is hard to claim that the architecture, even a purely functional one, would suffer to a large extent if you need to add attributes to the tradesman. In other words, tradesman is variable but not volatile. This is also true for any subset of attributes of the tradesman (e.g., skill sets). Maybe the tradesman is not volatile in isolation. Perhaps there exists a more generic volatility, such as membership management or regulations, that has affinity with the tradesman. It is important to discuss the volatility candidates this way and even challenge them. If you cannot clearly state what the volatility is, why it is volatile, and what risk the volatility poses in terms of likelihood and effect, then you need to look further. Identifying tradesman as an area of volatility signals decomposition along domain lines (see Figure 5-12).

- **Education certificates.** Is the certification process volatile? If so, what exactly is the true volatility from the point of view of the business and the system? In this case, the volatility arises in the workflow of matching the regulations governing required certifications for projects with appropriately certified tradesman. The certification itself is just an attribute of the tradesman. From the business's perspective, certification management will forever be secondary to the core added value of being a tradesmen brokerage.

- **Projects.** Is project volatility deserving of its own *Manager*? A `Project Manager` implies a project context. A `Market Manager` is better because some activities that the system needs to manage may not require a context of a running project to execute. For example, you can ask the market to propose a match without having a specific project in mind, or maybe a match may require involving multiple projects. Perhaps to maintain a valuable tradesman you wish to pay the tradesman a retainer, irrespective of any project. Identifying projects as a volatility manifests as domain decomposition. The core volatility is the marketplace, not the projects.

There is nothing wrong with suggesting certain areas of volatility, and then examining the resultant architecture. If the result produces a spiderweb of interactions or is asymmetric, then the design is unlikely to be good. You will probably sense whether the design is correct or not.

Sometimes an area of volatility may reside outside the system. For example, while payments may very well be a volatile area due to the various ways in which you could issue payments, TradeMe as a software project was not about implementing a payment system. The payments are ancillary to the core value of the system. The system will likely use a number of external payments systems as *Resources*. *Resources* may be whole systems, each with its own volatilities, but these are outside the scope of this system.

The design team produced the following list of areas volatile enough to affect the architecture. The list also identifies the corresponding components of the architecture that encapsulate the areas of volatility:

- **Client applications.** The system should allow several distinct client environments to evolve separately at their own pace. The clients cater to different users (tradesmen, contractors, marketplace reps, or education centers) or to background processes, such as a timer that periodically interacts with the system. These client applications may use different UI technologies, devices, or APIs (perhaps the education portal is a mere API); they may be accessed locally or across the Internet (tradesmen versus reps); they may be connected or disconnected; and so on. As expected, the clients are associated with a lot of volatility. Each one of these volatile client environments is encapsulated in its own *Client* application.
- **Managing membership.** There is volatility in the activities of adding or removing tradesmen and contractors, and even the benefits or discounts they get. Membership management changes across locales and over time. These volatilities are encapsulated in the `Membership Manager`.
- **Fees.** All the possible ways TradeMe can make money, combining volume and spread, are encapsulated in the `Market Manager`.
- **Projects.** Project requirements and size not only change but also are volatile and affect the required behavior. Small projects may require different workflows from large projects. The system encapsulates projects in the `Market Manager`.
- **Disputes.** When dealing with people, at best misunderstandings will arise; at worst outright fraud happens. The volatility in handling dispute resolution is encapsulated by the `Membership Manager`.
- **Matching and approvals.** Two volatilities come into play here. The volatility of how to find a tradesman that matches the project needs is encapsulated in the `Search Engine`. The volatility of search criteria and the definition thereof is encapsulated in the `Market Manager`.
- **Education.** There is volatility in matching a training class to a tradesman and in searching for an available class or a required class. Managing the education workflow volatility is encapsulated in the `Education Manager`. Searching for

classes and certifications is encapsulated in the `Search Engine`. Compliance with regulatory certification is encapsulated in the `Regulation Engine`.

- **Regulations.** Regulations are likely to change in any given country as time goes by. In addition, the regulations can be internal to the company. This volatility is encapsulated in the `Regulation Engine`.

- **Reports.** All the requirements of reporting and auditing with which the system needs to comply are encapsulated in the `Regulation Engine`.

- **Localization.** Two distinct volatilities relate to localization. UI elements of the *Clients* encapsulate the volatility in language and culture. For TradeMe, the stakeholders considered this a good enough solution. In other cases, localization could be a strong enough volatility that it would merit its own subsystem (e.g., *Manager*, *Resources*). Localization may even affect the design of the *Resources*. The volatility in regulations between countries is captured in the `Regulation Engine`.

- **Resources.** The *Resources* may be portals to external systems (such as payment) or store various elements such as lists of tradesman and projects. The exact nature of the store is volatile, potentially ranging from cloud-based database to a local store to a whole other system.

- **Resource access.** *ResourceAccess* components encapsulate the volatility of accessing the *Resources* such as the location of the storage, its type, and access technology. The *ResourceAccess* components convert atomic business verbs such as "*pay*" (e.g., paying a tradesman) into accessing the relevant *Resources* such as storage and payment systems.

- **Deployment model.** The deployment model is volatile. Sometimes data cannot leave a geographic area, or the company may wish to deploy parts or whole systems in the cloud. These volatilities are encapsulated in the composition of the subsystems and the `Message Bus` utility. The advantages of this modular composable interaction pattern in the system operational concepts are described later.

- **Authentication and authorization.** The system can authenticate the *Clients* in a number of ways, whether they are users or even other systems, and there are multiple options for representing credentials and identities. Authorization is nearly open-ended, with many ways of storing roles or representing claims. These volatilities are encapsulated in the `Security` *Utility* component.

Note that the mapping of areas of volatilities to components of the architecture is not 1:1. For example, the preceding list maps three areas of volatilities to the `Market Manager`. Recall from Chapter 3 that a *Manager* encapsulates the volatility of a family of logically related use cases, not just a single use case. In the case of the `Market Manager`, these market use cases are managing projects, matching tradesmen to projects, and charging the fees for the match.

Weak Volatiles

Two additional, weaker areas of volatility are not reflected in the architecture:

- **Notification.** How the *Clients* communicate with the system and how the system communicates with the outside world could be volatile. The use of the `Message Bus` *Utility* encapsulates that volatility. If the company had a strong need for open-ended forms of transports such as email or fax, then perhaps a `Notification Manager` would have been necessary.

- **Analysis.** TradeMe could analyze the requirements of projects and verify the requested tradesmen or even propose them in the first place. In this way, TradeMe could optimize the tradesmen assignment to projects. The system could analyze projects in various ways, with such analysis clearly being a volatile area. However, the design team rejected analysis as an area of volatility in the design because, as stated, the company is not in the business of optimizing projects. Providing optimizations, therefore, falls into speculative design. Any analysis activity required is folded into the `Market Manager`.

STATIC ARCHITECTURE

Figure 5-14 shows the static view of the architecture.

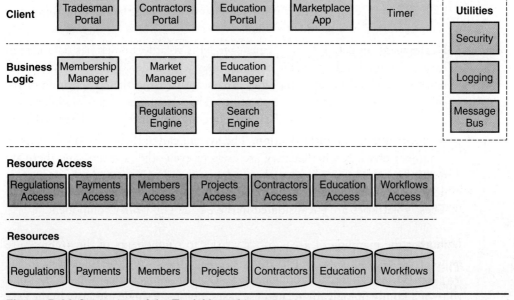

Figure 5-14 Static view of the TradeMe architecture

The *Clients*

The client tier contains a portal for each type of member, the tradesmen and the contractors. There is also a portal for the education center to issue or validate tradesman credentials and a marketplace application for the back-end users to administer the marketplace. In addition, the client tier contains external processes such as a scheduler or a timer that periodically initiates some behavior with the system. These are included in the architecture for reference, but are not part of the system.

Business Logic Services

In the business logic tier are the `Membership Manager` and `Market Manager`, encapsulating the respecting volatilities discussed previously. In short, the `Membership Manager` manages the volatility in the execution of the membership use cases, while the `Market Manager` is in charge of the use cases pertaining to the marketplace. Note that the use cases of membership (such as adding or removing a tradesman) are both logically related to each other and distinct from those related to the marketplace such as matching a tradesman to a project. The `Education Manager` encapsulates the volatility in the execution of use cases related to continuing education such as coordinating training and reviewing the education certificates.

There are only two *Engines*, which encapsulate some of the acute volatilities listed previously. The `Regulation Engine` encapsulates the regulation and compliance volatility between different countries and even in the same country over time. The `Search Engine` encapsulates the volatility in producing a match, something that can be done in an open-ended number of ways, ranging from a simple rate lookup, to safety and quality record considerations, to AI and machine learning techniques for the assignments.

ResourceAccess and *Resources*

The entities required when managing a marketplace, such as payments, members, and projects, all have some storage and corresponding *ResourceAccess* components. There is also workflows storage, as discussed later.

Utilities

The system requires three *Utilities*: `Security`, `Message Bus`, and `Logging`. Any future *Utilities* (e.g., instrumentation) would go in the *Utility* bar as well.

MESSAGE BUS

A message bus is merely a queued Pub/Sub (Figure 5-15). Any message posted to the bus is broadcast to any number of subscribing parties. As such, a message bus provides for general-purpose, queued, N:M communication, where N and M can be any non-negative integers. If the message bus is down, or if the posting party becomes disconnected, messages are queued in front of the message bus, and then processed when connectivity is restored. This provides for availability and robustness. If the subscribing party is down or disconnected (such as a mobile device), the messages are posted to a private queue per subscriber, and are processed when the subscriber becomes available. If both the posting publisher and the subscriber are connected and available, then the messages are asynchronous.

The choice of technology for the message bus has little to do with architecture and, therefore, is outside the scope of this book. However, specific features provided by a particular message bus may greatly affect ease of implementation, so choosing the right one requires careful consideration. Not all message buses are created equal, including those from brand-name vendors. At the very least, the message bus must support queuing, duplicating messages and multicast broadcasting, headers and context propagation, securing both posting and retrieving of messages, off-line work, disconnected work, delivery failure handling, processing failure handling, poison message handling, transactional processing, high throughput, a service-layer API, multiple-protocol support (especially non-HTTP-based protocols), and reliable messaging. Optional features that may be relevant include message filtering, message inspection, custom interception, instrumentation, diagnostics, automated deployment, easy integration with credentials stores, and remote configuration. No single message bus product will provide all these features. To mitigate the risk of choosing poorly, you should start with a plain, easy-to-use, free message bus, and implement the architecture initially with that message bus. This tactic allows you to better understand the desired qualities and attributes, and to prioritize them. Only then can you choose the best of breed that truly meets your needs.

Adding a message bus to your architecture does not eliminate the need to impose architectural constraints on the communications patterns. For example, you should disallow *Client*-to-*Client* communication across the bus.

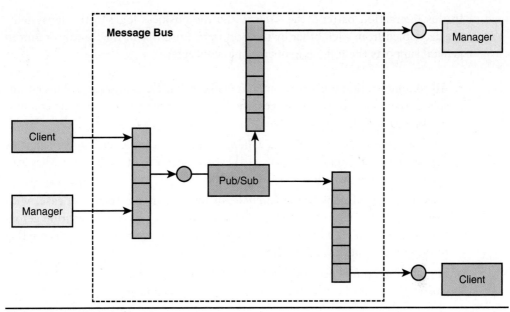

Figure 5-15 The message bus

OPERATIONAL CONCEPTS

With TradeMe, all communication between all *Clients* and all *Managers* takes place over the `Message Bus` *Utility*. Figure 5-16 illustrates this operational concept.

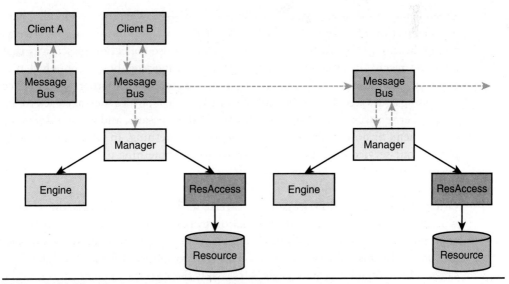

Figure 5-16 The abstract system interaction pattern

In this interaction pattern, the *Clients* and the business logic in the subsystems are decoupled from each other by the `Message Bus`. Use of the `Message Bus` in general supports the following operational concepts:

- All communication utilizes a common medium (the `Message Bus`). This encapsulates the nature of the messages, the location of the parties, and the communication protocol.

- No use case initiator (such as *Clients*) and use case executioner (such as *Managers*) ever interact directly. If they are unaware of each other, they can evolve separately, which fosters extensibility.

- A multiplicity of concurrent *Clients* can interact in the same use case, with each performing its part of the use case. There is no lock-step execution across *Clients* and system. This, in turn, leads to timeline separation and decoupling of the components along the timeline.

- High throughput is possible because the queues underneath the `Message Bus` can accept a very large number of messages per second.

The Message Is the Application

The operational concepts that a message bus supports are certainly nice to have, but by themselves may not justify the increased complexity. The main reason for choosing a message bus is because it supports the most important operational concept of TradeMe: the **Message Is the Application** design pattern.

When using this design pattern, the "application" is nowhere to be found. There is no collection of components or services that you can point to and identify as the application. Instead, the system comprises a loose collection of services that post and receive messages to one another (over a message bus, although that is secondary consideration). These messages are related to each other. Each service processing a message does some unit of work, and then posts a message back to the bus. Other services will subsequently examine the message, and some of them (or one of them, or none of them) will decide to do something. In effect, the message post by one service triggers another service to do something unbeknownst to the posting service. This stretches decoupling almost to the limit.

Often the same logical message may traverse all the services. Likely the services will add additional contextual information to the message (such as in the headers), modify previous context, pass context from the old message to a new one, and so on. In this way, the services act as transformation functions on the messages. The paramount aspect of the Message Is the Application pattern is that the required behavior of the application is the aggregate of those transformations plus the local work done by the individual services. Any required behavior changes induce changes in the way your services respond to the messages, rather than the architecture or the services.

The business objectives for TradeMe justified the use of this pattern because of the required extensibility. The company can extend the system by adding message processing services, thereby avoiding modification of existing services and risk to a working implementation. This correctly supports the directive from Chapter 3 that you should always build systems incrementally, not iteratively. The objective of forward-looking design is also well served here because nothing in this pattern ties the system to the present requirements. This pattern is also an elegant way of integrating external systems—yet another business objective.

FUTURE-LOOKING DESIGN

The use of granular services integrated over a message bus with the Message Is the Application design pattern is one of the best ways of preparing the system for the future. By "preparing the system for the future," I specifically refer to the next epoch in software engineering, the use of the actor model. Over the next decade the software industry will likely adopt a very granular use of services called actors. While actors are services, they are very simple services. Actors reside in a graph or grid of actors, and they only interact with each other using messages. The resulting network of actors can perform calculations or store data. The program is not the aggregate of the code of the actors; instead, the program or the required behavior consists of the progression of messages through the network. To change the program, you change the network of actors, not the actors themselves.

Building systems this way offers fundamental benefits such as better affinity to real-life business models, high concurrency without locking, and the ability to build systems that are presently out of reach, such as smart power grids, command and control systems, and generic AI. Using current-day technology and platforms along with the Message Is the Application is very much aligned—if not most of the way there—with the actor model. For example, in TradeMe, tradesmen and contractors are actors. Projects are networks of these actors, and other actors (such as `Market Manager`) compose the network. Adopting the TradeMe architecture today prepared the company for the future without compromising on the present.[a]

[a] For more on the actor model, see Juval Lowy, *Actors: The Past and Future of Software Engineering* (YouTube/IDesignIncTV, 2017).

As with everything in life, implementing this pattern comes with a cost. Not every organization can justify using the pattern or even having a message bus. The cost will almost always take the form of additional system complexity and moving parts, new APIs to learn, deployment and security issues, intricate failure scenarios, and more. The upside is an inherently decoupled system geared toward requirements churn, extensibility, and reuse. In general, you should use this pattern when you can invest in a platform and have the backing of your organization both top-down and bottom-up. In many cases, a simpler design in which the *Clients* just queue up calls to the *Managers* would be a better fit for the development team. Always calibrate the architecture to the capability and maturity of the developers and management. After all, it is a lot easier to morph the architecture than it is to bend the organization. Once the organizational capabilities have matured, you can incorporate a full Message Is the Application pattern.

WORKFLOW MANAGER

With *The Method*, the *Managers* encapsulate the volatility in the business workflows. Nothing prevents you from simply coding the workflows in the *Mangers* and then, when the workflows change, changing the code in the *Managers*. The problem with this approach is that the volatility in the workflows may exceed the developers' ability, as measured in time and effort, to catch up using just code.

The next operational concept in TradeMe is the use of workflow *Managers*. I hinted at this concept in Chapter 2 in the discussion of the stock trading system, but this chapter codifies it as another operational pattern. All *Managers* in TradeMe are workflow *Managers*. A **workflow *Manager*** is a service that enables you to create, store, retrieve, and execute workflows. In theory, it is just another *Manager*. In practice, however, such *Managers* almost always utilize some sort of third-party workflow execution tool and workflow storage. For each *Client* call, the workflow *Manager* loads not just the correct workflow type but also a specific instance of it, with a particular state and context; executes the workflow; and persists it back to the workflow store. Loading and saving the workflow instance each time supports long-running workflows. The *Manager* also does not have to maintain any kind of a session with the *Client* while remaining state-aware. Each call from the same user in the same workflow execution can come from a different device on a different connection and carries with it the unique ID of the instance of the workflow that the *Manager* should load and execute, as well as information about the client such as its address (e.g., URI).

To add or change a feature, you simply add or change the workflows of the *Managers* involved, but not necessarily the implementation of the individual participating services. This is a clean way to provide features as aspects of integration (as discussed in Chapter 4) and is a tangible aspect of the mission statement for the system, allowing you to illustrate how the architecture supports the business.

The real necessity for using a workflow *Manager* arises when the system must handle high volatility. With a workflow *Manager*, you merely edit the required behavior and deploy the newly generated code. The nature of this editing is specific to the workflow tool you choose. For example, some tools use script editors, whereas others use visual workflows that look like activity diagrams and generate or even deploy the workflow code.

You can even (with the right safeguards) have the product owners or the end users edit the required behavior. This drastically reduces the cycle time for delivering features and allows the software development team to focus on the core services as opposed to chasing changes in the requirements.

The business needs for TradeMe justified the use of this pattern because the objective of a quick turnaround for features is impossible to meet using hand-crafted coding by a small, thinly spread team. Use of workflow *Manager* enables a high degree of customization across markets, satisfying another objective for the system.

Again, evaluate carefully whether this concept is applicable to your particular case. Make sure the level of workflow volatility justifies the additional complexity, learning curves, and changes to the development process.

CHOOSING A WORKFLOW TOOL

The choice of technology for the workflow tool has little to do with architecture, so it is outside the scope of this book. However, if the architecture calls for it, you had better choose the right workflow tool. Literally dozens of workflow solutions exist, with the various tools offering a very wide set of features. At the very least, the workflow tool should support visual editing of workflows, persisting and rehydrating workflow instances, calling services from within the workflow across multiple protocols, posting messages to the message bus, exposing workflows as services across multiple protocols, nesting workflows, creating libraries of workflows, defining common templates of recurring workflow patterns that can be customized later on, and debugging workflows. It would also be nice to have the ability to play back, instrument, and profile the workflows and to integrate them with a diagnostics system.

DESIGN VALIDATION

You must know before work commences whether the design can support the required behaviors. As Chapter 4 explains, to validate your design, you need to show that the design can support the core use cases by integrating the various areas of volatility encapsulated in your services. You validate the design by showing the respective call chain or sequence diagram for each use case. You may require more than one diagram to complete a use case.

It is important to demonstrate that your design is valid not just to yourself, but also to others. If you cannot validate your architecture, or if the validation is too ambiguous, you need to go back to the drawing board.

As mentioned previously, the few company-provided use cases for TradeMe included just a single candidate for a core use case: Match Tradesmen. The architecture of TradeMe was modular and decoupled from all the use cases to such an extent that the design team could demonstrate that it supported all the provided use cases, not just the core Match Tradesman use case. The next section illustrates the validation of the TradeMe use cases and the operational concept of the new system.

ADD TRADESMAN/CONTRACTOR USE CASE

The Add Tradesman/Contractor use case involves several areas of volatility: the tradesman (or contractor) *Client* applications, the workflow of adding a member, compliance with regulations, and the payment system used. You can rearrange and simplify the use case from Figure 5-1 by adding swim lanes to the diagram, as shown in Figure 5-17.

Figure 5-17 shows that the execution of the use case requires interaction between a *Client* application and the membership subsystem. This is evident in the actual call chains of Figure 5-18 (the Adding Contractor use case is identical but with the contractor's application, the Contractors Portal). Following the operational concepts of TradeMe, in Figure 5-18 the *Client* application (in this case, either the Tradesman Portal when the member is applying directly or the Marketplace App when the back-end rep is adding the member) posts the request to the Message Bus.

Upon receiving the message, the Membership Manager (which is a workflow *Manager*) loads the appropriate workflow from the workflow storage. This either kicks off a new workflow or rehydrates an existing one to carry on with the

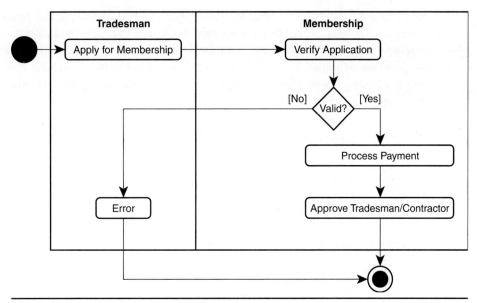

Figure 5-17 The Add Tradesman/Contractor use case with swim lanes

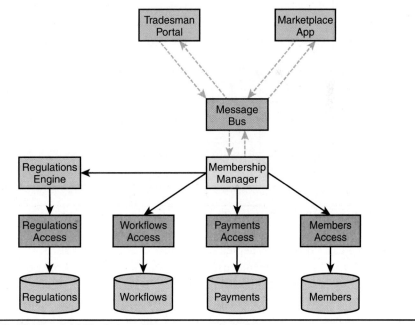

Figure 5-18 The Add Tradesman/Contractor call chain

workflow execution. Once the workflow has finished executing the request, the `Membership Manager` posts a message back into the `Message Bus` indicating the new state of the workflow, such as its completion, or perhaps indicating that some other *Manager* can start its processing now that the workflow is in a new state. *Clients* can monitor the `Message Bus` as well and update the users about their requests. The `Membership Manager` consults the `Regulation Engine` that is verifying the tradesman or contractor, adds the tradesman or contractor to the `Members` store, and updates the *Clients* via the `Message Bus`.

REQUEST TRADESMAN USE CASE

The Request Tradesman use case includes two areas of interest: the contractor and the market (Figure 5-19). After initial verification of the request, this use case triggers another use case, Match Tradesman.

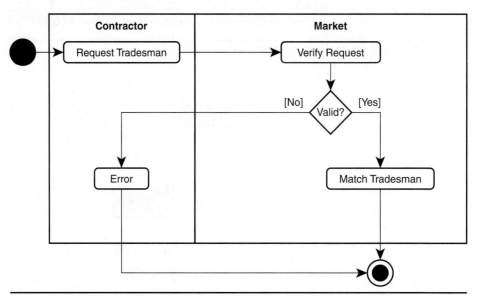

Figure 5-19 The Request Tradesman use case with swim lanes

The call chains are depicted in Figure 5-20. *Clients* such as the `Contractors Portal` or the internal user of the `Marketplace App` post a message to the bus requesting a tradesman. The `Market Manager` receives that message. The `Market Manager` loads the workflow corresponding to this request, and performs actions such as consulting with the `Regulation Engine` about what may be valid for this request or updating the project with the request for a tradesman. The `Market Manager` can then post back to the `Message Bus` that someone is

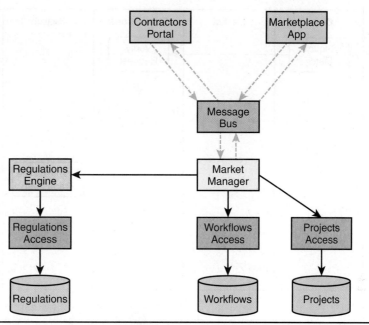

Figure 5-20 Request Tradesman call chains (until matching)

requesting a tradesman. This will trigger the matching and assignment workflows, all separated on the timeline.

MATCH TRADESMAN USE CASE

The Match Tradesman core use case involves multiple areas of interest. The first is who initiated the tradesman request that has triggered the match use case. That initiator could be a *Client* (a contractor or the marketplace reps), as in Figure 5-20, but it could also be a timer or any other subsystem that kicks off the match workflow. The other areas of interest are the market, regulations, search, and ultimately membership, as shown in Figure 5-21.

Once you realize that regulations and search are all elements of the market, you can refactor the activity diagram to that shown in Figure 5-22. This enables easy mapping to your subsystems design.

Figure 5-23 depicts the corresponding call chain. Again, this call chain is symmetrical with other call chains, in the sense that the first action is to load the appropriate workflow and execute it. The last call of the call chain to the `Message Bus` and to the `Membership Manager` triggers the Assign Tradesman use case.

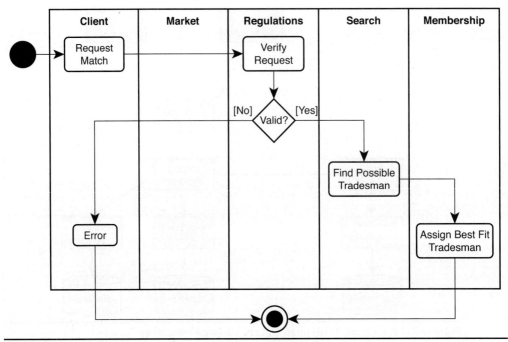

Figure 5-21 The Match Tradesman use case with swim lanes

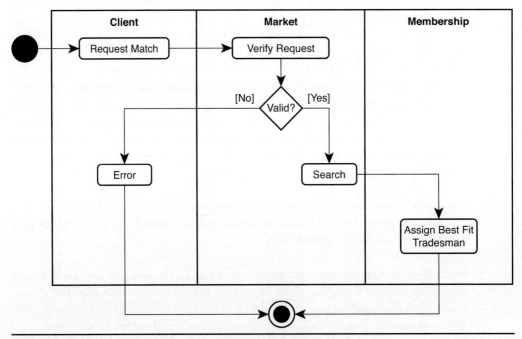

Figure 5-22 Refactored swim lanes for the Match Tradesman use case

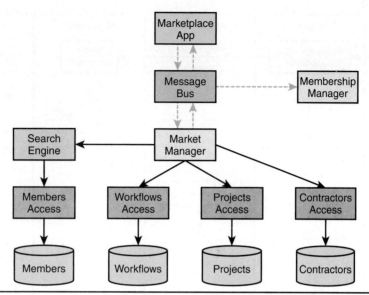

Figure 5-23 Call chains for the Match Tradesman use case

Notice the composability of this design. For example, suppose the company really does need to handle acute volatility in analyzing the project's needs. The call chain for finding a match allows for separating search from analysis. You would add an `Analysis Engine` to encapsulate the separate set of analysis algorithms. The business can even leverage TradeMe for some business intelligence to answer questions like "Could we have done things better?" For example, a call chain similar to Figure 5-23 could be used for the much more involved scenario of "Analyze all projects between 2016 and 2019" and the design of the components would not have to change at all. The number of these use cases is likely open, and that is the whole point: You have an open-ended design that can be extended to implement any of these future scenarios, a true composable design.

ASSIGN TRADESMAN USE CASE

The Assign Tradesman use case involves four areas of interest (Figure 5-24): client, membership, regulations, and market. Note that the use case is independent of who triggered it, whether an actual internal user or just a request message off the bus from another subsystem. For example, the Match Tradesman use case could trigger the assignment use case as a direct continuation of the workflow in the case of automatic match and assignment.

Again, after refactoring the activity diagram, it is easy to map to subsystems (Figure 5-25).

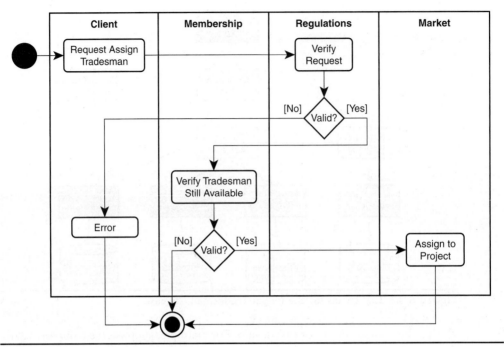

Figure 5-24 The Assign Tradesman use case swim lanes

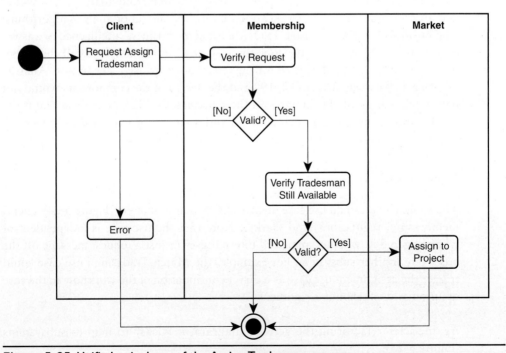

Figure 5-25 Unified swim lanes of the Assign Tradesman use case

As with all previous call chains, Figure 5-26 shows how the Membership Manager is executing the workflow that ultimately leads to assigning the tradesman to the project. This is a collaborative work between the Membership Manager and the Market Manager, with each managing its respective subsystem. Note that the Membership Manager is unaware of the Market Manager—it just posts a message to the bus. The Market Manager receives that message and updates the project according to its internal workflow. The Market Manager may, in turn, post another message to the Message Bus to trigger another use case, such as issuing a report on the project, or billing for the contractor, or pretty much anything. This is what the Message Is the Application design pattern is all about: The logical "assignment" message weaves its way between the services, triggering local behaviors as it goes. The *Client* can also monitor the Message Bus and may advise the user that the assignment is in progress.

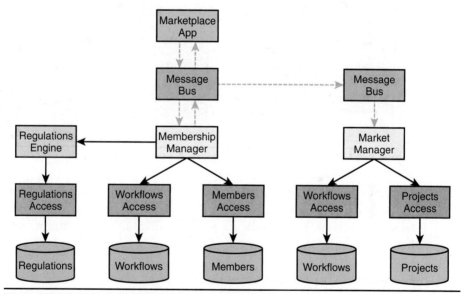

Figure 5-26 Call chains for the Assign Tradesman use case

TERMINATE TRADESMAN USE CASE

In the previous use cases, the initial diagram swim lanes included the regulations area, which was subsequently consolidated into the membership subsystem. Since this was such a recurring pattern, Figure 5-9 shows the refactored diagram for the Terminate Tradesman use case. This diagram still provides enough differentiation to allow for clear mapping to the design.

Figure 5-27 shows the call chain for terminating a tradesman. The Market Manager initiates the termination workflow and notifies the Membership Manager of the termination.

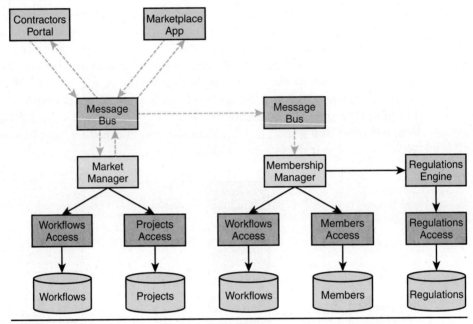

Figure 5-27 Call chains for the Terminate Tradesman use case

Any error condition or deviation from the "happy path" would add a dashed gray arrow from the Membership Manager back to the Message Bus and ultimately back to the client. Figure 5-28 is a sequence diagram demonstrating this interaction, without the calls between the *ResourceAccess* services and the *Resources*.

Finally, the call chain diagram in Figure 5-27 (or the sequence diagram of Figure 5-28) assumes the termination use case is triggered when a project is completed, and the contractor terminates the assigned tradesmen. But it can also be triggered by the tradesman posting a message from the Tradesman Portal to the Membership Manager, which would cause the call chain to flow in the opposite direction (Membership Manager to Market Manager and on to the *Client* apps). Again, this is a testimony to the versatility of the design.

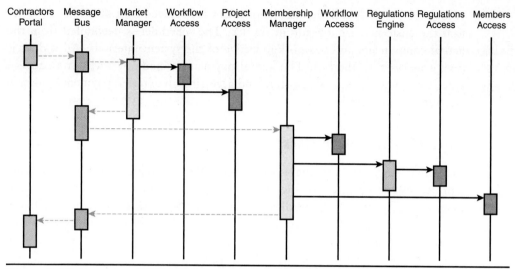

Figure 5-28 Sequence diagram for the Terminate Tradesman use case

PAY TRADESMAN USE CASE

The rest of the use cases closely follow the interactions and design pattern of the use cases described thus far, so only brief descriptions of them appear here. Also note the high degree of self-similarity or symmetry in the call chains. Figure 5-6 showed the Pay Tradesman use case, and its validating call chain is in Figure 5-29.

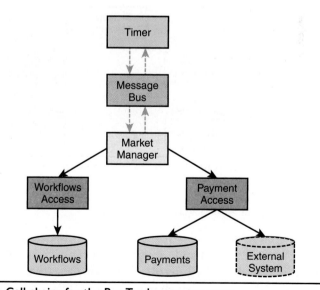

Figure 5-29 Call chains for the Pay Tradesman use case

Unlike the previous call chains, the payment is triggered by a scheduler or timer that the customer has already in service. The scheduler is decoupled from the actual components and has no knowledge of the system internals: All it does is post a message to the bus. The actual payment is made by `PaymentAccess` when updating the `Payments` store and accessing an external payment system, a *Resource* to TradeMe.

CREATE PROJECT USE CASE

In another simple use case, the `Market Manager` responds to the request to create a project by executing a corresponding workflow (see Figure 5-30 and the use case diagram in Figure 5-7). Regardless of how many steps this takes, or how many errors are involved, the nature of the workflow *Manager* pattern allows for as many permutations as needed.

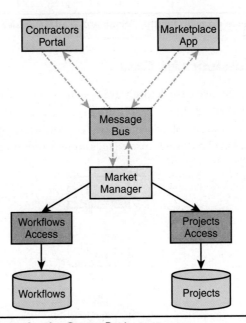

Figure 5-30 Call chains for the Create Project use case

CLOSE PROJECT USE CASE

The Close Project use case involves both the `Market Manager` and the `Membership Manager` (see Figure 5-31 and the use case in Figure 5-8). Again, TradeMe accomplishes this task with the interplay between these two major abstractions; the interaction is identical to that shown in Figure 5-27.

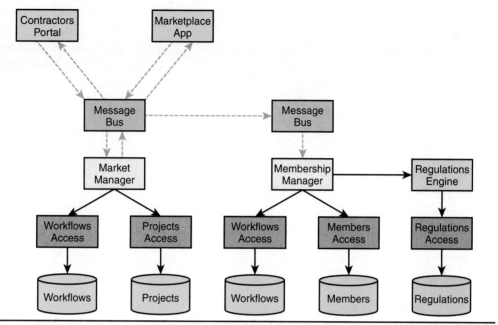

Figure 5-31 Call chains for the Close Project use case

> **Note**   Chapter 13 demonstrates designing the project for TradeMe, based on the architecture described in this chapter. As with the demonstration of system design, it is a comprehensive case study that walks through various permutations in determining the project design that will provide the best time, cost, and risk for the project.

WHAT'S NEXT?

This lengthy system design case study concludes the first part of this book. Having the system design in hand is just the first ingredient of success. Next comes project design. You should strike while the iron is hot: Always follow system design with project design, ideally back-to-back, as a continuous design effort.

Part II
PROJECT DESIGN

MOTIVATION

Much as you design the software system, you must *design* the project to build the system. This includes accurately calculating the planned duration and cost, devising several good execution options, scheduling resources, and even validating your plan to ensure it is sensible and feasible. Project design requires understanding the dependencies between services and activities, the critical path of integration, the staff distribution, and the risks involved. All of these challenges stem from your system design, and addressing them properly is an engineering task. As such, it is up to you, the software architect, as the engineer in charge, to design the project.

You should think of project design as a continuation of the system design effort. Combining system design and project design yields a nonlinear effect that drastically improves the likelihood of success for the project. It is also important to note that project design is not part of project management. Instead, project design is to project management what architecture is to programming.

The second part of this book is all about project design. The following chapters present conventional ideas along with my original, battle-proven techniques and methodologies, covering the core body of knowledge of modern software project design. This chapter provides the background and essential motivation for project design.

WHY PROJECT DESIGN?

No project has infinite time, money, or resources. All sound project plans always trade some time for money, or vice versa. Furthermore, for any given project, there are numerous possible combinations of schedule and cost. If you have one developer or four developers, if you have two years or six months, or if you try to minimize risks and maximize the probability for success, you will have different projects.

When you design a project you must provide management with several viable options trading schedule, cost, and risk, allowing management and other decision makers to choose up front the solution that best fits their needs and expectations. Providing options in project design is the key to success. Finding a balanced solution and even an optimal solution is a highly engineered design task. I say it is "engineered" not just because of the design and calculations involved, but because engineering is all about tradeoffs and accommodating reality.

Adding to the challenge of project design is the reality that no single correct solution exists even for the same set of constraints, much as there are always several possible design approaches for any system. Projects designed to meet an aggressive schedule will cost more and be far more risky and complex than projects designed to reduce cost and minimize risk. There is no "THE Project"; there are only options. Your task is to narrow this spectrum of near-countless possibilities to several good project design options, such as the following:

- The least expensive way to build the system
- The fastest way to deliver the system
- The safest way of meeting your commitments
- The best combination of schedule, cost, and risk

The following chapters will show you how to identify good project design options. If you do not provide these options, you will have no one to blame but yourself for conflicts with management. How often do you labor on the design of the system and then present it to management, only to have managers ordain, "You have a year and four developers." Any correlation between that year, the four developers, and what it really takes to deliver the system is accidental—and so are your chances of success. However, if you present the same architecture, accompanied by three to four project design options, all of them doable, but reflecting different tradeoffs of schedule, cost, and risk, a completely different dynamic will rule the meeting. Now the discussion will revolve around which of these options to choose.

You must provide an environment in which managers can make good decisions. The key is to provide them with only good options. Whichever option they do choose will then be a good decision.

PROJECT DESIGN AND PROJECT SANITY

Project design allows you to shed light on dark corners—that is, to have up-front visibility on the true scope of the project. Project design forces managers to think through work before it begins, to recognize unsuspected relationships and limits, to represent all activities, and to recognize several options for building the system. It allows the organization to determine whether it even wants to get the project done. After all, if the true cost and duration will exceed the acceptable limits, why start the work in the first place, only to have the project canceled once you run out of money or time?

Once project design is in place, you eliminate the commonplace gambling with costs, development death marches, wishful thinking about project success, and horrendously expensive trials and errors. After work commences, a well-designed project also lays the foundation for decision makers to evaluate and think through the effect of a proposed change on the schedule and the budget.

ASSEMBLY INSTRUCTIONS

Project design involves much more than just proper decision making. Project design also serves as the system assembly instructions. To use an analogy, would you buy a well-designed IKEA furniture set without the assembly instructions booklet? Regardless of how comfortable or convenient the item is, you would recoil at the mere thought of trying to guess where each of the dozens of pins, bolts, screws, and plates go, and in which order.

Your software system is significantly more complex than furniture, yet often architects presume developers and projects managers can just go about assembling the system, figuring it out as they go along. This ad hoc approach is clearly not the most efficient way of assembling the system. As you will see in the next chapters, project design changes the situation, since the only way to know how long it will take and how much it will cost to deliver the system is to figure out first how you will build it. Consequently, each project design option comes with its own set of assembly instructions.

HIERARCHY OF NEEDS

In 1943, Abraham Maslow published a pivotal work on human behavior, known as Maslow's hierarchy of needs.[1] Maslow ranked human needs based on their relative importance and suggested that only once a person has satisfied a lower-level need could that person develop an interest in satisfying a higher-level need. This hierarchal approach can describe another category of complex beings—software projects. Figure 6-1 shows a software project's hierarchy of needs in the shape of a pyramid.

---

1. A. H. Maslow, "A Theory of Human Motivation," *Psychological Review* 50, no. 4 (1943): 370–396.

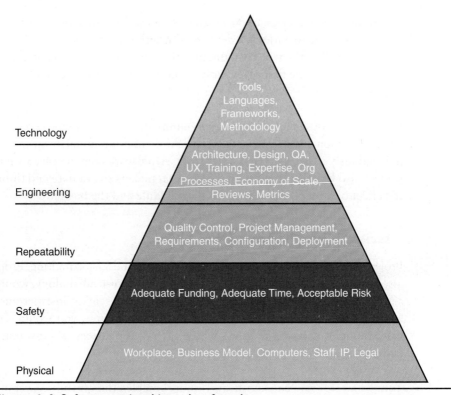

Figure 6-1 Software project hierarchy of needs

The project needs can be classified into five levels: physical, safety, repeatability, engineering, and technology.

1. **Physical.** This is the lowest level in the project pyramid of needs, dealing with physical survival. Much as a person must have air, food, water, clothing, and shelter, a project must have a workplace (even a virtual one) and a viable business model. The project must have computers to write and test the code, as well as people assigned to perform these tasks. The project must have the right legal protection. The project must not infringe on existing external intellectual property (IP), yet must also protect its own IP.

2. **Safety.** Once the physical needs are satisfied, the project must have adequate funding (often in the form of allocated resources) and enough time to complete the work. The work itself must be performed with acceptable risk—not too safe (because low-risk projects are likely not worth doing) and not too risky (because high-risk projects will likely fail). In short, the project must be reasonably safe. Project design operates at this level in the pyramid of needs.

3. **Repeatability.** Project repeatability describes the development organization's ability to deliver successfully time and again, and is the foundation for control and execution. It assures that if you plan for and commit to a certain schedule and cost, you will deliver on those commitments. Repeatability captures the credibility of the team and the project. To gain repeatability, you must manage requirements, manage and track the project's progress against the plan, employ quality control measures such as unit and system testing, have an effective configuration management system, and actively manage deployment and operations.

4. **Engineering.** Once the repeatability of the project effort is secured, the software project can, for the first time, turn its attention to the enticing aspects of software engineering. This includes architecture and detail design, quality assurance activities such as root cause analysis and correction (on a systemic level), and preventive work using hardened operating procedures. The first part of this book, which was devoted to system design, operates at this level of the pyramid.

5. **Technology.** At this level are development technology, tools, methodology, operating systems, and related hard-core technical aspects. This is the very pinnacle of the pyramid of needs, and it can express itself to its full potential only once the lower needs are fully addressed.

In a hierarchy of needs, higher-level needs serve the lower-level needs. For example, according to Maslow, food is a lower-level need than employment, yet most people work so that they can eat, as opposed to eat so that they can work. Similarly, the technology serves the engineering needs (such as the architecture), and the engineering needs serve the safety needs (those that project design provides). It also means that chronologically you have to design the system first; only then can you design the project to build it.

You can validate the pyramid by listing all necessary ingredients for success of a typical software project. You then prioritize, sort, and finally group them into categories of needs.

As an experiment in this process, consider the following two projects. The first has a tightly coupled design, a high cost of maintenance, and a low level of reuse, and is difficult to extend. However, there is adequate time to perform the work, and the project is properly staffed. The second project has an amazing architecture that is modular, extensible, and reusable; addresses all the requirements; and is future-proof. However, the team is understaffed, and even if the people were available, there is not enough time to safely develop the system. Ask yourself: Which project you would like to be part of?

The answer is unequivocally the first project. Consequently, project design must rank lower (i.e., be more foundational) in the pyramid of needs than architecture. A classic reason for failure for many software projects is an inverted pyramid of needs. Imagine Figure 6-1 turned on its head. The development team focuses almost exclusively on technology, frameworks, libraries, and platforms; spends next to nothing on architecture and design; and completely ignores the fundamental issues of time, cost, and risk. This makes the pyramid of needs unstable, and it is small wonder that such projects fail. By investing in the safety level of the pyramid using the tools of project design, you stratify the needs of the project, provide the foundation that stabilizes the upper levels, and drive the project to success.

7

PROJECT DESIGN OVERVIEW

The following overview describes the basic methodology and techniques you apply when designing a project. A good project design includes your staffing plan, scope and effort estimations, the services' construction and integration plan, the detailed schedule of activities, cost calculation, viability and validation of the plan, and setup for execution and tracking.

This chapter covers most of these concepts of project design, while leaving certain details and one or two crucial concepts for later chapters. However, even though it serves as a mere overview, this chapter contains all the essential elements of success in designing and delivering software projects. It also provides the development process motivation for the design activities, while the rest of the chapters are more technical in nature.

DEFINING SUCCESS

Before you continue reading, you must understand that project design is about success and what it takes to succeed. The software industry at large has had such a poor track record that the industry has changed its very definition of success: Success today is defined as anything that does not bankrupt the company right now. With such a low bar, literally anything goes and nothing matters, from low quality to deceiving numbers and frustrated customers. My definition of success is different, though it is also a low bar in its own way. I define **success** as meeting your commitments.

If you call for a year for the project and $1 million in costs, I expect the project to take one year, not two, and for the project to cost $1 million, not $3 million. In the software industry, many people lack the skills and training it takes to meet even this low bar for success. The ideas presented in this chapter are all about accomplishing just that.

A higher bar is to deliver the project the fastest, least costly, and safest way. Such a higher bar requires the techniques described in the following chapters. You can raise the bar even further and call for having the system architecture remain good for decades and be maintainable, reusable, extensible, and secure across its entire long and prosperous life. That would inevitably require the design ideas of the first part of this book. Since, in general, you need to walk before you can run, it is best to start with the basic level of success and work your way up.

REPORTING SUCCESS

Part 1 of this book stated a universal design rule: Features are always and everywhere aspects of integration, not implementation. As such, there are no features in any of the early services. At some point you will have integrated enough to start seeing features. I call that point the **system**. The system is unlikely to appear at the very end of the project since there may be some additional concluding activities such as system testing and deployment. The system typically appears toward the end because it requires most of the services as well as the clients. When using *The Method*, this means only once you have integrated inside the *Managers*, the *Engines*, the *ResourceAccess*, and the *Utilities* can you support the behaviors that the *Clients* require.

While the system is the product of the integration, not all the integration happens inside the *Managers*. Some integration happens before the *Managers* are complete (such as the *Engines* integrating *ResourceAccess*) and some integration happens after the *Managers* (such as between the *Clients* and the *Managers*). There might also be explicit integration activities, such as developing a client of a service against a simulator and then integrating the client with the real service.

The problem with the system appearing only toward the end of the project is pushback from management. Most people tasked with managing software development do not understand the design concepts in this book and simply want features. They would never stop to think that if a feature can appear early and quickly, then it does not add much value for the business or the customers because the company or the team did not spend much effort on the feature. Usually, management uses features as the metric to gauge progress and success, and tends to cancel sick projects that do not show progress. As such, the project faces a serious risk: It could be perfectly on schedule but because the system only appears at the end, if the project bases its progress report on features, it is asking to be canceled. The solution is simple:

Never base progress reports on features. Always base progress reports on integration.

A *Method*-based project performs a lot of integration along the project. These integrations are small and doable. As a result, there is the potential for a constant stream of good news coming out of the project, building trust and avoiding cancellation.

> **Note** This approach to progress reporting is common practice in other industries. For example, a contractor building a home shows the homeowner the foundations, the walls bolted to the foundation, the house connected to the utilities, and so on, to alleviate concerns and apprehensions about progress, not because the homeowner is interested in these details.

PROJECT INITIAL STAFFING

A good architecture does not happen on its own, is not a happenstance, and does not emerge organically in any reasonable amount of time or cost. Good architecture is the result of deliberate effort by the software architect. As such, the first act of wisdom in any software project is to assign a qualified and competent architect to the project. Nothing less will do, because the principal risk in any project is not having an architect accountable for the architecture. This risk far eclipses any other initial risk the project faces. It does not matter what the level of the developers' technical acumen is, how mature the technology is, or how pampering the development environment is. None of these will amount to anything if the system design is flawed. To use the house analogy, would you like to build a house from the best material, with the best construction crew, at the best location, but without any architecture or with a flawed architecture?

ARCHITECT, NOT ARCHITECTS

The architect will need to spend time gathering and analyzing the requirements, identifying the core use cases and the areas of volatility, and producing the system and the project design. While the design itself is not time-consuming (the architect can usually design both the system and the project in a week or two), it may take several months to get to the point that the architect can design the system and the project.

Most managers will recoil both at spending some three or four months on design and at skipping design entirely. They may wish to accelerate the design effort by having more architects participate. However, requirements analysis and architecture are contemplative, time-consuming activities. Assigning more architects to these activities does not expedite them at all, but instead will make matters worse. Architects are typically senior self-confident personnel, used to working independently. Assigning multiple architects only results in them contesting with each other, rather than in system and project design blueprints.

One way of resolving the multiple architects conflict is to appoint a design committee. Unfortunately, the surest way of killing anything is to appoint a committee to oversee it. Another option is to carve up the system and assign each architect a specific area to design. With this option, the system is likely to end as a Chimera—a mythological Greek beast that has the head of a lion, the wings of a dragon, the front legs of an ox, and the hind legs of a goat. While each part of the Chimera is well designed and even highly optimized, the Chimera is inferior at anything it attempts: It does not fly as well as a dragon, run as fast as a lion, pull as much as an ox, or climb as well as a goat. The Chimera lacks design integrity—and the same is true when multiple architects design the system, each responsible for their part.

A single architect is absolutely crucial for design integrity. You can extend this observation to the general rule that the only way to allow for design integrity is to have a single architect own the design. The opposite is also true: If no single person owns the design and can visualize it cover-to-cover, the system will not have design integrity.

Additionally, with multiple architects no one owns the in-betweens, the cross-subsystem or even cross-services design aspects. As a result, no one is accountable for the system design as a whole. When no one is accountable for something, it never gets done, or at best is done poorly.

With a single architect in charge, that architect is accountable for the system design. Ultimately, being accountable is the only way to earn the respect and trust of management. Respect always emerges out of accountability. When no one is accountable, as is the case with a group of architects, management intuitively has often nothing but scorn for the architects and their design effort.

> **Caution**   A single architect in charge does not mean the architect's work is exempt from review by other professional architects. Being accountable for the design does not imply working in isolation or avoiding constructive criticism. The architect should seek out such reviews to verify that the design is adequate.

Junior Architects

Most software projects need only a single architect. This is true regardless of the project size and is essential for success. However, large projects very easily saturate the architect with various responsibilities, preventing the architect from focusing on the key goal of designing the system and keeping the design from drifting away during development. Additionally, the role of architect involves technical leadership, requirements review, design review, code review for each service in the system, design documents updates, discussion of feature requests from marketing, and so on.

Management can address this overload by assigning a junior architect (or more than one) to the project. The architect can offload many secondary tasks to the junior architect, allowing the architect to focus on the design of the system and the project at the beginning and on keeping the system true to its design throughout the project. The architect and the junior architect are unlikely to compete because there is no doubt who is in charge, and there are clearly delineated lines of responsibilities. Having junior architects is also a great way of grooming and mentoring the next generation of architects for the organization.

THE CORE TEAM

As vital as the architect is to the project, the architect cannot work in isolation. On day 1, the project must have a **core team** in place. The core team consists of three roles: project manager, product manager, and architect. These are logical roles and may or may not map to three individuals. When they do not, you may see the same person as both the architect and the project manager, or a project with several product managers.

Most organizations and teams have these roles, but the job titles they use may be different. I define these roles as follows:

- **The project manager.** The job of the **project manager** is to shield the team from the organization. Most organizations, even small ones, create too much noise. If that noise makes its way into the development team, it can paralyze the team. A good project manager is like a firewall, blocking the noise, allowing only sanctioned communication through. The project manager tracks progress and reports status to management and other project managers, negotiates terms, and deals with cross-organization constraints. Internally, the project manager assigns work items to developers, schedules activities, and keeps the project on schedule, on budget, and on quality. No one in the organization other than the project manager should assign work activity or ask for status from developers.

- **The product manager.** The **product manager** should encapsulate the customers. Customers are also a constant source of noise. The product manager acts as a proxy for the customers. For example, when the architect needs to clarify the required behaviors, the architect should not chase customers; instead, the product manager should provide the answers. The product manager also resolves conflicts between customers (often expressed as mutually exclusive requirements), negotiates requirements, defines priorities, and communicates expectations about what is feasible and on what terms.

- **The architect.** The **architect** is the technical manager, acting as the design lead, the process lead, and the technical lead of the project. The architect not only designs the system, but also sees it through development. The architect needs to work with the product manager to produce the system design and with the project manager to produce the project design. While the collaboration with both the product manager and the project manager is essential, the architect is held responsible for both of these design efforts. As a process lead, the architect has to ensure the team builds the system incrementally, following the system and the project design with a relentless commitment to quality. As a technical lead, the architect often has to decide on the best way of accomplishing technical tasks (the what-to-do) while leaving the details (the how-to-do) to developers. This requires continuous hands-on mentoring, training, and reviews.

Perhaps the most glaring omission from this definition of the core team are developers. Developers (and testers) are transient resources that come and go across projects—a very important point that this chapter revisits as part of the discussion of scheduling activities and resource assignment.

Unlike developers, the core team stays throughout the project since the project needs all three roles from beginning to end. However, what these roles do in the project changes over time. For example, the project manager shifts from negotiating with stakeholders to providing status reports, and the product manager shifts from gathering requirements to performing demos. The architect shifts from designing the system and the project to providing ongoing technical and process leadership, such as conducting design and code reviews at the service level and resolving technical conflicts.

The Core Mission

The mission of the core team at the beginning is to design the project. This means reliably answering the questions of how long it will take and how much it will cost. It is impossible to know the answers to these key questions without project design, and to design the project you require the architecture. In this respect, the architecture is merely a means to an end: project design. Since the architect needs to work with the product manager on the architecture and with the project manager on the project design, the project requires the core team at the beginning of the project.

The Fuzzy Front End

The core team designs the project in the **fuzzy front end** leading to development. The fuzzy front end is a general term[1] in all technical projects referring to the very start of the project. The front end commences when someone has an idea about the project, and it concludes when developers start construction. The front end often lasts considerably longer than most people recognize: By the time they become involved in the project, the front end may have been in progress for several years. There is a large degree of variance across projects, which leads to the fuzziness about the exact duration of the front end. The duration of the front end is most heavily dependent on the constraints applied to the project. The more constrained the project is, the less time you need to spend in the front end. Conversely, the fewer the constraints, the more time you should invest in figuring out what lies ahead and how to go about it.

Software projects are never constraint-free. All projects face some constraints on time, scope, effort, resources, technology, legacy, business context, and so on. These constraints can be explicit or implicit. It is vital to invest the time in both verifying the explicit constraints and discovering the implicit constraints. Designing a system and project that violates a constraint is a recipe for failure. From my experience, a software project should spend roughly between 15% and 25% of the entire duration of the project in the front end, depending on constraints.

EDUCATED DECISIONS

It is pointless to approve a project without knowing its true schedule, cost, and risk. After all, you would not buy a house without knowing how much it costs. You would not buy a house that you can afford up front but whose upkeep and taxes you cannot pay. In any walk of life, it is obvious that you commit time and capital only after the scope is known. Many software projects recklessly proceed with no idea of the real time and cost required.

It is just as pointless to staff a project with resources before the organization is committed to the project and certain to have the required time and money. In fact,

---

1. https://en.wikipedia.org/wiki/Front_end_innovation

staffing a project before the commitment is made has a tendency to force the project ahead regardless of affordability. If the right thing to do is to avoid doing the project in the first place, the organization will only be wasting good money. A rush to commit the resources will almost always be accompanied by a poor functional design and no plan at all—hardly the ingredients of success.

The key to success is to make educated decisions, based on sound design and scope calculations. Wishful thinking is not a strategy, and intuition is not knowledge, especially when dealing with complex software systems.

> **Note**   The inability to make educated decisions about time and cost is a constant source of frustration for business stakeholders when working with software teams. The business people in charge simply want to know the cost involved and when they can realize the value of the effort. Avoiding these questions eventually creates tension, suspicion, and animosity between the team and management. Business-side people are used to planning and budgeting. Their fair expectation of software professionals is that they should have the expertise to do the same.

PLANS, NOT PLAN

The result of project design is a set of plans, not a single plan. As described in the previous chapter, the project plan is not a single coordinate of time and cost. There are always multiple possible ways of building any system, and only one option will offer the right combination of time, cost, and risk. The architect may be tempted to simply ask management what the design parameters of the project are and just design that single option. The problem is that managers often do not say what they mean or mean what they say.

For example, consider a 10-man-year project—that is, a project where the sum of effort across all activities is 10 man-years. Suppose management asks for the least costly way of building the system. Such a project would have one person working for 10 years, but management is unlikely to be willing to wait 10 years. Now suppose that management asks for the quickest possible way to build the system. Imagine it is possible to build the same system by engaging 3650 people for 1 day (or even 365 people for 10 days). Management is unlikely to hire so many people for such short durations. Similarly, management will never ask for the safest way of building the system (because anything worth doing requires risk, and safe projects are not worth doing) or knowingly go for the riskiest way of doing the project.

SOFTWARE DEVELOPMENT PLAN REVIEW

The only way to resolve the ambiguity about what management really wants is to present a buffet of good options from which to choose, with each option being a viable combination of time, cost, and risk. You present these options to management in a dedicated meeting unofficially called the Feed Me/Kill Me meeting. As the name implies, the purpose of this meeting is for management to choose one of the project design options and commit the required resources (the "Feed Me" route). One of the options is always that of not doing the project (the "Kill Me" route). Officially, the name of the meeting should be the **Software Development Plan Review**, or SDP review. It makes no difference if your process does not have an SDP review point: Just call a meeting (no manager can refuse a meeting request whose subject line is "Software Development Plan Review").

Once the desired option is identified, management must literally sign off on the SDP document. This document now becomes your project's life insurance policy because, as long as you do not deviate from the plan's parameters, there is no reason to cancel your project. This does require proper tracking (as described in Appendix A) and project management.

If no option is palatable, then you need to drive the right decision—in this case, killing the project. A doomed project, a project that from inception did not receive adequate time and resources, will do no one any good. The project will eventually run out of time or money or both, and the organization will have wasted not just the funds and time but the opportunity cost of devoting these resources to another doable project. It is also detrimental to the careers of the core team members to be on a project that never has a chance. Since you have only a few years to make your mark and move ahead, every project must count and be a feather in your cap. Spending a year or two on a sideways move that failed will limit your career prospects. Killing such a project before development starts is beneficial for all involved.

SERVICES AND DEVELOPERS

With the project design in hand (but only after management has chosen a specific option), the team can start constructing the system. Typically this requires assigning services (or modules, components, classes, etc.) to developers. The exact assignment methodology deserves a section on its own later on in the chapter. For now, recognize that you should always assign services to developers in a 1:1 ratio. The 1:1 ratio does not mean that a developer works on only one service, but rather that if you do a cross-section of the team at any moment in time, you will see a developer working on one and only one service. It is perfectly fine for a developer to finish one service and move to the next. However, you should never see a developer working on more than one service at a time or more than one developer working concurrently on the same service. Any other way of assigning services to developers will result in failure. Examples of the poor assignment options include:

- **Multiple developers per service.** The motivation for assigning two (or more) developers to one service is not a surplus of developers, but rather the desire to complete the work sooner. However, two people cannot really work on the same thing at the same time, so some subscheme must be used:
  - **Serialization.** The developers could work serially so that only one of them is working on the service at a time. This takes longer due to the context switch overhead—that is, the need to figure out what happened with the service since the current developer looked at it last. This defeats the purpose of assigning the two developers in the first place.
  - **Parallelization.** The developers could work in parallel and then integrate their work. This scheme will take much longer than just having a single developer working on the service. For example, suppose a service estimated as one month of effort is assigned to two developers who will work in parallel. One might be tempted to assume that the work will be complete after two weeks, but that is a false assumption. First, not all units of work can be split this way. Second, the developers would have to allocate at least another week to integrate their work. This integration is not at all guaranteed to succeed if the developers worked in parallel and did not collaborate during development. Even if the integration is possible, it would void all the testing effort that went into each part due to the integration changes. Testing the service as a whole also would require additional time. In all, the effort will take at least a month (and likely more). Meanwhile, other developers who are working on dependent services and expect the service to be ready after two weeks will be further delayed.

- **Multiple services per developer.** The option of assigning two (or more) services to a single developer is just as bad. Suppose two services, A and B, each estimated as a month of work, are assigned to a single developer, with the developer expected to finish both after a single month. Since the sum of work is two months, not only will the services be incomplete after one month, but finishing them will take much longer. While the developer is working on the A service, the developer is not working on the B service, causing the developers dependent on the B service to demand that the developer work on the B service. The developer might switch to the B service, but then those dependent on the A service would demand some attention. All this switching back and forth drastically reduces the developer's efficiency, prolonging the duration to much more than two months. In the end, perhaps after three or four months, the A and B services may be complete.

Either assigning more than one developer per service or assigning multiple services per developer causes a mushroom cloud of delays to propagate throughout the project, mostly due to delayed dependencies affecting other developers. This, in turn, makes accurate estimations very difficult. The only option that has any semblance of accountability and a chance of meeting the estimation is a 1:1 assignment of services to developers.

> **Note**   The 1:1 assignment of services to developers does not preclude pair programming. Even though pair programming doubles the number of developers assigned concurrently to a single service, the pair still will not serialize their work or work in parallel.

DESIGN AND TEAM EFFICIENCY

When using 1:1 assignments of services to developers, it follows that the interaction between the services is isomorphic to the interaction between the developers. Consider Figure 7-1.

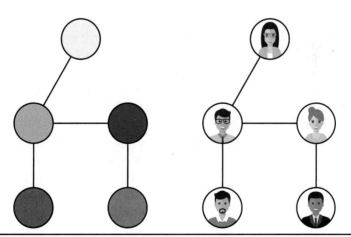

Figure 7-1 The system's design is the team's design. (Images: Sapann Design/ Shutterstock)

The relationship between the services, their interactions and communication, dictates the relationships and interactions between the developers. When using 1:1 assignment, the design of the system is the design of the team.

Next, consider Figure 7-2. While the number of services and their size has not changed from Figure 7-1, no one could claim it is a good design.

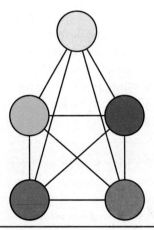

Figure 7-2 Tightly coupled system and team

A good system design strives to reduce the number of interactions between the modules to their bare minimum—the exact opposite of what happens in Figure 7-2. A loosely coupled system design such as that in Figure 7-1 has minimized the number of interactions to the point that removing one interaction makes the system inoperable.

The design in Figure 7-2 is clearly tightly coupled, and it also describes the way the team operates. Compare the teams from Figure 7-1 and Figure 7-2. Which team would you rather join? The team in Figure 7-2 is a high-stress, fragile team. The team members are likely territorial and resist change because every change has ripple effects that disrupt their work and the work of everybody else. They spend an inordinate amount of time in meetings to resolve their issues. In contrast, the team in Figure 7-1 can address issues locally and contain them. Each team member is almost independent from the others and does not need to spend much time coordinating work. Simply put, the team in Figure 7-1 is far more efficient than the team in Figure 7-2. As a result, the team with the better system design has far better prospects of meeting an aggressive deadline.

This last observation is paramount: Most managers just pay lip service to system design because the benefits of architecture (maintainability, extensibility, and reusability) are down-the-road benefits. Future benefits do not help a manager who is facing the harsh reality of scant resources and a tight schedule. If anything, it behooves the manager to reduce the scope of work as much as possible to meet the deadline. Since system design is supposedly not helping with the current objectives, the manager will throw overboard any meaningful investment in design. Sadly, by doing so, the manager loses all chance of meeting the commitments, because the only way to meet an aggressive deadline is with a world-class design that yields the most efficient team. When striving to get management support for your design effort, show how design helps with the immediate objective. The long-term benefits will flow out of that.

Personal Relationships and Design

While the way the design affects the team efficiency may be self-evident, the team also affects the design. In Figure 7-1, if two developers do not talk with each other, then that area of the design will be weak. You should assign two coupled services to two developers who naturally work effectively with each other.

Task Continuity

When assigning services (or activities such as UI development), try to maintain **task continuity**, a logical continuation between tasks assigned to each person. Often, such task assignments follow the service dependency graph. If service A depends on service B, then assign A to the developer of B. One advantage is that the A developer who is already familiar with B needs less ramp-up time. An important, yet often overlooked advantage of maintaining task continuity is that the project and the developer's win criteria are aligned. The developer is motivated to do an adequate job on B to avoid suffering when it is time to do A. Perfect task continuity is hardly ever possible, but it should be the goal.

Finally, take the developers' personal technical proclivities into account when making assignments. For example, it will likely not work well to have the security expert design the UI, to have the database expert implement the business logic, or to have junior developers implement the utilities such as message bus or diagnostics.

Effort Estimations

Effort **estimation** is how you try to answer the question of how long something will take. There are two types of estimations: individual activity estimation (estimating the effort for an activity assigned to a resource) and overall project estimation. The two types of estimations are unrelated, because the overall duration of the project is not the sum of effort across all activities divided by number of resources. This is due to the inherent inefficiency in utilizing people, the internal dependencies between activities, and any risk mitigation you may need to put in place.

In many software teams, engaging in estimations is at best a nice ritual and at worst an exercise in futility. The poor results of estimations in the software industry are due to several reasons:

1. Uncertainty in how long activities take, and even uncertainty in the list of activities, is the primary reason for poor accuracy of estimations. Do not confuse cause and effect: The uncertainty is the cause, and poor estimation accuracy is the result. You must proactively reduce the uncertainty, as described later in this chapter.

2. Few people in software development are trained in simple and effective estimation techniques. Most are left to rely on bias, guesswork, and intuition.

3. Many people overestimate or underestimate in an attempt to compensate for the uncertainty, which results in far worse outcomes.

4. Most people tend to look at just the tip of the iceberg when listing activities. Naturally, if you omit activities that are essential to success, your estimations will be off. This is true both when omitting activities across the project and when omitting internal phases inside activities. For example, estimators may list just the coding activities or, inside coding activities, account for coding but not design or testing.

CLASSIC MISTAKES

As just mentioned, people tend to overestimate and underestimate in an attempt to compensate for uncertainty. Both of these are deadly when it comes to project success.

Overestimation never works because of Parkinson's law.[2] For example, if you give a developer three weeks to perform a two-week activity, the developer will simply not work on it for two weeks and then be idle for a week. Instead, the developer will work on the activity for three weeks. Since the actual work consumed only two of those three weeks, in the extra week the developer will engage in gold plating—adding bells and whistles, aspects, and capabilities that no one needs or wants, and that were not part of the design. This gold plating significantly increases the complexity of the task, and the increased complexity drastically reduces the probability of success. Consequently, the developer labors for four or six weeks to finish the original task. Other developers in the project, who expect to receive the code after three weeks, are now delayed, too. Furthermore, the team now owns, perhaps for years and across multiple versions, a code module that is needlessly more complex than what it should have been in the first place.

---

2. Cyril N. Parkinson, "Parkinson's Law," *The Economist* (November 19, 1955).

Underestimation guarantees failure just as well. Undoubtedly, giving a developer two days to perform a two-week coding activity will preclude any gold plating. The problem is that the developer will try to do the activity quick-and-dirty, cutting corners and disregarding all known best practices. This is as sensible as asking a surgeon to operate on you quick-and-dirty or a contractor to build a house quick-and-dirty.

Sadly, there is no quick-and-dirty with any intricate task. Instead, the two options are quick-and-clean and dirty-and-slow. Because the developer is missing all the best practices in software development, from testing to detailed design to documentation, the developer is now trying to perform the task in the worst possible way. Consequently, the developer will not work on the activity for the nominal two weeks it could have taken, assuming the work was performed correctly, but will work on it for four or six (or more) weeks due to the low quality and increased complexity. As with overestimation, other developers in the project who expected the code after the scheduled two days are much delayed. Furthermore, the team now has to own, perhaps for years and across multiple versions, a code module that is done the worst possible way.

Probability of Success

While these conclusions may make common sense, what many miss is the magnitude of these classic mistakes. Figure 7-3 plots in a qualitative manner the probability of success as a function of the estimation. For example, consider a 1-year project. With proper architecture and project design, the project's normal estimation is 1 year, indicated by point N in Figure 7-3. What would be the probability of success if you give this project a day? A week? A month? Clearly, with sufficiently aggressive estimations, the probability of success is zero. How about 6 months? While the probability of a 1-year project completing in 6 months is extremely low, it is not zero because maybe a miracle will happen. The probability of success if you estimate at 11 months and 3 weeks is actually very high, and it is also fairly high for 11 months. However, it is unlikely the project can complete in 9 months. Therefore, to the left of the normal estimation is a tipping point where the probability of success drastically improves in a nonlinear way. Similarly, this 1-year project could last 13 months, and even 14 months is reasonable. But if you give this project 18 or 24 months, you will surely kill it because Parkinson's law will kick in: Work will expand to fill the allotted time, and the project will fail due to the increased complexity. Therefore, another tipping point exists to the right of the normal estimation, where the probability of success again collapses in a nonlinear way.

Figure 7-3 illustrates the paramount importance of good nominal estimations because they maximize the probability of success, in a nonlinear way. In the past, you were likely to hurt yourself and others when you both underestimated and over-estimated. These are not just common, classic mistakes—they are cardinal mistakes.

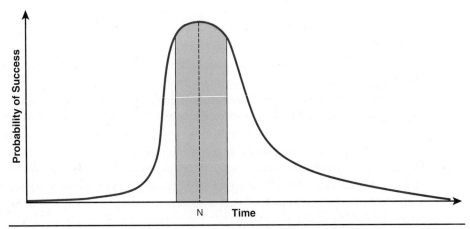

Figure 7-3 Probability of success as a function of estimation [Adopted and modified from Steve McConnell, *Rapid Development* (Microsoft Press, 1996).]

ESTIMATION TECHNIQUES

The poor track record with estimations in the software industry persists even though a decent set of effective estimation techniques have been available for decades and across multiple other industries. I have yet to see a team that has practiced estimations correctly and was also off the mark with their project design and commitments. Instead of trying to review all of these techniques, this section highlights some of the ideas and techniques I have found over the years to be the most simple and effective.

Accuracy, Not Precision

Good estimations are accurate, but not precise. For example, consider an activity that actually took 13 days and had 2 estimations: 10 days or 23.8 days. While the second estimation is far more precise, clearly the first estimation is better because it is more accurate. With estimations, accuracy counts more than precision. Since most software projects significantly veer off from their commitments at delivery (sometimes by multiples of the initial estimations), it is nonsensical when the people involved those projects estimate the activities down to the hour or the day.

Estimations also must match the tracking resolution. If the project manager tracks the project on a weekly basis, any estimation less than a week is pointless because it is smaller than the measurement resolution. Doing so makes as much sense as estimating the size of your house down to the micron when using a measuring tape for the actual measurement.

Even when an activity is actually 13 days in duration, it is better to estimate it as 15 days rather than 12.5 days. Any decent-size project will likely have several dozens of activities; by opting for accuracy, you will probably overestimate (a little) on some activities and underestimate (a little) on others. On average, though, your estimations will be fairly accurate. If you are trying to be precise, you can accumulate errors because you do not allow for errors in the estimations to cancel each other out. In addition, if you ask people for precise estimations, they will endlessly agonize and deliberate on them. If you ask for accurate estimations, the estimations will be easy, simple, and quick to make.

Reduce Uncertainty

Uncertainty is the leading cause of missed estimations. It is important not to confuse the unknown with the uncertain. For example, while the exact day of my demise is unknown, it is far from uncertain, and a whole industry (life insurance) is based on the ability to estimate that date. While the estimation may not be precise when it comes to me specifically, the life insurance industry has sufficient customers to make it accurate enough.

When asking people to estimate, you should help them overcome their fear of estimations. Many may have had their poor estimations used against them in the past. You may even encounter refusal to estimate in the form of "I don't know" or "Estimations never work." Such attitudes may indicate fear of entrapment, or trying to avoid the effort of estimating, or being ignorant and inexperienced in estimation techniques, rather than a fundamental inability to estimate.

Confronted with the uncertain, take these steps:

• Ask first for the order of magnitude: Is the activity more like a day, a week, a month, or a year? With the magnitude known, narrow it down using factor of 2 to zoom in. For example, if the answer to the first question was a month as the type of unit, ask if it is more like two weeks, one month, two months, or four months. The first answer rules out eight months (since that is more like a year as an order of magnitude), and it cannot be one week because that was not provided in the first place as an order of magnitude.

- Make an explicit effort to list the areas of uncertainty in the project and focus on estimating them. Always break down large activities into smaller, more manageable activities to greatly increase the accuracy of the estimations.
- Invest in an exploratory discovery effort that will give insight into the nature of the problem and reduce the uncertainty. Review the history of the team or the organization, and learn from your own history how long things have taken in the past.

PERT Estimations

One estimation technique dealing specifically with high uncertainly is part of Program Evaluation and Review Technique (PERT).[3] For every activity, you provide three estimations: the most optimistic, the most pessimistic, and the most likely. The final estimation is provided by this formula:

$$E = \frac{O + 4 * M + P}{6}$$

where:

- E is the calculated estimation.
- O is the optimistic estimation.
- M is the most likely estimation.
- P is the pessimistic estimation.

For example, if an activity has an optimistic estimation of 10 days, a pessimistic estimation of 90 days, and a most likely estimation of 25 days, the PERT estimation for it would be 33.3 days:

$$E = \frac{10 + 4 * 25 + 90}{6} = 33.3$$

OVERALL PROJECT ESTIMATION

Estimating the project as a whole is useful primarily for project design validation, but can also be beneficial when initiating project design. When you finish the detailed project design, compare it to the overall project estimation. The two need not match perfectly but should be congruent and validate each other. For example,

---

3. https://en.wikipedia.org/wiki/Program_evaluation_and_review_technique

if the detailed project design was 13 months and the overall project estimation was 11 months, then the detailed project design is valid. But if the overall estimation was 18 months, then at least one of these numbers is wrong, and you must investigate the source of the discrepancy. You can also utilize the overall project estimation when dealing with a project with very few up-front constraints. Such a clean canvas project has a great deal of unknowns, making it difficult to design. You can use the overall project estimation to work backward to box in certain activities as a way of initiating the project design process.

Historical Records

With overall project estimation, your track record and history matter the most. With even a modest degree of repeatability (see Figure 6-1), it is unlikely that you could deliver the project faster or slower than similar projects in the organization's past. The dominant factor in throughput and efficiency is the organization's nature, its own unique fingerprint of maturity, which is something that does not change overnight or between projects. If it took your company a year to deliver a similar project in the past, then it will take it a year in the future. Perhaps this project could be done in six months somewhere else, but with your company it will take a year. There is some good news here, though: Repeatability also means the company likely will not take two or three years to complete the project.

Estimation Tools

A great yet little-known technique for overall project estimation is leveraging project estimation tools. These tools typically assume some nonlinear relationship exists between size and cost, such as a power function, and use a large number of previously analyzed projects as their training data. Some tools even use Monte Carlo simulations to narrow down the range of the variables based on your project attributes or historical records. I have used such tools for decades, and they produce accurate results.

Broadband Estimation

The broadband estimation is my adaptation of the Wideband Delphi[4] estimation technique. The broadband estimation uses multiple individual estimations to identify the average of the overall project estimation, then adds a band of estimations above and below it. You use the estimations outside the band to gain insight into the nature of the project and refine the estimations, repeating this process until the band and the project estimations converge.

---

4. Barry Boehm, *Software Engineering Economics* (Prentice Hall, 1981).

To start any broadband estimation effort, first assemble a large group of project stakeholders, ranging from developers to testers, managers, and even support people—diversity of the group is key with the broadband technique. Strive for a mix of newcomers and veterans, devil's advocates, experts and generalists, creative people, and worker bees. You want to tap into the group's synergy of knowledge, intelligence, experience, intuition, and risk assessment. A good group size is between 12 and 30 people. Using fewer than 12 participants is possible, but the statistical element may not be strong enough to produce good results. With more than 30 participants, it is difficult to finish the estimation in a single meeting.

Begin the meeting by briefly describing the current state and phase of the project, what you have already accomplished (such as architecture), and additional contextual information (such as the system's operational concepts) that may not be known to stakeholders who were not part of the core team. Each participant needs to estimate two numbers for the project: how long will it take in months and how many people it will require. Have the estimators write these numbers, along with their name, on a note. Collect the notes, enter them in a spreadsheet, and calculate both the average and the standard deviation for each value. Now, identify the estimations (both in time and people) that were at least one standard deviation removed from the average—that is, those values outside the broadband of consensus (hence the name of the technique). These are the outliers.

Instead of culling the outliers from the analysis (the common practice in most statistical methods), solicit input from those who produced them—because they may know something that the others do not. This is a great way of identifying the uncertainties. Once the outliers have voiced their reasoning for the estimation and all have heard it, you conduct another round of estimations. You repeat this process until all estimations fall within one standard deviation, or the deviation is less than your measurement resolution (such as one person or one month). Broadband estimation typically converges this way by the third round.

> **Caution** During the broadband meeting, it is important to maintain a free, collegial atmosphere. Those who produce the outliers (both high and low) are known to all involved in the process, and their estimations must not be perceived as criticism of management and the organization.

A Word of Caution

Overall project estimation, whether done by using historical records, estimation tools, or the broadband method, tends to be accurate, if not highly accurate. You should compare the various overall estimations to ensure that you do, indeed, have a good estimation. Unfortunately, while these overall estimations are accurate, they merely augment and verify your detailed project design effort. They serve only as reinforcement and a sanity check because they are not actionable on their own. You may be fairly certain that the project requires 18 months and 6 people, but as yet you have no idea how to utilize those resources to finish the project on that schedule. You have to design the project to learn this information.

ACTIVITY ESTIMATIONS

You start the project design with the estimated duration of the individual activities in the project. Before you estimate individual activities, you must prepare a meticulous list of all activities in the project, both coding and noncoding activities alike. In a way, even that list of activities is an estimation of the actual set of activities, so the same rationale about reducing uncertainties holds true here. Avoid the temptation to focus on the structural coding activities indicated by the system architecture, and actively look below the waterline at the full extent of the iceberg. Invest time in looking for activities, and ask other people to compile that list so you could compare it with your own list. Have colleagues review, critique, and challenge your list of activities. You may be surprised by what you actually missed.

Since accuracy is superior to precision, a best practice is to always use a quantum of 5 days in any activity estimation. Activities that take 1 or 2 days should not be part of the plan. Activities that are 3 or 4 days are always estimated at 5 days. Activities are either 5, 10, 15, 20, 25, 30, or 35 days long. Activities estimated at 40 or more days may be good candidates to break down into smaller activities to reduce the uncertainty. Using 5 days for each activity aligns the project nicely on week boundaries and reduces waste of parts of weeks before or after an activity. This practice also matches real life—no activity has ever started on a Friday.

The reduction in uncertainty benefits even regular-size activities. Force yourself and others to break down each activity into tasks in addition to coding, such as learning curves, test clients, installation, integration points, peer reviews, and documentation. Again, by avoiding focusing on coding and examining the full scope of the work ahead, you greatly reduce the uncertainty of individual activity estimations.

The Estimation Dialog

If you ask others to estimate an activity, you must maintain a correct estimation dialog with them. Never dictate duration by saying, "You have two weeks!" Not only is that based on nothing, but the owner of the activity also does not feel accountable to actually finish in two weeks. When people are unaccountable, progress and quality will be lacking. Avoid leading questions, such as "It is going to take two weeks, right?" While this is somewhat better than dictating the estimation, you now bias the other party toward your estimation. Even if the person agrees, he or she still will not feel accountable to your estimation. A far better question is the open question, "How long will it take?" Do not accept an immediate answer. Always force people to get back to you later with the answer because you want them to itemize what is really involved and to reflect and contemplate on the answer. You must have good estimations to maximize the probability of success and people's accountability (see Figure 7-3).

CRITICAL PATH ANALYSIS

To calculate the actual duration of a project as well several other key aspects of the project, you need to find the project's critical path. Critical path analysis is the single most important project design technique. However, you cannot perform this analysis without the following prerequisites:

- **The system architecture.** You must have the decomposition of the system into services and other building blocks such as *Clients* and *Managers*. While you could design a project with even a bad architecture, that is certainly less than ideal. A bad system design will keep changing, and with it, your project design will change. It is crucial that the system architecture be valid, so that it holds true over time.

- **A list of all project activities.** Your list must contain both coding and noncoding activities. It is straightforward to derive the list of most coding activities by examining the architecture. The list of noncoding activities is obtained as discussed previously and is also a product of the nature of the business. For example, a banking software company will have compliance and regulatory activities.

- **Activity effort estimation.** Have an accurate estimation of the effort for each activity in the list of activities. You should use multiple estimation techniques to drive accuracy.

- **Services dependency tree.** Use the call chains to identify the dependencies between the various services in the architecture.

- **Activity dependencies.** Beyond the dependencies between your services, you must compile a list of how all activities depend on other activities, coding and noncoding alike. Add explicit integration activities as needed.

- **Planning assumptions.** You must know the resources available for the project or, more correctly, the staffing scenarios that your plan calls for. If you have several such scenarios, then you will have a different project design for each availability scenario. The planning assumptions will include which type of resource is required at which phase of the project.

PROJECT NETWORK

You can graphically arrange the activities in the project into a network diagram. The **network diagram** shows all activities in the project and their dependencies. You first derive the activity dependencies from the way the call chains propagate through the system. For each of the use cases you have validated, you should have a call chain or sequence diagram showing how some interaction between the system's building blocks supports each use case. If one diagram has Client A calling Manager A and a second diagram has Client A calling Manager B, then Client A depends on both Manager A and Manager B. In this way, you systematically discover the dependencies between the components of the architecture. Figure 7-4 shows the dependency chart of the code modules in a sample *Method-based* architecture.

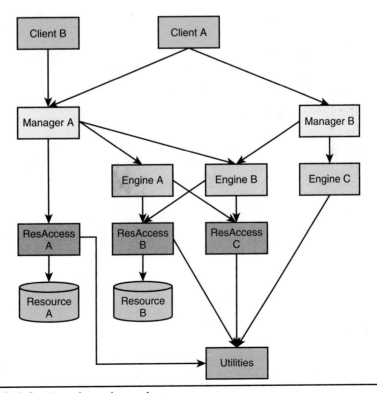

Figure 7-4 Services dependency chart

The dependency chart shown in Figure 7-4 has several problems. First, it is highly structural and is missing all the nonstructural coding and noncoding activities. Second, it is graphically bulky and with larger projects would become visually too crowded and unmanageable. Third, you should avoid grouping activities together, as is the case with the *Utilities* in the figure.

You should turn the diagram in Figure 7-4 into the detailed abstract chart shown in Figure 7-5. That chart now contains all activities, coding and noncoding alike, such as architecture and system testing. You may want to also add a side legend identifying the activities for easy review.

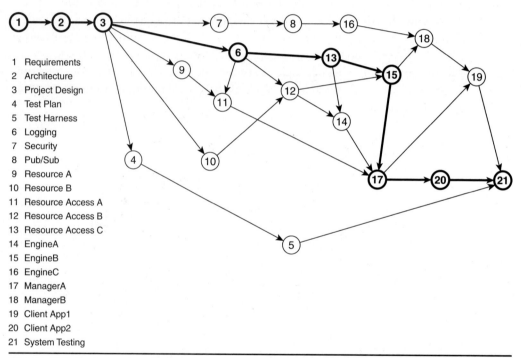

1   Requirements
2   Architecture
3   Project Design
4   Test Plan
5   Test Harness
6   Logging
7   Security
8   Pub/Sub
9   Resource A
10 Resource B
11 Resource Access A
12 Resource Access B
13 Resource Access C
14 EngineA
15 EngineB
16 EngineC
17 ManagerA
18 ManagerB
19 Client App1
20 Client App2
21 System Testing

Figure 7-5 Project network

Activity Times

The effort estimation for an activity alone does not determine when that activity will complete: Dependencies on other activities also come into play. Therefore, the time to finish each activity is the product of the effort estimation for that activity plus the time it takes to get to that activity in the project network. The time to get to an activity, or the time it takes to be ready to start working on the activity, is the maximum of time of all network paths leading to that activity. In a more formal manner, you calculate the time for completing activity i in the project with this recursive formula:

$$T_i = E_i + Max(T_{i-1}, T_{i-2}, ..., T_{i-n})$$

where:

- T_i is the time for completing activity i.
- E_i is the effort estimation for activity i.
- n is the number of activities leading directly to activity i.

The time for each of the preceding activities is resolved the same way. Using regression, you can start with the last activity in the project and find the completion time for each activity in the network. For example, consider the activity network in Figure 7-6.

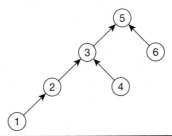

Figure 7-6 Project network used in the time calculation example

In the diagram in Figure 7-6, activity 5 is the last activity. Thus, the set of regression expressions that define the time to finish activity 5 are:

$$T_5 = E_5 + Max(T_3, T_6)$$
$$T_6 = E_6$$
$$T_3 = E_3 + Max(T_2, T_4)$$
$$T_4 = E_4$$
$$T_2 = E_2 + T_1$$
$$T_1 = E_1$$

Note that the time to finish activity 5 depends on the effort estimation of the previous activities as much as it depends on the network topology. For example, if all the activities in Figure 7-6 are of equal duration, then:

$$T_5 = E_1 + E_2 + E_3 + E_5$$

However, if all activities except activity 6 are estimated at 5 days, and activity 6 is estimated at 20 days, then:

$$T_5 = E_6 + E_5$$

While you could manually calculate the activity times for small networks such as Figure 7-6, this calculation quickly gets out of hand with large networks. Computers excel at regression problems, so you should use tools (such as Microsoft Project or a spreadsheet) to calculate activity times.

THE CRITICAL PATH

By calculating the activity times, you can identify the longest possible path in the network of activities. In this context, the longest path means the path with greatest duration, not necessarily the one with the greatest number of activities. For example, the project network in Figure 7-7 has 17 activities, each of different estimated duration (the numbers in Figure 7-7 are just the activity IDs; durations are not shown).

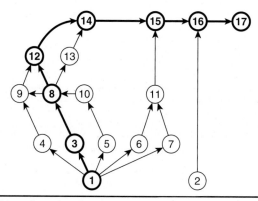

Figure 7-7 Identifying the critical path

Based on the effort estimation for each activity and the dependencies, using the formula given earlier and starting from activity 17, the longest path in the network is shown in bold. That longest path in the network is called the **critical path**. You should highlight the critical path in your network diagrams using a different color or bold lines. Calculating the critical path is the only way to answer the question of how long it will take to build the system.

Because the critical path is the longest path in the network, it also represents the shortest possible project duration. Any delay on the critical path delays the entire project and jeopardizes your commitments.

No project can ever be accelerated beyond its critical path. Put another way, you must build the system along its critical path to build the system the quickest possible way. This is true in any project, regardless of technology, architecture, development methodology, development process, management style, and team size.

In any project with multiple activities on which multiple people are working, you will have a network of activities with a critical path. The critical path does not care if you acknowledge it or not; it is just there. Without critical path analysis, the likelihood of developers building the system along the critical path is nearly zero. Working this way is likely to be substantially slower.

> **Note**   While the discussion so far has referred to the critical path of the project as a singular path, a project can absolutely have multiple critical paths (all of equal duration), including having all network paths as critical paths. Projects with multiple critical paths are risky because any delay on any of these paths will delay the project.

ASSIGNING RESOURCES

During project design, the architect assigns abstract resources (such as `Developer 1`) to each of the project design options. Only after the decision makers have chosen a particular project design option can the project manager assign actual resources. Since any delay in the critical path will delay the project, the project manager should always assign resources to the critical path first. You should take matters a step further by always assigning your best resources to the critical path. By "best," I mean the most reliable and trustworthy developers, the ones who will not fail to deliver. Avoid the classic mistake of first assigning developers to high-visibility but noncritical activities, or to activities that the customer or management care the most about. Assigning development resources first to noncritical activities does nothing to accelerate the project. Slowing down the critical path absolutely slows down the project.

Staffing Level

During project design, for each project design option the architect needs to find out how many resources (such as developers) the project will require overall. The architect discovers the required staffing level iteratively. Consider the network in Figure 7-7, where the critical path is already identified, and assume each node is a service. How many developers are required on the first day of the project? If you were given just a single developer, that developer is by definition your best developer, so the single developer goes to activity 1. If you are given two developers, then you can assign the second developer to activity 2, even though that activity is not required until much later. If you are given three developers, then the third developer is at best idle, and at worst disrupting the developer working on activity 1. Therefore, the answer to the question of how many developers are required on day 1 of the project is at most two developers.

Next, suppose activity 1 is complete. How many developers are required now? The answer is at most six (activities 3, 4, 5, 6, 7, and 2 are available). However, asking for six developers is less than ideal since by the time you have progressed up the critical path to the level of activities 8 or 12, you need only three or even two developers. Perhaps it is better to ask for just four developers instead of six developers once activity 1 is complete. Utilizing only four as opposed to six developers has two significant advantages. First, you will reduce the cost of the project. A project with four developers is 33% less expensive than a project with six developers. Second, a team of four developers is far more efficient than a team of six developers. The smaller team will have less communication overhead and less temptation for interference from the idle hands.

Based on this criterion alone, a team of three or even two developers would be better than a team of four developers. However, when examining the network of Figure 7-7 it is likely impossible to build the system with just three developers and keep the same duration. With so few developers, you will paint yourself into a corner in which a developer on the critical path needs a noncritical activity that is simply not ready yet (such as activity 15 needing activity 11). This promotes a noncritical activity to a critical activity, in effect creating a new and longer critical path. I call this situation **subcritical staffing**. When the project goes subcritical, it will miss its deadline because the old critical path no longer applies.

The real question is not how many resources are required. The question to ask at any point of the project is:

What is the lowest level of resources that allows the project to progress unimpeded along the critical path?

Finding this lowest level of resources keeps the project critically staffed at all points in time and delivers the project at the least cost and in the most efficient way. Note that the critical level of staffing can and should change throughout the life of the project.

Imagine a group of developers without project design. The likelihood of that group constituting the lowest level of resources required to progress unimpeded along the critical path is nearly zero. The only way to compensate for the unknown staffing needs of the project is by using horrendously wasteful and inefficient overcapacity staffing. As illustrated previously, working this way cannot be the fastest way of completing the project—and now you see it also cannot be the least costly way of building the system. My experience is that overcapacity can be more expensive than the lowest cost level by many multiples.

Float-Based Assignment

Returning to the network in Figure 7-7, once you have concluded that you could try to build the system with only four developers, you face a new challenge: Where and when will you deploy these four developers? For example, with activity 1 complete, you could assign the developers to activities 3, 4, 5, 6 or 3, 5, 6, 7, or 3, 4, 6, 2, and so on. Even with a simple network, the combinatorial spectrum of possibilities is staggering. Each of these options would have its own set of possible downstream assignments.

Fortunately, you do not have to try any of these combinations. Examine activity 2 in Figure 7-7. You can actually defer assigning resources to activity 2 until the day that activity 16 (which is on the critical path) must start, minus the estimated duration of activity 2. Activity 2 can "float" to the top (remain unassigned and not start) until it bumps against activity 16. All noncritical activities have **float**, which is the amount of time you could delay completing them without delaying the project. Critical activities have no float (or more precisely, their float is zero) since any delay in these activities would delay the project. When you assign resources to the project, follow this rule:

Always assign resources based on float.

To figure out how to assign developers in the previous example once activity 1 is complete, calculate the float of all activities that are possible once activity 1 is complete, and assign the four developers based on the float, from low to high. First, assign a developer to the critical path, not because it is special but because it has the lowest possible float. Now, suppose activity 2 has 60 days of float and activity 4 has 5 days of float. This means that if you defer getting to activity 4 by more than 5 days, you will derail the project. By contrast, you could defer getting to activity 2 by at most 60 days, so you assign the next developer to activity 4. During the intervening time while activity 2 remains unassigned, you are in effect consuming the activity's float. Perhaps by the time the float of activity 2 has become 15 days, you will be finally able to assign a developer to this activity.

CLASSIC PITFALL

As observed by Tom Demarco,[a] most organizations incentivize their managers to do the wrong thing when it comes to project staffing, even when starting with the best of intentions. Managers can correctly assign developers to the project only after project design, which is possible only after the architecture is complete. These design activities, while short in nature, conclude the fuzzy front end of the project, which itself may take months of scoping the work, prototyping, evaluating technologies, interviewing customers, analyzing requirements, and more. There is no point in hiring developers until the project manager can assign them based on the plan, because otherwise they will have nothing to do.

However, empty offices and desks, for months on end, reflect poorly on the manager, making it seem as if the manager is just slacking. The manager fears that when (not if) the project is late (as software projects are known to be), the manager will get the blame because the manager did not hire the developers at the beginning of the project. To avoid this liability, as soon as the fuzzy front end starts, the manager will hire developers to avoid empty offices. The developers still have nothing to do, so they will play games, read blogs, and take long lunch breaks. Unfortunately, this behavior reflects even worse on the manager than the empty offices, because now the perception is that the manager does not know how to delegate and manage, and the organization has to pay for it, too.

Again, the manager fears that if the project is late, the manager will be the one left holding the bag. As soon as the front end starts, the manager will staff the project and assign feature A to the first developer, feature B to the second developer, and so on, even though the project lacks a sound architecture or critical path analysis. When several weeks or months later the architect produces the architecture and the project design, they will be irrelevant, since the developers have been working on a completely different system and project. The project will grossly miss the schedule and blow through any set budget, not just because of the lack of architecture and critical path analysis, but also because what took place instead was both functional decomposition of the system and functional decomposition of the team.

The arguments from Chapter 2 about system decomposition could easily be made about team decomposition, too. The project now has the worst possible combination of system design and team design. The manager will continually be pleading for more time and resources from top management. When the project is late (again as most projects are in the software industry), the manager looks no worse than any other manager in the organization.

Doing the right thing is a lot easier the second time around, when you have already proven that you know how to deliver on time and on budget. The organization may never understand how it worked (or why the way other managers always try it does not work), but cannot argue with results. The first time going this route, and without a track record of success, you will face a struggle. The best action is to confront this pitfall head on and make resolving it part of your project design, as described in Chapter 11.

a. Tom Demarco, The Deadline (Dorset House, 1997).

The nature of this process is iterative both because initially the lowest level of staffing is unknown and because using float-based assignment changes the floats of the activities. Start by attempting to staff the project with some resource level, such as six resources, and then assign these resources based on float. Every time a resource is scheduled to finish an activity, you scan the network for the nearest available activities, choosing the activity with the lowest float as the next assignment for that resource. If you successfully staff the project, try again, this time with a reduced staffing level such as five or even four resources. At some point, you will have an excess of activities compared with the available resources. If those unassigned activities have high enough float, you could defer assigning resources to them until some resources become available. While these activities are unassigned, you will be consuming their float. If the activities become critical, then you cannot build the project with that staffing level, and you must settle for a higher level of resources.

Another key advantage of float-based assignment relates to risk reduction. Activities with the least float are the riskiest, the ones most capable of delaying the project. Assigning resources to these activities first allows you to staff a project in the safest possible way and reduce the overall risk associated with any given staffing level. Again, without project design, the likelihood that a project manager or a group of developers will assign activities based on float is nearly zero. Working this way is not just slow and expensive, but also risky.

Network and Resources

The discussion so far has focused on the dependencies between the activities as the way to construct the network. However, the resources also affect the network.

For example, if you were to assign the network depicted in Figure 7-7 to a single developer, the actual network diagram would be a long string, not Figure 7-7. The dependency on the single resource drastically changes the network diagram. Therefore, the network diagram is actually not just a network of activities, but first and foremost a network of dependencies. If you have unlimited resources and very elastic staffing, then you can rely only on the dependencies between the activities. Once you start consuming float, you must add the dependencies on the resources to the network. The key observation here is:

Resource dependencies are dependencies.

The actual way of assigning resources to the project network is a product of multiple variables. When you assign resources you must take the following into account:

- Planning assumptions
- Critical path
- Floats
- Available resources
- Constraints

These will always result in several project design options, even for straightforward projects.

SCHEDULING ACTIVITIES

Together, the project network, the critical path, and the float analysis allow you to calculate the duration of the project as well as when each activity should start with respect to the project beginning. However, the information in the network is based on workdays, not on calendar dates. You need to convert the information in the network to calendar dates by scheduling the activities. This is a task that you can easily perform by using a tool (such as Microsoft Project). Define all activities in the tool, then add dependencies as predecessors, and assign the resources according to your plan. Once you select a start date for the project, the tool will schedule all activities. The output may also include a Gantt chart, but that is incidental to the core piece of information you can now glean from the tool: the planned start and completion dates for each activity in the project.

> **Caution**   Gantt charts in isolation are detrimental because they may give management the illusion of planning and control. A Gantt chart is merely one view of the project network, and it does not encompass the full project design.

STAFFING DISTRIBUTION

The required staffing for your project is not constant with time. At the beginning, you need only the core team. Once management selects a project design option and approves the project, you can add resources such as developers and testers.

Not all resources are needed all at once due to the dependencies and the critical path. Much the same way, not all resources are retired uniformly. The core team is required throughout, but developers should not be needed through the last day of the project. Ideally, you should phase in developers at the beginning of the project as more and more activities become possible, and phase out the developers toward the end of the project.

This approach of phasing in and phasing out resources has two significant advantages. First, it avoids the feast-or-famine cycles experienced by many software projects. Even if you have the required average level of staffing for the project, you could be understaffed in one part of the project and overstaffed in another part. These cycles of idleness or intense overtime are demoralizing and very inefficient. Second (and more importantly), phasing resources offers the possibility of realizing economy of scale. If you have several projects in the organization, then you could arrange them such that developers are always phasing out of one project while phasing into another. Working this way yields a hundreds of percent increase in productivity, the classic "doing much more with less."

> **Note**   Phasing in and phasing out resources across projects is predicated on sound system and project design that ensures a consistent system structure which decouples specific developers from specific components.

Staffing Distribution Chart

Figure 7-8 depicts the typical staffing distribution chart of a well-designed and properly staffed project. At the start of the project is the front end, during which the core team is working on the system and project design; this phase ends with the

SDP review. If the project is terminated at that point, the staffing goes to zero and the core team is available for other projects. If the project is approved, an initial ramp-up in staffing occurs in which developers and other resources are working on the lowest-level activities in the project that enable other activities. When those activities become available, the project can absorb additional staff. At some point you have phased in all the resources the project ever needs, reaching peak staffing. For a while, the project is fully staffed. The system tends to appear at the end of this phase. Now the project can phase out resources, and those left are working on the most dependent activities. The project concludes with the level of staffing required for system testing and release.

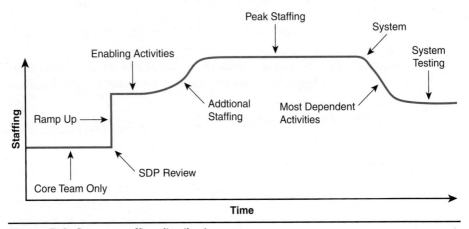

Figure 7-8 Correct staffing distribution

Figure 7-9 shows a staffing distribution chart that demonstrates the behavior of Figure 7-8. You produce a chart such as Figure 7-9 by first staffing the project, then listing all the **dates of interest** (unique dates when activities start and end) in chronological order. You then count how many resources are required for each category of resources in each time period between dates of interest. Do not forget to include in the staffing distribution resources that do not have specific activities but are nonetheless required, such as the core team, quality control, and developers between coding activities. This sort of stacking bar diagram is trivial to do in a spreadsheet. The files accompanying this book contain several example projects and templates for these charts.

Since the dates of interest may not be regularly spaced, the bars in the staffing distribution chart may vary in time resolution. However, in most decent-size projects with enough activities, the overall shape of the chart should follow that of

Figure 7-8. By examining the staffing distribution chart, you get a quick and valuable feedback on the quality of your project design.

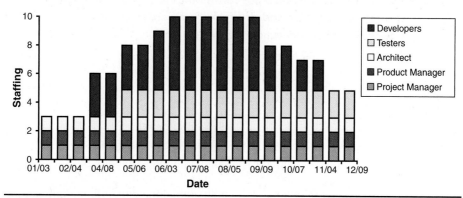

Figure 7-9 Sample staffing distribution

Staffing Mistakes

Several common project staffing mistakes may be evident in the staffing distribution chart. If the chart looks rectangular, it implies constant staffing—a practice against which I have already cautioned.

A staffing distribution with a huge peak in the middle of the chart (as shown in Figure 7-10) is also a red flag: Such a peak always indicates waste.

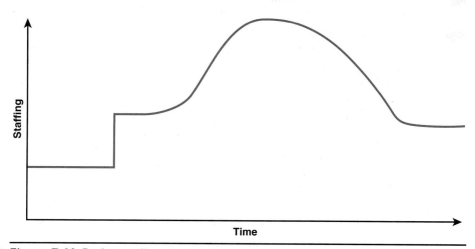

Figure 7-10 Peak in staffing distribution

Consider the effort expended in hiring people and training them on the domain, architecture, and technology when you use them for only a short period of time. A peak is usually caused by not consuming enough float in the project, resulting in a spike in resource demand. If the project were to trade some float for resources, the curve would be smoother. Figure 7-11 depicts a sample project with a peak in staffing.

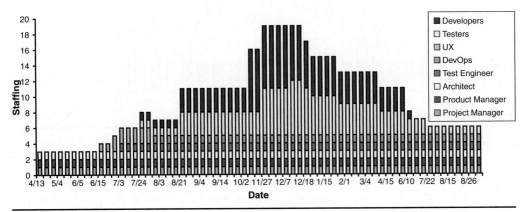

Figure 7-11 Sample peak in staffing distribution

A flat line in the staffing distribution chart (as shown in Figure 7-12) is yet another classic mistake. The flat line indicates the absence of the high plateau of Figure 7-8. The project is likely subcritical and is missing the resources to staff the noncritical activities of the original plan.

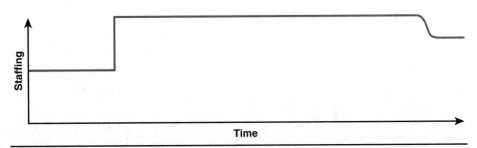

Figure 7-12 Flat subcritical staffing distribution

Figure 7-13 shows the staffing distribution for a sample subcritical project. This project goes subcritical at a level of 11 or 12 resources. It is not just missing the plateau, but has a valley instead.

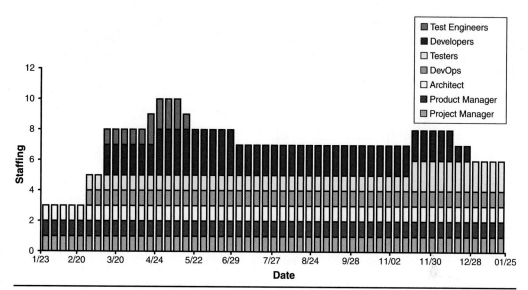

Figure 7-13 Sample subcritical staffing distribution

Erratic staffing distributions (as in Figure 7-14) are yet another distress signal. Projects that are designed with this kind of elasticity in mind are due for a disappointment (see Figure 7-15) because staffing can never be that elastic. Most projects cannot conjure people out of thin air, have them be instantly productive, and then dispose of them a moment later. In addition, when people constantly come and go from a project, training (or retraining) them is very expensive. It is difficult to hold people accountable or retain their knowledge under such circumstances.

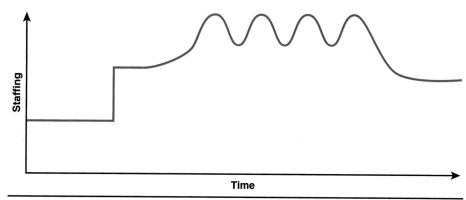

Figure 7-14 Erratic staffing distribution

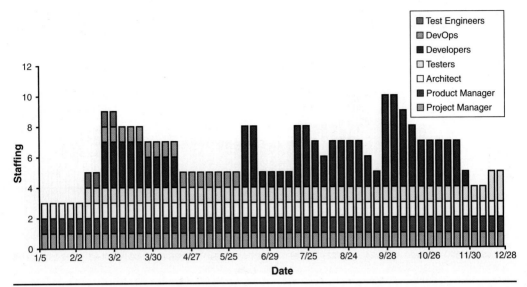

Figure 7-15 Sample erratic staffing distribution

Figure 7-16 illustrates another staffing distribution to avoid, the high ramp-up coming into the project. While this figure does not include any numbers, the chart clearly indicates wishful thinking. No team can instantly go from zero to peak staffing and have everyone add value and deliver high-quality, production-worthy code. Even if the project initially has that much parallel work, and even if you have the resources, the network downstream throttles how many resources the project can actually absorb beyond that, and the required staffing fizzles out.

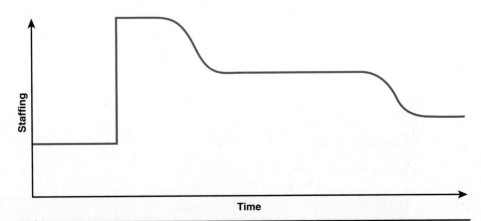

Figure 7-16 High ramp-up in staffing distribution

Figure 7-17 demonstrates such a project. This plan expects instantaneously to get to 11 people, and shortly afterward deflates to around six people until the end of

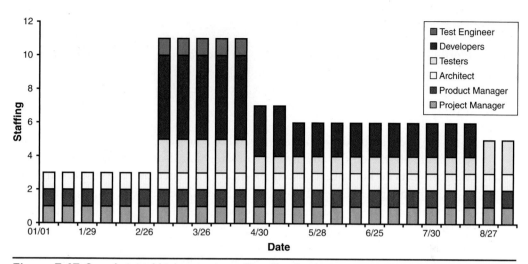

Figure 7-17 Sample initial high ramp in staffing distribution

the project. It is improbable that any team can ramp up this way, and the available resources are used inefficiently due to the oversized team.

Smoothing the Curve

A key observation from the visual indicators of mistakes in the charts is that good projects have smooth staffing distributions. Life is much better when you are cruising along through your project rather than negotiating sharp turns or experiencing screaming acceleration and emergency braking.

As just mentioned, the two root causes of incorrect staffing are assuming too elastic staffing and not consuming float when assigning resources. When considering staffing elasticity, you have to know your team and have a good grasp on what is feasible as far as availability and efficiency. The degree of staffing elasticity also depends on the nature of the organization and the quality of the system and project design. The better the designs, the more quickly developers can come to terms with the new system and activities. Consuming float is easy to do in most projects and likely to reduce both the volatility in the staffing and the absolute level of the required staffing. Being more realistic about staffing elasticity and consuming float often eliminate the peaks, the ups-and-downs, and the high ramp-ups.

> **Note** Do not confuse smoothing the staffing distribution chart (without extending the project or its cost) with load leveling. **Load leveling** is a technique that extends the duration of the project to conform to a lower level of resources. Load leveling is another term for subcritical staffing as defined in this chapter.

PROJECT COST

Plotting the staffing distribution chart for each project design option is a great validation aid in reflecting on the option and seeing if it makes sense. With project design, if something does not feel right, more often than not, something is indeed wrong.

Drawing the staffing distribution chart offers another distinct benefit: It is how you figure out the cost of the project. Unlike physical construction projects, software projects do not have a cost of goods or raw materials. The cost of software is overwhelmingly in labor. This labor includes all team members, from the core team to the developers and testers. Labor cost is simply the staffing level multiplied by time:

$$Cost = Staffing * Time$$

Multiplying staffing by time is actually the area under the staffing distribution chart. To calculate the cost, you need to calculate that area.

The staffing distribution chart is a discrete model of the project that has vertical bars (the staffing level) in each time period between dates of interest. You calculate the area under the staffing distribution chart by multiplying the height of each vertical bar (the number of people) by the duration of the time period between its dates of interest (Figure 7-18). You then sum the results of these multiplications.

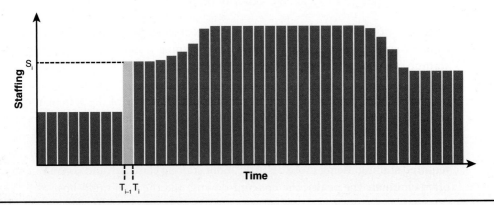

Figure 7-18 Calculating project cost

The formula for the calculation of the area under the staffing chart is:

$$\text{Cost} = \sum_{i=1}^{n}(S_i {}^* (T_i - T_{i-1}))$$

where:

- S_i is the staffing level at date of interest i.
- T_i is the date of interest i (T_0 is the start date).
- n is the number of dates of interest in the project.

Finding the area under the staffing distribution chart is the only way to answer the question how much the project will cost.

If you use a spreadsheet to produce the staffing distribution chart, you just need to add another column with a running sum to calculate the area under the chart (in essence, a numerical integration). The support files accompanying this book contain several examples of this calculation.

Since cost is defined as staffing multiplied by time, the units of cost should be effort and time, such as man-month or man-year. It is better to use these units as opposed to currency to neutralize differences in salary, local currencies and budgets. It then becomes possible to objectively compare the cost of different project design options.

Given the architecture, the initial work breakdown, and the effort estimation, it is a matter of a few hours to a day at the most to answer the questions of how long it will take and how much it will cost to build the system. Sadly, most software projects are running blind. This is as sensible as playing poker without ever looking at the cards—except, instead of chips, you have your project, your career prospects, or even the company's future on the line.

PROJECT EFFICIENCY

Once the project cost is known, you can calculate the project efficiency. The **efficiency** of a project is the ratio between the sum of effort across all activities (assuming perfect utilization of people) and the actual project cost. For example, if the sum of effort across all activities is 10 man-months (assuming 30 workdays in a month), and the project cost is 50 man-months (of regular workdays), then the project efficiency is 20%.

The project efficiency is a great indicator of the quality and sanity of the project's design. The expected efficiency of a well-designed system, along with a properly designed and staffed project, ranges between 15% and 25%.

These efficiency rates may seem appallingly low, but higher efficiency is actually a strong indicator of an unrealistic project plan. No process in nature can ever even approach 100% efficiency. No project is free from constraints, and these constraints prevent you from leveraging your resources in the most efficient way. By the time you add the cost of the core team, the testers, the Build and DevOps, and all the other resources associated with your project, the portion of the effort devoted to just writing code is greatly diminished. Projects with high efficiency such as 40% are simply impossible to build.

Even 25% efficiency is on the high side and is predicated on having a correct system architecture that will provide the project with the most efficient team (see Figure 7-1) and a correct project design that uses the smallest level of resources and assigns them based on floats. Additional factors required for delivering on high efficiency expectations include a small, experienced team whose members are accustomed to working together, and a project manager who is committed to quality and can handle the complexity of the project.

Efficiency also correlates with staffing elasticity. If staffing were truly elastic (i.e., you could always get resources just when you need them and let them go at the precise moment when you no longer need them), the efficiency would be high. Of course, staffing is never that elastic, so sometimes resources will be idle while still assigned to the project, driving the efficiency down. This is especially the case when utilizing resources outside the critical path. If a single person is working on all critical activities, that person is actually at peak efficiency because the person works on activities back-to-back, and the cost of that effort approaches the sum of the cost of the critical activities. With noncritical activities, there is always float. Since staffing is never truly elastic, the resources outside the critical path can never be utilized at very high efficiency.

If the project design option has a high expected efficiency, you must investigate the root cause. Perhaps you assumed too liberal and elastic staffing or the project network is too critical. After all, if most network paths are either critical or near-critical (most activities have low float), then you would get a high efficiency ratio. However, such a project is obviously at high risk of not meeting its commitments.

Efficiency as Overall Estimation

The efficiency of software projects is tightly correlated with the nature of the organization. Inefficient organizations do not turn efficient overnight, and vice versa. Efficiency also relates to the nature of the business. The overhead required in a project that produces software for a medical device will differ from that of a small startup developing a social media plug-in.

You can use efficiency as yet another broad project estimation technique. Suppose you know that historically your projects were 20% efficient. Once you have your individual activity breakdown and their estimations, simply multiply the sum of effort (assuming perfect utilization) across all activities by 5 to produce a rough overall project cost.

EARNED VALUE PLANNING

Another insightful project design technique is earned value planning. Earned value is a popular means of tracking a project, but you can also use it as a great project design tool. With earned value planning you assign value to each activity toward the completion of project, and then combine it with the schedule of each activity to see how you plan to earn value as a function of time.

The formula for the planned earned value is:

$$EV(t) = \frac{\sum_{i=1}^{m} E_i}{\sum_{i=1}^{N} E_i}$$

where:

- E_i is the estimated duration for activity i.
- m is the number of activities completed at time t.
- N is the number of activities in the project.
- t is a point in time.

The **earned value** at time t is the ratio between the sum of estimated duration of all activities completed by time t divided by the sum of the estimated durations of all activities.

Consider, for example, the very simple project in Table 7-1.

Table 7-1 Sample project earned value

Activity	Duration (days)	Value (%)
Front End	40	20
Access Service	30	15
UI	40	20
Manager Service	20	10
Utility Service	40	20
System Testing	30	15
Total	200	100

The sum of estimated duration across all activities in Table 7-1 is 200 days. The UI activity, for example, is estimated at 40 days. Since 40 is 20% of 200, you could state that by completing the UI activity, you have earned 20% toward the completion of the project. From your scheduling of activities you also know when the UI activity is scheduled to complete, so you can actually calculate how you plan to earn value as a function of time (Table 7-2).

Table 7-2 Sample planned earned value as function of time

Activity	Completion Date	Value (%)	Earned Value (%)
Start	0	0	0
Front End	t_1	20	20
Access Service	t_2	15	35
UI	t_3	20	55
Manager Service	t_4	10	65
Utility Service	t_5	20	85
System Testing	t_6	15	100

Such a chart of planned progress is shown in Figure 7-19. By the time the project reaches the planned completion date, it should have earned 100% of the value. The key observation in Figure 7-19 is that the pitch of the planned earned value curve represents the throughput of the team. If you were to assign exactly the same project to a better team, they would meet the same 100% of earned value sooner, so their line would be steeper.

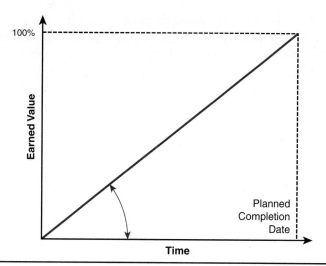

Figure 7-19 Planned earned value chart

CLASSIC MISTAKES

The realization that you can gauge the expected throughput of the team from the earned value chart enables you to quickly discern mistakes in your project plan. For example, consider the planned earned value chart in Figure 7-20. No team in the world could ever deliver on such a plan. For much of the project, the expected throughput was shallow. What kind of miracle of productivity would deliver the rocket launch of earned value toward the end of the project?

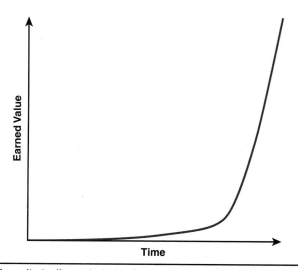

Figure 7-20 Unrealistically optimistic plan

Such unrealistic, overly optimistic plans are usually the result of back-scheduling. The plan may even start with the best of intentions, progressing along the critical path. Unfortunately, you find that someone has already committed the project on a specific date with no regard for a project design or the actual capabilities of the team. You then take the remaining activities and cram them against the deadline, basically back-scheduling from that. Only by plotting the planned earned value will you be able to call attention to the impracticality of this plan and try to avert failure. Figure 7-21 depicts a project with such behavior.

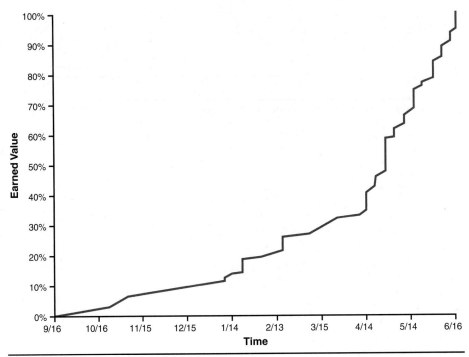

Figure 7-21 Sample unrealistically optimistic plan

In much the same way, you can detect unrealistically pessimistic plans such as that shown in Figure 7-22. This project starts out well, but then productivity is expected to suddenly diminish—or more likely, the project was given much more time than was required. The project in Figure 7-22 will fail because it allows for gold plating and complexity to raise their heads. You can even extrapolate from the healthy part of the curve when the project should have finished (somewhere above the knee in the curve).

THE SHALLOW S CURVE

A project utilizing a fixed-size team would always results in a straight line on the planned earned value chart. As mentioned already, you should not keep the team size fixed. A properly staffed and well-designed project always results in a shallow S curve for the earned value chart, as shown in Figure 7-23.

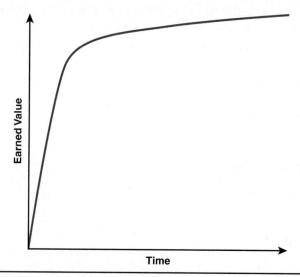

Figure 7-22 Unrealistically pessimistic plan

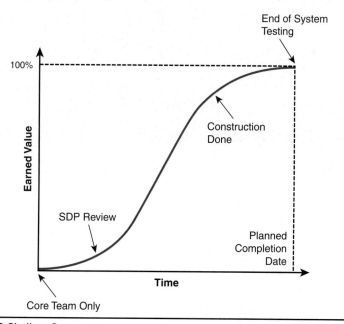

Figure 7-23 Shallow S curve

The shape of the planned earned value curve is related to the planned staffing distribution. At the beginning of the project, only the core team is available, so not much measurable value is added at the front end, and the pitch of the earned value curve is almost flat. After the SDP review, the project can start adding people. As you increase the size of the team, you will also increase its throughput, so the earned value curve gets steeper and steeper. At some point you reach peak staffing. For a while the team size is mostly fixed, so there is a straight line at maximum throughput in the center of the curve. Once you start phasing out resources, the earned value curve levels off until the project completes. Figure 7-24 shows a sample shallow S curve.

THE LOGISTIC FUNCTION

The shallow S curve of the planned earned value is a special case of the logistic function.[a] The generic form of the logistic function can take any S shape (S, mirror S, inverted S, ascending or descending), can span any range of values, and can even be asymmetric.

Every process that involves change can be modeled using a logistic function. For example, the temperature in a room rises and falls according to a logistic function, as does your body weight, the market share of a company, radioactive decay, the risk of burning your skin as a function of distance from a flame, statistical distributions, population growth, effectiveness of design, the intelligence of neural networks, and pretty much everything else. The logistic function is the single most important function known to mankind because it enables us to quantify and model the world—a world that is highly dynamic.

The standard logistic function is defined by this expression:

$$F(x) = \frac{1}{1+e^{-x}}$$

Figure 7-25 plots the standard logistic function. The standard logistic function approaches 0 and 1 asymptotically, crossing the y-axis when $x = 0$ and $y = 0.5$.

Subsequent chapters will refer to the logistic function in a qualitative manner when putting it to good use for risk and complexity modeling.

a. https://en.wikipedia.org/wiki/Logistic_function

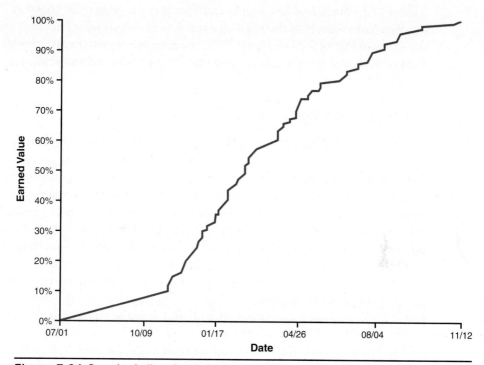

Figure 7-24 Sample shallow S curve

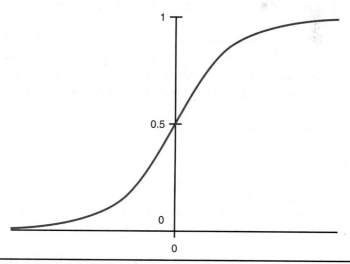

Figure 7-25 Standard logistic function

The earned value curve is a simple and easy way to answer the question: "Does the plan make sense?" If the planned earned value is a straight line, or it exhibits the issues of Figure 7-20 or Figure 7-22, the project is in danger. If it looks like a shallow S, then at least you have hope that the plan is sound and sensible.

ROLES AND RESPONSIBILITIES

It is up to the architect to design both the system and the project to build that system. The architect is likely the only member of the team with the insight and perspective on the correct architecture, the limits of the technology, the dependencies between the activities, the design constraints of both the system and the project, and the relative resource skills. It is futile to expect management, project managers, product managers, or developers to design the project. All of them simply lack the insight, information, and training required to design a project. Furthermore, designing the project is not part of their job. However, the architect does need the input, insight, and perspective of the project manager on the resources cost, the availability scenarios, planning assumptions, priorities, feasibility, and even the politics involved, just as the product manager is essential in producing the architecture.

The architect designs the project as a continuous design effort following the system design. This process is identical to that used in every other engineering discipline: The design of the project is part of the engineering effort and is never left for the construction workers and foremen to figure out on-site or on the factory floor.

The architect is not responsible for managing and tracking the project. Instead, the project manager assigns the actual developers to the project and tracks their progress against the plan. When things change during execution, both the project manager and the architect need to close the loop together and redesign the project.

The realization that the architect should design the project is part of the maturity of the role of the architect. The demand for architects has emerged in the late 1990s in response to the increased cost of ownership and complexity of software systems. Architects are now required to design systems that enable maintainability, reusability, extensibility, feasibility, scalability, throughput, availability, responsiveness, performance, and security. All of these are design attributes, and the way to address them is not via technology or keywords, but with correct design.

However, that list of design attributes is incomplete. This chapter started with the definition of success, and to succeed you must add to that list schedule, cost, and risk. These are design attributes as much as the others, and you provide them by designing the project.

8

NETWORK AND FLOAT

The project network acts as a logical representation of the project for planning purposes. The technique for analyzing the network is called the critical path method, although it has as much to do with the noncritical activities as it does with the critical ones. Critical path analysis is admirably suited for complex projects, ranging from physical construction to software systems, and it has a decades-long proven track record of success. By performing this analysis, you find the project duration and determine where and when to assign your resources.

Because the project network is so instrumental to project design, this chapter expands on a few of the concepts that were introduced in Chapter 7, in the project design overview. You will see recurring techniques, terms, and universal concepts that are independent of any specific project or even any industry. The ideas of this short chapter enable objective and repeatable analysis of the project. Any two architects analyzing the same project network should produce very comparable results.

THE NETWORK DIAGRAM

An **activity** in a software project is any task that requires both time and a resource. Activities may include architecture, project design, service construction, system testing, and even training classes. The project is a collection of related activities, and the network diagram captures these activities and their dependencies. In network diagrams, there is no notion of order of execution or concurrency between the activities.

Network diagrams are often deliberately not shown to scale so that you can focus purely on dependencies and general topology of the network. Avoiding scale in most cases also simplifies the design of the project. Attempts to keep the network diagram to scale will impose a serious burden when estimations change, when you add or remove activities, or when you reschedule activities.

There are two possible representations of a project network diagram: a node diagram and an arrow diagram (Figure 8-1).

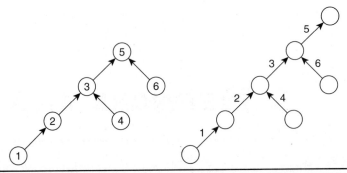

Figure 8-1 A node diagram (left) and the equivalent arrow diagram (right)

THE NODE DIAGRAM

With a node diagram, each node in the chart represents an activity. For example, on the left side of Figure 8-1, every circle is an activity. The arrows in a node diagram represent dependencies between the activities, and the length of the arrow is irrelevant. There is no time spent along the arrows; instead, all time is spent inside the nodes. There is no simple way of drawing node diagrams to scale other than by increasing the radius of the nodes. Doing so tends to clutter the diagram and makes it difficult to interpret correctly.

THE ARROW DIAGRAM

With an arrow diagram, arrows represent activities, and the nodes represent dependencies on the entering activities, as well as events that occur when all the entering activities complete, as shown on the right side of Figure 8-1. Note that both diagrams in Figure 8-1 depict the same network, illustrating that the two diagram types are equivalent (i.e., any network can be rendered using either notation). Since the nodes in an arrow diagram represent events, no time is ever spent inside a node; that is, the events are instantaneous. As with node diagrams, time passes in the direction of the arrows. To draw an arrow diagram to scale, you would scale time to the length of the arrow. That stated, typically the arrow's length is irrelevant (in this book, unless explicitly stated, all network diagrams are not to scale).

With an arrow diagram, all activities must have a start event and a completion event. It is also good practice to add an overall start and completion event for the project as a whole.

Dummy Activities

Suppose in the network of Figure 8-1, activity 4 also depends on activity 1. If activity 2 already depends on activity 1, the arrow diagram has a problem, because you cannot split the arrow of activity 1. The solution is to introduce a dummy activity between the completion event of activity 1 and the start event of 4 (shown as a dashed arrow in Figure 8-2). The **dummy** activity is an activity of zero duration whose sole purpose is to express the dependency on its tail node.

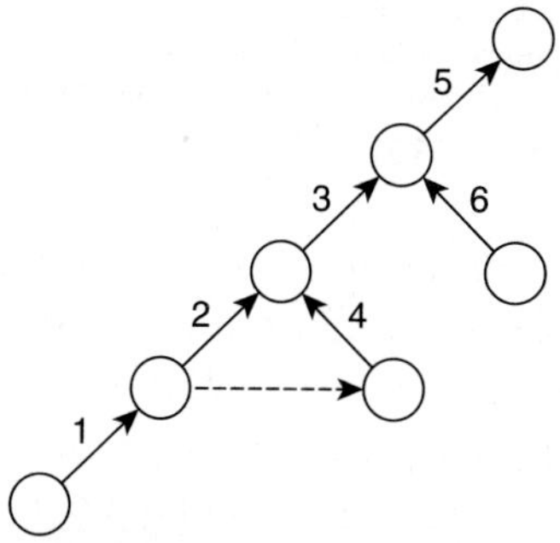

Figure 8-2 Use of a dummy activity

ARROW VERSUS NODE DIAGRAMS

While the two notations are equivalent, there are distinct pros and cons for each. One point favoring arrow diagrams is that the completion events are a natural place to designate milestones. A **milestone** is an event denoting the completion of a significant part of the project. With node diagrams you typically have to add activities of zero duration as milestones.

Nearly everyone requires a bit of practice to correctly draw and read an arrow diagram, whereas people intuitively draw node diagrams and understand them, giving node diagrams what appears to be a clear advantage. Node diagrams at first seem to have no need for a dummy activity because you can just add another dependency arrow (such as another arrow between activities 1 and 4 on the left side of Figure 8-1). For these simplistic reasons, the vast majority of tools for drawing network diagrams use node diagrams.

In contrast, at least four of IDesign's customers have developed arrow diagramming tools (and two of these tools are available along with the support files for this book). They invested in the tools for arrow diagrams due to a crucial flaw in all node diagrams. Consider the networks in Figure 8-3.

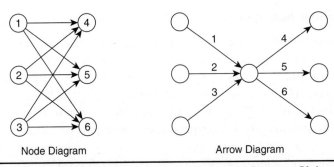

Node Diagram   Arrow Diagram

Figure 8-3 Repeated dependencies in node versus arrow diagrams [Adopted and modified from James M. Antill and Ronald W. Woodhead, *Critical Path in Construction Practice*, 4th ed. (Wiley, 1990).]

Figure 8-3 depicts two identical networks, both comprising six activities; 1, 2, 3, 4, 5, 6. Activities 4, 5, and 6 all depend on activities 1, 2, and 3. With an arrow diagram the network is straightforward and easy to understand, while the corresponding node diagram is an entangled cat's cradle. You can clean up the node diagram by introducing a dummy node of zero duration, but that may get confused with a milestone.

As it turns out, the situation in Figure 8-3 is very common in well-designed software systems in which you have repeated dependencies across the layers of the architecture. For example, activities 1, 2, and 3 could be *ResourceAccess* services, and activities 4, 5 and 6 could be some *Managers* and *Engines*, each using all three *ResourceAccess* services. With node diagrams, it is difficult to figure out what is going on even in a simple project network like that shown in Figure 8-3. By the time you add *Resources*, *Clients*, and *Utilities*, the diagram becomes utterly incomprehensible.

It is pointless to draw unintelligible network diagrams. The primary purpose of the network diagram is communication: You strive to communicate your project design to others or even to yourself. Having a model that no one can understand and to which no one can relate defeats the purpose of having the network diagram in the first place.

Consequently, you should avoid node diagrams and use arrow diagrams. The initial arrow diagram learning curve is more than offset by the benefits of having a concise, clear, clutter-free model of your project. The lack of widely available tool support for arrow diagrams, which forces you to draw your arrow diagram manually, is not necessarily a bad thing. Drawing the network by hand is valuable because in the process you review and verify activity dependencies, and it may even unveil additional insights about the project.

HISTORY OF THE CRITICAL PATH METHOD

The ideas of a network of activities and the critical path as a way of discovering how to build the project, how long it will take, and how much it will cost are not new. The physical construction industry has been using it successfully for decades. The critical path method originated at DuPont as part of the Manhattan Project in the 1940s[a] and in the U.S. Navy in the 1950s with the Polaris submarine missile project.[b] In both of these cases, critical path analysis was used to rein in out-of-control complexity and issues similar to those plaguing large modern software projects. In 1959, James Kelley published a short paper[c] based on the DuPont experience in designing industrial plants. The first eight pages contained all the familiar elements of the methodology, such as the critical path, arrow diagrams, dummies, floats, and even an ideal time–cost curve.

In the 1960s, NASA used the critical path method as the principal planning tool for catching up and winning the race to the moon.[d] The critical path method gained in reputation after the role it played in salvaging the much delayed Sydney Opera House project,[e] and in ensuring the rapid construction of the World Trade Center in New York City (then the tallest buildings in the world), both completed in 1973.

a. https://en.wikipedia.org/wiki/Critical_path_method#history
b. https://en.wikipedia.org/wiki/Program_evaluation_and_review_technique#history
c. James E. Kelley and Morgan R. Walker, "Critical Path Planning and Scheduling," *Proceedings of the Eastern Joint Computer Conference*, 1959.
d. https://ntrs.nasa.gov/search.jsp?R=19760036633
e. James M. Antill and Ronald W. Woodhead, *Critical Path in Construction Practice*, 4th ed. (Wiley, 1990).

FLOATS

Activities on the critical path must complete as soon as planned to avoid delaying the project. Noncritical events may be delayed without slipping the schedule; in other words, they can float until they must begin. A project without any float, where all network paths are critical, could in theory meet its commitments, but in practice any misstep anywhere will cause a delay. From a design perspective, floats are the project's safety margins. When designing a project, you always want to reserve enough float in the network. The development team can then consume this float to compensate for unforeseen delays in noncritical activities. Low-float projects are at high risk of delays. Anything more than a minor delay on a low-float activity will cause that activity to become critical and derail the project.

The discussion of floats so far was somewhat simplistic because there are actually several types of floats. This chapter discusses two types: total float and free float.

TOTAL FLOAT

An activity's **total float** is by how much time you can delay the completion of that activity without delaying the project as a whole. When the completion of an activity is delayed by an amount less than its total float, its downstream activities may be delayed as well, but the completion of the project is not delayed. This means that total float is an aspect of a chain of activities, not just particular activities. Consider the network in the top part of Figure 8-4, which shows the critical path in bold lines and a noncritical path or chain of activities above it.

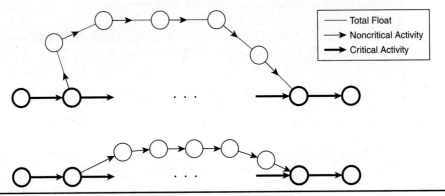

Figure 8-4 Float as an aspect of a chain of activities

For the purpose of this discussion, Figure 8-4 is drawn to scale so that the length of each line corresponds to each activity's duration. The noncritical activities all have the same amount of total float, indicated by the red line at the end of the activity's arrow. Imagine that the start of the first noncritical activity in the top half of the figure is delayed or that the activity takes longer than its estimation. While that activity executes, the delay in completing the upstream activity consumes the total float of the downstream activities (shown in the bottom half of the figure).

All noncritical activities have some total float, and all activities on the same noncritical chain share some of the total float. If the activities are also scheduled to start as soon as possible, then all activities on the same chain will have the same amount of total float. Consuming the total float somewhere further up a chain will drain it from the downstream activities, making them more critical and riskier.

Note   As you will see later in this chapter, the total float of each activity in the network is a key project design consideration. In the rest of this book, references to just "float" always refer to total float.

FREE FLOAT

An activity's **free float** is by how much time you can delay the completion of that activity without disturbing any other activity in the project. When the completion of an activity is delayed by an amount less or equal to its free float, the downstream activities are not affected at all, and of course the project as a whole is not delayed. Consider Figure 8-5.

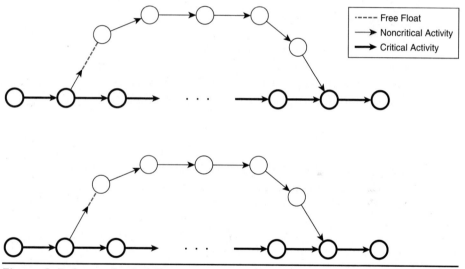

Figure 8-5 Consuming free float

Again, for the purpose of this discussion, Figure 8-5 is drawn to scale. Suppose the first activity in the noncritical chain in the top part of the figure has some free float, indicated by the dotted red line at the end of the activity's arrow. Imagine that the activity is delayed by an amount of time less than (or equal to) its free float. You can see that the downstream activities are unaware of that delay (bottom part of diagram).

Interestingly, while any noncritical activity always has some total float, an activity may or may not have free float. If you schedule your noncritical activities to start as soon as possible, back to back, then even though these activities are noncritical, their free float is zero because any delay will disrupt the other noncritical activities on the chain. However, the last activity on a noncritical chain that connects back to the critical path always has some free float (or it would be a critical activity, too).

Free float has little use during project design, but it can prove very useful during project execution. When an activity is delayed or exceeds its effort estimation, the free float of the delayed activity enables the project manager to know how much time is available before other activities in the project will be affected, if at all. If the delay is less than the delayed activity's free float, nothing really needs to be done. If the delay is greater than the free float (but less than the total float), the project manager can subtract the free float from the delay and accurately gauge the degree by which the delay will interfere with downstream activities and take appropriate actions.

CALCULATING FLOATS

The floats in the project network are a function of the activity durations, their dependencies, and any delays you may introduce. None of these have to do with actual calendar dates when you schedule these activities. You can calculate the floats even if the actual start date of the project is as yet undecided.

In most decent-size networks, such float calculations, if done manually, are error prone, get quickly out of hand, and are invalidated by any change to the network. The good news is that these are purely mechanical calculations, and you should use tools for calculating the floats.[1] With the total float values at hand, you can record them on the project network as shown in Figure 8-6. This figure shows a sample project network in which the numbers in black are each activity's ID, and the numbers in blue below the arrows are the total float for the noncritical activities.

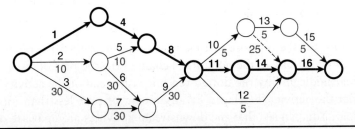

Figure 8-6 Recording total floats on the network

---

1. You can use Microsoft Project to calculate the floats for each activity by inserting the Total Slack and the Free Slack columns, which correspond to the total and free float. To learn how to manually calculate floats, see James M. Antill and Ronald W. Woodhead, *Critical Path in Construction Practice*, 4th ed. (Wiley, 1990).

While only total float is required for project design, you can also record free float in the network diagram. The project manager will find this information invaluable during project execution.

VISUALIZING FLOATS

Capturing the information about the floats on the network diagram, as shown in Figure 8-6, is not ideal. Human beings process alphanumeric data slowly and have a hard time relating to such data. It is difficult to examine complex networks (or even simple ones, like that in Figure 8-6) and at a glance to assess the criticality of the network. The **criticality** of the network indicates where the risky areas are and how close the project is to an all-critical network. Total floats are better visualized by color-coding the arrows and nodes—for example, using red for low float values, yellow for medium float values, and green for high float values. You can partition the three float value ranges in several ways:

- **Relative criticality.** Relative criticality divides the maximum value of the float of all activities in the network into three equal parts. For example, if the maximum float is 45 days, then red would be 1 to 15 days, yellow would be 16 to 30 days, and green would be 31 to 45 days of float. This technique works well if the maximum float is a large number (such as greater than 30 days) and the floats are uniformly distributed up to that number.

- **Exponential criticality.** Relative criticality assumes that the risk for delay is somewhat equally spread across the range of float. In reality, an activity with 5 days of float is much more likely to derail the project than an activity with 10 days of float, even though both may be classified as red by relative criticality. To address this issue, the exponential criticality divides the range of the maximum float into three unequal, exponentially smaller ranges. I recommend making the divisions at 1/9 and 1/3 of the range: These divisions are reasonably sized but more aggressive than those produced by 1/4 and 1/2, and the divisors are proportional to the number of colors. For example, if the maximum float is 45 days, then red would be 1 to 5 days, yellow would be 6 to 15 days, and green would be 16 to 45 days of float. As with relative criticality, the exponential criticality works well if the maximum total float is a large number (such as greater than 30 days) and the floats are uniformly distributed up to that number.

- **Absolute criticality.** The absolute criticality classification is independent of both the value of the maximum float and how uniformly the floats are distributed along the range. The absolute criticality sets an absolute float range for each color classification. For example, red activities would be those with 1 to 9 days of float, yellow would be 10 to 26 days of float, and green activities would be 27 days of float (or more). Absolute criticality classification is straightforward and works well in most projects. The downside is that it may require customizing the ranges to the project at hand to reflect the risk. For example, 10 days may be green in a 2-month project but red in a year-long project.

Figure 8-7 shows the same network as in Figure 8-6 with color coding for absolute criticality classification using the absolute float ranges just suggested. The critical activities in black have no float.

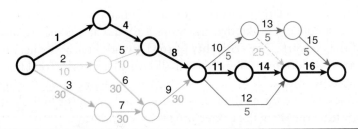

Figure 8-7 Floats color coding

Compare the ease with which you can interpret the visual information in Figure 8-7 versus the same textual information in Figure 8-6. You can immediately see that the second part of the project is risky.

PROACTIVE PROJECT MANAGEMENT

Most competent project managers actively manage their projects against the critical path. Because any delay along this path will derail the project, the project manager watches the critical path like a hawk. When well-managed projects still miss deadlines, those delays hardly ever occur because of slipping critical activities. My observation is that the primary reason that well-managed projects slip is because noncritical activities become critical. This usually happens because the originally noncritical activities did not get the resources on the planned schedule, causing the activities to bleed out their total float, become critical, and delay the project.

To avoid being blindsided by the noncritical activities, the project manager should proactively track the total float of all noncritical activity chains. The project manager can calculate the total float for each chain on a regular basis and even extrapolate a trend line to see at what point it becomes critical. The project manager should track the chains at relatively high resolution (such as weekly) because the float of a chain often behaves as a step function with nonlinear degradation due to dependencies on other activities or resources.

FLOATS-BASED SCHEDULING

As stated in Chapter 7, the safest and most efficient way to assign resources to activities is based on float—or, given the definition of this chapter, total float. This is the safest method because you address the riskier activities first, and it is the most efficient because you maximize the percentage of time for which the resources are utilized.

Consider the snapshot of a scheduling chart shown in Figure 8-8. Here the length of each colored bar represents the time-scaled duration of that activity, and the right or left position is aligned with the schedule.

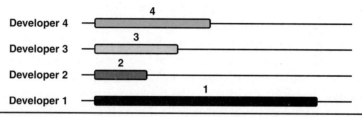

Figure 8-8 Maximizing resource demand when not consuming float

The figure has four activities: 1, 2, 3, 4. All activities are ready to start on the same date. Due to downstream activities (not shown), activity 1 is critical, while activities 2, 3, and 4 have various levels of total float indicated by their color coding: 2 is red (low float), 3 is yellow (medium float), and 4 is green (high float). Suppose these are all development activities that all developers can perform equally well, and that there are no task continuity issues. When staffing this project, you first must assign a developer to the critical activity 1. If you have a second developer, you should assign that developer to activity 2, which has the lowest float of all other activities. This way, you can utilize as many as four developers, working on each of the activities as soon as possible.

Alternatively, you can staff the project with only two developers (see Figure 8-9). As before, the first developer works on activity 1. The second developer starts with activity 2 as soon as possible because there is no point in postponing a near-critical activity and making it critical.

Once activity 2 is complete, the second developer moves to the remaining activity with the lowest float, activity 3. This requires rescheduling 3 further down the timeline, until the second developer is available after completing activity 2. This is only possible by consuming (reducing) the float of activity 3; due to some

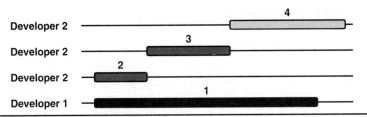

Figure 8-9 Trading float for resources

downstream dependencies in this example, this causes activity 3 to become red. Once activity 3 is complete, the second developer proceeds to work on activity 4. This, too, is possible only by consuming the available float of activity 4; while acceptable in this example, this turns the float of activity 4 from green to yellow.

This form of staffing trades float for resources and, in effect, for cost. When assigning resources, you use floats in two ways: You assign resources to available activities based on floats, low to high, and if needed, you consume activities' float to staff the projects with a smaller level of resources without delaying the project.

> **Note** Pushing activity 3 down the timeline until the developer who worked on activity 2 is available is identical to making activity 3 dependent on activity 2. This is a good way of changing the network to reflect a dependency on a resource. Recall from Chapter 7 that the network diagram is not merely a network of activities but a network of dependencies, and that resource dependencies are dependencies.

FLOAT AND RISK

As just stated, assigning resources based on float allows you to trade float for cost. You may be tempted to trade all the project's float for lower cost, but that is rarely a good idea because a project with little float has less tolerance for delays. When you trade resources for float, you reduce the cost but increase the risk. In effect, you are not merely trading float for lower cost, but lower cost for higher risk. The float trade therefore is a three-way trade. In the example of Figure 8-9, using two developers rather than four has reduced cost but, as a side effect, made the project risker. During project design you should constantly manage the remaining float, and by doing so manage the risk of the project. This allows you to craft several options that offer different blends of schedule, cost, and risk.

9

TIME AND COST

The fastest way to deliver any system is to build it along its critical path. A well-designed project also efficiently assigns the minimally required resources along its critical path, but the project's duration is still bounded by the critical path. You can accelerate the execution by adopting software engineering practices that facilitate quick and clean development. Beyond these development best practices, this chapter discusses what you can do to reduce the schedule by compressing the critical path. The primary technique for this type of schedule reduction is redesigning the project by producing several shorter, ever-more-compressed project design solutions. You will then see the fundamental concept of the time–cost curve and how time and cost interplay in a project. The result is a set of project design options that enable you both to best fit up front the wishes of management for time and cost and to pivot quickly in case things change.

ACCELERATING SOFTWARE PROJECTS

Contrary to what many believe, the best way of meeting a deadline hardly ever involves just working harder or throwing more people on the project. It does involve working smarter, cleanly, and correctly while embracing a wide set of best practices. In general, the following techniques are possible in any software project and will accelerate the project as a whole:

- **Assure quality.** Most teams incorrectly refer to their quality control and testing activities as quality assurance (QA). True QA has little to do with testing. It typically involves a single, senior expert who answers the question: What will it take to assure quality? The answer must include how to orient the entire development process to assure quality, how to prevent problems from ever happening, and how to track the root causes of problems and to fix them. The presence of a QA person is a sign of organizational maturity and is almost always indicative of commitment to quality, of understanding that quality does not happen on its own, and of acknowledging that the organization must actively pursue quality. The QA person is sometimes responsible for designing the process and authoring procedures for key phases. Since quality leads to productivity, proper QA always accelerates the schedule, and it sets organizations that practice QA apart from the rest of the industry.

- **Employ test engineers.** Test engineers are not testers, but rather full-fledged software engineers who design and write code whose objective is to break the system's code. Test engineers, in general, are a higher caliber of engineer than regular software engineers, because writing test engineering code often involves more difficult tasks: developing fake communication channels; designing and developing regression testing; and designing test rigs, simulators, automation, and more. Test engineers are intimately familiar with the architecture and inner workings of the system, and they take advantage of that knowledge to try to break the system at every turn. Having such an "anti-system" system ready to tear your product apart does wonders for quality because you can discover problems as soon as they occur, isolate root causes, avoid ripple effects of changes, eliminate superimposition of defects masking other defects, and considerably shorten the cycle time of fixing problems. Having a constant, defect-free codebase accelerates the schedule like nothing else ever does.

- **Add software testers.** In most teams, the developers outnumber the testers. In projects with too few testers, the one or two testers cannot afford to scale up with the team, and they are frequently reduced to performing testing that has little added value. Such testing is repetitive, does not vary with the team size or the system's growing complexity, and often treats the system as a black box. This does not mean that good testing does not take place, but rather that the bulk of the testing is shifted onto developers. Changing the ratio of testers to developers, such as 1:1 or even 2:1 (in favor of testers), allows the developers to spend less time testing and more time adding direct value to the project.

- **Invest in infrastructure.** All software systems require common utilities in the form of security, message queues and message bus, hosting, event publishing, logging, instrumentation, diagnostics, and profiling, as well as regression testing and test automation. Modern software systems need configuration management, deployment scripts, a build process, daily builds, and smoke tests (often lumped under DevOps). Instead of having every developer write his or her own unique infrastructure, you should invest in building (and maintaining) a framework for the entire team that accomplishes most or all of the items listed here. This focuses the developers on business-related coding tasks, provides great economy of scale, makes it easier to onboard new developers, reduces stress and friction, and decreases the time it takes to develop the system.

- **Improve development skills.** Today's software environments are characterized by a very high rate of change. This rate of change exceeds many developers' ability to keep up with the latest language, tools, frameworks, cloud platforms, and other innovations. Even the best developers are perpetually coming to terms with technology, and they spend an inordinate amount of time stumbling, figuring things out in a nonstructured, haphazard way. Even worse, some developers are so overwhelmed that they resort to copy-and-paste of code from the web, without any real understanding of the short- or long-term implications (including legal ones) of their actions. To ameliorate this problem, you should dedicate the time and resources to train developers on the technology, methodology, and tools at hand. Having competent developers will accelerate the time it takes to develop any software.

- **Improve the process.** Most development environments suffer from a deficient process. They go through the motions for the sake of doing the process, but lack any real understanding or appreciation of the reasoning behind the activities. There are no real benefits from these hollow activities, and they often make things worse, in a cargo-cult culture[1] manner. Volumes have been written about software development processes. Educate yourself on the battle-proven best practices and devise an improvement plan that will address the quality, schedule, and budget issues. Sort the best practices in the improvement plan by effect and ease of introduction, and proactively address the reasons why there were absent in the first place. Write standard operating procedures, and have the team and yourself follow the standard operating procedures, and even enforce them if necessary. Over time, this will make projects more repeatable and able to deliver on the set schedule.

- **Adopt and employ standards.** A comprehensive coding standard addresses naming conventions and style, coding practices, project settings and structure, framework-specific guidelines, your own guidelines, your team's dos and don'ts, and known pitfalls. The standard helps to enforce development best practices and to avoid mistakes, elevating novices to the level of veterans. It makes the code uniform and eases any issues created when one developer works on another's code. By complying with the standard, developers increase the chances of success and decrease the time it would otherwise take to develop the system.

- **Provide access to external experts.** Most teams will not have world-class experts as members. The team's job is to understand the business and deliver the system, not to be very good in security, hosting, UX, cloud, AI, BI, Big Data, or database architecture. Reinventing the wheel is very time-consuming and is never as good as accessing readily available, proven knowledge (recall the 2% problem from Chapter 2). It is far better and faster to defer to external experts. Use these experts at specific places as required and avoid costly mistakes.

1. https://en.wikipedia.org/wiki/Cargo_cult

- **Engage in peer reviews.** The best debugger is the human eye. Developers often detect problems in each other's code much faster than it takes to diagnose and eliminate the problems once the code is part of the system. This is also true when it comes to defects in the requirements or in the design and test plan of each of the services in the system. The team should review all of these to ensure the highest-quality codebase.

> **Note**   The software development industry is so chaotic that this list of common-sense basic practices may look foreign to most developers today. However, ignoring them and doing more of the same will not accelerate the schedule. The same actions that caused the problem cannot be the ones used to solve it. Over time, by employing some or all of these practices, the team will become hyperproductive, addicted to success, and able to tackle aggressive schedules with confidence.

These software engineering best practices will accelerate the project as a whole, irrespective of specific activities or the project network itself. They are effective in any project, in any environment, and with any technology. While it might appear costly to improve the project this way, it can very well end up costing less. The reduction in the time it takes to develop the system pays for the cost of the improvements.

SCHEDULE COMPRESSION

The issue with the items in the previous list of schedule acceleration techniques is that none is a quick fix for the schedule; all of them take time to be effective. However, you can do two things to immediately accelerate the schedule—either work with better resources or find ways of working in parallel. By employing these techniques you will compress the schedule of the project. Such schedule compression does not mean doing the same work faster. Schedule **compression** means accomplishing the same objectives faster, often by doing more work to finish the task or the project sooner. You can use these two compression techniques in combination with each other or in isolation, on parts of the project, on the project as a whole, or on individual activities. Both compression techniques end up increasing the direct cost (defined later) of the project while reducing the schedule.

WORKING WITH BETTER RESOURCES

Senior developers will deliver their part of the system faster than junior developers. However, it is a common misconception that this difference is because they code faster. Often, junior developers code much faster than senior developers. Senior developers spend as little of their time as possible coding, instead spending the bulk of their time designing the code module, the interactions, and the approaches they intend to use for testing. Senior developers write testing rigs, simulators, and emulators for the components they are working on and for the services they consume. They document their work, they contemplate the implications of each coding decision, and they look at maintainability and extensibility of their services, as well as other aspects such as security. Therefore, while per unit of time such senior developers code more slowly than junior developers do, they complete the task more quickly. As you might suspect, senior developers are at high demand and command higher compensation than do junior developers. You should assign these better resources only to critical activities since leveraging them outside the critical path will not alter the schedule.

WORKING IN PARALLEL

In general, whenever you take a sequential set of activities and find ways of performing these activities in parallel, you accelerate the schedule. There are two possible ways of working in parallel. The first is by extracting internal phases of an activity and moving them elsewhere in the project. The second way is by removing dependencies between activities so that you could work in parallel on these activities (assigning multiple people to the same activity at the same time does not work, as explained in Chapter 7).

Splitting Activities

Instead of performing the internal phases of an activity sequentially, you can split up the activity. You schedule some of the less-dependent phases in parallel to other activities in the project, either before or after the activity. Good candidates for internal phases to extract upstream in the project (i.e., prior to the rest of the activity) include the detailed design, documentation, emulators, service test plan, service test harness, API design, UI design, and so on. Candidates for internal phases to move downstream in the project include integration with other services, unit testing, and repeated documentation. Splitting an activity reduces the time it occupies on the critical path and shortens the project.

Removing Dependencies

Instead of working sequentially on dependent activities, you can look for ways to reduce or even eliminate dependencies between activities and work on the activities in parallel. If the project has activity A that depends on activity B, which in turn depends on activity C, the duration of the project would be the sum of the durations of these three activities. However, if you could remove the dependency between A and B, then you could work on A in parallel to B and C and compress the schedule accordingly.

Removing dependencies often involves investing in additional activities that enable the parallel work in the first place:

- **Contract design.** By having a separate design activity for a service contract, you can provide the interface or the contract to its consumers and then start working on those before the service they depend upon is completed. Providing the contract may not remove the dependency completely, but it could enable some level of parallel work. The same goes for the design of UI, messages, APIs, or protocols between subsystems or even systems.

- **Emulators development.** Given the contract design, you could write a simple service that emulates the real service. Such implementation should be very simple (always returning the same results and without errors) and could further remove the dependencies.

- **Simulators development.** Instead of a mere emulator, you could develop a complete simulator to a service or services. The simulator could maintain state, inject errors, and be indistinguishable from the real service. Sometimes writing a good simulator can be more difficult than constructing the real service. However, the simulator does remove the dependency between the service and its clients, allowing a high degree of parallel work.

- **Repeated integration and testing.** Even with a great simulator for a service, a client developed against only that simulator should be a cause for concern. Once the real service is completed, you must repeat the integration and testing between that service and all clients that were developed against the simulator.

Parallel Work Candidates

Sometimes the best candidates for parallel work are evident in the staffing distribution chart. If the chart contains several pulses, perhaps you can decouple these pulses.

Consider the chart in Figure 9-1, which exhibits three pulses. In the original plan, all three were done sequentially due to the dependencies between the outputs of each pulse as the inputs to the next one. If you can find some way of removing those dependencies, you can work on one or two of the pulses in parallel to the other one, significantly compressing the schedule.

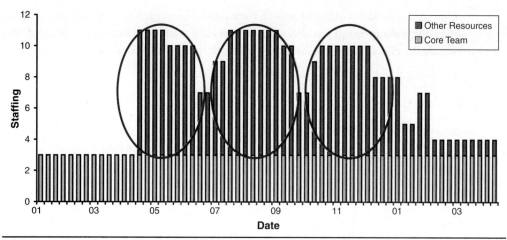

Figure 9-1 Candidates for parallel work

PARALLEL WORK AND COST

Both forms of parallel work—splitting activities or removing dependencies between activities—often require additional resources. The project will need more resources to perform the extracted phases in parallel to other activities. The project also will require more resources to work on the additional activities that enable the parallel work, such as additional developers for the repeated integration, and additional testers for the repeated testing. This will increase the cost of the project and the workload. In particular, the additional resources will result in a larger team, higher peak team size, increased noise, and less efficient execution. The reduced efficiency will drive the cost up even further because you get less from each team member.

The team at hand may be incapable of parallel work for a variety of reasons (lack of an architect, lack of senior developers, or an inadequate team size), forcing you to resort to expensive high-grade, external talent. Even if you can afford the total cost of the project, the parallel work will increase the cash flow rate and may make the project unaffordable. In short, parallel work is not free.

Perils of Parallel Work

In general, removing dependencies between activities is like defusing a bomb—something you should do very carefully. Parallel work often increases the execution complexity of the project, and by doing so drastically increases the demands on the project manager in charge of the project. Before engaging in parallel work, you should invest in infrastructure that accelerates all activities in the project without changing cross-activities dependencies. This is likely safer and easier than parallel work.

That said, parallel work will reduce the overall time to market. When deciding on pursuing a compressed parallel option, carefully weigh the incurred risks and cost of parallel execution with the expected reduction in the schedule.

TIME–COST CURVE

At least initially, adding cost allows delivering any project faster. In most projects, the trade of time-for-cost is not a linear trade, but rather looks ideally like the curve in Figure 9-2.

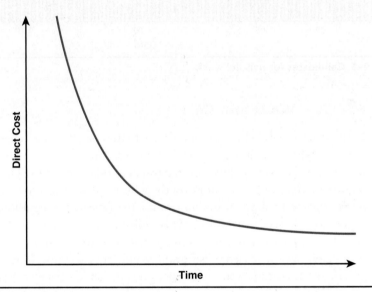

Figure 9-2 Idealized time–cost curve

For example, consider a 10-man-year project consisting only of coding activities. Assigning this project to a single developer will take 10 years to complete and cost 10 man-years. However, assigning the same project to two developers will likely take 7 years or more, not 5. To complete this project in 5 years, you will need at least 3 developers, and more likely 5 or even 6 developers. These costs (10 years for 10 man-years of cost, 7 years for 14 man-years, and 5 years for 30 man-years) are indeed the expression of nonlinear trades of cost for time.

POINTS ON TIME–COST CURVE

The time–cost curve depicted in Figure 9-2 is both ideal and unrealistic. It assumes that given a large enough budget, the project could be done nearly instantaneously. Common sense tells you that assumption is wrong. For example, no amount of money can deliver a 10-man-year project in a month (or, for that matter, in a year). There is a natural limit to all compression efforts. Similarly, the time–cost curve of Figure 9-2 indicates that given more time, the cost of the project goes down, while (as discussed in Chapter 7) giving projects more time than is required actually drives up their cost.

While the time–cost curve of Figure 9-2 is incorrect, it is possible to discuss points on the time–cost curve that are present across all projects. These points are the result of a few classic planning assumptions. Figure 9-3 shows the actual time–cost curve.

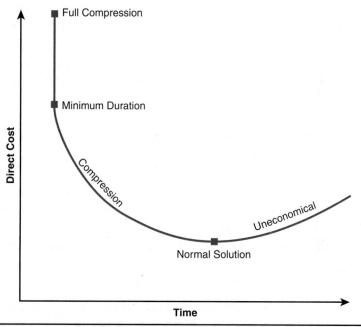

Figure 9-3 Actual time–cost curve [Adopted and modified from James M. Antill and Ronald W. Woodhead, *Critical Path in Construction Practice*, 4th ed. (Wiley, 1990).]

The Normal Solution

You can always design a project by assuming you have unlimited resources and that every resource will be available when required. At the same time, you should design the project with an eye for minimum cost, and avoid asking for more resources than are really required. As explained in Chapter 7, you can find the lowest level of resources that will allow you to progress unimpeded along the critical path. This will give you both the least expensive way of building the system and the most efficient team. Such a project design option is called the **normal solution**. The normal solution represents the most unconstrained or natural way of building the system.

The Uneconomical Zone

Suppose the duration of the normal solution of the project is a year. Giving the same project more than a year to complete always costs more. The additional cost comes from employing resources for longer periods of time, from the accumulated overhead, from gold plating, from increased complexity, and from the reduction of the probability of success. Therefore, points to the right of normal on the time–cost curve belong to the **uneconomical zone** of the project.

Compressed Solutions

You can compress the normal solution by using some or all of the compression techniques described earlier in this chapter. While all of the resulting compressed solutions are of shorter duration, they also cost more, likely in nonlinear ways. Obviously, you should focus your compression effort only on activities on the critical path, because compressing noncritical activities does nothing for the schedule. Each compressed solution is to the left of the normal solution on the time–cost curve.

Minimum Duration Solution

As you compress the project, the cost keeps escalating. At some point the critical path will be fully compressed because there are no more candidates for parallel work and you have already employed the best people on the critical activities. When you reach this point, you have the **least time** or **minimum duration** solution of the project. Every project always has such a minimum duration point, where no amount of money, effort, or willpower can deliver it any faster.

Full Compression Solution

While you cannot build the project any faster than its shortest possible duration, you can always waste money. Nothing prevents you from compressing all activities in the project, critical and noncritical alike. The project will not complete any faster than minimum duration, but it will certainly cost more. This point on the time–cost curve is called the **full compression** point.

> **Note** My personal experience indicates that 30% compression is likely the upper compression limit for any software project, and even that level of compression is hard to achieve. You can use this limit to validate any deadline constraint. For example, if the project has a normal solution of 12 months and a deadline set at 7 months, then the project cannot be built since that requires 41% schedule compression.

DISCRETE MODELING

The actual time–cost curve shown in Figure 9-3 offers infinite points between the normal solution and the minimum duration solution. Yet no one has the time to design an infinite number of project solutions, nor is there any need to do so. Instead, the architect and the project manager must provide management with one or two practical points in between the normal solution and the minimum duration solution. These options represent some reasonable trade of time for cost from which management can choose and are always be the result of some network compression. As a result, the curve you actually produce during project design is a discrete model, as shown in Figure 9-4. While the time–cost curve of Figure 9-4 has far fewer points than Figure 9-3, it has enough information to discern correctly how the project behaves.

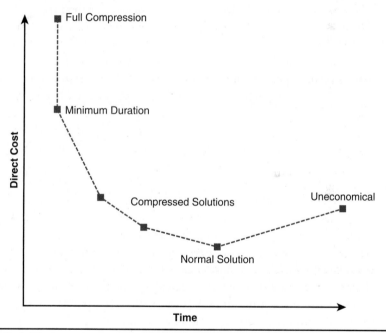

Figure 9-4 Discrete time–cost curve [Adopted and modified from James M. Antill and Ronald W. Woodhead, *Critical Path in Construction Practice*, 4th ed. (Wiley, 1990).]

AVOIDING CLASSIC MISTAKES

You should present the impractical full compression and the uneconomical solutions to management, because many managers are simply unaware of their impracticality. Managers may have the wrong mental model of how a project behaves—most likely the mental model depicted in Figure 9-2. When you have the wrong mental model, you always make the wrong decisions.

Suppose schedule is the utmost priority, and the manager does not mind spending whatever it takes to meet the commitment. The manager may think that it is possible to throw money and people on the project to push the team toward a deadline, even though no amount of money can deliver below minimum duration.

It is also just as common to find managers with a constrained budget but more amendable schedule. Such a manager may attempt to cut the cost by subcritically staffing the project or by not giving the project the required resources. Doing so pushes the project right of the normal solution into the uneconomical zone, again causing it to cost much more.

PROJECT FEASIBILITY

The time–cost curve shows a paramount aspect of the project: feasibility. Project design solutions of time and cost representing points at or above the curve are doable. For example, consider the point A in Figure 9-5. The A solution calls for T_2 time and C_1 cost. While A is a feasible solution, it is suboptimal. If T_2 is an acceptable deadline, then the project could also be delivered for C_2 cost, the value of the time–cost curve at the time of T_2. Because A is above the curve, it follows that $C_2 < C_1$. Conversely, if the cost of C_1 is acceptable, then for the same cost it is also possible to deliver the project in a time of T_1, the value of the time–cost curve at the time of C_1. Since A is to the right of the curve, it follows that $T_1 < T_2$.

The points on the time–cost curve simply represent the most optimal trade of time for cost. The time–cost curve is optimal because it is always better to deliver the project faster (for the same cost) or at lower cost (for the same deadline). You could do worse, but not better than the time–cost curve. This also implies that points under the time–cost curve are impossible. For example, consider the point B in Figure 9-6. The B solution calls for T_3 time and C_4 cost. However, to deliver the project at time of T_3 would require at least the cost of C_3. Since B is below the time–cost curve, it follows that $C_3 > C_4$. If C_4 is all you can afford, then the project would require at least the time of T_4. Since B is left of the time–cost curve, it follows that $T_4 > T_3$.

The Death Zone

If the points on the time–cost curve are simply minimum cost for any duration, then the time–cost curve divides the area into two zones. The first is the feasible solutions zone, covering solutions above or at the time–cost curve. The second zone is the **death zone**, encompassing all solutions below the time–cost curve, as shown in Figure 9-7.

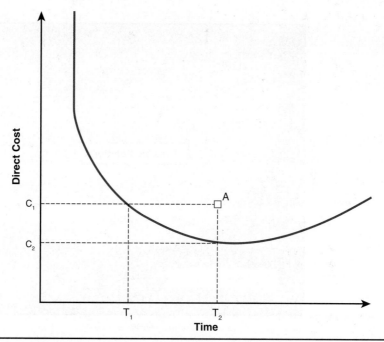

Figure 9-5 Suboptimal solution above the time–cost curve

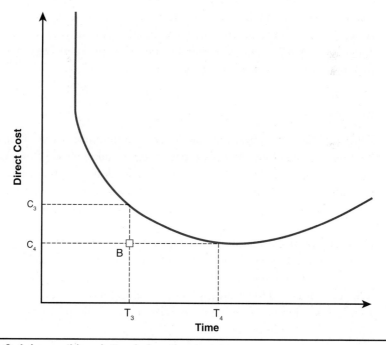

Figure 9-6 Impossible solution below the time–cost curve

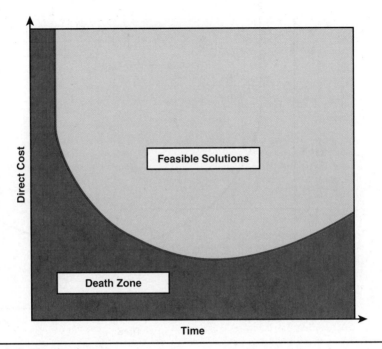

Figure 9-7 The death zone

I cannot stress enough how important it is not to design a project in the death zone. Projects in the death zone have failed before anyone writes the first line of code. The key to success is neither architecture nor technology, but rather avoiding picking a project in the death zone.

FINDING NORMAL SOLUTIONS

When searching for the normal solution, the minimum level of staffing required to proceed unimpeded along the critical path is often unknown up front. For example, the fact that you could staff the project with 12 developers does not mean you could not have done so with 8 or even 6 developers without delaying the project. Consequently, finding the normal level of staffing is an iterative process, as shown in Figure 9-8.

For each iterative attempt at a normal solution, you progressively trade more float for resources. This trade will naturally increase the risk of the project due to the reduced float. It also means that the true normal solution already has a considerable level of risk. However, the lowest staffing level required for the true normal solution is often good enough risk-wise, because sufficient float remains to meet the project's commitments.

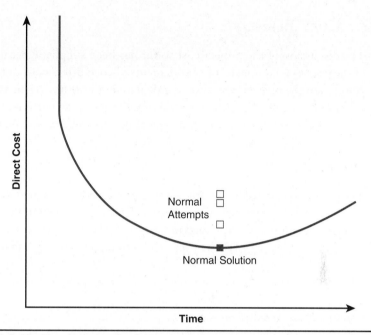

Figure 9-8 Finding the normal solution

Accommodating Reality

When looking for the staffing level of the normal solution, you should make minor accommodations for reality. For example, in a year-long project, if you could avoid hiring another resource by extending the schedule by a week, then you should probably take that trade. It is also a good idea to find ways of simplifying the project execution or reducing its integration risk in exchange for a slight extension of the duration or a small increase in cost. You should always prefer these accommodations for reality. As a result, the intermediate normal attempts may not be aligned exactly vertically atop each other (as in Figure 9-8), but rather may drift a little to the right or to the left.

What constitutes a minor adjustment to accommodate reality and what qualifies as a distortion of the intent in finding the normal solution is a judgment call. My rule of thumb is that anything less than 2–3% of the schedule or the cost is at the noise level and is fair game for such modifications. The 2–3% guideline is related to the project design and tracking resolution. If activities are only as granular as one week, and if the project is tracked on a weekly basis, then over a year, the design and measurement resolution is 2%, making anything more precise just noise. Chapter 11 and Chapter 13 demonstrate such accommodations.

PROJECT COST ELEMENTS

The discussion of the project cost so far has been simplistic because the total cost of the project is composed of two elements of cost: direct cost and indirect cost. As you design the project, you should calculate both of these elements of cost as well as the project's total cost. Understanding the interplay between the cost elements of the project is crucial for sound project design and decision making.

DIRECT COST

The project's **direct cost** comprises activities that add direct measurable value to the project. These are the same explicit project activities shown in the project's planned earned value chart. As explained in Chapter 7, the planned earned value (and hence the direct cost) varies over the project's lifetime, resulting in a shallow S curve.

The direct cost of a software project typically includes the following items:

- Developers working on services
- Testers performing system testing
- Database architect designing a database
- Test engineers designing and building a test harness
- UI/UX experts designing the user interface and the user experience
- The architect designing the system or the project

The direct cost curve of the project looks like Figure 9-3.

INDIRECT COST

The project's **indirect cost** comprises activities that add indirect immeasurable value to the project. Such activities are typically ongoing, and are not shown in the earned value charts or the project plan.

The indirect cost of a software project typically includes the following items:

- The core team (i.e., architect, project manager, product manager) after the SDP review
- Ongoing configuration management, daily build and daily test, or DevOps in general
- Vacations and holidays
- Committed resources between assignments

The indirect cost of most projects is largely proportional to the duration of the project. The longer the project takes, the higher the indirect cost. If you were to plot the indirect cost of the project over time, you should get roughly a straight line.

It is wrong to think of indirect cost as needless overhead. The project will fail without a dedicated architect and a project manager, yet after the SDP review, they have no explicit activities in the plan.

ACCOUNTING VERSUS VALUE

The concepts of direct and indirect costs are overloaded. Some regard direct cost as costs associated with direct team members and indirect cost as costs of external consultants or subcontractors. Others define direct cost simply as that for which they must pay, and indirect cost as that for which other people or organizations must pay. However, the question of who ends up paying for the resources is an accounting question, not a project design question. The definitions in this chapter are strictly from a value perspective: Does a resource or an activity add a measurable or immeasurable value?

TOTAL, DIRECT, AND INDIRECT COSTS

The **total cost** of the project is the sum of its direct and indirect costs:

$$\text{Total Cost} = \text{Direct Cost} + \text{Indirect Cost}$$

Given the definitions of direct and indirect costs, Figure 9-9 shows the two elements of cost and the resulting total cost of the project.

The indirect cost is shown as a straight line, and the direct cost curve is the same curve shown in the previous figures. Both the direct and indirect curves in Figure 9-9 are the product of discrete solutions, and the total cost curve is the sum of the direct and indirect costs at each of these points.

Revisiting the Death Zone

As with the direct cost curve, solutions above the total cost curve are feasible, while solutions below it are impossible. Therefore, the area below the total cost curve is the actual death zone of the project because it takes into account both the indirect cost and the direct cost. Merely being above the death zone on the direct cost curve may not mean the project is out of danger because you still have to pay for the indirect cost. Spend the time to model the total cost curve and then simply observe if the parameters you are given leave any chance for success. You will see how to do just that in Chapter 11.

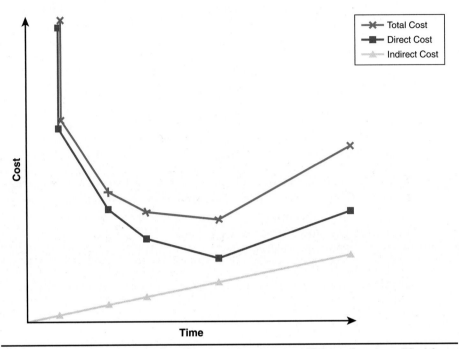

Figure 9-9 Project direct, indirect, and total cost curves [Adopted and modified from James M. Antill and Ronald W. Woodhead, *Critical Path in Construction Practice*, 4th ed. (Wiley, 1990).]

COMPRESSION AND COST ELEMENTS

A compressed project design solution will reduce the duration of the project and, therefore, will also reduce the indirect cost of the project. This, in turn, tends to offset the cost of compressing the project. For example, in Figure 9-9, consider the segments on all three curves between the normal solution (the lowest point on the direct cost curve) and the compressed solution to its left. On the direct cost curve, the compressed solution has a substantial additional cost between these two points. However, on the total cost curve, once you factor in the indirect cost, the difference in total cost is much reduced. For a little increase in total cost between the normal solution and the first compression point, you would get the same reduction of schedule. The accumulated indirect cost makes compressing more compelling, at least initially, because compression will tend to pay for itself. In many projects the reduction in indirect cost may be of an even a greater benefit than the schedule reduction.

THE FIRST ACTUAL TIME–COST CURVE

Fixing the software industry for the most part requires adopting engineering ideas and practices that originated in other industries. One exception is the actual time–cost curve, which originated from the computer and software industry.

In the early 1960s, General Electric developed the GE-225 computer, the world's first commercial transistor-based computer.[a] The GE-225 project was a hotspot of innovation. It introduced the world's first time-sharing operating system (which influenced the design of all modern operating systems), direct memory access, and the programming language BASIC.

In 1960, General Electric published a paper detailing its insights on the relationship between time and cost from the GE-225 project.[b] That paper contained the first actual time–cost curve (similar to Figure 9-4) and the breakdown into direct and indirect costs (as shown in Figure 9-9). These ideas were quickly adopted as-is by the physical construction industry.[c] James Kelley, the co-author of the first paper on the critical path method, consulted on the GE-225 project.

Incidentally, the architect of the GE-225 was Arnold Spielberg[d] (the father of the movie director Steven Spielberg). In 2006, the IEEE society recognized Spielberg with the prestigious Computer Pioneer Award.

a. https://en.wikipedia.org/wiki/GE-200_series
b. Børge M. Christensen, "GE 225 and CPM for Precise Project Planning" (General Electric Company Computer Department, December 1960).
c. James O'Brien, *Scheduling Handbook* (McGraw-Hill, 1969); and James M. Antill and Ronald W. Woodhead, *Critical Path in Construction Practice*, 2nd ed. (Wiley, 1970).
d. https://www.ge.com/reports/jurassic-hardware-steven-spielbergs-father-was-a-computing-pioneer/

Normal Solution and Minimum Total Cost

With the direct cost curve, the normal point is by definition also the minimum cost solution. To its right is the uneconomical zone, and to its left are the compressed solutions that trade time for additional cost. However, once you have added the indirect cost to find the total cost of the project for each of the designed solutions, the minimum total cost solution will no longer be the normal solution. Adding the indirect cost will shift the minimum total cost point somewhere to the left of the normal solution. Moreover, the steeper the slope of the indirect cost line, the more significant the shift to the left of the minimum total cost point.

As an example, consider Figure 9-10. On the direct cost curve the normal solution is clearly the point of minimum cost. However, on the total cost curve, the point of minimum cost is the first compressed solution to the left of the normal solution. In this case, compressing the project has actually reduced the cost of the project. This makes the point of minimum total cost of the project the optimal project design option from a time–cost perspective because it completes the project faster than normal and at a lower total cost.

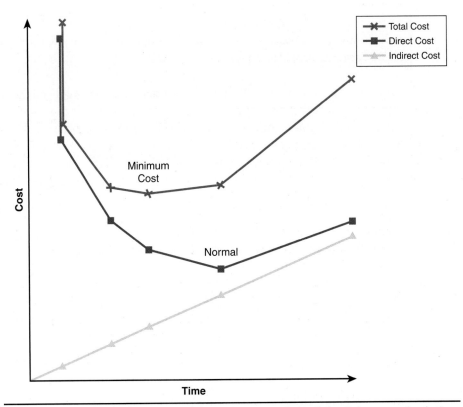

Figure 9-10 A high indirect cost shifts minimum total cost left of the normal solution

In Figure 9-10, the shift to the left of the point of minimum total cost is accentuated because of the discrete nature of the charts. That said, there is always a shift to the left, even with a continuous chart such as Figure 9-11, which has a lower slope of the indirect cost line than that shown in Figure 9-10.

Because you will only ever develop a small set of project design solutions, the time–cost curve you build will always be a discrete model of the project. With the solutions you have (and the level of indirect cost), the normal solution may indeed be the point of minimum total cost, as in Figure 9-9. However, that outcome is misleading and is simply an artifact of missing some unknown design solution slightly left of normal.

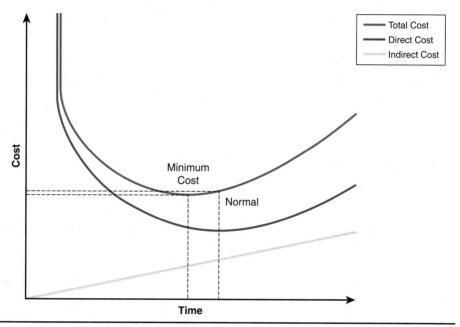

Figure 9-11 Shift to the left on a continuous time–cost curve

Figure 9-12 is the same as Figure 9-9 except that it adds that unknown point immediately to the left of the normal solution to illustrate the shift to the left of the point of minimum total cost.

The problem with this situation is that you have no idea how to make that solution: You do not know what combination of resources and compression yields this point. While such a solution always exists in theory, in practice for most projects you can equate the total cost of the normal solution with the minimum total cost of the project. The difference between the total cost of the normal solution and the point of true minimum total cost often does not justify the effort required to find that exact point.

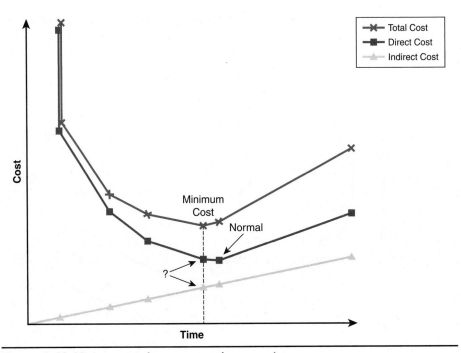

Figure 9-12 Minimum total cost as an unknown point

Indirect Cost and Risk

The steeper the slope of the indirect cost line, the more profound the shift to the left of the point of minimum total cost is. With a high indirect cost, one of the compressed solutions will likely be the optimal point of the project since its cost will be lower than the normal solution while delivering on a shorter schedule. However, this presents a problem: The more compressed project design solutions typically carry a higher risk. This risk can be due both to the criticality of the project and to its increased execution complexity. A high indirect cost therefore means that the optimal design point of the project is likely to be a high-risk option. Having your best option be a risky option is hardly a recipe for success. The implication is that projects with high indirect cost are almost always also high-risk projects. You will see how to address these risks in the following chapters.

STAFFING AND COST ELEMENTS

For each of your project design solutions, you must account for both direct and indirect cost. As established in Chapter 7, the total cost of a software project is the area under the staffing distribution chart. If you know the project total cost and one of the cost elements such as the direct cost, you can extract the other cost element by subtracting it from the total cost. For each project design solution, you first staff the project, then draw the planned earned value chart and the planned staffing distribution chart. Next, you calculate the area under the staffing distribution chart for the total cost, and you also sum up the effort across all direct cost activities (the ones you show on the earned value chart). The indirect cost is simply the difference between the two.

Graphically, Figure 9-13 shows a typical breakdown of the cost elements under the staffing distribution chart (also refer to Figure 7-8). In the front end of the project, only the core team is engaged, and much of that work involves indirect cost. The rest of the effort expended by the core team does have some direct value, such as designing the system and the project. However, past the SDP review, the core team turns into pure indirect cost. After the SDP review, the project has additional ongoing indirect costs such as DevOps, daily build, and daily tests. The rest of the staffing is a direct cost, such as developers building the system.

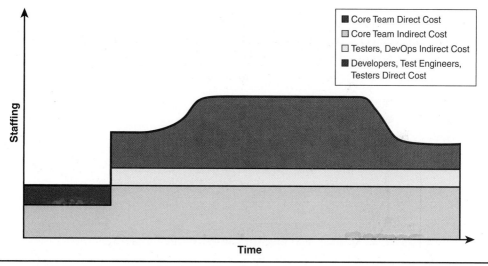

Figure 9-13 Cost elements under the staffing distribution

Direct versus Indirect Cost

As you can see from Figure 9-13, a typical software project will have more indirect cost than direct cost. Most people fail to recognize just how much indirect cost is required to deliver a high-quality, complex software system. A ratio of 1:2 of direct cost to indirect cost is quite common, but this ratio can easily be higher. The exact ratio of direct cost to indirect cost is often an aspect of the nature of the business. For example, you would expect a higher indirect cost in a company that produces avionics compared with one that produces a regular line of business systems.

Indirect Cost versus Total Cost

In a software project the indirect cost is often the dominant element of the total cost. This leads to a key observation: All things being equal, shorter projects always cost less simply because they incur less indirect cost. This is the case regardless of how you achieve the shorter schedule—whether by compressing the project or by employing the best practices which opened this chapter. A shorter project costs less even when compressing the project requires additional resources or even more expensive resources.

Unfortunately, many managers are simply unaware that shorter projects will cost less, which leads to a classic mistake. When faced with a tight budget, the manager will try to reduce the cost by throttling the resources (i.e., either the quality or the quantity of the resources). This will make the project longer, so that it ends up costing much more.

FIXED COST

Software projects have yet another element of cost that is fixed with time. **Fixed cost** might include computer hardware and software licenses. The fixed cost of the project is expressed as a constant shift up of the indirect cost line (Figure 9-14).

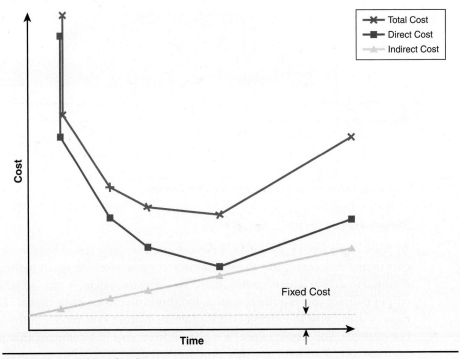

Figure 9-14 Adding fixed cost

Because the fixed cost merely shifts the total time–cost curve up, it adds nothing to the decision-making process, as it affects all options almost equally (it may change slightly with the team size). In most decent-size software projects, the fixed cost will be approximately 1–2% of the total cost, so it is typically negligible.

NETWORK COMPRESSION

Compressing the project will change the project network. Compression should be an iterative process in which you constantly look for the best next step. You start compressing the project from its normal solution. The normal solution should respond well to compression because it is at the minimum of the time–cost curve. As noted, initially the compression may even end up paying for itself. In addition, immediately to the left of the normal solution, the time–cost curve is the most flat. This means that your first one or two compression points will provide the best return on investment (ROI) of the compression cost. However, as you compress the project further, you will start climbing up the time–cost curve, eventually experiencing diminishing returns on the cost of compression. The project will offer less and less reduction in schedule while incurring ever higher cost, as if the project resists more compression. When compressing the project as a whole, you should attempt to compound the effect by compressing a previously compressed solution, not just trying a new compression technique on the baseline normal solution.

COMPRESSION FLOW

You should avoid compressing activities that will not respond well to compression regardless of the cost spent on them (such as architecture) or activities that are already fully compressed. Since even individual activities have their own time–cost curve, initially an activity may be easy to compress, but subsequent compression will require additional cost to climb the activity's own time–cost curve. At some point the activity will be impossible to compress any further. For this reason, it is better, in general, to compress other activities than to repeatedly compress the same activity.

Ideally, you should compress only activities on the critical path. There is hardly ever any point in compressing activities outside the critical path because doing so will just drive the cost up without shortening the schedule. At the same time, you should not blindly compress all activities on the critical path. The best candidates for compression are activities that offer the best ROI for the compression. Compression of these activities will yield the most reduction in schedule for the least additional cost. The duration of the activity also matters, because all compression techniques are disruptive and will increase the risk and complexity of the project. It is better to incur these effects on a large critical activity and gain the most reduction in schedule. It is also generally advisable to split large activities into smaller ones—a nice side effect of compressing a large activity.

As you compress the critical path, you will shorten it. As a result, another path may now be the longest in the project network; that is, a new critical path emerges. You should constantly evaluate the project network to detect the emergence of the new critical path and compress that path instead of the old critical path. If multiple critical paths arise, you must find ways of compressing these concurrently and by identical amounts. For example, if an activity or a set of activities caps all critical paths, then the next compression iteration would target them.

You can keep repeatedly compressing the project until one of the following conditions is met:

- You have met the desired deadline so there is so point in designing even more expensive and shorter projects.
- The calculated cost of the project exceeds the budget set for the project.
- The compressed project network is so complex that it is unlikely any project manager or team could deliver on it.
- The duration of the compressed solution is more than 30% (or even 25%) shorter than that of the normal solution. As noted earlier, there is a natural limit to how much in practice you can compress any project.
- The compressed solutions are too risky or risk is decreasing slightly because you are past the point of maximum risk. This requires the ability to quantify the risk of the project design solutions (discussed in the next chapter).
- You have run out of ideas or options for compressing the project any further. There is nothing more to compress.
- Too many critical paths have emerged or all network paths have become critical.
- You can find ways of compressing activities only outside the critical path. The compressed solution is at the same duration as the previous one but is more expensive. You have reached the full compression point of the project.

Understanding the Project

The series of compressed project solutions allows you to better model the project and to understand how it behaves in the face of changes to its boundary conditions of time and cost. Often, it takes only two or three points left of the normal solution to understand how the project behaves. The more complex or expensive the project, the more you should invest in understanding the project, because even minute mistakes have drastic implications.

10

RISK

As demonstrated in Chapter 9, every project always has several design options that offer different combinations of time and cost. Some of these options will likely be more aggressive or riskier than other options. In essence, each project design option is a point in a three-dimensional space whose axes are time, cost, and risk. Decision makers should be able to take the risk into account when choosing a project design option—in fact, they must be able to do so. When you design a project, you must be able to quantify the risk of the options.

Most people recognize the risk axis but tend to ignore it since they cannot measure or quantify it. This invariably leads to poor results caused by applying a two-dimensional model (time and cost) to a three-dimensional problem (time, cost, and risk). This chapter explores how to measure risk objectively and easily using a few modeling techniques. You will see how risk interacts with time and cost, how to reduce the risk of the project, and how to find the optimal design point for the project.

> **Note** Risk calculation involves simple math. To automate the algebra and avoid error-prone manual calculations, the support files accompanying this book contain examples in spreadsheet form that perform the risk calculations.

CHOOSING OPTIONS

The ultimate objective of risk modeling is to weigh project design options in light of risk as well as time and cost so as to evaluate the feasibility of these options. In general, risk is the best criterion for choosing between options.

For example, consider two options for the same project: The first option calls for 12 months and 6 developers, and the second option calls for 18 months and 4 developers. If this is all that you know about the two options, most people will choose the first option since both options end up costing the same (6 man-years) and the first option delivers much faster (provided you have the cash flow to afford it). Now suppose you know the first option has only a 15% chance of success and the second option has a 70% chance of success. Which option would you choose? As an even more extreme example, suppose the second option calls for 24 months and 6 developers with the same 70% chance of success. Although the second option now costs twice as much and takes twice as long, most people will intuitively choose that option. This is a simple demonstration that often people choose an option based on risk, rather than based on time and cost.

PROSPECT THEORY

In 1979, the psychologists Daniel Kahneman and Amos Tversky developed prospect theory,[a] one of the most important concepts in behavioral psychology on decision making. Kahneman and Tversky discovered that people make decisions based on the risk involved as opposed to the expected gain. Given a measurable identical loss or gain, most people disproportionally suffer more for the loss than they would enjoy for the same gain. As a result people seek to reduce the risk as opposed to maximize gains, even when it would logically be better to take the risk. This observation went against conventional wisdom that held that people act rationally to maximize their gains based on expected value. Prospect theory underscores the importance of adding risk to time and cost in the decision-making process. In 2002, Daniel Kahneman won the Nobel Memorial Prize in Economics for his work developing prospect theory.

a. Daniel Kahneman and Amos Tversky, "Prospect Theory: An Analysis of Decision under Risk," *Econometrica*, 47, no. 2 (March 1979): 263–292.

TIME–RISK CURVE

Just as the project has a time–cost curve, it also has a time–risk curve. The ideal curve is shown in Figure 10-1 by the dashed line.

As you compress the project, the shorter project design solutions carry with them an increased level of risk, and the rate of increase is likely nonlinear. This is why the dashed line in Figure 10-1 curves up toward the vertical risk axis and relaxes downward with time. However, this intuitive dashed line is wrong. In reality, a time–risk curve is a logistic function of some kind, the solid line in Figure 10-1.

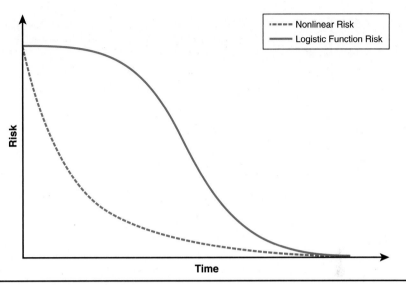

Figure 10-1 Ideal time–risk curves

The logistic function is a superior model because it more closely captures the general behavior of risk in complex systems. For example, if I were to plot the risk of me burning dinner tonight due to compressing the normal preparation time, the risk curve would look like the solid line in Figure 10-1. Each compression technique—such as setting the oven temperature too high, placing the tray too close to the heating element, choosing easier-to-cook but more flammable food, not preheating the oven, and so on—increases the risk of burning dinner. As shown by the solid line, the risk of a burnt dinner due to the cumulative compression at some point is almost maximized and even flattens out, because dinner is certain to burn. Similarly, if I decide not to even enter the kitchen, then the risk would drop precipitously. If the risk was dictated by the dashed line, I would always have some chance of not burning dinner since I could always keep increasing the risk by compressing it further.

Note that the logistic function has a tipping point where the risk drastically increases (the analog to the decision to enter the kitchen). The dashed line, by contrast, keeps increasing gradually and does not have a noticeable tipping point.

ACTUAL TIME–RISK CURVE

It turns out that even the logistic function in Figure 10-1 is still an idealized time–risk curve. The actual time–risk curve is more like that shown in Figure 10-2. The reason for the shape of this curve is best explained by overlaying it with the project's direct cost curve. Since the project behavior is three-dimensional, Figure 10-2 relies on a secondary *y*-axis for the risk.

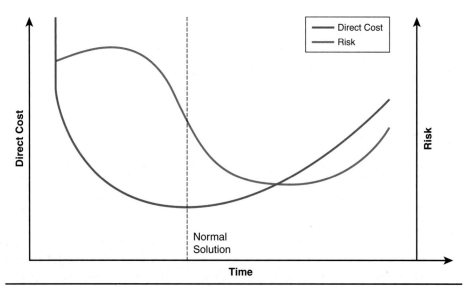

Figure 10-2 Actual time–cost–risk curve

The vertical dashed line in Figure 10-2 indicates the duration of the normal solution as well as the minimum direct cost solution for the project. Note that the normal solution usually trades some amount of float to reduce staffing. The reduction in float manifests in an elevated level of risk.

To the left of the normal solution are the shorter, compressed solutions. The compressed solutions are also riskier, so the risk curve increases to the left of the normal solution. The risk rises and then levels off (as is the case with the ideal logistic function). However, unlike the ideal behavior, the actual risk curve gets maximized before the point of minimum duration and even drops a bit, giving it a concave shape. While such behavior is counterintuitive, it occurs because in general, shorter projects are somewhat safer, a phenomenon I call the **da Vinci effect**. When investigating the tensile strength of wires, Leonardo da Vinci found that shorter wires are stronger than longer wires (it is because the probability of a defect is proportional to the length of the wire).[1] In analogy, the same is true for projects. To illustrate the point, consider two possible ways of delivering a 10-man-year project: 1 person for 10 years or 3650 people for 1 day. Assuming both are viable projects (that the people are available, that you have the time, and so on), the 1-day project is much safer than the 10-year project. The likelihood of something bad happening in a single day is

---

1. William B. Parsons, *Engineers and Engineering in the Renaissance* (Cambridge, MA: MIT Press, 1939); Jay R. Lund and Joseph P. Byrne, *Leonardo da Vinci's Tensile Strength Tests: Implications for the Discovery of Engineering Mechanics* (Department of Civil and Environmental Engineering, University of California, Davis, July 2000).

open for debate, but it is a near certainty with 10 years. I provide a more quantified explanation for this behavior later in this chapter.

To the right of the normal solution, the risk goes down, at least initially. For example, giving an extra week to a one-year project will reduce the risk of not meeting that commitment. However, if you keep giving the project more time, at some point Parkinson's law will take effect and drastically increase the risk. So, to the right of the normal solution, the risk curve goes down, becomes minimized at some value greater than zero, and then starts climbing again, giving it a convex shape.

RISK MODELING

This chapter presents my techniques for modeling and quantifying risk. These models complement each other in how they measure the risk. You often need more than one model to help you choose between options—no model is ever perfect. However, each of the risk models should yield comparable results.

Risk values are always relative. For example, jumping off a fast-moving train is risky. However, if that train is about to go over a cliff, jumping is the most sensible thing to do. Risk has no absolute value, so you can evaluate it only in comparison with other alternatives. You should therefore talk about a "riskier" project as opposed to a "risky" project. Similarly, nothing is really safe. The only safe way of doing any project is not doing it. You should therefore talk about a "safer" project rather than a "safe" project.

NORMALIZING RISK

The whole point of evaluating risk is to be able to compare options and projects, which requires comparing numbers. The first decision I made when creating the models was to normalize risk to the numerical range of 0 to 1.

A risk value of 0 does not mean that the project is risk-free. A risk value of 0 means that you have minimized the risk of the project. Similarly, a risk value of 1 does not mean that the project is guaranteed to fail, but simply that you have maximized the risk of the project.

The risk value also does not indicate a probability of success. With probability, a value of 1 means a certainty, and a value of 0 means an impossibility. A project with a risk value of 1 can still deliver, and a project with a risk value of 0 can still fail.

RISK AND FLOATS

The floats of the various activities in the network provide an objective way of measuring the risk of the project, and the previous chapters have referred to floats when discussing risk. Two different project design options will differ in their floats and, therefore, may drastically differ in their risk as well. As an example, consider the two project design options shown in Figure 10-3.

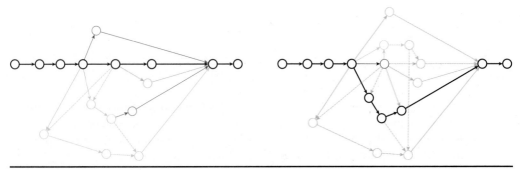

Figure 10-3 Two project options

Both of these options are valid project design options for building the same system. The only information available in Figure 10-3 is the color-coded floats of the two networks. Now, ask yourself: With which project would you rather be involved? Everyone to whom I have shown these two charts preferred the greener option on the right-hand side of Figure 10-3. What is interesting is that no one has ever asked what the difference in duration and cost between these two options was. Even when I volunteered that the greener option was both 30% longer and more expensive, that information did not affect the preference. No one chose the low-float, high-stress, and high-risk project shown on the left in Figure 10-3.

Design Risk

Your project faces multiple types of risk. There is staffing risk (Will the project actually gets the level of staffing it requires?). There is duration risk (Will the project be allowed the duration it requires?). There is technological risk (Will the technology be able to deliver?). There are human factors (Is the team technically competent and can they work together?). There is always an execution risk (Can the project manager execute correctly the project plan?).

These types of risk are independent of the kind of risk you assess using floats. Any project design solution always assumes that the organization or the team will have what it takes to deliver on the planned schedule and cost and that the project will receive the required time and resources. The remaining type of risk pertains to how well the project will handle the unforeseen. I call this kind of risk **design risk**.

Design risk assesses the project's sensitivity to schedule slips of activities and to your ability to meet your commitments. Design risk therefore quantifies the fragility of the project or the degree to which the project resembles a house of cards. Using floats to measure risk is actually quantifying that design risk.

RISK AND DIRECT COST

The project risk measurements usually correlate to the direct cost and duration of the various solutions. In most projects, the indirect cost is independent of the project risk. The indirect cost keeps mounting with the duration of the project even if the risk is very low. Therefore, this chapter refers to only direct cost.

CRITICALITY RISK

The **criticality risk** model attempts to quantify the intuitive impression of risk when you evaluate the options of Figure 10-3. For this risk model you classify activities in the project into four risk categories, from most to least risk:

- **Critical activities.** The critical activities are obviously the riskiest activities because any delay with a critical activity always causes schedule and cost overruns.
- **High risk activities.** Low float, near-critical activities are also risky because any delay in them is likely to cause schedule and cost overruns.
- **Medium risk activities.** Activities with a medium level of float have medium level of risk and can sustain some delays.
- **Low risk activities.** Activities with high floats are the least risky and can sustain even large delays without derailing the project.

You should exclude activities of zero duration (such as milestones and dummies) from this analysis because they add nothing to the risk of the project. Moreover, unlike real activities, they are simply artifacts of the project network.

Chapter 8 showed how to use color coding to classify activities based on their float. You can use the same technique for evaluating the sensitivity or fragility of activities by color coding the four risk categories. With the color coding in place, assign a weight to the criticality of each activity. The weight acts as a risk factor. You are, of course, at liberty to choose any weights that signify the difference in risk. One possible allocation of weights is shown in Table 10-1.

Table 10-1 Criticality risk weights

Activity Color	Weight
Black (critical)	4
Red (high risk)	3
Yellow (medium risk)	2
Green (low risk)	1

The criticality risk formula is:

$$\text{Risk} = \frac{W_C{}^*N_C + W_R{}^*N_R + W_Y{}^*N_Y + W_G{}^*N_G}{W_C{}^*N}$$

where:

- W_C is the weight of the black, critical activities.
- W_R is the weight of red, low-float activities.
- W_Y is the weight of yellow, medium-float activities.
- W_G is the weight of green, high-float activities.
- N_C is the number of the black, critical activities.
- N_R is the number of red, low-float activities.
- N_Y is the number of yellow, medium-float activities.
- N_G is the number of green, high-float activities.
- N is the number of activities in the project ($N = N_C + N_R + N_Y + N_G$).

Substituting the weights from Table 10-1, the criticality risk formula is:

$$\text{Risk} = \frac{4{}^*N_C + 3{}^*N_R + 2{}^*N_Y + 1{}^*N_G}{4{}^*N}$$

Applying the criticality risk formula to the network in Figure 10-4 yields:

$$\text{Risk} = \frac{4{}^*6 + 3{}^*4 + 2{}^*2 + 1{}^*4}{4{}^*16} = 0.69$$

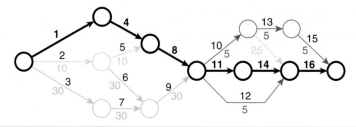

Figure 10-4 Sample network for risk calculation

Criticality Risk Values

The maximum value of the criticality risk is 1.0; it occurs when all activities in the network are critical. In such a network, N_R, N_Y, and N_G are zero, and N_C equals N:

$$\text{Risk} = \frac{W_C{}^*N + W_R{}^*0 + W_Y{}^*0 + W_G{}^*0}{W_C{}^*N} = \frac{W_C}{W_C} = 1.0$$

The minimum value of the criticality risk is W_G over W_C; it occurs when all activities in the network are green. In such a network, N_C, N_R, and N_Y are zero, and N_G equals N:

$$\text{Risk} = \frac{W_C{}^*0 + W_R{}^*0 + W_Y{}^*0 + W_G{}^*N}{W_C{}^*N} = \frac{W_G}{W_C}$$

Using the weights from Table 10-1, the minimum value of risk is 0.25. The criticality risk, therefore, can never be zero: A weighted average such as this will always have a minimum value greater than zero as long as the weights themselves are greater than zero. This is not necessarily a bad thing, as the project risk should never be zero. The formula implies the lowest range of risk values is too low to achieve, which is reasonable since anything worth doing requires risk.

Choosing Weights

As long as you can rationalize your choice of weights, the criticality risk model will likely work. For example, the set of weights [21, 22, 23, 24] is a poor choice because 21 is only 14% smaller than 24; thus, this set does not emphasize the risk of the green versus the critical activities. Furthermore, the minimum risk using these weights (W_g/W_c) is 0.88, which is obviously too high. I find the weights set [1, 2, 3, 4] to be as good as any other sensible choice.

Customizing Criticality Risk

The criticality risk model often requires some customization and judgment calls. First, as mentioned in Chapter 8, the ranges of the various colors (the criteria for red, yellow, and green activities) must be appropriate for the duration of your project. Second, you should consider defining very-low-float or near-critical activities (such as those with 1 day of float) as critical because these basically have the same risk as critical activities. Third, even if some activities' floats are not near-critical, you should examine the chain on which the activities reside and adjust it accordingly. For example, if you have a year-long chain of many activities and the chain has only 10 days of float, you should classify each activity on the chain as a critical activity for risk calculation. A slip with one activity up that chain will consume all float, turning all downstream activities into critical activities.

FIBONACCI RISK

The Fibonacci series is a sequence of numbers in which every item in the series equals the sum of the previous two, with the exception that the first two values are defined as 1.

$$\text{Fib}_n = \text{Fib}_{n\text{-}1} + \text{Fib}_{n\text{-}2}$$
$$\text{Fib}_2 = \text{Fib}_1 = 1$$

This recursive definition yields the series of 1, 1, 2, 3, 5, 8, 13, ….

The ratio between two (sufficiently large) consecutive Fibonacci numbers is an irrational number known as phi (the Greek letter φ), whose value is 1.618…, and the series is expressed as:

$$\text{Fib}_i = \varphi * \text{Fib}_{i\text{-}1}$$

Since ancient times, φ has been known as the golden ratio. It is observed throughout nature and human enterprises alike. Two famous (and quite disparate) examples based on the golden ratio are the way the invertebrate nautilus's shell spirals and the way markets retrace their former price levels.

Notice that the weights in Table 10-1 are similar to the beginning values of the Fibonacci series. As an alternative to Table 10-1, you can choose any four consecutive members from the Fibonacci series (such as [89, 144, 233, 377]) as weights. Regardless of your choice, when you use them to evaluate the network in

Figure 10-4, the risk will always be 0.64 because the weights maintain the ratio of φ. If W_G is the weight of the green activities, the other weights are:

$$W_Y = \varphi {}^* W_G$$
$$W_R = \varphi^2 {}^* W_G$$
$$W_C = \varphi^3 {}^* W_G$$

and the criticality risk formula can be written as:

$$\text{Risk} = \frac{\varphi^3 {}^* W_G {}^* N_C + \varphi^2 {}^* W_G {}^* N_R + \varphi {}^* W_G {}^* N_Y + W_G {}^* N_G}{\varphi^3 {}^* W_G {}^* N}$$

Since W_G appears in all elements of the numerator and the denominator, the equation can be simplified:

$$\text{Risk} = \frac{\varphi^3 {}^* N_C + \varphi^2 {}^* N_R + \varphi {}^* N_Y + N_G}{\varphi^3 {}^* N}$$

Approximating the value of φ, the formula is reduced to:

$$\text{Risk} = \frac{4.24 {}^* N_C + 2.62 {}^* N_R + 1.62 {}^* N_Y + N_G}{4.24 {}^* N}$$

I call this risk model the **Fibonacci risk** model.

Fibonacci Risk Values

The maximum value that the Fibonacci risk formula can reach is 1.0 in an all-critical network. The minimum value that it can reach is 0.24 (1/4.24), slightly less than the minimum criticality risk model value of 0.25 (when using the set [1, 2, 3, 4] for weights). This supports the notion that risk has a natural lower limit of about 0.25.

ACTIVITY RISK

The criticality risk model uses broad risk categories. For example, if you define float greater than 25 days as green, then two activities—one with 30 days of float and the other with 60 days of float—will be placed in the same green bin and will have the same risk value. To better account for the risk contribution of each individual activity, I created the **activity risk** model. This model is a far more discrete than the criticality risk model.

The activity risk formula is:

$$\text{Risk} = 1 - \frac{F_1 + \ldots + F_i + \ldots + F_N}{M^*N} = 1 - \frac{\sum_{i=1}^{N} F_i}{M^*N}$$

where:

- F_i is the float of activity i.
- N is the number of activities in the project.
- M is the maximum float of any activity in the project or $\text{Max}(F_1, F_2, \ldots, F_N)$.

As with the criticality risk, you should exclude activities of zero duration (milestones and dummies) from this analysis.

Applying the activity risk formula to the network in Figure 10-4 yields:

$$\text{Risk} = 1 - \frac{30 + 30 + 30 + 30 + 10 + 10 + 5 + 5 + 5 + 5}{30^*16} = 0.67$$

Activity Risk Values

The activity risk model is undefined when all activities are critical. However, at the limit, given a large network (large N) that includes only one noncritical activity with float M, the model approaches 1.0:

$$\text{Risk} \approx 1 - \frac{F_1}{M^*N} = 1 - \frac{M}{M^*N} = 1 - \frac{1}{N} \approx 1 - 0 = 1.0$$

The minimum value of the activity risk is 0 when all activities in the network have the same level of float, M:

$$\text{Risk} = 1 - \frac{\sum_{i=1}^{N} M}{M^*N} = 1 - \frac{M^*N}{M^*N} = 1 - 1 = 0$$

While activity risk can in theory reach zero, in practice it is unlikely that you will encounter such a project because all projects always have some non-zero amount of risk.

Calculation Pitfall

The activity risk model works well only when the floats of the projects are more or less uniformly spread between the smallest float and the largest float in the network. An outlier float value that is significantly higher than all other floats will skew the calculation, producing an incorrectly high-risk value. For example, consider a one-year project that has a single week-long activity that can take place anywhere between the beginning and the end of the project. Such an activity will have almost a year's worth of float, as illustrated in the network in Figure 10-5.

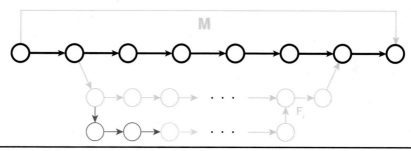

Figure 10-5 Network with outlier high float activity

Figure 10-5 shows the critical path (bold black) and many activities with some color-coded level of float (F_i) below. The activity shown above the critical path itself is short but has an enormous amount of float M.

Since M is much larger than any other F_i, the activity risk formula yields a number approaching 1:

$$M \gg F_i$$

$$\text{Risk} = 1 - \frac{\sum_{i=1}^{N} F_i}{M*N} \approx 1 - \frac{F_i*N}{M*N} \approx 1 - \frac{F_i}{M} \approx 1 - 0 = 1.0$$

The next chapter demonstrates this situation and provides an easy and effective way of detecting and adjusting the float outliers.

The activity risk also produces an incorrectly low activity risk value when the project does not have many activities and the floats of the noncritical activities are all of similar or even have identical value. However, except for these rare, somewhat contrived examples, the activity risk model measures the risk correctly.

CRITICALITY VERSUS ACTIVITY RISK

For decent-size real-life projects, the criticality and activity risk models yield very similar results. Each model has pros and cons. In general, criticality risk reflects human intuition better, while activity risk is more attuned to the differences between individual activities. Criticality risk modeling often requires calibration or judgment calls, but it is indifferent to how uniformly the floats are spread. Activity risk is sensitive to the presence of large outlier floats, but it is easy to calculate and does not require much calibration. You can even automate the adjustment of float outliers.

> **Note**   When the activity risk and the criticality risk differ greatly, you should determine the root cause. Perhaps the calibration of the criticality risk was incorrect or the activity risk is skewed because the floats are not spread uniformly. If nothing stands out, you may want to use the Fibonacci risk model as the arbitrating risk model.

COMPRESSION AND RISK

As discussed previously, risk decreases slightly with high compression, reflecting the intuitive observation that shorter projects are safer. Quantified risk modeling offers an explanation for this phenomenon. The only practical way of highly compressing a software project is to introduce parallel wor0k. Chapter 9 listed several ideas for engaging in parallel work, such as splitting activities and performing the less-dependent phases in parallel to other activities or introducing additional activities that enable the parallel work. Figure 10-6 shows this effect in a qualitative manner.

Figure 10-6 depicts two networks, with the bottom diagram being the compressed version of the top diagram. The compressed solution has fewer critical activities, a shorter critical path, and more noncritical activities in parallel. When measuring the risk of such compressed projects, the presence of more of activities with float and fewer critical activities will decrease the risk value produced by both the criticality and activity risk models.

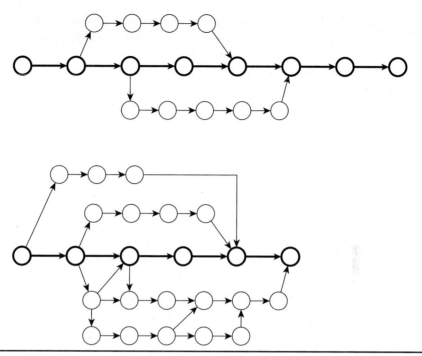

Figure 10-6 High compression makes the network more parallel

EXECUTION RISK

While the design risk of a highly parallel project may be lower than the design risk of a less compressed solution, such a project is more challenging to execute because of the additional dependencies and the increased number of activities that need to be scheduled and tracked. Such a project will have demanding scheduling constraints and require a larger team. In essence, a highly compressed project has converted design risk into execution risk. You should measure the execution risk as well as the design risk. A good proxy for the expected execution risk is the complexity of the network. Chapter 12 discusses how to quantify execution complexity.

RISK DECOMPRESSION

While compressing the project is likely to increase the risk, the opposite is also true (up to a point): By relaxing the project, you can decrease its risk. I call this technique **risk decompression**. You deliberately design the project for a later delivery date by introducing float along the critical path. Risk decompression is the best way to reduce the project's fragility, its sensitivity to the unforeseen.

You should decompress the project when the available solutions are too risky. Other reasons for decompressing the project include concerns about the present prospects based on a poor past track record, facing too many unknowns, or a volatile environment that keeps changing its priorities and resources.

As discussed in Chapter 7, a classic mistake when trying to reduce risk is to pad estimations. This will actually make matters worse and decrease the probability of success. The whole point of decompression is to keep the original estimations unchanged and instead increase the float along all network paths.

At the same time, you should not over-decompress. Using the risk models, you can measure the effect of the decompression and stop when you reach your decompression target (discussed later in this section). Excessive decompression will have diminishing returns when all activities have high float. Any additional decompression beyond this point will not reduce the design risk, but will increase the overall overestimation risk and waste time.

You can decompress any project design solution, although you typically decompress only the normal solution. Decompression pushes the project a bit into the uneconomical zone (see Figure 10-2), increasing the project's time and cost. When you decompress a project design solution, you still design it with the original staffing. Do not be tempted to consume the additional decompression float and reduce the staff—that defeats the purpose of risk decompression in the first place.

How to Decompress

A straightforward way of decompressing the project is to push the last activity or the last event in the project down the timeline. This adds float to all prior activities in the network. In the case of the network depicted in Figure 10-4, decompressing activity 16 by 10 days results in a criticality risk of 0.47 and an activity risk of 0.52. Decompressing activity 16 by 30 days results in a criticality risk of 0.3 and an activity risk of 0.36.

A more sophisticated technique is to also decompress one or two key activities along the critical path, such as activity 8 in Figure 10-4. In general, the further down the network you decompress, the more you need to decompress because any slip in an upstream activity can consume the float of the downstream activities. The earlier in the network you decompress, the less likely it is that all of the float you have introduced will be consumed.

DECOMPRESSION TARGET

When decompressing a project, you should strive to decompress until the risk drops to 0.5. Figure 10-7 demonstrates this point on the ideal risk curve using a logistic function with asymptotes at 1 and 0.

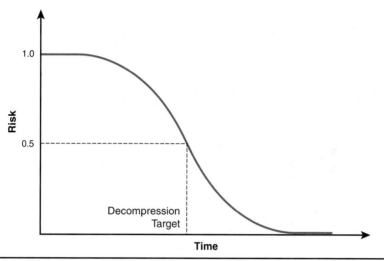

Figure 10-7 The decompression target on the ideal risk curve

When the project has a very short duration, the value of risk is almost 1.0, and the risk is maximized. At that point the risk curve is almost flat. Initially, adding time to the project does not reduce the risk by much. With more time, at some point the risk curve starts descending, and the more time you give the project, the steeper the curve gets. However, with even more time, the risk curve starts leveling off, offering less reduction in risk for additional time. The point at which the risk curve is the steepest is the point with the best return on the decompression—that is, the most reduction in risk for the least amount of decompression. This point defines the risk **decompression target**. Since the logistic function in Figure 10-7 is a symmetric curve between 0 and 1, the tipping point is at a risk value of exactly 0.5.

To determine how the decompression target relates to cost, compare the actual risk curve with the direct cost curve (Figure 10-8). The actual risk curve is confined to a narrower range than the ideal risk curve and never approaches either 0 or 1, although it behaves similarly to a logistic function between its maximum and minimum values. As discussed at the beginning of this chapter, the steepest point of the risk curve (where concave becomes convex) is at minimum direct cost, which coincides with the decompression target (Figure 10-8).

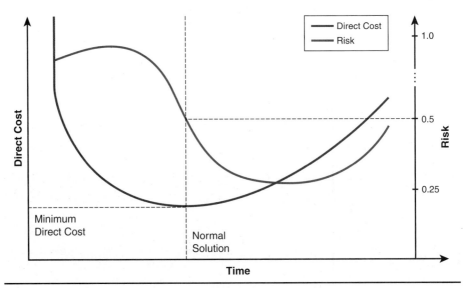

Figure 10-8 Minimum direct cost coincides with risk at 0.5

Since the risk keeps descending to the right of 0.5, you can think of 0.5 as a minimum decompression target. Again, you should monitor the behavior of the risk curve and not over-decompress.

If the minimum direct cost point of the project is also the best point risk-wise, this makes it the optimal design point for the project, offering the least direct cost at the best risk. This point is neither too risky nor too safe, benefiting as much as possible from adding time to the project.

> **Note** In theory, the minimum direct cost point of the project coincides with the normal solution and the steepest point on the risk curve. In practice, that is rarely the case because the model is fundamentally a discrete model, and you usually make concessions for reality. Your normal solution may be close to the minimum point of direct cost, but not exactly at it. This means you often have to decompress the normal solution to the tipping point of the risk curve.

RISK METRICS

To end this chapter, here are a few easy-to-remember metrics and rules of thumb. As is the case with every design metric, you should use them as guidelines. A violation of the metrics is a red flag, and you should always investigate its cause.

- **Keep risk between 0.3 and 0.75.** Your project should never have extreme risk values. Obviously, a risk value of 0 or 1.0 is nonsensical. The risk should not be too low: Since the criticality risk model cannot go below 0.25, you can round the lower possible limit of 0.25 up to 0.3 as the lower bound for any project. When compressing the project, long before the risk gets to 1.0 (a fully critical project), you should stop compressing. Even a risk value of 0.9 or 0.85 is still high. If the bottom quarter of 0 to 0.25 is disallowed, then for symmetry's sake you should avoid the top quarter of risk values between 0.75 and 1.0.

- **Decompress to 0.5.** The ideal decompression target is a risk of 0.5, as it targets the tipping point in the risk curve.

- **Do not over-decompress.** As discussed, decompression beyond the decompression target has dismissing returns, and over-decompression increases the risk.

- **Keep normal solutions under 0.7.** While elevated risk may be the price you pay for a compressed solution, it is inadvisable for a normal solution. Returning to the symmetry argument, if risk of 0.3 is the lower bound for all solutions, then risk of 0.7 is the upper bound for a normal solution. You should always decompress high-risk normal solutions.

You should make both risk modeling and risk metrics part of your project design. Constantly measure the risk to see where you are and where you are heading.

11

PROJECT DESIGN IN ACTION

The difficulty facing many project design novices is not the specific design techniques and concepts, but rather the end-to-end flow of the design process. It is also easy to get mired in the details and to lose sight of the objective of the design effort. Without experience, you may be stumped when you encounter the first snag or situation that does not behave as prescribed. It is impractical to try to cover all possible contingencies and responses. Instead, it is better to master the thought process involved in project design.

This chapter demonstrates the thought process and the mindset via a comprehensive walkthrough of the design effort. The emphasis is on the systematic examination of the steps and iterations. You will see observations and rules of thumb, how to alternate between project design options, how to home in on what makes sense, and how to evaluate tradeoffs. As this chapter evolves, it demonstrates ideas from the previous chapters as well as the synergy gained by combining project design techniques. It also covers additional aspects of project design such as planning assumptions, complexity reduction, staffing and scheduling, accommodating constraints, compression, and risk and planning. As such, the objective of this chapter is teaching project design flow and techniques, as opposed to providing a real-life example.

THE MISSION

Your mission is to design a project to build a typical business system. This system was designed using *The Method*, but that fact is immaterial in this chapter. In general, the input to the project design effort should include the following ingredients:

- **The static architecture.** You use the static architecture to create the initial list of coding activities.
- **Call chains or sequence diagrams.** You produce the call chains or sequence diagrams by examining the use cases and how they propagate through the system. These provide the rough cut of structural activity dependencies.

- **List of activities.** You list all activities, coding and noncoding alike.
- **Duration estimation.** For each activity, you accurately estimate the duration (and resources) involved (or work with others to do so).
- **Planning assumptions.** You capture the assumptions you have about staffing, availability, ramp-up time, technology, quality, and so on. You typically will have several such sets of assumptions, with each set resulting in a different project design solution.
- **Some constraints.** You write down all the explicitly known constraints. You should also include possible or likely constraints, and plan accordingly. You will see multiple examples in this chapter for handling constraints.

THE STATIC ARCHITECTURE

Figure 11-1 shows the static architecture of the system. As you can tell, the system is fairly limited in size. It includes two *Clients*, five business logic components, three *ResourceAccess* components, two *Resources*, and three *Utilities*.

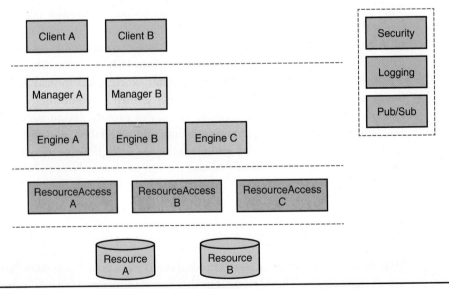

Figure 11-1 The system static architecture

While the system in Figure 11-1 was inspired by a real system, the merits of this particular architecture are irrelevant in this chapter. When designing the project, you should avoid turning the project design effort into a system design review. Even poor architectures should have adequate project design to maximize the chance of meeting your commitments.

THE CALL CHAINS

The system has only two core use cases and two call chains. The first call chain, shown in Figure 11-2, concludes with publishing an event. The second call chain in Figure 11-3, depicts the processing of that event by the subscribers.

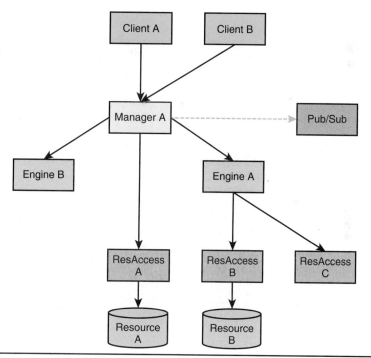

Figure 11-2 Call chain 1

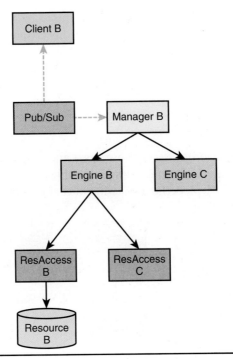

Figure 11-3 Call chain 2

Dependency Chart

You should examine the call chains, and lay out a first draft of the dependencies between components in the architecture. You start with all the arrows connecting components, regardless of transport or connectivity, and consider each as a dependency. You should account for any dependency exactly once. However, typically the call chain diagrams do not show the full picture because they often omit repeated implicit dependencies. In this case, all components of the architecture (except the *Resources*) depend on Logging, and the *Clients* and *Managers* depend on the Security component. Armed with that additional information, you can draw the dependency chart shown in Figure 11-4.

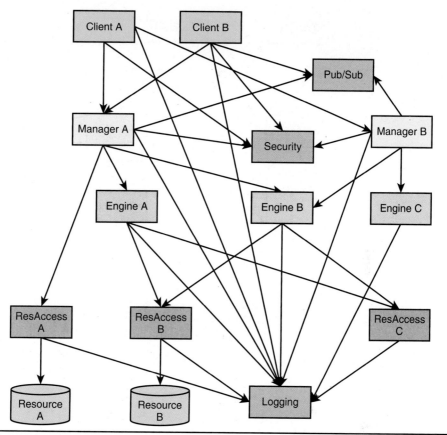

Figure 11-4 Initial dependency chart

As you can see, even with a simple system having only two use cases, the dependency chart is cluttered and hard to analyze. A simple technique you can leverage to reduce the complexity is to eliminate dependencies that duplicate **inherited dependencies**. Inherited dependencies are due to transitive dependencies[1]—those dependencies that an activity implicitly inherits by depending on other activities. In Figure 11-4, Client A depends on Manager A and Security; Manager A also depends on Security. This means you can omit the dependency between Client A and Security. Using inherited dependencies, you can reduce Figure 11-4 to Figure 11-5.

---

1. https://en.wikipedia.org/wiki/Transitive_dependency

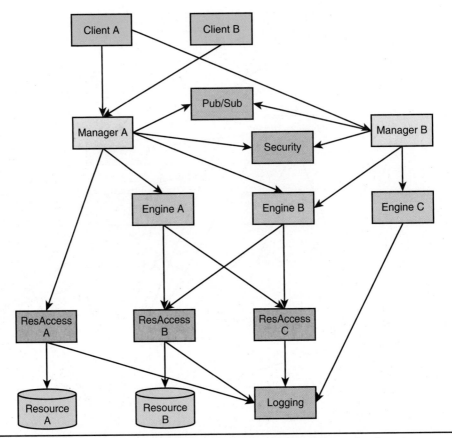

Figure 11-5 Dependency chart after consolidating inherited dependencies

LIST OF ACTIVITIES

While Figure 11-5 is certainly simpler than Figure 11-4, it is still inadequate because it is highly structural in nature, showing only the coding activities. You must compile a comprehensive list of all activities in the project. In this case, the list of noncoding activities includes additional work on requirements, architecture (such as technology verification or a demo service), project design, test plan, test harness, and system testing. Table 11-1 lists all activities in the project, their duration estimation, and their dependencies on preceding activities.

Table 11-1 Activities, duration, and dependencies

ID	Activity	Duration (days)	Depends On
1	Requirements	15	
2	Architecture	20	1
3	Project Design	20	2
4	Test Plan	30	3
5	Test Harness	35	4
6	Logging	15	3
7	Security	20	3
8	Pub/Sub	5	3
9	Resource A	20	3
10	Resource B	15	3
11	ResourceAccess A	10	6,9
12	ResourceAccess B	5	6,10
13	ResourceAccess C	15	6
14	Engine A	20	12,13
15	Engine B	25	12,13
16	Engine C	15	6
17	Manager A	20	7,8,11,14,15
18	Manager B	25	7,8,15,16
19	Client App1	25	17,18
20	Client App2	35	17
21	System Testing	30	5,19,20

NETWORK DIAGRAM

With the list of activities and dependencies at hand, you can draw the project network as an arrow diagram. Figure 11-6 shows the initial network diagram. The numbers in this figure correspond to the activity IDs in Table 11-1. The bold lines and numbers indicate the critical path.

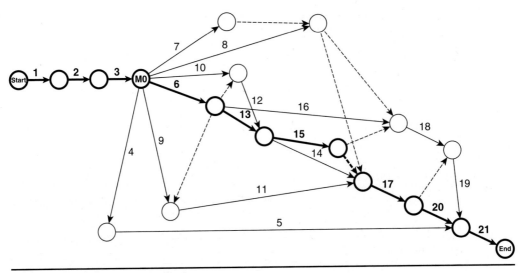

Figure 11-6 Initial network diagram

About Milestones

As defined in Chapter 8, a milestone is an event in the project denoting the completion of a significant part of the project, including major integration achievements. Even at this early stage in the project design, you should designate the event completing Project Design (activity 3) as the SDP review milestone, M0. In this case, M0 is the completion of the front end (short for fuzzy front end) of the project, comprising requirements, architecture, and project design. This makes the SDP review an explicit part of the plan. You can have milestones on or off the critical path, and they can be public or private. Public milestones demonstrate progress for management and customers, while private milestones are internal hurdles for the team. If a milestone is outside the critical path, it is a good idea to keep it private since it could move as a result of a delay somewhere upstream from it. On the critical path, milestones can be both private and public, and they correlate directly with meeting the commitments of the project in terms of both time and cost. Another use for milestones is to force a dependency even if the call chains do not specify such a dependency. The SDP review is such a milestone—none of the construction activities should start before the SDP review. Such forced-dependency milestones also simplify the network, and you will see another example shortly.

Initial Duration

You can construct the network of activities listed in Table 11-1 in a project planning tool, which gives you a first look at project duration. Doing so gives a duration of 9.0 months for this project. However, without resource assignment, it is not yet possible to determine the cost of the project.

> **Note**   The support files accompanying this book contain Microsoft Project files and associated Excel spreadsheets for each permutation and iteration discussed in this chapter. The following text contains explanation and summary information only.

PLANNING ASSUMPTIONS

To proceed with the design, you itemize the planning assumptions, especially the planned staffing requirements, in a list such as the following:

- One project manager is required throughout the project.
- One product manager is required throughout the project.
- One architect is required throughout the project.
- One developer is required per service for any coding activity. Once that service is complete, the developer can move to another activity.
- One database architect is required for each of the *Resources*. This work is independent of the code development work and can be done in parallel.
- One tester is required from the start of construction of the system services until the end of testing.
- One additional tester is required during system testing.
- One test engineer is required for the test plan and test harness activities.
- One DevOps specialist is required from the start of construction until the end of testing.

This list is, in fact, the list of resources you need to complete the project. Also note the structure of the list: "one X for Y." If you cannot state the required staffing this way, you probably do not understand your own staffing requirements, or you are missing a key planning assumption.

You should explicitly make two additional planning assumptions about the developers regarding testing time and idle time. First, in this example project, developers will produce such high-quality work that they will not be needed during system testing. Second, developers between activities are considered a direct cost. Strictly speaking, idle time should be accounted for as an indirect cost because it is not associated with project activities, yet the project must pay for it. However, many project managers strive to assign idle developers some activities in support of other development activities, even if that means more than one developer is temporarily assigned per service. Under this planning assumption, you still account for developers between activities as direct cost.

Project Phases

Each activity in a project always belongs to a **phase**, or a type of activities. Typical phases include the front end, design, infrastructure, services, UI, testing, and deployment, among others. A phase may contain any number of activities, and the activities in a phase can overlap on the timeline. What is less obvious is that the phases are not sequential and can themselves overlap or even start and stop. The easiest way of laying out phases is to structure the planning assumptions list into a role/phase table; Table 11-2 provides an example.

Table 11-2 Roles and phases

Role	Front End	Infrastructure	Services	Testing
Architect	X	X	X	X
Project Manager	X	X	X	X
Product Manager	X	X	X	X
DevOps		X	X	X
Developers		X	X	
Testers			X	X

In much the same way, you could add other roles that are required for the duration of an entire phase, such as UX (user experience) or security experts. However, you should not include roles that are required only for specific activities, such as the test engineer.

Table 11-2 is a crude form of a staffing distribution view. The relationship between roles and phases is essential when building the staffing distribution chart because you must account for the use of all the resources, regardless of whether they are assigned to specific project activities. For example, in Table 11-2, an architect is required throughout the project. In turn, in the staffing distribution chart, you would show the architect across the duration of the project. In this way, you can account for all resources necessary to produce the correct staffing distribution chart and cost calculation.

> **Note** Rarely will someone hand you the planning assumptions on a silver platter, as is the case in this chapter. Some form of discovery, back-and-forth, and negotiation always takes place at the front end of the project as you try to distill your specific planning assumptions. You can even reverse this flow: Start with your take on the planning assumptions and staffing distributions, captured as suggested here, and then ask for feedback and comments.

FINDING THE NORMAL SOLUTION

With the list of activities, dependencies, and planning assumptions in hand, you proceed to iteratively find the normal solution. For the first pass, assume that you have unlimited resources at your disposal, but you will utilize only as many resources as required to progress unimpeded along the critical path. This provides the least constrained way of building the system at the lowest level of resources.

UNLIMITED RESOURCES (ITERATION 1)

Initially, also assume that you have unlimited staffing elasticity. You could make very minor (if any) adjustments for reality. For example, there is no point in hiring a person for a single week if you can trade some float and avoid any need for that resource. You assume that every special skill set is available when needed. These liberal assumptions should yield the same project duration as you had before assigning resources. Indeed, after staffing the project this way, the duration remains at 9.0 months and yields the planned earned value chart shown in Figure 11-7. This chart exhibits the general shape of a shallow S curve but it is not as smooth as it should be.

Following the process outlined in Chapter 7, Figure 11-8 shows the corresponding project staffing distribution chart. This plan uses as many as four developers and two database architects, uses one test engineer, and does not consume any float. The calculated project total cost is 58.3 man-months.

Recall from Chapter 9 that finding the normal solution is an iterative process (see Figure 9-8) simply because the lowest level of staffing is not known at the beginning of the design effort. Therefore, this first set of results is not yet the normal solution. In the next iteration you should accommodate reality, consume float to decrease staffing volatility, address any obvious design flaws, and reduce complexity if possible.

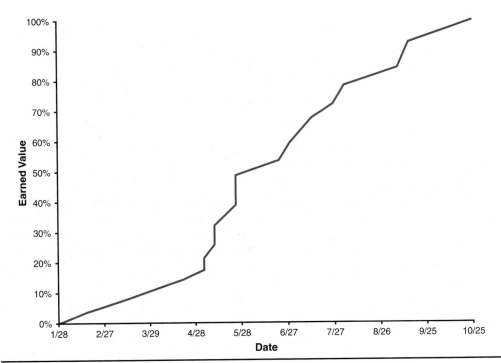

Figure 11-7 Planned earned value with unlimited resources

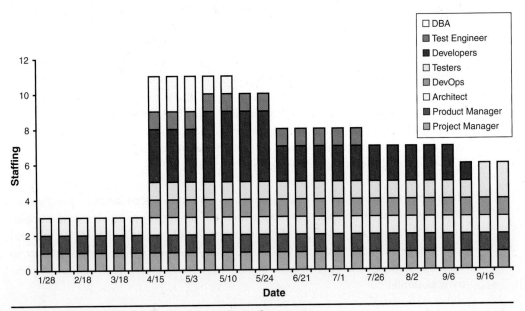

Figure 11-8 Staffing distribution with unlimited resources

NETWORK AND RESOURCE PROBLEMS

The first iteration on the normal solution suffers from several key problems. First, it assumes unlimited and readily available resources, including those with special skills. Clearly, resources are not limitless, and special skills are rare. Second, the planned staffing distribution chart (see Figure 11-8) displays a concerning sign (identified in Chapter 7)—namely, a high ramp coming into the project. You should expect this behavior due to the assumptions about staffing availability and elasticity. Third, over its duration, the project engages some resources only for short periods of time. This is asking for trouble as far as availability and necessary onboarding time. While you could plan to mitigate that by using subcontractors, you should not create problems that you need to solve. The staffing distribution should be smooth, and you should avoid high ramps and sharp drops. You should create other project variations that have some resource constraints and entertain a more realistic staffing elasticity. Often, this will also smooth both the staffing distribution and the planned earned value charts.

The last problem with the solution so far is the integration pressure on the *Manager* services. From Table 11-1 and the network diagram of Figure 11-6, you can see that the *Managers* (activities 17 and 18) are expected to integrate with four or five other services. Ideally, you should integrate only one or two services at a time. Integrating more than two services concurrently will likely result in a nonlinear increase in complexity because any issues across services will be superimposed on each other. The problem is further compounded because the integrations occur toward the end of the project, when you have little runway left to fix issues.

INFRASTRUCTURE FIRST (ITERATION 2)

A common technique to simplify the project is to move the infrastructure services (*Utilities* such as `Logging`, `Security`, and `Pub/Sub`, and any additional infrastructure activity such as build automation) to the beginning of the project, regardless of their natural dependencies in the network. In other words, immediately after M0, the developers will work on these infrastructure services. You can even introduce a milestone called M1 denoting when the infrastructure is complete, making all other services depend on M1, as shown in the subnetwork in Figure 11-9.

Completing the infrastructure first reduces the complexity in the network (decreases the number of dependencies and crossing lines) and alleviates the integration pressure at the *Managers*. Overriding the original dependencies in this way typically reduces the initial staffing demand because none of the other services can start until M1 is complete. It also reduces the staffing volatility and usually results in a smoother staffing distribution and a gradual ramp-up at the beginning of the project.

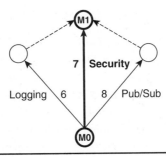

Figure 11-9 Infrastructure first

Another important advantage of developing the infrastructure first is the early access it provides to key infrastructure components. This allows developers to integrate their work with the infrastructure as they construct the system, rather than having to retrofit and test infrastructure services (such as Logging or Security) after the fact. Having the infrastructure services available before the business-related components (*ResourceAccess*, *Engines*, *Managers*, and *Clients*) is almost always an excellent idea, even if the need is not evident at first.

Developing the infrastructure first changes the initial staffing to three developers (one per service) until after M1, at which point the project can absorb a fourth developer (note you are still working on an staffing plan with unlimited resources). Repeating the prior steps, the infrastructure first plan extends the schedule by 3% to 9.2 months and incurs 2% of additional total cost, to 59 man-months. In exchange for the negligible additional cost and schedule, the project gains early access to key services and a simpler, more realistic plan. Going forward, this new project becomes the baseline for the next iteration.

LIMITED RESOURCES

The resources you ask for may not always be available when you need them, so it is prudent to plan for fewer resources (at least initially) to mitigate that risk. How will the project behave if three developers are unavailable at the beginning of the project? If no developers at all are available, the architect can develop the infrastructure, or the project can engage subcontractors: The infrastructure services do not require domain knowledge, so they are good candidates for such external and readily available resources. If only one developer is available at the beginning, then that single developer can do all infrastructure components serially. Perhaps only a single developer is available initially, and then a second developer can join in after the first activity is complete.

Infrastructure First with Limited Resources (Iteration 3)

Choosing the latter, somewhat middle-of-the-road scenario of one and then two developers, recalculate the infrastructure-first project to see how the project behaves with limited resources. Instead of three parallel activities (one critical) at the beginning, as shown in Figure 11-9, you now have one activity that is critical, then two activities in parallel (one critical). Serializing activities in this way increases the duration of the project. This variation extends the schedule by 8% to 9.9 months and increases the total cost by 4% to 61.5 man-months. Figure 11-10 shows the resulting staffing distribution chart. Note the gradual phasing in of the developers, from one, to two, to four.

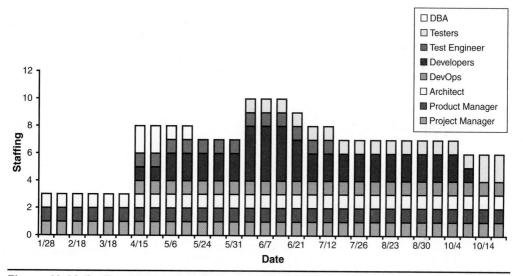

Figure 11-10 Staffing distribution of infrastructure-first with limited resources

Extending the critical path by limiting the resources also increases the float of the noncritical activities that span that section of the network. Compared with unlimited resources, the float of the Test Plan (activity 4 in Figure 11-6) and Test Harness (activity 5 in Figure 11-6) is increased by 30%, the float of Resource A (activity 9 in Figure 11-6) is increased by 50%, and the float of Resource B (activity 10 in Figure 11-6) is increased by 100%. This is noteworthy because a seemingly minute change in resource availability has increased the float dramatically. Be aware that this knife can cut both ways: Sometimes a seemingly innocuous change can cause the floats to collapse and derail the project.

No Database Architects (Iteration 4)

On top of limiting the initial availability of the developers, suppose the project did not get the database architects called for in the previous solutions. This is certainly a real-life scenario—such qualified resources are often hard to come by. In this case, developers design the databases to the best of their abilities. To see how the project responds to this new limit, instead of just adding developers, constrain the project to no more than four developers (allowing for more developers would be identical to having the database architects). Surprisingly, this does not change the duration and results with a total cost of 62.7 man-months, a mere 2% increase. The reason is that the same four developers start working earlier and do not even have to consume float.

Further Limited Resources (Iteration 5)

Since the project could easily cope with four developers, the next limited-resources plan caps the available developers at three. This also does not change the duration of the project because it is possible to trade the fourth developer for some float. As for cost, there is a 3% reduction in cost to 61.1 man-months due to the more efficient use of developers. Figure 11-11 shows the resulting staffing distribution chart.

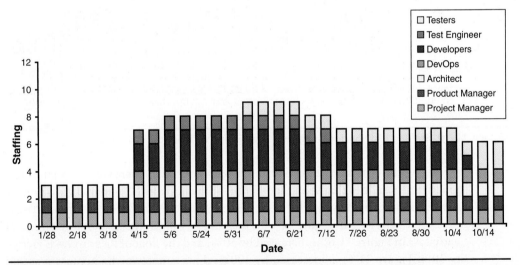

Figure 11-11 Staffing distribution with three developers and one test engineer

Note the use of the test engineer along with the three developers. Figure 11-11 is the best staffing distribution so far, looking very much like the expected pattern from Chapter 7 (see Figure 7-8).

Figure 11-12 shows the shallow S curve of the planned earned value. The figure shows a fairly smooth shallow S curve. If anything, the shallow S is almost too shallow. You will see the meaning of that later on.

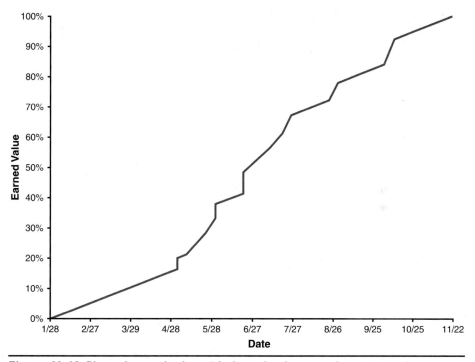

Figure 11-12 Planned earned value with three developers and one test engineer

Figure 11-13 shows the corresponding network diagram, using the absolute criticality float color-coding scheme described in Chapter 8. This example project uses 9 days as the upper limit for red activities and 26 days as the upper limit for the yellow activities. The activity IDs appear above the arrows in black, and the float values are shown below the line in the arrow's color. The test engineer's activities—that is, the Test Plan (activity 4) and the Test Harness (activity 5)—have a very high float of 65 days. Note the M0 milestone terminating the front end and the M1 milestone at the end of the infrastructure. The diagram also shows the phasing in of the resources between M0 and M1 to build the infrastructure (activities 6, 7, and 8).

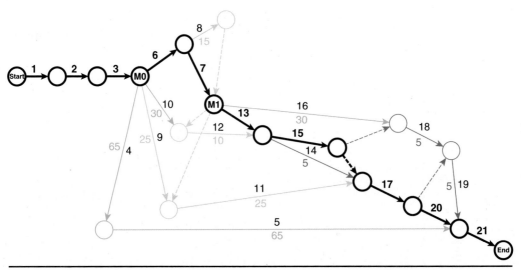

Figure 11-13 Network diagram with three developers and one test engineer

No Test Engineer (Iteration 6)

The next experiment in resource reduction is to remove the test engineer but keep the three developers. Once again, this design solution results in no change to the duration and cost of the project. The third developer simply takes over the test engineer's activities after completing other lower-float activities already assigned. The problem is that deferring the Test Plan and Test Harness activities to much later consumes 77% of their float (from 65 days to 15 days). This is very risky because if the float drops by 100%, the project is delayed.

> **Caution** Every software project should have a test engineer. Test engineers are so crucial to success that you should consider letting go of developers before you give up on professional test engineering.

GOING SUBCRITICAL (ITERATION 7)

Chapter 9 explained the importance of presenting the effects of subcritical staffing to decision makers. Too often, decision makers are unaware of the impracticality of cutting back on resources to supposedly reduce costs. The example project becomes subcritical by limiting the number of developers to just two and eliminating the test engineer. By the time activities on the critical path are scheduled to start, some supporting noncritical activities are not ready yet, so they impede the old critical path. The limiting factor now is not the duration of the critical path, but rather the availability of the two developers. Consequently, the old network (and specifically the old critical path) no longer applies. You must therefore redraw the network diagram to reflect the dependency on the two developers.

Recall from Chapter 7 that resource dependencies are dependencies and that the project network is a dependency network, not just an activity network. You therefore add the dependency on the resources to the network. You actually have some flexibility in designing the network: As long as the natural dependency between the activities is satisfied, the actual order of the activities can vary. To create the new network, you assign the two resources, as always, based on float. Each developer takes on the next lowest-float activity available after finishing with the current activity. At the same time, you add a dependency between the developer's next activity and the current one to reflect the dependency on the developer. Figure 11-14 shows the subcritical network diagram for the example project.

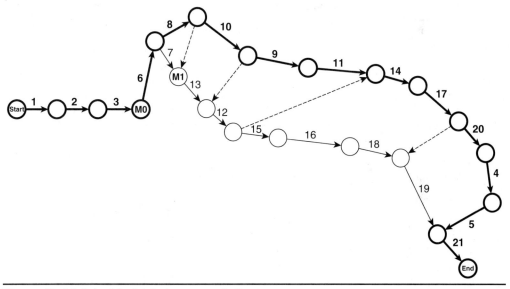

Figure II-14 Subcritical solution network diagram

Given that only two developers are performing most of the work, the subcritical network diagram looks like two long strings. One string of activities is the long critical path; the other string is the second developer back-filling on the side. This long critical path increases the risk to the project because the project now has more critical activities. In general, subcritical projects are always high-risk projects.

In the extreme case of having only a single developer, all activities in the project are critical, the network diagram is one long string, and the risk is 1.0. The duration of the project equates to the sum of all activities, but, due to the maximum risk, even that duration is likely to be exceeded.

Subcritical Cost and Duration

Compared with the limited-resources solution of three developers and one test engineer, the project duration is extended by 35% to 13.4 months due to the serialization of the activities. While using a smaller development team, the project total cost is increased by 25% to 77.6 man-months due to the longer duration and the mounting indirect cost. This result clearly demonstrates the point: There really is no cost saving with subcritical staffing.

Planned Earned Value

Figure 11-15 shows the subcritical planned earned value. You can see that the supposed shallow S curve is almost a straight line.

In the extreme case of only a single developer doing all the work, the planned earned value is a straight line. In general, a lack of curvature in the planned earned value chart is a telltale sign for a subcritical project. Even the somewhat anemic shallow S curve in Figure 11-12 indicates the project is close to becoming subcritical.

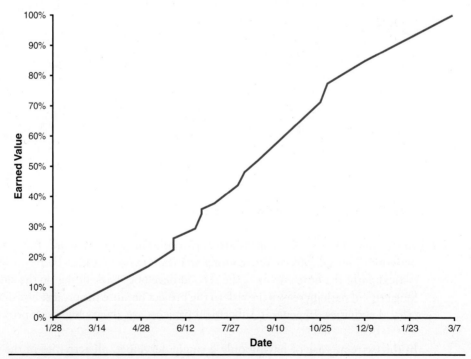

Figure 11-15 Subcritical planned earned value

DEDICATED RESOURCES AND FLOAT

The past several iterations have repeatedly constrained access to dedicated resources such as database architects or the test engineer without any material effect on the schedule or the cost. Some managers expect this behavior instinctively. When architects or other project leads plead for access to expert resources, management often denies that request on the grounds that the extra cost would not expedite the schedule. In that respect, the managers are justified. However, constraining access to dedicated experts reduces the float of the activities designated for those experts and, by doing so, drastically increases the risk of the project. Most managers miss this consequence completely. Highly constrained projects that have only developers are always high-risk projects. In addition, developers should be (and typically are) business domain experts. Expecting developers to be jacks-of-all trades is impractical and often leads to disappointing results.

CHOOSING THE NORMAL SOLUTION

The search for the normal solution has involved several attempts using combinations of resources and network designs. Out of all of these, the best solution so far was Iteration 5 (which relied on three developers and one test engineer) for several reasons:

- This solution complies with the definition of the normal solution by utilizing the lowest level of resources that allows the project to progress unimpeded along the critical path.
- This solution works around limitations of access to experts such as database architects while not compromising on a key resource, the test engineer.
- This solution does not expect all the developers to start working at once.
- Both the staffing distribution chart and the planned earned value chart exhibit acceptable behavior.

The front end of this solution encompasses, as expected, 25% of the duration of the project, and the project has an acceptable efficiency of 23%. Recall from Chapter 7 that the efficiency number should not exceed 25% for most projects.

The rest of the chapter uses Iteration 5 as the normal solution and as the baseline for the other iterations. Table 11-3 summarizes the various project metrics of the normal solution.

Table 11-3 Project metrics of the normal solution

Project Metric	Value
Total cost (man-months)	61.1
Direct cost (man-months)	21.8
Duration (months)	9.9
Average staffing	6.1
Peak staffing	9
Average developers	2.3
Efficiency	23%
Front End	25%

NETWORK COMPRESSION

With the normal solution in place, you can try to compress the project and see how well certain compression techniques work. There is no single correct way of compressing a project. You will have to make assumptions about availability, complexity, and cost. Chapter 9 discussed a variety of compression techniques. In general, the best strategy is to start with the easier ways of compressing the project. For demonstration purposes, this chapter shows how to compress the project using several techniques. Your specific case will be different. You may choose to apply only a few of the techniques and the ideas discussed here, weighing carefully the implications of each compressed solution.

COMPRESSION USING BETTER RESOURCES

The simplest way of compressing any project is to use better resources. This requires no changes to the project network or the activities. Although the simplest form of compression, it may not be the easiest due to the availability of such resources (more on that in Chapter 14). The purpose here is to gauge how the project will respond to compressing with better resources, or even if it is worth pursuing, and, if it is, how to do so.

Compression Using a Top Developer (Iteration 8)

Suppose you have access to a top developer who can perform coding activities 30% faster than the developers you already have. Such a top developer is likely to cost much more than 30% of the cost of a regular developer. In this project you can assume the top developer costs 80% more than a regular developer.

Ideally you would assign such a resource only on the critical path, but that is not always possible (recall the discussion of task continuity from Chapter 7). The normal baseline solution assigns two developers to the critical path, and your goal is to replace one of them with the top resource. To identify which one, you should consider both the number of activities and the number of days spent on the critical path per person.

Table 11-4 lists the two developers in the normal solution who touch the critical path, the number of critical activities versus noncritical activities each has, and the total duration on the critical path and off the critical path. Clearly, it is best to replace Developer 2 with the top developer.

Table 11-4 Developers, critical activities, and duration

Resource	Noncritical Activities	Noncritical Duration (days)	Critical Activities	Critical Duration (days)
Developer 1	4	85	2	35
Developer 2	1	5	4	95

Next, you need to revisit Table 11-1 (the duration estimations for each activity), identify the activities for which Developer 2 is responsible, and adjust their duration downward by 30% (the expected productivity gain with the better resource) using 5-day resolution. With the new activity durations, repeat the project duration and cost analysis while accounting for the additional 80% markup for Developer 2.

Figure 11-16 shows the critical path on the network diagram before and after compressing with the top developer.

The new project duration is 9.5 months, only 4% shorter than the duration of the original normal solution. The difference is so small because a new critical path has emerged, and that new path holds the project back. Such miniscule reduction in duration is a fairly common result. Even if that single resource is vastly more productive than the other team members, and even if all activities assigned to that top resource are done much faster, the durations of the activities assigned to regular team members are unaffected by the top resource, and those activities simply stifle the compression.

In terms of cost, the compressed project cost is unchanged, despite having a top resource that costs 80% more. This, too, is expected because of the indirect cost. Most software projects have a high indirect cost. Reducing the duration even by a little tends to pay for the cost of compression, at least with the initial compression attempts, because the minimum of the total cost curve is to the left of the normal solution (see Figure 9-10).

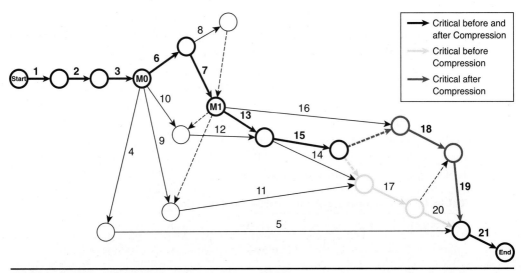

Figure 11-16 New critical path with one top developer

Compression Using a Second Top Developer (Iteration 9)

You could try compressing with multiple top resources. In this example, it makes sense to ask for just a second top developer to replace Developer 1 because a third top developer could be assigned only outside the critical path. With a second top resource, the compression has a more noticeable effect: The schedule is reduced by an additional 11% to 8.5 months, and the total cost is reduced by 3% to 59.3 man-months.

INTRODUCING PARALLEL WORK

Often, the only meaningful way of accelerating projects is to introduce parallel work. There are multiple ways of working in parallel in a software project, some more challenging than others. Parallel work increases the project complexity, so here too you should consider the simplest and easiest techniques first.

Low-Hanging Fruit

The best candidates for parallel work in most well-designed systems are the infrastructure and the *Client* designs because both are independent of the business logic. Earlier, you saw this independence play out in Iteration 2, which pushed the infrastructure to start immediately after the SDP review. To enable parallel work with the *Clients*, you split the *Clients* into separate design and development activities. Such *Client*-related design activities typically include the UX design, the UI design, and the API or SDK design (for external system interactions). Splitting the *Clients* also supports better separation of *Client* designs from the back-end system because the *Clients* should provide the best experience for the consumers of the services, not merely reflect the underlying system. You can now move the infrastructure development and the *Client* design activities to be parallel to the front end.

This move has two downsides, however. The lesser downside is the higher initial burn rate, which increases simply because you need developers as well as the core team at the beginning. The larger downside is that starting the work before the organization is committed to the project tends to make the organization decide to proceed, even if the smart thing to do is to cancel the project. It is human nature to disregard the sunk cost or to have an anchoring bias[2] attached to shining UI mockups.

I recommend moving the infrastructure and the *Client* designs to the front end only if the project is guaranteed to proceed and the purpose of the SDP review is solely to select which option to pursue (and to sign off on the project). You could mitigate the risk of biasing the SDP decision by moving only the infrastructure development to be in parallel to the front end, proceeding with the *Client* designs after the SDP review. Finally, make sure that the *Client* design activities are not misconstrued as significant progress by those who equate UI artifacts with progress. You should combine the work in the front end with project tracking (see Appendix A) to ensure decision makers correctly interpret the status of the project.

AVOIDING THE PITFALL

Moving the infrastructure development and the *Client* designs to the beginning of the front end has a great benefit above and beyond compressing the project. Chapter 7 discussed a classic pitfall in which the organization incentivizes managers to do the wrong thing by staffing the project and assigning features to the developers as soon as the front end starts. Since the underlying motivation of the managers is to avoid empty offices and idle hands, assigning infrastructure development and *Client* designs to the developers will keep them busy, giving the core team the time required to design the system and the project. If the SDP review (which concludes the front end) kills the project before the infrastructure or the *Client* designs is complete, you just abort those activities and write off the cost involved.

---

2. https://en.wikipedia.org/wiki/Anchoring

Adding and Splitting Activities

Identifying additional opportunities for parallel work is more challenging else-where in the project. You have to be creative and find ways of eliminating dependencies between coding activities. This almost always requires investing in additional activities that enable parallel work such as emulators, simulators, and integration activities. You also have to split activities and extract out of them new activities for the detailed design of contracts, interfaces, messages or the design of dependent services. These explicit design activities will take place in parallel to other activities.

There is no set formula for this kind of parallel work. You could do it for a few key activities or for most activities. You could perform the additional activities up-front or on-the-go. Very quickly you will realize that eliminating all dependencies between coding activities is practically impossible because there are diminishing returns on compression when all paths are near-critical. You will be climbing the direct cost curve of the project, which, near the minimum duration point (see Figure 9-3), is characterized by a steep slope, requiring even more cost for less and less reduction in schedule.

Infrastructure and *Client* Designs First (Iteration 10)

Returning to the example, the next iteration of project design compression moves the infrastructure in parallel to the front end. It also splits the *Client* activities into some up-front design work (e.g., requirements, test plan, UI design) and actual *Client* development, and moves the *Client* designs to the front end. In this example project you can assume that the *Client* design activities are independent of the infrastructure and are unique per *Client*.

Table 11-5 lists the revised set of activities, their duration, and their dependencies for this compression iteration.

Note that Logging (activity 6), and therefore the rest of the infrastructure activities, along with the new *Client* design activities (activities 24 and 25), can start at the beginning of the project. Note also that the actual *Client* development activities (activities 19 and 20) are shorter now and depend on the completion of the respective *Client* design activities.

Table 11-5 Activities with infrastructure and *Client* designs first

ID	Activity	Duration (days)	Depends On
1	Requirements	15	
2	Architecture	20	1
3	Project Design	20	2
4	Test Plan	30	22
5	Test Harness	35	4
6	Logging	10	
7	Security	15	6
8	Pub/Sub	5	6
9	Resource A	20	22
10	Resource B	15	22
11	ResourceAccess A	10	9,23
12	ResourceAccess B	5	10,23
13	ResourceAccess C	10	22,23
14	EngineA	15	12,13
15	EngineB	20	12,13
16	EngineC	10	22,23
17	ManagerA	15	14,15,11
18	ManagerB	20	15,16
19	Client App1	15	17,18,24
20	Client App2	20	17,25
21	System Testing	30	5,19,20
22	M0	0	3
23	M1	0	7,8
24	Client App1 Design	10	
25	Client App2 Design	15	

Several potential issues arise when compressing this project by moving the infrastructure and the *Client* design activities to the front end. The first challenge is cost. The duration of the front end now exceeds the duration of the infrastructure and the *Client* design activities, even when done serially by the same resources. Therefore, starting that work simultaneously with the front end is wasteful because the developers will be idle toward the end. It is more economical to defer the start of the infrastructure and the *Client* designs until they become critical. This will increase the risk of the project, but reduce the cost while still compressing the project.

In this iteration, you can reduce the cost further by using the same two developers to develop the infrastructure first; after completing the infrastructure, they follow with the *Client* design activities. Since resource dependencies are dependencies, you make the *Client* design activities depend on the completion of the infrastructure (M1). To maximize the compression, the two developers used in the front end proceed to other project activities (the *Resources*) immediately after the SDP review (M0). In this specific case, to calculate the floats correctly, you also make the SDP review dependent on the completion of the *Client* design activities. This removes the dependency on the *Client* design activities from the *Clients* themselves and allows the *Clients* to inherit the dependency from the SDP review instead. Again, you can afford to override the dependencies of the network in this case only because the front end is longer than the infrastructure and the *Client* design activities combined. Table 11-6 shows the revised dependencies of the network (changes noted in red).

Table II-6 Revised dependencies with infrastructure and *Client* designs first

ID	Activity	Duration (days)	Depends On
1	Requirements	15	
...	...	...	...
19	Client App1	15	17,18,~~24~~
20	Client App2	20	17,~~25~~
21	System Testing	30	5,19,20
22	M0	0	3,24,25
23	M1	0	7,8
24	Client App1 Design	10	23
25	Client App2 Design	15	23

The other challenge with splitting activities is the increased complexity of the *Clients* as a whole. You could compensate for that complexity by assigning the *Client* design activities and development to the same two top developers from the previous compression iteration. This compounds the effect of compression with top resources. However, since the *Clients* and the project are now more complex and demanding, you should further compensate for that by assuming there is no 30% reduction in the time it takes to build the *Clients* (but the developers still cost 80% more). These compensations are already reflected in the duration estimation of activities 19 and 20 in Table 11-5 and Table 11-6.

The result of this compression iteration is a cost increase of 6% from the previous solution to 62.6 man-months and a schedule reduction of 8% to 7.8 months. Figure 11-17 shows the resulting network diagram.

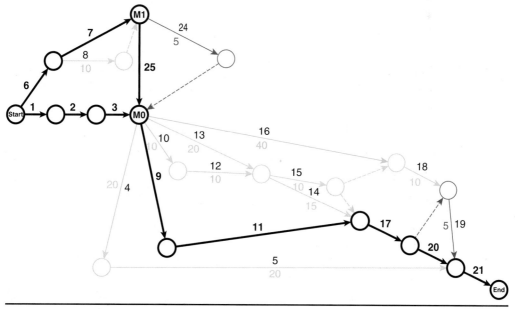

Figure 11-17 Network diagram for infrastructure and *Client* designs first

> **Note** Figure 11-17 has a long chain of activities [10, 12, 15, 18, 19] that has a mere 5 to 10 days of float. Given the length of the project, you should consider long chains with only 5 (or even 10) days of float as critical paths when calculating risk.

Compression with Simulators (Iteration II)

Examining Figure 11-17 reveals that a near-critical path (activities 10, 12, 15, 18, and 19) has developed alongside the critical path. This means any further compression requires compressing both of these paths to a similar degree. Compressing just one of them will have little effect because the other path then dictates the duration of the project. In this kind of situation, it is best to look for a **crown**—that is, a large activity that sits on top of both paths. Compressing the crown compresses both paths. In this example project, the best candidates are the development of the *Client* apps (activities 19 and 20) and the *Manager* services (activities 17 and 18). The *Clients* and *Managers* are relatively large activities, and they crown both paths. You could try to compress the *Clients*, the *Managers,* or both.

Compressing the *Clients* becomes possible when you develop simulators (see Chapter 9) for the *Manager* services on which they depend and move the development of the *Clients* somewhere upstream in the network, in parallel to other activities. Since no simulator is ever a perfect replacement for the real service, you also need to add explicit integration activities between the *Clients* and the *Managers*, once the *Managers* are complete. This in effect splits each *Client* development into two activities: The first is a development activity against the simulators, and the second is an integration activity against the *Managers*. As such, the *Clients* development may not be compressed, but the overall project duration is shortened.

You could mimic this approach by developing simulators for the *Engines* and *ResourceAccess* services on which the *Managers* depend, which enables development of the *Managers* earlier in the project. However, in a well-designed system and project, this would usually be far more difficult. Although simulating the underlying services would require many more simulators and make the project network very complex, the real issue is timing. The development of these simulators would have to take place more or less concurrently with the development of the very services they are supposed to simulate, so the actual compression you can realize from this approach is limited. You should consider simulators for the inner services only as a last resort.

In this example project, the best approach is to simulate the *Managers* only. You can compound the previous compression iteration (infrastructure and *Client* designs at the front end) by compressing it with simulators. A few new planning assumptions apply when compressing this iteration:

- **Dependencies.** The simulators could start after the front end, and they also require the infrastructure. This is inherited with a dependency on M0 (activity 22).

- **Additional developers.** When using the previous compression iteration as the starting point, two additional developers are required for the development of simulators and the *Client* implementations.

- **Starting point.** It is possible to reduce the cost of the two additional developers by deferring the work on the simulators and the *Clients* until they become critical. However, networks containing simulators tend to be fairly complex. You should compensate for that complexity by starting with the simulators as soon as possible and have the project benefit from higher float as opposed to lower cost.

Table 11-7 lists the activities and the changes to dependencies, while using the previous iteration as the baseline solution and incorporating its planning assumptions (changes noted in red).

Table 11-7 Activities with *Manager* simulators

ID	Activity	Duration (days)	Depends On
1	Requirements	15	
...	...	...	...
17	ManagerA	15	...
18	ManagerB	20	...
19	Client App1 Integration	15	17,18,28
20	Client App2 Integration	20	17,29
...	...	...	...
26	ManagerA Simulator	15	22
27	ManagerB Simulator	20	22
28	Client App1	15	26,27
29	Client App2	20	26

Figure 11-18 shows the resulting staffing distribution chart. You can clearly see the sharp jump in the developers after the front end and the near-constant utilization of the resources. The average staffing in this solution is 8.9 people, with peak staffing of 11 people. Compared with the previous compression iteration, the simulators solution results in a 9% reduction in duration to 7.1 months, but increases the total cost by only 1% to 63.5 man-months. This small cost increase is due to the reduction in the indirect cost and the increased efficiency and expected throughput of the team when working in parallel.

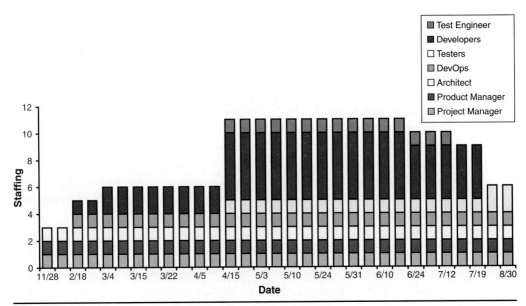

Figure 11-18 The simulators solution staffing distribution chart

Figure 11-19 shows the simulators solution network diagram. You can see the high float for the simulators (activities 26 and 27) and *Client* development (activities 28 and 29). Also observe that virtually all other network paths are critical or near critical and there is high integration pressure toward the end of the project. This solution is fragile to the unforeseen, and the network complexity drastically increases the execution risk.

END OF COMPRESSION ITERATIONS

Compared with the normal solution, the simulators solution reduces the schedule by 28% while increasing the cost by only 4%. Due to the high indirect cost, the compression ends up practically paying for itself. The direct cost, by comparison, increases by 59%, twice the reduction in the duration from a percentage standpoint. As noted in Chapter 9, the maximum expected compression of a software project is at most 30%, making the simulators solution as compressed as this project is ever likely to get.

While further compression is theoretically possible (by compressing the *Managers*), in practice this is as far as the project design team should go. There is a low probability of success from compressing any further, and the core team will be wasting time designing improbable projects.

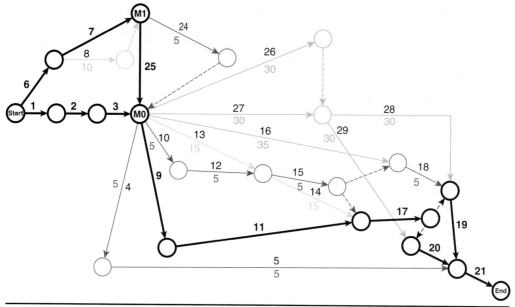

Figure 11-19 The simulators solution network diagram

THROUGHPUT ANALYSIS

It is important to recognize how compression affects the expected throughput of the team compared with the normal solution. As explained in Chapter 7, the pitch of the shallow S curve represents the throughput of the team. Figure 11-20 plots the shallow S curves of the planned earned value for the normal solution and each of the compressed solutions on the same scale.

As expected, the compressed solutions have a steeper shallow S since they complete sooner. You can quantify the difference in the required throughput by replacing each curve with its respective linear regression trend line and examining the equation of the line (see Figure 11-21).

The trend lines are straight lines, so the coefficient of the x term is the pitch of the line and, therefore, the expected throughput of the team. In the case of the normal solution, the team is expected to operate at 39 units of productivity, while the simulators solution calls for 59 units of productivity (0.0039 versus 0.0059, scaled to integers). The exact nature of these units of productivity is immaterial. What is important is the difference between the two solutions: The simulators solution expects a 51% increase in the throughput of the team (59 − 39 = 20, which is 51% of 39). It is unlikely that any team, even by increasing its size, could increase its throughput by such a large factor.

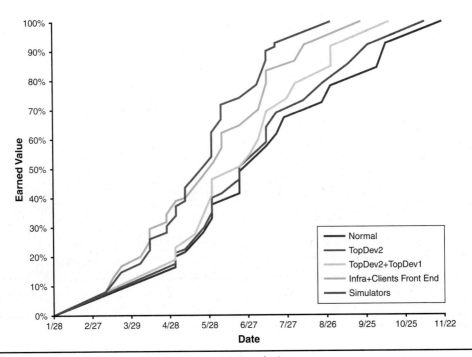

Figure 11-20 Planned earned value of the project solutions

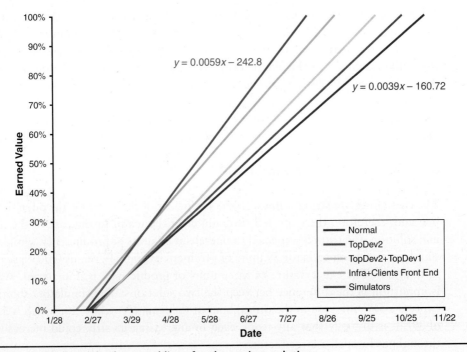

Figure 11-21 Earned value trend lines for the project solutions

Although not a hard-and-fast rule, comparing the ratio of average-to-peak staffing from one solution to another can give you some sense whether the throughput difference is realistic. For the simulators solution, this ratio is 81%, compared to 68% for the normal solution; in other words, the simulators solution expects more intense utilization of the resources. Since the simulators solution also requires a larger average team size (8.9 versus 6.1 of the normal solution) and since larger teams tend to be less efficient, the prospect of achieving the 51% increase in throughput is questionable, especially when working on a more complex project. This further cements the idea that the simulators solution is a bar set too high for most teams.

EFFICIENCY ANALYSIS

The efficiency of each project design solution is a fairly easy number to calculate— and a very telling one. Recall from Chapter 7 that the efficiency number indicates both the expected efficiency of the team and how realistic the design assumptions are regarding constraints, staffing elasticity, and criticality of the project. Figure 11-22 shows the project solutions efficiency chart for the example project.

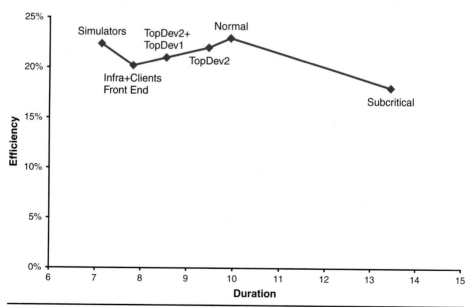

Figure 11-22 The project efficiency chart

Observe in Figure 11-22 that peak efficiency is at the normal solution, resulting from the lowest level of resources utilization without any compression cost. As you compress the project, efficiency declines. While the simulators solution is on par with the normal solution, I consider it unrealistic since the project is much more complex and its feasibility is in question (as indicated by the throughput analysis). The subcritical solution is awful when it comes to efficiency due to the poor ratio of direct cost to the indirect cost. In short, the normal solution is the most efficient.

TIME–COST CURVE

Having designed each solution and produced its staffing distribution chart, you can calculate the cost elements for each solution, as shown in Table 11-8.

Table 11-8 Duration, total cost, and cost elements for the various options

Design Option	Duration (months)	Total Cost (man-months)	Direct Cost (man-months)	Indirect Cost (man-months)
Simulators	7.1	63.5	34.8	28.7
Infra+Clients Front End	7.8	62.6	30.4	32.2
TopDev1+TopDev2	8.5	59.3	26.6	32.7
TopDev2	9.5	61.1	24.2	36.9
Normal	9.9	61.1	21.8	39.2
Subcritical	13.4	77.6	20.9	56.7

With these cost numbers, you can produce the project time–cost curves shown in Figure 11-23. Note that the direct cost curve is a bit flat due to the scaling of the chart. The indirect cost is almost a perfect straight line.

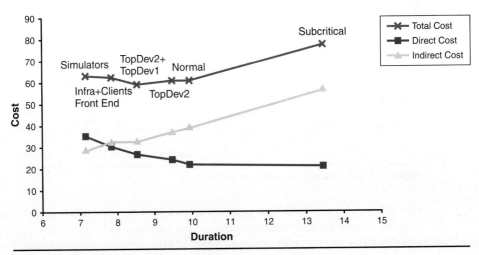

Figure 11-23 The project time–cost curves

TIME–COST CORRELATION MODELS

The time–cost curves of Figure 11-23 are discrete, and they can only hint at the behavior of the curves outside the specific solutions. However, with the discrete time–cost curves at hand, you can also find correlation models for the curves. A **correlation model** or a **trend line** is a mathematical model that produces a curve that best fits the distribution of the discrete data points (tools such as Microsoft Excel can easily perform such analysis). Correlation models allow you to plot the time–cost curves at any point, not just at the known discrete solutions. For the points in Figure 11-23, these models are a straight line for the indirect cost, and a polynomial of the second degree for the direct and indirect costs. Figure 11-24 shows these correlation trend lines in dashed lines, along with their equations and R^2 values.

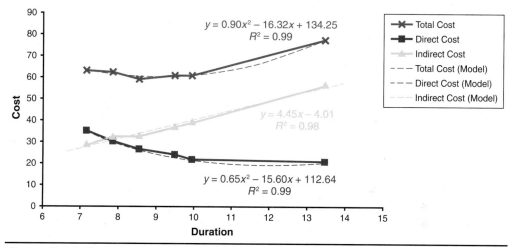

Figure 11-24 The project time–cost trend lines

The R^2 (also known as the coefficient of determination) is a number between 0 and 1 that represents the quality of the model. Numbers greater than 0.9 indicate an excellent fit of the model to the discrete points. In this case, the equations within the range of the project design solutions depict their curves very precisely.

Figure 11-24 provides the equations for how cost changes with time in the example project. For the direct and indirect costs, the equations are:

$$\text{Direct Cost} = 0.65t^2 - 15.6t + 112.64$$
$$\text{Indirect Cost} = 4.45t - 4.01$$

where t is measured in months. While you also have a correlation model for the total cost, that model is produced by a statistical calculation, so it is not a perfect sum of the direct and indirect costs. You produce the correct model for the total cost by simply adding the equations of the direct and indirect models:

$$\text{Total Cost} = \text{Direct Cost} + \text{Indirect Cost}$$
$$= 0.65t^2 - 15.6t + 112.64 + 4.45t - 4.01$$
$$= 0.65t^2 - 11.15t + 108.63$$

Figure 11-25 plots the modified total cost correlation model along with the direct and indirect models.

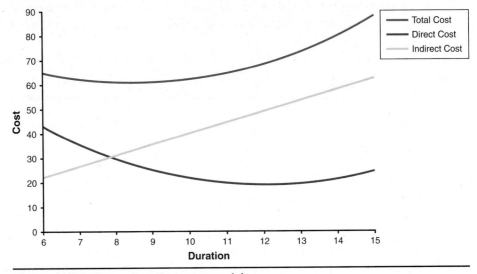

Figure 11-25 The project time–cost models

THE DEATH ZONE

Chapter 9 introduced the concept of the death zone—that is, the area under the time–cost curve. Any project design solution that falls in that area is impossible to build. Having the model (or even the discrete curve) for the project total cost enables you to visualize the project death zone, as shown in Figure 11-26.

Identifying the death zone allows you to answer intelligently quick questions and avoid committing to impossible projects. For example, suppose management asks if you could build the example project in 9 months with 4 people. According to the total cost model of the project, a 9-month project costs more than 60 man-months and requires an average of 7 people:

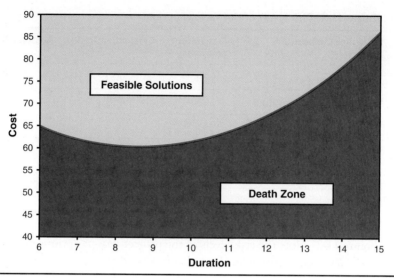

Figure 11-26 The project death zone

$$\text{Total Cost} = 0.65^*9^2 - 11.15^*9 + 108.63 = 61.2$$
$$\text{Average Staff} = 61.2/9 = 6.8$$

Assuming the same ratio of average-to-peak staffing as the normal solution (68%), a solution that delivers at 9 months peaks at 10 people. Any fewer than 10 people causes the project at times to go subcritical. The combination of 4 people and 9 months (even when utilized at 100% efficiency 100% of the time) is 36 man-months of cost. That particular time–cost coordinate is not even visible in Figure 11-26 because it is so deep within the death zone. You should present these findings to management and ask if they want to commit under these terms.

> **Note**   Many times, architects or project managers intuitively feel that some arbitrary management edict is infeasible, but they lack the tools or the numbers to refute it. Project design is an objective, nonconfrontational way of presenting the facts and discussing reality.

PLANNING AND RISK

Each project design solution carries some level of risk. Using the risk modeling techniques described in Chapter 10, you can quantify these risk levels for the solutions, as shown in Table 11-9.

Table 11-9 Risk levels of the various options

Design Option	Duration (months)	Criticality Risk	Activity Risk
Simulators	7.1	0.81	0.76
Infra+Clients Front End	7.8	0.77	0.81
TopDev1+TopDev2	8.5	0.79	0.80
TopDev2	9.5	0.70	0.77
Normal	9.9	0.73	0.79
Subcritical	13.4	0.79	0.79

Figure 11-27 plots the risk levels of the project design options along with the direct cost curve. The figure offers both good and bad news regarding risk. The good news is that criticality risk and activity risk track closely together in this project. It is always a good sign when different models concur on the numbers, giving credence to the values. The bad news is that all project design solutions so far are high-risk options; even worse, they are all similar in value. This means the risk is elevated and uniform regardless of the solution. Another problem is that Figure 11-27 contains the subcritical point. The subcritical solution is definitely a solution to avoid, and you should remove it from this and any subsequent analysis.

In general, you should avoid basing your modeling on poor design options. To address the high risk, you should decompress the project.

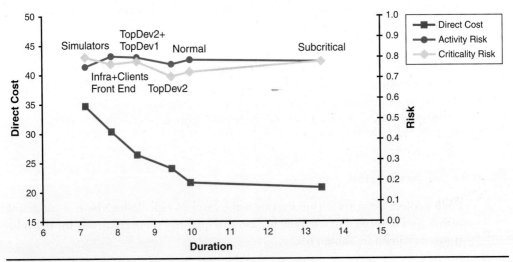

Figure 11-27 Direct cost and risk of the various options

RISK DECOMPRESSION

Since in this example project all project design solutions are of high risk, you should decompress the normal solution and inject float along the critical path until the risk drops to an acceptable level. Decompressing a project is an iterative process because you do not know up front by how much to decompress or how well the project will respond to decompression.

Somewhat arbitrarily, the first iteration decompresses the project by 3.5 months, from the 9.9 months of the normal solution to the furthest point of the subcritical solution. This result reveals how the project responds across the entire range of solution durations. Doing so produces a decompression point called D1 (total project duration of 13.4 months) with criticality risk of 0.29 and activity risk of 0.39. As explained in Chapter 10, 0.3 should be the lowest risk level for any project, which implies this iteration overly decompressed the project.

The next iteration decompresses the project by 2 months from the normal duration, roughly half the decompression amount of D1. This produces D2 (total project duration of 12 months). The criticality risk is unchanged from 0.29, because these 2 months of decompression are still larger than the lower limit used in this project for green activities. Activity risk is increased to 0.49.

Similarly, halving the decompression of D2 yields D3 with a 1-month decompression (total project duration of 10.9 months), criticality risk of 0.43, and activity risk of 0.62. Half of D3 produces D4, a 2-week decompression (total project duration of 10.4 months) with criticality risk of 0.45 and activity risk at 0.7. Figure 11-28 plots the decompressed risk curves for the project.

Adjusting Outliers

Figure 11-28 features a conspicuous gap between the two risk models. This difference is due to a limitation of the activity risk model—namely, the activity risk model does not compute the risk values correctly when the floats in the project are not spread uniformly (see Chapter 10 for more details). In the case of the decompressed solutions, the high float values of the test plan and the test harness skew the activity risk values higher. These high float values are more than one standard deviation removed from the average of all the floats, making them **outliers**.

When computing activity risk at the decompression points, you can adjust the input by replacing the float of the outlier activities with the average of all floats plus one standard deviation of all floats. Using a spreadsheet, you can easily automate the adjustment of the outliers. Such an adjustment typically makes the risk models correlate more closely.

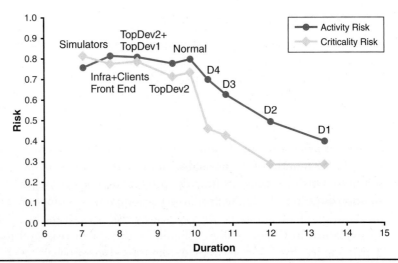

Figure 11-28 Risk decompression curves

Figure 11-29 shows the adjusted activity risk curve along with the criticality risk curve. As you can see, the two risk models now concur.

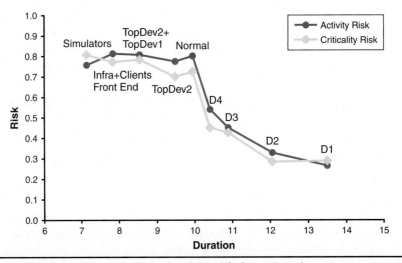

Figure 11-29 Criticality and adjusted activity risk decompression curves

Risk Tipping Point

The most important aspect of Figure 11-29 is the risk tipping point around D4. Decompressing the project even by a little to D4 decreases the risk substantially. Since D4 is right at the edge of the tipping point, you should be a bit more conservative and decompress to D3 to pass the knee in the curves.

Direct Cost and Decompression

To compare the decompressed solutions to the other solutions, you need to know their respective cost. The problem is that the decompression points provide only the duration and the risk. No project design solutions produce these points—they are just the risk value of the normal solution network with additional float. You have to extrapolate both the indirect and direct cost of the decompressed solutions from the known solutions.

In this example project, the indirect cost model is a straight line, and you can safely extrapolate the indirect cost from that of the other project design solution (excluding the subcritical solution). For example, the extrapolation for D1 yields an indirect cost of 51.1 man-months.

The direct cost extrapolation requires dealing with the effect of delays. The additional direct cost (beyond the normal solution that was used to create the decompressed solutions) comes from both the longer critical path and the longer idle time between noncritical activities. Because staffing is not fully dynamic or elastic, when a delay occurs, it often means people on other chains are idle, waiting for the critical activities to catch up.

In the example project's normal solution, after the front end, the direct cost mostly consists of developers. The other contributors to direct cost are the test engineer activities and the final system testing. Since the test engineer has very large float, you can assume that the test engineer will not be affected by the schedule slip. The staffing distribution for the normal solution (shown in Figure 11-11) indicates that staffing peaks at 3 developers (and even that peak is not maintained for long) and goes as low as 1 developer. From Table 11-3, you can see that the normal solution uses 2.3 developers, on average. You can therefore assume that the decompression affects two developers. One of them consumes the extra decompression float, and the other one ends up idle.

The planning assumptions in this project stipulate that developers between activities are accounted for as a direct cost. Thus, when the project slips, the slip adds the direct cost of two developers times the difference in duration between the normal solution and the decompression point. In the case of the furthest decompression point D1 (at 13.4 months), the difference in duration from the normal solution (at 9.9 months) is 3.5 months, so the additional direct cost is 7 man-months. Since the normal solution has 21.8 man-months for its direct cost, the direct cost at D1 is 28.8 man-months. You can add the other decompression points by performing similar calculations. Figure 11-30 shows the modified direct-cost curve along with the risk curves.

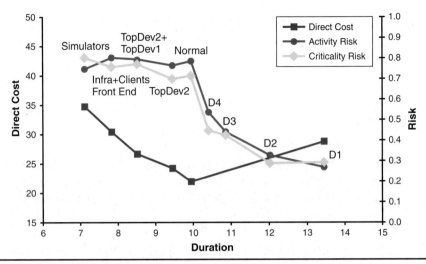

Figure 11-30 Modified direct cost curve and the risk curves

REBUILDING THE TIME–COST CURVE

With the new cost numbers for D1, you can rebuild the time–cost curves, while excluding the bad data point of the subcritical solution. This yields a better time–cost curve based on possible solutions. You can then proceed to calculate the correlation models as before. This process produces the following cost formulas:

$$\text{Direct Cost} = 0.99t^2 - 21.32t + 136.57$$
$$\text{Indirect Cost} = 3.54t + 3.59$$
$$\text{Total Cost} = 0.99t^2 - 17.78t + 140.16$$

These curves have a R^2 of 0.99, indicating an excellent fit to the data points. Figure 11-31 shows the new time–cost curves models as well as the points of minimum total cost and the normal solution.

With a better total cost formula now known, you can calculate the point of minimum total cost for the project. The total cost model is a second order polynomial of the form:

$$y = ax^2 + bx + c$$

Recall from calculus that the minimum point of such a polynomial is when its first derivative is zero:

$$y' = 2ax + b = 0$$

$$x_{min} = -\frac{b}{2a} = -\frac{-17.78}{2*0.99} = 9.0$$

As discussed in Chapter 9, the point of minimum total cost always shifts to the left of the normal solution. While the exact solution of minimum total cost is unknown, Chapter 9 suggested that for most projects finding that point is not worth the effort. Instead, you can, for simplicity's sake, equate the total cost of the normal solution with the minimum total cost for the project. In this case, the minimum total cost is 60.3 man-months and the total cost of the normal solution according to the model is 61.2 man-months, a difference of 1.5%. Clearly, the simplification assumption is justified in this case. If minimizing the total cost is your goal, then both the normal solution and the first compression solution with a single top developer are viable options.

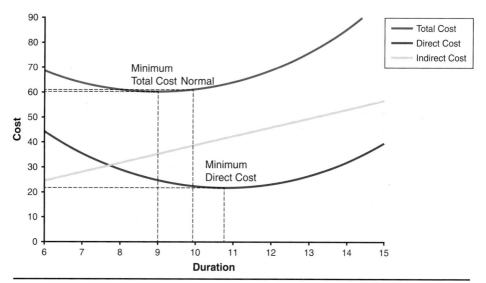

Figure 11-31 Rebuilt time–cost curve models

Minimum Direct Cost

Following similar steps with the direct cost formula, you can easily calculate the point in time of minimum direct cost as 10.8 months. Ideally, the normal solution is also the point of minimum direct cost. In the example project, however, the normal solution is at 9.9 months. The discrepancy is partially due to the differences between a discrete model of the project and the continuous model (see Figure 11-30, where the normal solution is also minimum direct cost, versus Figure 11-31). A more meaningful reason is that the point has shifted due to rebuilding the time–cost curve to accommodate the risk decompression points. In practice, the normal solution is often offset a little from the point of minimum direct cost due to accommodating constraints. The rest of this chapter uses the duration of 10.8 months as the exact point of minimum direct cost.

MODELING RISK

You can now create trend line models for the discrete risk models, as shown in Figure 11-32. In this figure, the two trend lines are fairly similar. The rest of the chapter uses the activity risk trend line because it is more conservative: It is higher across almost all of the range of options.

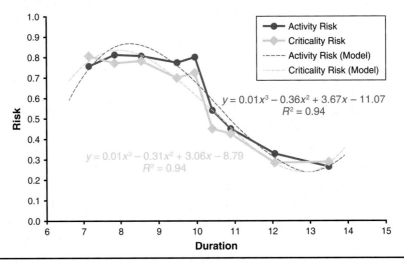

Figure 11-32 The project time–risk trend lines

Fitting a polynomial correlation model, you now have a formula for risk in the project:

$$R = 0.01t^3 - 0.36t^2 + 3.67t - 11.07$$

where t is measured in months.

> **Note**   The small coefficient of the first term in the polynomial combined
> with its high degree (third) means that for this risk formula, more precision
> is required. While not shown in the text, all the remaining calculations in
> this chapter use eight decimal digits.

With the risk formula you can plot the risk model side by side with the direct cost
model, as in Figure 11-33.

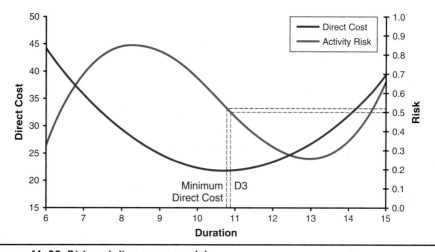

Figure 11-33 Risk and direct cost models

Minimum Direct Cost and Risk

As mentioned earlier, the minimum of the direct cost model is at 10.8 months.
Substituting that time value into the risk formula yields a risk value of 0.52; that
is, the risk at the point of minimum direct cost is 0.52. Figure 11-33 visualizes this
with the dashed blue lines.

Recall from Chapter 10 that ideally the minimum direct cost should be at 0.5
risk and that this point is the recommended decompression target. The example
project is off that mark by 4%. While this project does not have project design
solution with a duration of exactly 10.8 months, the known D3 decompression
point comes close, with a duration of 10.9 months (see the dashed red lines in
Figure 11-33). In a practical sense, these points are identical.

Optimal Project Design Option

The risk model value at D3 is at 0.50, meaning that D3 is the ideal target of risk
decompression as well as practically the point of minimum direct cost. This makes

D3 the optimal point in terms of direct cost, duration, and risk. The total cost at D3 is only 63.8 man-months, virtually the same as the minimum total cost. This also makes D3 the optimal point in terms of total cost, duration, and risk.

Being the optimal point means that the project design option has the highest probability of delivering on the commitments of the plan (the very definition of success). You should always strive to design around the point of minimum direct cost. Figure 11-34 visualizes the float of the project network at D3. As you can see, the network is a picture of health.

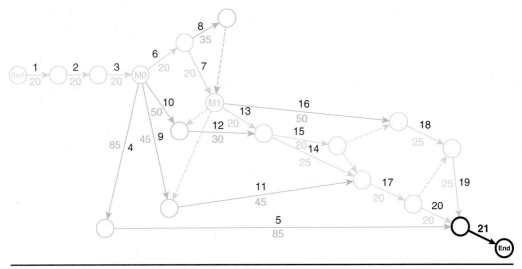

Figure 11-34 Float analysis of the optimal design solution

Minimum Risk

Using the risk formula, you can also calculate the point of minimum risk. This point comes at 12.98 months and a risk value of 0.248. Chapter 10 explained that the minimum risk value for the criticality risk model is 0.25 (using the weights [1, 2, 3, 4]). While 0.248 is very close to 0.25, it was produced using the activity risk formula, which, unlike the criticality risk model, is unaffected by the choice of weights.

RISK INCLUSION AND EXCLUSION

The discrete risk curve of Figure 11-29 indicates that while compression shortens the project, it does not necessarily increase the risk substantially. Compressing this example project even reduced the risk a bit on the activity risk curve. The main increase in risk was due to moving left of D3 (or minimum direct cost), and all compressed solutions have high risk.

Using the risk model, Figure 11-35 shows how all the project design solutions map to the risk curve of the project. You can see that the second compressed solution is almost at maximum risk, and that the more compressed solutions have the expected decreased level of risk (the da Vinci effect introduced in Chapter 10). Obviously, designing anything to or past the point of maximum risk is ill advised. You should avoid even approaching the point of maximum risk for the project—but where is that cutoff point? The example project has a maximum risk value of 0.85 on the risk curve, so project design solutions approaching that number are not good options. Chapter 10 suggested 0.75 as the maximum level of risk for any solution. With risk higher than 0.75, the project is typically fragile and likely to slip the schedule.

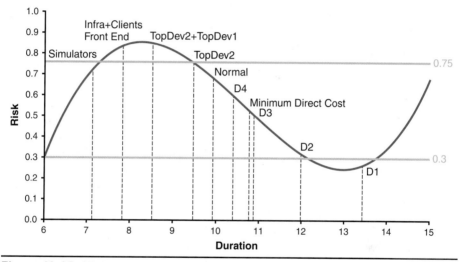

Figure 11-35 All design solutions and risk

Using the risk formula, you will find that the point of 0.75 risk is at duration of 9.49 months. While no project design solution exactly matches this point, the first compression point has a duration of 9.5 months and risk of 0.75. This suggests that the first compression is the upper practical limit in this example project. As discussed previously, 0.3 should be the lowest level of risk, which excludes the D1 decompression point at 0.27 risk. The D2 decompression point at 0.32 is possible, but borderline.

SDP REVIEW

All the detailed project design work culminates in the SDP review, where you present the project design options to the decision makers. You should not only drive educated decisions, but also make the right choice obvious. The best project design option so far was D3, a one-month decompression offering both minimum cost and risk of 0.50.

When presenting your results to decision makers, list the first compression point, the normal solution, and the optimal one-month decompression from the normal solution. Table 11-10 summarizes these viable project design options.

Table 11-10 Viable project design options

Design Option	Duration (months)	Total Cost (man-months)	Risk
One Top Developer	9.5	61.1	0.75
Normal Solution	9.9	61.1	0.68
One-Month Decompression	10.9	63.8	0.50

PRESENTING THE OPTIONS

You should not actually present the raw information as shown in Table 11-10. It is unlikely that anyone has ever seen this level of precision, so you will lack credibility. You should also add the subcritical solution. Since the subcritical solution ends up costing more (as well as being risky and taking longer), you want to dispel such notions as early as possible.

Table 11-11 lists the project options you should present at the SDP review. Note the rounded schedule and cost numbers. The rounding was performed with a bit of a license to create a more prominent spread. While this will not change anything in the decision-making process, it does lend more credibility to the numbers.

Table 11-11 Project design options for review

Project Option	Duration (months)	Total Cost (man-months)	Risk
One Top Developer	9	61	0.75
Normal Solution	10	62	0.68
One-Month Decompression	11	64	0.50
Subcritical Staffing	13	77	0.78

The risk numbers are not rounded because risk is the best way of evaluating the options. It is nearly certain that the decision makers have never seen risk in a quantified form as a tool for driving educated decisions. You must explain to them that the risk values are nonlinear; that is, using the numbers from Table 11-11, 0.68 risk is a lot more risky than 0.5 risk, not a mere 36% increase. To illustrate nonlinear behavior, you can use an analogy between risk and a more familiar nonlinear domain, the Richter scale for earthquake strength. If the risk numbers were levels of earthquakes on the Richter scale, an earthquake of 6.8 is 500 times more powerful than an earthquake of 5.0 magnitude, and a 7.5 quake is 5623 times more powerful. This sort of plain analogy steers the decision toward the desired point of 0.50 risk.

12

ADVANCED TECHNIQUES

Project design is an intricate discipline, and the previous chapters covered only the basic concepts. This was deliberate, to allow for a moderate learning curve. There is more to project design, and in this chapter you will find additional techniques useful in almost any project, not just the very large or the very complex. What these techniques have in common is that they give you a better handle on risk and complexity. You will also see how to successfully handle even the most challenging and complex projects.

GOD ACTIVITIES

As the name implies, **god activities** are activities too large for your project. "Too large" could be a relative term, when a god activity is too large with respect to other activities in the project. A simple criterion for such a god activity is having an activity with a duration that differs by at least one standard deviation from the average duration of all the activities in the project. But god activities can be too large in absolute respect. Durations in the 40–60 days range (or longer) are too large for a typical software project.

Your intuition and experience may already tell you to avoid such activities. Typically, god activities are mere placeholders for some great uncertainty lurking under the cover. The duration and effort estimation for a god activity is almost always low-grade. Consequently, the actual activity duration may be longer, potentially enough to derail the project. You should confront such dangers as soon as possible to ensure that you have a chance of meeting your commitments.

God activities also tend to deform the project design techniques shown in this book. They are almost always part of the critical path, rendering most critical path management techniques ineffective because the critical path's duration and its position in the network gravitate toward the god activities. To make matters worse, the risk models for projects with god activities result in misleadingly low risk numbers. Most of the effort in such a project will be spent on the critical god activities, making the project for all practical purposes a high-risk project. However, the risk calculation will be skewed lower because the other activities orbiting the critical god activities will have high float. If you removed these satellite activities, the risk number would shoot up toward 1.0, correctly indicating the high risk resulting from the god activities.

HANDLING GOD ACTIVITIES

The best course of action with god activities is to break them down into smaller independent activities. Subdividing god activities will markedly improve the quality of the estimation, reduce the uncertainty, and provide the correct risk value. But what if the scope of work is truly huge? You should treat such activities as mini-projects and compress them. Start by identifying internal phases of the god activities and finding ways of working in parallel across these phases inside each god activity. If that is not possible, you should look for ways of making the god activities less critical by getting them out of the way of the other activities in the project.

For instance, developing simulators for the god activities reduces other activities' dependencies on the god activities themselves. This will enable working in parallel to the god activities, making the god activities less (or maybe not at all) critical. Simulators also reduce the uncertainty of the god activities by placing constraints on them that reveal hidden assumptions, making the detailed design of the god activities easier.

You should also consider ways of factoring the god activities into separate side projects. Factoring into a side project is important especially if the internal phases of the god activity are inherently sequential. This makes project management and progress tracking much easier. You must design integration points along the network to reduce the integration risk at the end. Extracting the god activities this way tends to increase the risk in the rest of the project (the other activities have much less float once the god activities are extracted). This is typically a good thing because the project would otherwise have deceptively low risk numbers. This situation is so common that low risk numbers are often a signal to look for god activities.

RISK CROSSOVER POINT

The case study in Chapter 11 used the simple guidelines of risk lower than 0.75 and higher than 0.3 to include and exclude project design options. You can be more precise than general rules of thumb when deciding on your project design options.

In Figure 11-33, at the point of minimum direct cost and immediately to its left, the direct cost curve is basically flat, but the risk curve is steep. This is an expected behavior because the risk curve typically reaches its maximum value before the direct cost reaches its maximum value with the most compressed solutions. The only way to achieve maximum risk before maximum direct cost is if, initially, left of minimum direct cost, the risk curve rises much faster than the direct cost curve. At the point of maximum risk (and a bit to its right), the risk curve is flat or almost flat, while the direct cost curve is fairly steep.

It follows that there must be a point left of minimum direct cost where the risk curve stops rising faster than the direct cost curve. I call that point the **risk crossover point**. At the crossover point, the risk approaches its maximum. This indicates you should probably avoid compressed solutions with risk values above the crossover. In most projects, the risk crossover point will coincide with the value of 0.75 on the risk curve.

The risk crossover point is a conservative point both because it is not at maximum risk and because it is based on the behavior of the risk and direct cost, rather than an absolute value of risk. That said, given the track record of most software projects, a bit of caution is never a bad thing.

Deriving the Crossover Point

Finding the risk crossover point requires comparing the rate of growth of the direct cost curve and the risk curve. You can do that analytically using some basic calculus, graphically in a spreadsheet, or using a numerical equation solver. The files accompanying this chapter contain all three techniques almost in a template manner so that you can easily find the risk crossover point.

The rate of growth of a curve is expressed by its first derivative, so you have to compare the first derivative of the risk curve with the first derivative of the direct cost curve. The risk model in the example project of Chapter 11 is in the form of a polynomial of the third degree with the following form:

$$y = ax^3 + bx^2 + cx + d$$

The first derivative of that polynomial is in the form of this second-degree polynomial:

$$y' = 3ax^2 + 2bx + c$$

With the example project, the risk formula is:

$$R = 0.01t^3 - 0.36t^2 + 3.67t - 11.07$$

Therefore, the first derivative of the risk is:

$$R' = 0.03t^2 - 0.72t + 3.67$$

With the example project, the direct cost formula is:

$$C = 0.99t^2 - 21.32t + 136.57$$

Therefore, the first derivative of the direct cost is:

$$C' = 1.98t - 21.32$$

There are two issues you need to overcome before you can compare the two derivative equations. The first issue is that the ranges of values between maximum risk and minimum direct cost in both curves are monotonically decreasing (meaning the rates of growth of the two curves will be negative numbers), so you must compare the absolute values of the rates of growth. The second issue is that the raw rates of growth are incompatible in magnitude. The risk values range between 0 and 1, while the cost values are approximately 30 for the example project. To correctly compare the two derivatives, you must first scale the risk values to the cost values at the point of maximum risk.

The recommended scaling factor is given by

$$F = \frac{R(t_{mr})}{C(t_{mr})}$$

where:

- t_{mr} is the time for maximum risk.
- $R(t_{mr})$ is the project's risk formula value at t_{mr}.
- $C(t_{mr})$ is the project's cost formula value at t_{mr}.

The risk curve is maximized when the first derivative of the risk curve, R', is zero. Solving the project's risk equation for t when $R' = 0$ yields a t_{mr} of 8.3 months. The corresponding risk value, R, is 0.85, and the corresponding direct cost value is

28 man-months. The ratio between these two values, F, is 32.93, the scaling factor for the example project.

The acceptable risk level for the project occurs when all of the following conditions are met:

- Time is to the left of the point of minimum risk of the project.
- Time is to the right of the point of maximum risk of the project.
- Risk rises faster than cost in absolute value to scale.

You can put these conditions together in the form of this expression:

$$F * |R'| > |C'|$$

Using the equations for the risk and direct cost derivatives as well as the scaling factor yields:

$$32.93 * |0.03t^2 - 0.72t + 3.67| > |1.98t - 21.32|$$

Solving the equation provides the acceptable range for t:

$$9.03 < t < 12.31$$

The result is not one, but two crossover points, at 9.03 and 12.31 months. Figure 12-1 visualizes the behavior of the scaled risk and cost derivatives in absolute value. You can clearly see that the risk derivative in absolute value crosses over the cost derivative in absolute value in two places (hence crossover points).

Math aside, the reason why there are two risk crossover points has to do with the semantics of the points from a project design perspective. At 9.03 months, the risk is 0.81; at 12.31 months, the risk is 0.28. Superimposing these values on the risk curve and the direct cost curve in Figure 12-2 reveals the true meaning of the crossover points.

Project design solutions to the left of the 9.03-month risk crossover point are too risky. Project design solutions to the right of the 12.31-month risk crossover point are too safe. In between the two risk crossover points, the risk is "just right."

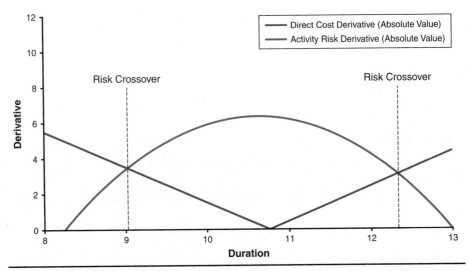

Figure 12-1 Risk crossover points

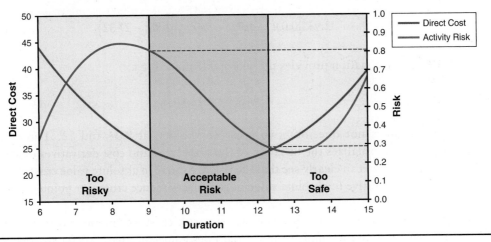

Figure 12-2 Risk inclusion and exclusion zones

Acceptable Risk and Design Options

The risk values at the crossover points of 0.81 and 0.28 agree closely with the rules of thumb of 0.75 and 0.30. For the example project, the acceptable risk zone includes the first compressed solution, the normal solution, and the decompression points of D4, D3, and D2 (see Figure 11-35). All of these points are practical design options. "Practical" in this context means the project stands a reasonable chance of meeting its commitments. The more compressed solutions are too risky, and the D1 point is too safe. You can further select between the decompression points by finding the best decompression target.

FINDING THE DECOMPRESSION TARGET

As Chapter 10 pointed out, the risk level of 0.5 is the steepest point in the risk curve. This makes it the ideal decompression target because it offers the best return—that is, for the least amount of decompression, you get the most reduction in risk. This ideal point is the tipping point of risk, and therefore it is the minimum point of decompression.

If you have plotted the risk curve, you can see where that tipping point is located, and if you have one, select a decompression point at the tipping point, or more conservatively, to its right. This technique was used in Chapter 11 to recommend D3 in Figure 11-29 as the decompression target. However, merely eyeballing a chart is not a good engineering practice. Instead, you should apply elementary calculus to identify the decompression target in a consistent and objective manner.

Given that the risk curve emulates a standard logistic function (at least between minimum and maximum risk), the steepest point in the curve also marks a twist or inflection point in the curve. To the left of that point the risk curve is concave, and to the right of it the risk curve is convex. Calculus tells us that at the inflection point, where concave becomes convex, the second derivative of the curve is zero. The ideal risk curve and its first two derivatives are shown graphically in Figure 12-3.

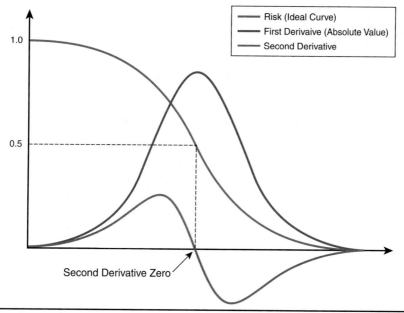

Figure 12-3 The inflection point as decompression target

Using the example project from Chapter 11 to demonstrate this technique, you have the risk equation as polynomial of the third degree. Its first and second derivatives are:

$$y = ax^3 + bx^2 + cx + d$$
$$y' = 3ax^2 + 2bx + c$$
$$y'' = 6ax + 2b$$

Equating the second derivative to zero provides this formula:

$$x = -\frac{b}{3a}$$

Since the risk model is:

$$R = 0.01t^3 - 0.36t^2 + 3.67t - 11.07$$

the point at which the second derivative is zero is at 10.62 months:

$$t = -\frac{-0.36}{3*0.01} = 10.62$$

At 10.62 months, the risk value is 0.55, which differs only 10% from the ideal target of 0.5. When plotted on the discrete risk curves in Figure 12-4, you can see that this value falls right between D4 and D3, substantiating the choice in Chapter 11 of D3 as the decompression target.

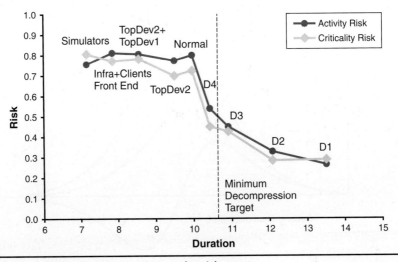

Figure 12-4 Decompression target on the risk curves

Unlike in Chapter 11, which used visualization of the risk chart and a judgment call to identify the tipping point, the second derivative provides an objective and repeatable criterion. This is especially important when there is no immediately obvious visual risk tipping point or when the risk curve is skewed higher or lower, making the 0.5 guideline unusable.

GEOMETRIC RISK

The risk models presented in Chapter 10 all use a form of arithmetic mean of the floats to calculate the risk. Unfortunately, the arithmetic mean handles an uneven distribution of values poorly. For example, consider the series [1, 2, 3, 1000]. The arithmetic mean of that series is 252, which does not represent the values in the series well at all. This behavior is not unique to risk calculations, and any attempt at using an arithmetic mean in the face of very uneven distribution will yield an unsatisfactory result. In such a case it is better to use a geometric rather than an arithmetic mean.

The **geometric mean** of a series of values is the product of multiplying all the values in the series of n values and then taking the nth root of the multiplication. Given a series of values a_1 to a_n, the geometric mean of that series would be:

$$\text{Mean} = \sqrt[n]{a_1 * a_2 * ... * a_n} = \sqrt[n]{\prod_{i=1}^{n} a_i}$$

For example, while the arithmetic mean of the series [2, 4, 6] is 4, the geometric mean is 3.63:

$$\text{Mean} = \sqrt[3]{2 * 4 * 6} = 3.63$$

The geometric mean is always less or equal to arithmetic mean of the same series of values:

$$\sqrt[n]{\prod_{i=1}^{n} a_i} \leq \frac{\sum_{i=1}^{n} a_i}{n}$$

The two means are equal only when all values in the series are identical.

While initially the geometric mean looks like an algebraic oddity, it shines when it comes to an uneven distribution of values. In the geometric mean calculation, extreme outliers have much less effect on the result. For the example series of [1, 2, 3, 1000], the geometric mean is 8.8 and is a better representation of the first three numbers in the series.

GEOMETRIC CRITICALITY RISK

As with the arithmetic criticality risk, you can use the float color coding and the corresponding number of activities to calculate the geometric criticality risk. Instead of multiplying the float weight by the number of activities, you raise it to that power. The geometric criticality formula is:

$$\text{Risk} = \frac{\sqrt[N]{(W_C)^{N_C} * (W_R)^{N_R} * (W_Y)^{N_Y} * (W_G)^{N_G}}}{W_C}$$

where:

- W_C is the weight of critical activities.
- W_R is the weight of red activities.
- W_Y is the weight of yellow activities.
- W_G is the weight of green activities.
- N_C is the number of critical activities.
- N_R is the number of red activities.
- N_Y is the number of yellow activities.
- N_G is the number of green activities.
- N is the number of activities in the project ($N = N_C + N_R + N_Y + N_G$).

Using the example network of Figure 10-4, the geometric criticality risk is:

$$\text{Risk} = \frac{\sqrt[16]{4^6 * 3^4 * 2^2 * 1^4}}{4} = 0.60$$

The corresponding arithmetic criticality risk for the same network is 0.69. As expected, the geometric criticality risk is slightly lower than the arithmetic criticality risk.

Risk Value Range

Like the arithmetic criticality risk, the geometric criticality risk has the maximum value of 1.0 when all activities are critical and a minimum value of W_G over W_C when all activities in the network are green:

$$\text{Risk} = \frac{\sqrt[N]{(W_C)^0 * (W_R)^0 * (W_Y)^0 * (W_G)^N}}{W_C} = \frac{\sqrt[N]{1 * 1 * 1 * (W_G)^N}}{W_C}$$

$$= \frac{W_G}{W_C}$$

GEOMETRIC FIBONACCI RISK

You can use the Fibonacci ratio between criticality weights to produce the geometric Fibonacci risk model. Given this definition of weights:

$$W_Y = \varphi * W_G$$
$$W_R = \varphi^2 * W_G$$
$$W_C = \varphi^3 * W_G$$

The geometric Fibonacci formula is:

$$\text{Risk} = \frac{\sqrt[N]{(\varphi^3 * W_G)^{N_C} * (\varphi^2 * W_G)^{N_R} * (\varphi * W_G)^{N_Y} * (W_G)^{N_G}}}{\varphi^3 * W_G}$$

$$= \frac{\sqrt[N]{\varphi^{3N_C + 2N_R + N_Y} * W_G^{N_C + N_R + N_Y + N_G}}}{\varphi^3 * W_G} = \frac{\sqrt[N]{\varphi^{3N_C + 2N_R + N_Y} * W_G^{N}}}{\varphi^3 * W_G} = \frac{\sqrt[N]{\varphi^{3N_C + 2N_R + N_Y}}}{\varphi^3}$$

$$= \varphi^{\frac{3N_C + 2N_R + N_Y}{N} - 3}$$

Risk Value Range

Like the arithmetic Fibonacci risk, the geometric Fibonacci risk has the maximum value of 1.0 when all activities are critical and a minimum value of 0.24 (φ^{-3}) when all activities in the network are green.

GEOMETRIC ACTIVITY RISK

The geometric activity risk formula uses a geometric mean of the floats in the project. Critical activities have zero float, which creates a problem because the geometric mean will always be zero. The common workaround is to add 1 to all values in the series and subtract 1 from the resulting geometric mean.

The geometric activity risk formula is therefore:

$$\text{Risk} = 1 - \frac{\sqrt[N]{\prod_{i=1}^{N}(F_i + 1)} - 1}{M}$$

where:

- F_i is the float of activity i.
- N is the number of activities in the project.
- M is the maximum float of any activity in the project or $\text{Max}(F_1, F_2, ..., F_N)$.

Using the example network of Figure 10-4, the geometric activity risk would be:

$$\text{Risk} = 1 - \frac{\sqrt[16]{1*1*1*1*1*1*31*31*31*31*11*11*6*6*6*6} - 1}{30} = 0.87$$

The corresponding arithmetic activity risk for the same network is 0.67.

Risk Value Range

The maximum value of the geometric activity model approaches 1.0 as more activities become critical, but it is undefined when all activities are critical. The geometric activity risk has a minimum value of 0 when all activities have the same level of float. Unlike the arithmetic activity risk, with the geometric activity risk there is no need to adjust outliers of abnormally high float, and the floats do not need to be uniformly spread.

GEOMETRIC RISK BEHAVIOR

Both the geometric criticality risk and the geometric Fibonacci risk models yield results that are very similar to their arithmetic counterparts. However, the geometric activity formula does not track well with its arithmetic kin, and its value is much higher across the range. The result is that the geometric activity risk values typically do not conform to the risk value guidelines provided in this book.

Figure 12-5 illustrates the difference in behavior between the geometric risk models by plotting all of the risk curves of the example project from Chapter 11.

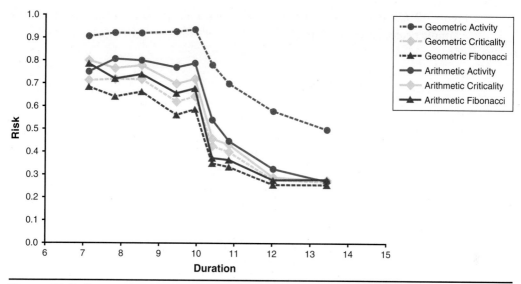

Figure 12-5 Geometric versus arithmetic risk models

You can see that the geometric criticality and geometric Fibonacci risk have the same general shape as the arithmetic models, only slightly lower, as expected. You can clearly observe the same risk tipping point. The geometric activity risk is greatly elevated, and its behavior is very different from the arithmetic activity risk. There is no easily discernable risk tipping point.

Why Geometric Risk?

The near-identical behavior of the arithmetic and geometric criticality (as well as Fibonacci) risk models illustrates that it does not matter much which one you use. The differences do not justify the time and effort involved in building yet another risk curve for the project. If anything, just for the sake of simplicity when explaining risk modeling to others, you should choose the arithmetic model. The geometric activity risk is clearly less useful than the arithmetic activity risk, but its utility in one case is why I decided to discuss geometric risk.

Geometric activity risk is the last resort when trying to calculate the risk of a project with god activities. Such a project in effect has very high risk since most of the effort is spent on the critical god activities. As explained previously, due to the size of the god activities, the other activities have considerable float, which in turn skews the arithmetic risk lower, giving you a false sense of safety. In contrast, the geometric activity risk model provides the expected high risk value for projects with god activities. You can produce a correlation model for the geometric activity risk and perform the same risk analysis as with the arithmetic model.

Figure 12-6 shows the geometric activity risk and its correlation model for the example project presented in Chapter 11.

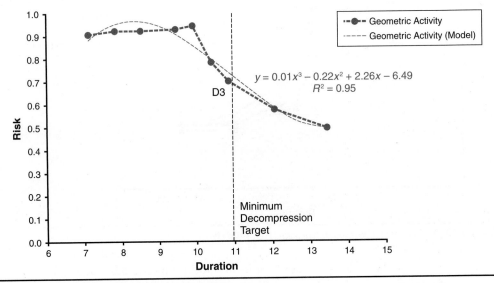

Figure 12-6 Geometric activity risk model

The point of maximum risk, 8.3 months, is shared by both the arithmetic and geometric models. The minimum decompression target for the geometric activity model (where the second derivative is zero) comes at 10.94 months, similar to the 10.62 months of the arithmetic model and just to the right of D3. The geometric risk crossover points are 9.44 months and 12.25 months—a slightly narrower range than the 9.03 months and 12.31 months obtained when using the arithmetic activity risk model. As you can see, the results are largely similar for the two models, even though the behavior of the risk curve is very different.

Of course, instead of finding a way to calculate the risk of a project with god activities, you should fix the god activities as discussed previously. Geometric risk, however, allows you to deal with things the way they are, not the way they should be.

EXECUTION COMPLEXITY

In the previous chapters, the discussion of project design focused on driving educated decisions before work starts. Only by quantifying the duration, cost, and risk can you decide if the project is affordable and feasible. However, two project design options could be similar in their duration, cost, and risk, but differ greatly in their execution complexity. Execution complexity in this context refers to how convoluted and challenging the project network is.

CYCLOMATIC COMPLEXITY

Cyclomatic complexity measures connectivity complexity. It is useful in measuring the complexity of anything that you can express as a network, including code and the project.

The cyclomatic complexity formula is:

$$Complexity = E - N + 2 * P$$

For project execution complexity:

- E is the number of dependencies in the project.
- N is the number of activities in the project.
- P is the number of disconnected networks in the project.

In a well-designed project, P is always 1 because you should have a single network for your project. Multiple networks (P > 1) make the project more complex.

To demonstrate the cyclomatic complexity formula, given the network in Table 12-1, E equals 6, N is 5, and P is 1. The cyclomatic complexity is 3:

$$Complexity = 6 - 5 + 2 * 1 = 3$$

Table 12-1 Example network with cyclomatic complexity of 3

ID	Activity	Depends On
1	A	
2	B	
3	C	1,2
4	D	1,2
5	E	3,4

PROJECT TYPE AND COMPLEXITY

While there is no direct way to measure the execution complexity of the project, you can use the cyclomatic complexity formula as its proxy. The more internal dependencies the project has, the riskier and more challenging it is to execute. Any of these dependencies can be delayed, causing cascading delays in multiple other places in the project. The maximum cyclomatic complexity of a project with N activities is on the order of N^2, a project where every one of the activities depends on all the other activities.

In general, the more parallel the project, the higher its execution complexity will be. At the very least, it is challenging to have a larger staff available in time for all the parallel activities. The parallel work (and the additional work required to enable the parallel work) increases both the workload and the team size. A larger team will be less efficient and more demanding to manage. Parallel work also results in higher cyclomatic complexity because the parallel work increases E faster than it increases N. At the extreme, a project with N activities starting at the same time and finishing together, where each activity is independent of all other activities and the activities are all done in parallel, has a cyclomatic complexity of N + 2. Such a project has a huge execution risk.

In much the same way, the more sequential the project, the simpler and less complex it will be to execute. At the extreme, the simplest project with N activities is a serial string of activities. Such a project has the minimum possible cyclomatic complexity of exactly 1. Subcritical projects with very few resources tend to resemble such long strings of activities. While the design risk of such a subcritical project is high (approaching 1.0), the execution risk is very low.

Empirically, I find that well-designed projects have a cyclomatic complexity of 10 or 12. While this level may seem low, you must understand that the chance of meeting your commitments is disproportionally related to the execution complexity. For example, a project with cyclomatic complexity of 15 may be only 25% more complex than a project with cyclomatic complexity of 12, but the lower-complexity project may be twice as likely to succeed. High execution complexity is therefore positively correlated to the likelihood of the failure. The more complex the project, the more likely you are to fail to meet your commitments. In addition, successfully delivering on one complex project is no guarantee that you will be able to repeat that success with another complex project.

It is certainly possible to repeatedly deliver projects with high cyclomatic complexity levels, but it takes time to build such capabilities across the organization. It requires a sound architecture, great project design within the risk guidelines, a team whose members are used to working together and are at peak productivity, and a top-notch project manager who pays meticulous attention to details and proactively handles conflicts. Lacking these ingredients, you should take active steps to reduce the execution complexity using the design-by-layers and network-of-networks techniques described later on in this chapter.

COMPRESSION AND COMPLEXITY

Complexity tends to increase with compression and is likely to do so in a nonlinear manner. Ideally, the complexity of your project design solutions as a function of their durations will look like the dashed curve of Figure 12-7.

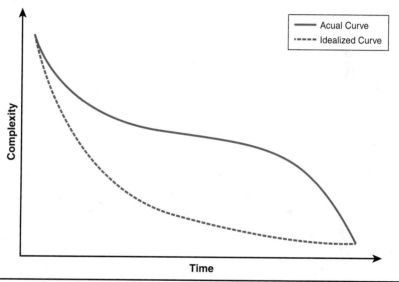

Figure 12-7 Project time–complexity curve

The problem with such a classic nonlinear behavior is it does not account for compressing the project by using more skilled resources without any change to the project network. The dashed line also presumes that complexity can be further reduced with ever-increasing allocation of time, but, as previously stated, complexity has a hard minimum at 1. A better model of the project complexity is some kind of a logistic function (the solid line in Figure 12-7).

The relatively flat area of the logistic function represents the case of working with better resources. The sharp rise on the left of the curve corresponds to parallel work and compressing the project. The sharp drop on the right of the curve represents the project's subcritical solutions (which also take considerably more time). Figure 12-8 demonstrates this behavior by plotting the complexity curve of the example project from Chapter 11.

Recall from Chapter 11 that even the most compressed solution was not materially more expensive than the normal solution. Complexity analysis reveals that the true cost of maximum compression in this case was a 25% increase in cyclomatic complexity—an indicator that the project execution is far more challenging and risky.

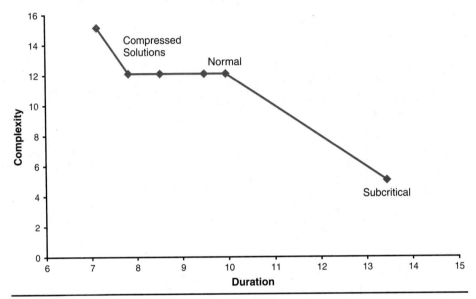

Figure 12-8 The example project time–complexity curve

VERY LARGE PROJECTS

The project design methodology in this book works well regardless of scale. It does, however, become more challenging as the project gets bigger. There is a maximum capacity of the human brain to maintain a mental picture of the details, constraints, and interdependencies within the project. At some project size, you will lose your ability to design the project. Most people can design a project that has up to 100 activities or so. With practice, this number can increase. A well-designed system and project make it possible to handle even a few hundreds of activities.

Megaprojects with many hundreds or even thousands of activities have their own level of complexity. They typically involve multiple sites, dozens or hundreds of people, huge budgets, and aggressive schedules. In fact, you typically see the last three in tandem because the company first commits to an aggressive schedule and then throws people and money at the project, hoping the schedule will yield.

The larger the project becomes, the more challenging the design and the more imperative it is to design the project. First, the larger the project, the more is at stake if it fails. Second, and even more importantly, you have to plan to work in parallel out of the gate because no one will wait 500 years—or, for that matter, even 5 years—for delivery. Making things worse, with a megaproject the heat will be on from the very first day, because such projects place the future of the company at stake, and many careers are on the line. You will be under the spotlight with managers swarming around like angry yellow jackets.

Almost without exception, all megaprojects end up as megafailures. Size maps directly to poor outcomes.[1] The larger the project, the larger the deviation will be from its commitments, with longer delays and higher and higher costs incurred relative to the initial schedule and budget. Megaprojects are modern-day failed ziggurats on a biblical scale.

COMPLEX SYSTEMS AND FRAGILITY

The fact that large projects are ordained to fail is not an accident, but rather a direct result of their complexity. In this context, it is important to distinguish between complex and complicated. Most software systems are complicated, not complex. A complicated system can still have deterministic behavior, and you can understand its inner workings exactly. Such a system will have known repeatable responses to set inputs, and its past behavior is indicative of its future behavior. In contrast to a complicated system, the weather, the economy, and your body are complex systems. Complex systems are characterized by lack of understanding of the internal mechanism at play and inability to predict behavior. This complex behavior is not necessarily due to numerous complicated internal parts. For example, three bodies orbiting one another are a complex nondeterministic system. Even a simple pendulum with a pivot is a complex system. While both of these examples are not complicated, they are still complex systems.

In the past, complex software systems were limited to mission-critical systems, where the underlying domain was inherently complex. Over the past two decades, due to increased systems connectivity, diversity, and the scale of cloud computing, enterprise systems and even just regular software systems now exhibit complex system traits.

A fundamental attribute of complex systems is that they respond in nonlinear ways to minute changes in the conditions. This is the last-snowflake effect, in which a single additional flake can cause an avalanche on a snow-laden mountain side.

---

1. Nassim Nicholas Taleb, *Antifragile* (Random House, 2012).

The single snowflake is so risky because complexity grows nonlinearly with size. In large systems, the increase in complexity causes a commensurate increase in the risk of failure. The risk function itself can be a highly nonlinear function of complexity, akin to a power law function. Even if the base of the function is almost 1, and the system grows slowly in size (one additional line of code at a time or one more snowflake on the mountain side), over time the growth in complexity and its compounding effect on risk will cause a failure due to a runaway reaction.

Complexity Drivers

Complexity theory[2] strives to explain why complex systems behave as they do. According to complexity theory, all complex systems share four key elements: connectivity, diversity, interactions, and feedback loops. Any nonlinear failure behavior is the product of these complexity drivers.

Even if the system is large, if the parts are disconnected, complexity will not raise its head. In a connected system with n parts, connectivity complexity grows in proportion to n^2 (a relationship known as Metcalfe's law[3]). You could even make the case for connectivity complexity on the order of n^n due to ripple effects, where any single change causes n changes and each of those causes n additional changes, and so on.

The system can still have connected parts and not be that complex to manage and control if the parts are clones or simple variations of one another. On the other hand, the more diverse the system is (such as having different teams with their own tools, coding standards, or design), the more complex and error prone that system will be. For example, consider an airline that uses 20 different types of airplanes, each specific for its own market, with unique parts, oils, pilots, and maintenance schedules. This very complex system is bound to fail simply because of diversity. Compare that with an airline that uses just a single generic type of airplane that is not designed for any market in particular and can serve all markets, passengers, and ranges. This second airline is not just simpler to run: It is more robust and can respond much more quickly to changes in the marketplace. These ideas should resonate with the advantages of composable design discussed in Chapter 4.

You can even control and manage a connected diverse system as long as you do not allow intense interactions between the parts. Such interactions can have destabilizing unintended consequences across the system, often involving diverse aspects such as schedule, cost, quality, execution, performance, reliability, cash flow,

---

2. https://en.wikipedia.org/wiki/Complex_system
3. https://en.wikipedia.org/wiki/Metcalfe's_law

customer satisfaction, retention, and morale. Unabated, these changes will trigger more interactions in the form of feedback loops. Such feedback loops magnify the problems to the point that input or state conditions that were not an issue in the past become capable of taking the system down.

> **Note** These complexity drivers also explain why functionally decomposed systems are complex and fragile. Functional decomposition is as diverse as the required functionality across all customers and points in time. The resulting huge diversity in the architecture leads directly to out-of-control complexity.

Size, Complexity, and Quality

The other reason large projects fail has to do with quality. When a complex system depends on the completion of a series of tasks (such as a series of interactions between services or activities in a project), and when the failure of any task causes failure of the whole, any quality issue produces severe side effects, even if the components are very simple. This was demonstrated in 1986 when a 30-cent O-ring brought down a $3 billion space shuttle.

When the quality of the whole depends on the quality of all the components, the overall quality is the product of the qualities of the individual elements.[4] The result is highly nonlinear decay behavior. For example, suppose the system performs a complex task composed of 10 smaller tasks, each having a near-perfect quality of 99%. In that case the aggregate quality is only 90% ($0.99^{10} = 0.904$).

Even this assumption of 99% quality or reliability is unrealistic because most software units are never tested to within 99% of all possible inputs, all possible interactions with all connecting components, all possible feedback loops of state changes, all deployments and customer environments, and so on. The realistic unit quality figures are probably lower. If each unit was tested and qualified within a 90% level, the system quality drops to 35%. A 10% decrease in quality per component degrades the overall outcome by 65%.

The more components the system has, the worse the effect becomes, and the more vulnerable the system becomes to any quality issues. This explains why large projects often suffer from poor quality to the point of being unusable.

---

4. Michael Kremer, "The O-Ring Theory of Economic Development," *Quarterly Journal of Economics* 108, no. 3 (1993): 551–575.

NETWORK OF NETWORKS

The key to success in large projects is to negate the drivers of complexity by reducing the size of the project. You must approach the project as a **network of networks**. Instead of one very large project, you create several smaller, less complex projects that are far more likely to succeed. The cost will typically increase at least by a little, but the likelihood of failure will decrease considerably.

With a network of networks, there is a proviso that the project is feasible, that it is somehow possible to build the project in this way. If the project is feasible, then there is a good probability that the networks are not tightly coupled and that the segmentation into separate subnetworks is possible. Otherwise, the project is destined to fail.

Once you have the network of networks, you design, manage, and execute each of them just like any other project.

> **Note** Approaching a large system as a collection of slices or subsystems (see Chapter 3) is another manifestation of the network-of-networks idea. Each slice stands alone and is far less complex than the system as a whole. This collection of subsystems has the additional distinct advantage that each subsystem involves far fewer components than a whole system and, therefore, is less sensitive to the cumulative quality degradation discussed previously.

DESIGNING A NETWORK OF NETWORKS

Since you do not know in advance if the segmentation is possible or what the network of networks looks like, you must engage in a preliminary mini-project whose mission is to discover the network of networks. There is never just one way of designing the network of networks; indeed, there are usually multiple possibilities for shape and structure. These possibilities are hardly ever equivalent because a few of them are likely to be easier to deal with than others. You must compare and contrast the various options.

As with all design efforts, your approach to designing the network of networks should be iterative. Start by designing the megaproject, and then chop it into individual manageable projects along and beside the mega critical path. Look for junctions where the networks interact. These junctions are a great place to start with the segmentation. Look for junctions not just of dependencies but also of time: If an entire set of activities would complete before another set could start, then there is a time junction, even if the dependencies are all intertwined. A more advanced technique is to look for a segmentation that minimizes the total cyclomatic complexity of the network of networks. In this case, P greater than 1 is acceptable for the total complexity, while each subnetwork has P of 1.

Figure 12-9 shows an example megaproject, and Figure 12-10 shows the resulting three independent subnetworks.

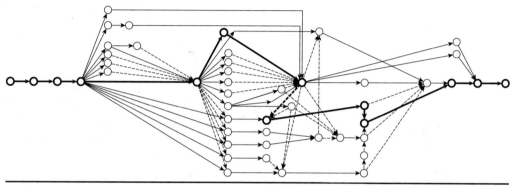

Figure 12-9 An example megaproject

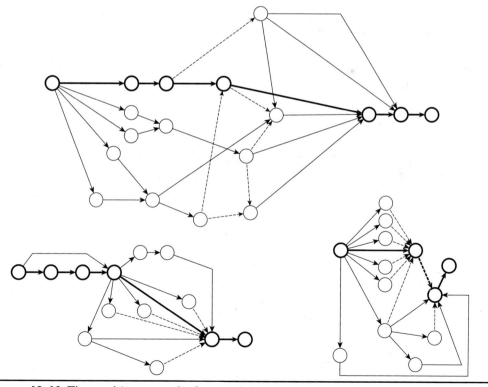

Figure 12-10 The resulting network of networks

Quite often, the initial megaproject is just too messy for such work. When this is the case, investing the time to simplify or improve the design of the megaproject will help you identify the network of networks. Look for ways to reduce complexity by introducing planning assumptions and placing constraints on the megaproject. Force certain phases to complete before others start. Eliminate solutions masquerading as requirements.

The diagram in Figure 12-9 underwent several complexity reduction iterations to reach the state shown. The initial diagram was incomprehensible and unworkable.

Decoupling Networks

The network of networks will likely include some dependencies that scuttle the segmentation or somehow prevent parallel work across all networks, at least initially. You can address these by investing in the following network-decoupling techniques:

- Architecture and interfaces
- Simulators
- Development standards
- Build, test, and deployment automation
- Quality assurance (not mere quality control)

Creative Solutions

Although there is no set formula for constructing the network of networks, the best guideline is to be creative. You will often find yourself resorting to creative solutions to nontechnical problems that stifle the segmentation. Perhaps political struggles and pushback concentrate parts of the megaproject instead of distributing them. In such cases, you need to identify the power structure and defuse the situation to allow for the segmentation. Perhaps cross-organizational concerns involving rivalries prevent proper communication and cooperation across the networks, manifesting as rigid sequential flow of the project. Or maybe the developers are in separate locations, and management insists on providing some work for each location, in a functional way. Such decomposition has nothing to do with the correct network of networks or where the real skills reside. You may need to propose a massive reorganization, including the possibility of relocating people, to have the organization reflect the network of networks, rather than the other way around (more on this topic in the next section on countering Conway's law).

Perhaps some legacy group is mandated to be part of the project due to personal favors. Instead of segmentation, this creates a choke point for the project because everything else now revolves around the legacy group. One solution might be to convert the legacy group into a cross-network group of domain expert test engineers.

Finally, try several renderings of the network of networks by different people, for the simple reason that some may see simplicity where others do not. Given what is at stake, you must pursue every angle. Take your time to carefully design the network of networks. Avoid rushing. This will be especially challenging since everyone else will be aching to start work. Due to the project's size, however, certain failure lurks without this crucial planning and structuring phase.

Countering Conway's Law

In 1968, Melvin Conway coined Conway's law,[5] which states that organizations that design systems always produce designs that are copies of the communication structures of these organizations. According to Conway, a centralized, top-down organization can produce only centralized, top-down architectures—never distributed architectures. Similarly, an organization structured along functional lines will conceive only functional decompositions of systems. Certainly, in the age of digital communication, Conway's law is not universal, but it is common.

If Conway's law poses a threat to your success, a good practical way to counter it is to restructure the organization. To do so, you first establish the correct and adequate design, and then you reflect that design in the organizational structure, the reporting structure, and the communication lines. Do not shy away from proposing such a reorganization as part of your design recommendations at the SDP review.

Although Conway referred originally to system design, his law applies equally well to project design and to the nature of the network. If your project design includes a network of networks, you may have to accompany your design with a restructuring of the organization that mimics those networks. The degree to which you will have to counter Conway's law even in a regular-size project is case-specific. Be aware of the organizational dynamics and devise the correct structure if your observation (or even your intuition) is telling you it is necessary.

SMALL PROJECTS

On the other side of the scale from very large projects are small (or even very small) projects. Counterintuitively, it is important to carefully design such small projects. Small projects are even more susceptible to project design mistakes than

---

5. Melvin E. Conway, "How Do Committees Invent?," *Datamation*, 14, no. 5 (1968): 28–31.

are regular-size projects. Due to their size they respond much more to changes in their conditions. For example, consider the effects of assigning a person incorrectly. With a team of 15 people, such a mistake affects about 7% of the available resources. With a team of 5 people, it affects 20% of the project resources. A project may be able to survive a 7% mistake, but a 20% mistake is serious trouble. A large project may have the resource buffer to survive mistakes. With a small project, every mistake is critical.

On the positive side, small projects may be so simple that they do not require much project design. For example, if you have only a single resource, the project network is a long string of activities whose duration is the sum of duration across all activities. With very minimal project design, you can know the duration and cost. There is also no need to build the time–cost curve or calculate the risk (it will be 1.0). Since most projects have some form of a network that differs from a simple string or two, and since you should avoid subcritical projects, in a practical sense you almost always design even small projects.

DESIGN BY LAYERS

All the project design examples so far in this book have produced their network of activities based on the logical dependencies between activities. I call this approach **design by dependencies**. There is, however, another option—namely, building the project according to its architecture layers. This is a straightforward process when using *The Method*'s architectural structure. You could first build the *Utilities*, then the *Resources* and the *ResourceAccess*, followed by *Engines*, *Managers*, and *Clients*, as shown in Figure 12-11. I call this technique **design by layers**.

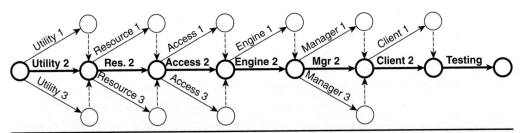

Figure 12-11 Project design by layers

As shown in Figure 12-11, the network diagram is basically a series of pulses, each corresponding to a layer in the architecture. While the pulses are sequential and often serialized, internally each pulse is constructed in parallel. *The Method*'s adherence to the closed architecture principle enables this parallel work inside a pulse.

When designing by layers, the schedule is similar to the same project designed by dependencies. Both cases result in a similar critical path composed of the components of the architecture across the layers.

Caution When designing by layers, do not forget to add nonstructural activities, such as explicit integration and system testing, to the network.

PROS AND CONS

A downside to designing by layers is the increase in risk. In theory, if all services in each layer are of equal duration, then they are all critical, and the risk number approaches 1.0. Even if that is not the case, any delay in the completion of any layer immediately delays the entire project because subsequent pulses are put on hold. When designing by dependencies, however, only the critical activities run such risk of delaying the project. The best (and nearly mandatory) way of addressing the high risk of a design-by-layers project is to use risk decompression. Because almost all activities will be critical or near critical, the project will respond very well to decompression, as all activities in each pulse gain the additional float. To further compensate for the implicit risk of design by layers, you should decompress the project so that its risk is less than 0.5, perhaps to 0.4. This level of decompression suggests that projects designed by layers will take longer than projects designed by dependencies.

Designing by layers can increase the team size and, in turn, the direct cost of the project. With design by dependencies, you find the lowest level of resources allowing unimpeded progress along the critical path by trading float for resources. With design by layers, you may need as many resources as are required to complete the current layer. The team has to work in parallel on all activities within each pulse and complete all of them before beginning the next pulse. You must assume all the components in the current layer are required by the next layer.

With that in mind, designing by layers has the clear advantage of producing a very simple project design to execute. It is the best antidote for a complex project network and can reduce overall cyclomatic complexity by half or more. In theory, since the pulses are sequential, at any moment in time the project manager has to contend with only the execution complexity of each pulse and the support activities. The cyclomatic complexity of each pulse roughly matches the number of parallel activities. In a typical *Method*-based system, this cyclomatic complexity is as low as 4 or 5, whereas the cyclomatic complexity of projects designed by dependencies can be 50 or more.

Many projects in the software industry tolerate both schedule slips and overcapacity; therefore their real challenge is complexity, not duration or cost. When possible, with *Method*-based systems, I prefer designing by layers to address the otherwise risky and complex execution. As with most things when it comes to project design, designing by layers is predicated on having the right architecture in the first place.

You can combine the techniques of both design by layers and design by dependencies. For example, the example project in Chapter 11 moved all of the infrastructure *Utilities* to the beginning of the project, despite the fact that their logical dependencies would have allowed them to take place much later in the project. The rest of the project was designed based on logical dependencies.

> **Note** Only the design methodology for the initial network dependencies differs for design by layers and design by dependencies. All other project design techniques from the previous chapters apply in exactly the same way.

LAYERS AND CONSTRUCTION

Designing and building by layers is a perfect example of the design rule from Chapter 4: Features are always and everywhere aspects of integration, not implementation. Only after all the layers are complete can you integrate them into features. This implies that designing by layers is well suited to regular projects rather than larger and more complex projects with multiple independent subsystems. To return to the house analogy, with a simple house the construction is always by layers—typically the foundation, plumbing, walls, roof, and so on. With a large multistory building, each floor is its own separate project that contains plumbing, walls, ceiling, and other tasks.

A final observation is that designing the project by layers basically breaks the project into smaller subprojects. These smaller projects are done sequentially and are separated by junctions of time. This is akin to breaking a megaproject into smaller networks and carries very similar benefits.

13

Project Design Example

While Chapter 11 illustrated an example project, its main purpose was to teach the thought process when using project design techniques and how they interrelate. Only secondarily did the example demonstrate end-to-end project design. The focus in this chapter is how to drive project design decisions in a real-life project and when to apply which project design techniques. The project designed here builds the TradeMe system, the example system from Chapter 5. As with the system design case study in Chapter 5, this chapter derives directly from the actual project that IDesign designed for one of its customers. The design team consisted of two IDesign architects (a veteran and an apprentice) and a project manager from the customer. While this example scrubs or obfuscates the specific business details, I present here the project design as it was. Both the system and the project design effort were completed in less than a week.

All of the data and calculations used in this chapter are available as part of the downloadable reference files for this book. However, when reading this chapter for the first time, I advise you to resist the temptation to crosscheck constantly between the text and the files. Instead, you should focus on the reasoning leading to those calculations and the interpretations of the results. Once those are in hand, you can use this chapter for reference as you explore the data in detail to confirm your understanding and to practice the techniques.

> **Caution** This chapter does not duplicate the previous chapters and avoids explaining specific project design techniques. A thorough understanding of the prior chapters will help you get the most out of this example.

ESTIMATIONS

The TradeMe project design effort performed two types of estimations: individual activity estimations and an overall project estimation. The individual activity estimations were used in the project design solutions, and the overall estimation served to validate the project design results.

INDIVIDUAL ACTIVITY ESTIMATIONS

Estimating the individual activities started by listing the types of activities in the project to avoid missing crucial activities. The team classified the TradeMe activities into three categories:

- Structural coding activities
- Nonstructural coding activities
- Noncoding activities

When building the list of activities, the design team expanded each list to include the individual activities and the duration estimation for each activity. The team also indicated the designated role responsible for each activity according to the customer's process or their own experience.

Estimation Assumptions

The design team clearly documented any initial constraints or assumptions on the estimations. The TradeMe project relied on the following estimation assumptions:

- **Detailed design.** The individual developers were capable of doing the detailed design, so each coding activity contained its own detailed design phase.
- **Development process.** The team was set to build the system quickly and cleanly, while relying on most of the best practices in this book.

Structural Activities

The structural activities of TradeMe derived directly from the system architecture (see Figure 5-14). These activities included *Utilities*, *Resources*, *ResourceAccess*, *Managers*, *Engines*, and *Clients*, and were mostly tasks for developers. The architect was responsible for the key activities of the `Message Bus` and the `Workflow Repository`. Table 13-1 lists the duration estimation for some of the structural coding activities of the project.

Nonstructural Coding Activities

The TradeMe design team identified a few coding activities that did not map directly to the architecture. These activities were the result of both the system operational concept and the company's development process. Table 13-2 lists the team's duration estimation for the non-structural coding activities of the project.

Table 13-1 Duration estimation for some of the structural coding activities

ID	Activity	Duration (days)	Role
14	Logging	10	Developer
15	Message Bus	15	Architect
16	Security	20	Developer
18	Payments DB	5	DB Architect
...	...	...	...
23	Workflow Repository	15	Architect
...	...	...	...
26	Payments Access	10	Developer
...	...	...	...
35	Search Engine	15	Developer
...	...	...	...
38	Market Manager	10	Developer
...	...	...	...
45	Marketplace App	25	Developer

Table 13-2 Duration estimation for nonstructural coding activities

ID	Activity	Duration (days)	Role
10	System Test Harness	25	Test Engineer
36	Abstract Manager	30	Developer
40	Regression Test Harness	10	Developer

The abstract *Manager* was a base service for the rest of the *Managers* in the system. It contained the bulk of the workflow management as well as the message bus interaction. Derived *Managers* executed specific workflows. The other two activities were both testing-related. The `System Test Harness` was owned by a test engineer, but the `Regression Test Harness` was owned by a developer.

Noncoding Activities

TradeMe had many noncoding activities, which tended to concentrate at the beginning or the end of the project. The noncoding activities were owned by various members of the core team, the test engineer, testers, or external experts such as a UX designer. These activities are shown in Table 13-3. This list was also driven by the company's development process, planning assumptions, and commitment to quality.

Table 13-3 Duration estimation for the noncoding activities

ID	Activity	Duration (days)	Role
2	Requirements	15	Architect, Product Manager
3	Architecture	15	Architect, Product Manager
4	Project Planning	10	Architect, Project Manager, Product Manager
5	Management Education	5	Architect, Project Manager, Product Manager
7	UX Design	10	UX/UI Expert
8	Dev Training	5	Architect
9	Test Plan	25	Test Engineer
11	Build and Setup	10	DevOps
12	UI Design	20	UX/UI Expert
13	Manual	20	Product Manager
25	Data Migration	10	Developer
46	Manual Polishing	10	Product Manager
47	System Testing	10	Quality Control
48	System Rollout	10	Architect, Project Manager, Product Manager, DevOps

OVERALL PROJECT ESTIMATION

The design team asked a group of 20 people to estimate the TradeMe project as a whole. The only input provided was the static architecture of TradeMe and the system's operational concept. The design team used the broadband estimation technique and came up with duration of 10.5 months and average staffing of 7.1 people. This equated to a total cost of 74.6 man-months.

DEPENDENCIES AND PROJECT NETWORK

The design team then proceeded to determine the dependencies between the various activities. The starting point for TradeMe was the architecture and the behavioral dependencies between the structural components. To those, the team added nonbehavioral dependencies such as noncoding activities or coding activities that were independent of the architecture. The design team also leveraged project design patterns and reasonable complexity reduction techniques both to simplify the network and to ease the upcoming project execution. The result was the first iteration of the project network.

BEHAVIORAL DEPENDENCIES

When building the first set of dependencies, the design team examined the use cases and the call chains supporting them. For each call chain, they listed all the components in the chain (often in the architecture hierarchy order, such as *Resources* first and *Clients* last) and then added the dependencies. For example, when they examined the Add Tradesman use case (see Figure 5-18), the design team observed that the `Membership Manager` calls the `Regulation Engine`, so they added the `Regulation Engine` as a predecessor to the `Membership Manager`.

Distilling dependencies from the use cases required multiple passes, because each call chain potentially revealed different dependencies. The design team even discovered some missing dependencies in the call chains. For example, based solely on the call chains of Chapter 5, the `Regulation Engine` required only the `Regulation Access` service. Upon further analysis, the design team decided that `Regulation Engine` depended on `Projects Access` and `Contractors Access` as well.

Abstract Structural Dependencies

The `Abstract Manager` encapsulated the common workflow management actions (e.g., persistence, state management). Therefore, the design team added a dependency between the `Abstract Manager` and the `Workflow Repository`. The other *Managers* themselves depended on the `Abstract Manager`. Similarly, the `Abstract Manager` provided the `Message Bus` dependency for all *Managers*.

Operational Dependencies

Some code dependencies were implicit in the call chains due to the system's operational concept. In TradeMe, all communication between *Clients* and *Managers* (and between *Managers* and other *Managers*) flowed over the message bus, creating an operational (not structural) dependency between them. The dependencies indicated that the *Clients* needed the *Managers* ready for test and deployment.

NONBEHAVIORAL DEPENDENCIES

TradeMe also contained dependencies that could not be traced directly to the required behavior of the system or its operational concept. These involved coding and noncoding activities alike. Such dependencies originated mostly with the company's development process and TradeMe's planning assumptions. For example, the new system had to carry forward the legacy data from the old system. Data migration necessitated that the new *Resources* (the databases) complete first, so the data migration activity depended on the *Resources*. Similarly, the completion of the *Managers* required the Regression Test Harness. In addition, at the time of the project's design, the plan still had to account for a few remaining front-end activities. Finally, the company had its own release procedures and internal dependencies, which were incorporated as dependencies between the concluding activities.

OVERRIDING SOME DEPENDENCIES

In TradeMe, a core operational concept was the use of a message bus. It was crucial to choose the right message bus technology and align the detailed design and coding activities of messages and contracts with the message bus. The call chain–derived dependencies showed that the project could defer the Message Bus activity until it was needed by the *Clients* and the *Managers*. However, that ran the risk that the message bus chosen by the development team might invalidate prior decisions about design or implementation. The team decided it was safer to address the Message Bus activity first in the project.

Similar logic applied to security. While the call chain analysis indicated that only the *Clients* and the *Managers* needed to take explicit security actions, security was so important that the project had to assure Security completed before all business logic activities. This ensured all activities had security support if they needed it and avoided security becoming an after-thought or a late-stage add-on.

Reducing Complexity

The project design team also overrode dependencies so that they could reduce the complexity of the emerging network. Specifically, they changed the following dependencies:

- **Implementing infrastructure first.** In TradeMe, most activities depended on *Utility* components such as `Logging`. Moving the infrastructure (which also included the `Build`) to the beginning of the project drastically reduced the number of dependencies in the project. It also had the benefit of making the infrastructure available to all components in case the need arose, especially those components that had no obvious need based on the call chains alone.

- **Adding milestones.** Even at this early stage of the project, the design team introduced three milestones. The `SDP Review` milestone concluded the front-end activities. The other two milestones were `Infrastructure Complete` and `Managers Complete`: All development activities depended on the infrastructure milestone, and all *Clients* depended on the completion of the *Managers*.

- **Consolidating inherited dependencies.** The design team consolidated dependencies into inherited dependencies where possible. For example, even though the *Clients* require the `Message Bus`, that dependency could be inherited via their *Manager* dependencies.

SANITY CHECKS

With the initial network laid out, the design team performed the following sanity checks:

1. Verified the TradeMe project had a single start activity and a single end activity.
2. Verified that every activity in the project resided on a path ending somewhere on the critical path(s).
3. Verified that the initial risk measurement yielded a relatively low risk number.
4. Calculated the duration of the project without any resource assignment. This came to 7.8 months and later would serve as important check of the normal solution.

THE NORMAL SOLUTION

The company provided the following planning assumptions:

- **Core team.** The core team was required throughout the project. The core team consisted of a single architect, a project manager, and a product manager. The core team was allowed to work directly on the project only infrequently. Such work included key high-risk activities done by the architect and producing the user manual, which was assigned to the product manager.

- **Access to experts.** The project had access to experts or specialists, such as test engineers, DB architects, and UX/UI designers.
- **Assignments.** There was a 1:1 assignment of developers to services or other coding activities. On top of assigning based on floats, whenever possible, TradeMe maintained task continuity (see Chapter 7).
- **Quality control.** A single quality control tester was required from the start of construction to the end of the project. The tester was treated as a direct cost only during the system test activity. One additional tester was required for the system testing activity.
- **Build and operations.** A single build, configuration, deployment, and DevOps specialist was required from start of construction until the end of the project.
- **Developers.** Developers between tasks were considered to be a direct cost rather than an indirect cost. TradeMe's high quality expectations eliminated the need for developers during system testing.

Table 13-4 outlines which roles were required in each phase of the project.

Table 13-4 Roles and phases of the project

Role	Front End	Infrastructure	Services	Testing
Architect	X	X	X	X
Project Manager	X	X	X	X
Product Manager	X	X	X	X
Testers		X	X	X
DevOps		X	X	X
Developers		X	X	

NETWORK DIAGRAM

Assigning resources to the various activities affected the project network. In several places, the network included dependencies on the resources in addition to the logical dependencies between the activities. After consolidating the inherited dependencies, the network diagram looked like Figure 13-1.

Figure 13-1 contains a couple of collapsed dependencies (indicated by two activity numbers per arrow) that simplified the diagram without affecting its nature. The most notable aspect of this network diagram is that it contains two critical paths.

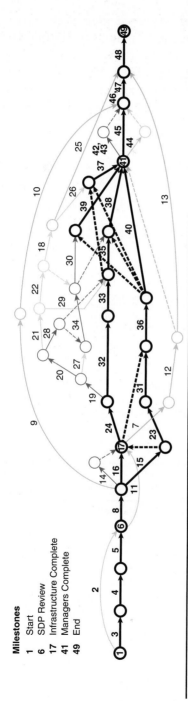

Milestones

1 Start
6 SDP Review
17 Infrastructure Complete
41 Managers Complete
49 End

Figure 13-1 Logical dependencies network diagram

PLANNED PROGRESS

Figure 13-2 captures the planned earned value of the first normal solution. The duration of this solution stood at 7.8 months, indicating that the staffing assignments had not extended the critical path. The chart in Figure 13-2 has the general shape of a shallow S curve but is not ideal. The project starts reasonably well, but the second half of the project is not very shallow. The steep planned earned value curve was also reflected in the somewhat elevated risk values. Both the activity risk and criticality risk were 0.7.

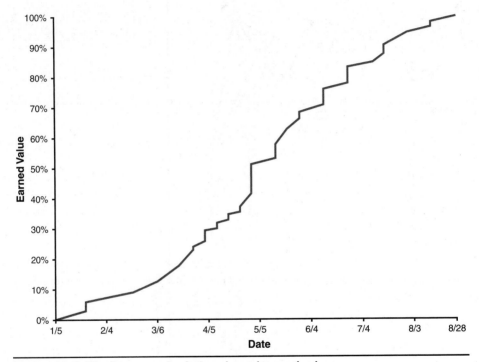

Figure 13-2 The first normal solution planned earned value

PLANNED STAFFING DISTRIBUTION

Figure 13-3 shows the staffing distribution chart of the first normal solution. As with the planned earned value chart, the distribution in Figure 13-3 is problematic. The distinct peak at the center of the project indicates waste and implies an unrealistic expectation of staffing elasticity (see Chapter 7 and Figure 7-10).

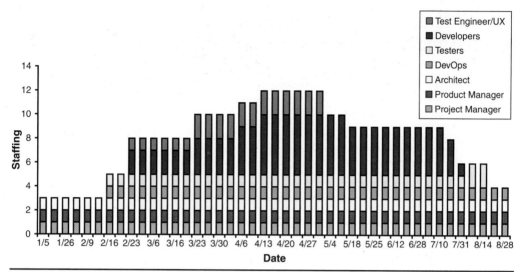

Figure 13-3 The first normal solution staffing distribution

COST AND EFFICIENCY

Based on the staffing distribution, the project total cost came to 59 man-months: 32 man-months of direct cost and 27 man-months of indirect cost. The higher direct cost compared to the indirect cost indicated that this solution likely was very much to the left side of the time–cost curve, where the indirect cost is still low.

The calculated project efficiency was 32%. Since the upper practical limit is 25%, such high efficiency was questionable. Taken together, the direct cost higher than the indirect cost, the conspicuous peak in the staffing distribution chart, and the high efficiency strongly indicated overly aggressive assumptions about staffing elasticity. The solution expected that across all the parallel network paths, resources would always be available at the right time to maintain progress. The rather steep planned earned value chart visualized this expectation. In short, this first attempt at the normal solution assumed a very efficient team, likely one too efficient to be practical.

RESULTS SUMMARY

Table 13-5 summaries the project metrics of this first normal solution.

Table 13-5 Project metrics of the first normal solution

Project Metric	Value
Duration (months)	7.8
Total cost (man-months)	59
Direct cost (man-months)	32
Peak staffing	12
Average staffing	7.5
Average developers	3.5
Efficiency	32%
Activity risk	0.7
Criticality risk	0.7

COMPRESSED SOLUTION

The next step was to consider options for accelerating the project. Due to the presence of the two critical paths, the best course of action was to compress this project by enabling parallel work.

From Figure 13-1, it was evident that the *Manager* services (activities 36, 37, 38, 39), along with the `Regression Test Harness` (activity 40), capped the two critical paths, as well as the two near-critical paths. The *Clients* (activities 42, 43, 44, 45), in turn, depended on the completion of all the *Managers*, prolonging the project. This made the *Clients* and the *Managers* natural candidates for compression.

ADDING ENABLING ACTIVITIES

For each *Manager* service, the design team added the following activities, which enabled the compression:

1. A contract design activity that decoupled the Clients from the Manager. The various contract design activities could perhaps have started after the SDP review, but it was deemed better to postpone them until after the infrastructure was complete. Estimated work per contract: 5 days.

2. A *Manager* simulator that provided a good-enough implementation of the *Manager*'s contract. The simulators had to enable full development of the *Clients*, which now depended on the simulators, not the actual *Managers*. The

simulators had no dependencies on lower-level services such as *ResourceAccess* or *Engines*. The simulators needed only the *Manager* contracts to simulate and the Message Bus. The contracts themselves depended on the infrastructure, which included the Message Bus. Estimated work per simulator: 15 days.

3. A dedicated activity that integrated and retested the *Clients* against the *Managers*. The integration activity depended on the completion of the actual *Manager* and its *Clients*. The system testing activity now required not just the *Clients* but also all the *Manager* integrations to be completed. Estimated work per integration activity: 5 days.

Figure 13-4 shows a simplified network diagram capturing the compression-related activities in red. In the compressed network, the *Managers* were only near-critical and were developed on a similar timeline to the normal solution. The most important change (which allowed the compression in the first place) was that the *Clients* now completed a month sooner. However, the reduction in the duration of the project was less than a month because of the additional integration activities following the *Managers*.

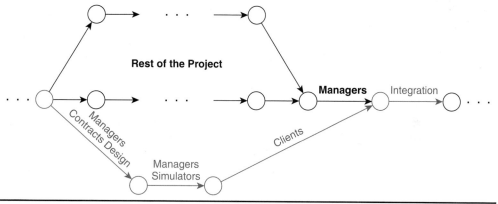

Figure 13-4 Simplified network diagram for the compressed solution

Managers' Duration Estimation

The duration estimation for the *Managers* themselves remained unchanged. In the normal solution, each *Manager* activity had to internally include some investment in designing the service contract. In theory, once the design team had extracted the contract design out of the *Managers* into separate activities, each *Manager* should have taken less time. However, in practice, this reduction is unlikely. Splitting activities is never 100% efficient, and inevitably some effort is lost due to the need to understand the contract and how it affected the internal implementation of the *Managers*. To compensate for these shortcomings, the design team kept the duration estimation of the *Managers* the same as for the normal solution.

ASSIGNING RESOURCES

The rest of the steps for the compressed solution were virtually identical to those for the normal solution. However, the design team discovered they could reduce the staff by two developers throughout the project by using the architect for one development activity and by pushing the schedule out one week. The company judged trading the slight delay for the reduced staff as acceptable given its challenge in securing more developers. The duration of the compressed solution came in at 7.1 months, a 3-week (9%) acceleration compared with the normal solution (7.8 months). The new resources did consume more of the floats, and the new risk number for the project was 0.74.

PLANNED PROGRESS

Figure 13-5 shows the planned earned value for the compressed solution. The curve now tapers somewhat at the end of the project, better than that in the normal solution.

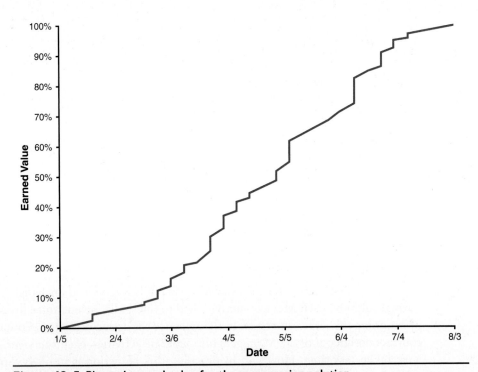

Figure 13-5 Planned earned value for the compression solution

PLANNED STAFFING DISTRIBUTION

Figure 13-6 shows the staffing distribution of the compressed solution. The staffing distribution looks solid for the most part. The initial ramp-up from 3 to 12 people is a bit challenging, but doable. Peak staffing of 12 is the same as the normal solution. Average staffing is at 8.2, compared with 7.5 of the normal solution.

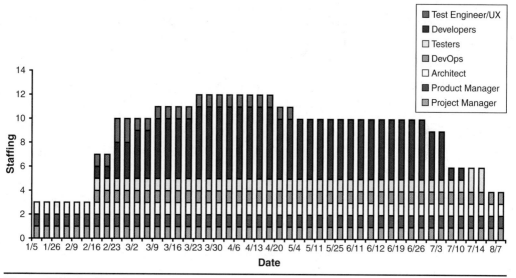

Figure 13-6 Staffing distribution for the compressed solution

COST AND EFFICIENCY

The cost of the compressed solution came in at 58.5 man-months, slightly less than the normal solution's cost of 59 man-months. Direct cost was 36.7 man-months compared with the normal solution's direct cost of 32 man-months. Although this project design solution was faster and at lower cost, the real difference from the normal solution was the expected project efficiency—37%. If the normal solution's efficiency of 32% required a highly efficient team, the compressed solution demanded nothing less than a team of heroes. Combined with the elevated risk of 0.74, this compressed solution was a disappointment waiting to happen.

RESULTS SUMMARY

Table 13-6 summarizes the metrics of the compressed solution. The compressed solution made an already challenging project (see Figure 13-1) more challenging and created an unrealistically high efficiency expectation. Its major downside, however, was the integration—not the increase in execution complexity. The multiple, parallel integrations occurring near the end of the project offered no leeway. If any of them went awry, the team had no time for repairs. The increase in both the execution complexity and the integration risk in exchange for less than a month of compression was not a good trade.

Table 13-6 Project metrics of the compressed solution

Project Metric	Value
Duration (months)	7.1
Total cost (man-months)	58.5
Direct cost (man-months)	36.7
Peak staffing	12
Average staffing	8.2
Average developers	4.7
Efficiency	37%
Activity risk	0.73
Criticality risk	0.75

Even so, this compression attempt was not a waste of time—it proved the compressed solution would be an exercise in futility. The compressed solution also helped the design team to better understand the project and provided another point on the time–cost curve.

DESIGN BY LAYERS

The main problem with the first normal solution was not the unrealistic efficiency but the complexity of the project network. That complexity is evident just by examining the (already simplified) network diagram in Figure 13-1. The cyclomatic complexity of the network is 33 units. Coupled with the high efficiency expected of the team, this implied a high execution risk.

Instead of confronting the high complexity, the design team chose to redesign the project by architecture layers, as opposed to the logical dependencies between the activities. This produced mostly a string of pulses of activities. The pulses corresponded to the layers of the architecture or the phase of the project: front end, infrastructure and foundational work, *Resources*, *ResourceAccess*, *Engines*, *Managers*, *Clients*, and release activities (Figure 13-7).

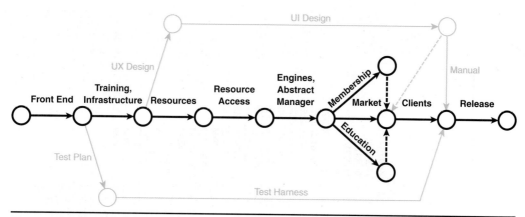

Figure 13-7 Design-by-layers network diagram

While the pulses were serialized and sequential to each other, internally the pulses were done in parallel. In Figure 13-7, all the pulses are collapsed except for the expanded *Manager*'s pulse. A few remaining support activities, such as UI Design and the Test Harness, were not part of the string of pulses, but they had very high float.

An instantly noticeable aspect of Figure 13-7 is how simple that network is compared with that of Figure 13-1. Since the pulses were sequential in time, the project manager would only have to contend with the complexity of each pulse and its support activities. In TradeMe, the complexity of the individual pulses was 2, 4, 5, 4, 4, 4, 4, and 2. The complexity of the support activities was 1 and, due to their high float, had essentially no effect on the execution complexity.

DESIGN BY LAYERS AND RISK

As discussed in Chapter 12, design by layers yields riskier projects. The design team found that with TradeMe, the risk of the design-by-layers solution was 0.76, up from the 0.7 of the original normal solution (which used design by dependencies). The risk went even higher to 0.79 when ignoring the high-float support activities.

STAFFING DISTRIBUTION

Figure 13-8 shows the planned staffing distribution for the design-by-layers solution. The overall shape of the staffing distribution chart was satisfactory. The project needed only 4 developers, and staffing peaked at 11 people.

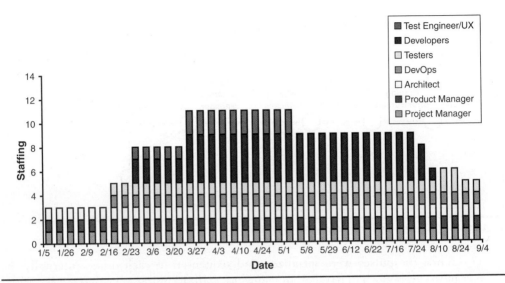

Figure 13-8 Design-by-layers staffing distribution

RESULTS SUMMARY

Table 13-7 shows the project metrics for designing TradeMe by layers.

Table 13-7 Project metrics for the design-by-layers solution

Project Metric	Value
Duration (months)	8.1
Total cost (man-months)	60.8
Direct cost (man-months)	32.2
Peak staffing	11
Average staffing	7.5
Average developers	3.4
Efficiency	31%
Activity risk	0.75
Criticality risk	0.76

SUBCRITICAL SOLUTION

The design-by-layers solution called for four developers. The company was concerned about what would happen if it was unable to get those four developers. It was therefore important to investigate the implications of going subcritical. The planning assumptions still allowed for access to external experts.

For this project, any design-by-layers solution with fewer than four developers became subcritical, so the design team chose to explore a two-developer solution. These developers were assigned the database design as well. The subcritical network diagram was similar to the one in Figure 13-7 except that internally each pulse consisted of only two parallel strings of activities.

DURATION, PLANNED PROGRESS, AND RISK

The subcritical solution extended the project to 11.1 months. The planned earned value curve (shown in Figure 13-9) was almost a straight line whose linear regression trend line had an R^2 of 0.98.

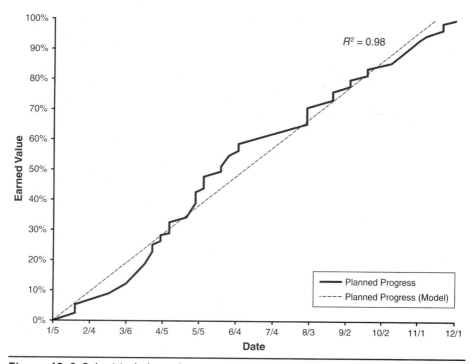

Figure 13-9 Subcritical planned progress

The subcritical nature of the solution was also reflected by its risk index of 0.84. If the company had to pursue this option, the design team recommended decompressing the project by at least a month. Decompression pushed the schedule into the 12-month range, 50% or more longer than the design-by-layers solution.

COST AND EFFICIENCY

The total cost of the subcritical solution was 74.1 man-months, with a direct cost of 30.4 man-months, and the expected efficiency was more reasonable at 25%. The staffing distribution chart (not shown) was missing the hump in the center, as is typical for subcritical solutions (see Chapter 7).

RESULTS SUMMARY

Table 13-8 shows the project metrics for the subcritical solution.

Table 13-8 Project metrics for the subcritical solution

Project Metric	Value
Duration (months)	11.1
Total cost (man-months)	74.1
Direct cost (man-months)	30.4
Peak staffing	9
Average staffing	6.7
Average developers	2
Efficiency	25%
Activity risk	0.85
Criticality risk	0.82

The subcritical time and cost metrics (11.1 months and 74.1 man-months) compared favorably to those for the overall estimation (10.5 months and 74.6 man-months), differing by about 5% in duration and less than 1% in cost. This correlation suggested that the subcritical solution numbers were the likely option for the project. The more realistic 25% efficiency also gave credence to the subcritical solution.

COMPARING THE OPTIONS

Analyzing the results of Table 13-5 and Table 13-7 revealed several telling observations. First, the project duration remained largely the same regardless of whether the team used design by layers or design by dependencies. As explained in Chapter 12, this similarity was expected. After all, call chain–based dependencies are principally a product of the layers, and the project duration is dictated by the longest path through the layers. Also, the average staffing level of developers and efficiency were unchanged. The main differences related to the drastically reduced execution complexity and the higher risk with the design-by-layers solution.

In short, for TradeMe, design by layers was comparable to or better than the first normal solution in every respect except risk. Even if the design-by-layers solution had cost more and taken longer, its execution simplicity made it the obvious choice for TradeMe. The design-by-layers solution was also far better than the subcritical solution derived from it. The subcritical solution cost more, took longer, and was riskier. The design team adopted the design-by-layers solution as the normal solution for the remainder of the analysis.

PLANNING AND RISK

At this point the design team had produced four solutions for building the system: the compressed solution, the normal solution by dependencies, the normal solution by layers, and the subcritical option of the design-by-layers solution. Since the subcritical solution was a fallback position for the design-by-layers solution, the design team excluded it from the risk analysis.

RISK DECOMPRESSION

The design-by-layers solution had elevated risk and critical pulses, which the design team mitigated by using risk decompression. Since the appropriate amount of decompression was unknown, the design team tried decompressing by 1 week, 2 weeks, 4 weeks, 6 weeks, and 8 weeks, and observed the risk behavior. Table 13-9 shows the risk values of the three design options and the five decompression points.

Table 13-9 Risk values for the options and decompression points

Option	Duration (months)	Criticality Risk	Activity Risk
Compressed	7.1	0.75	0.73
Design by Dependencies	7.8	0.70	0.70
Design by Layers	8.1	0.76	0.75
D1	8.3	0.60	0.65
D2	8.5	0.48	0.57
D3	9.0	0.42	0.46
D4	9.4	0.27	0.39
D5	9.9	0.27	0.34

Figure 13-10 plots these options and decompression points against the timeline. The criticality risk behaved as expected, and the risk dropped with decompression along some logistic function. The activity risk also dropped with decompression, but a gap appeared between the two curves because the activity risk model did not respond well to an uneven distribution of the floats. The calculations that produced the values in Table 13-9 addressed this issue by adjusting the float outliers as described in Chapter 11—that is, by replacing the outliers with the average of the floats plus one standard deviation of the floats. In this case, the adjustment was simply insufficient. A float adjustment at half a standard deviation aligned the curves perfectly. However, the design team chose to just use the criticality risk curve, which did not require any adjustments. The team observed that decompression beyond D4 was excessive because the risk curve was leveling out.

With the values in Table 13-9, the design team found a polynomial correlation model for the risk curve with R^2 of 0.96:

$$\text{Risk} = 0.09t^3 - 2.28t^2 + 19.19t - 52.40$$

where t is measured in months.

Using the risk model, maximum risk was at 7.4 months, with a risk value of 0.78. This point was between the deign-by-dependencies solution's 7.8 months and the compressed solution's 7.1 months (see Figure 13-11). The design team removed the compressed solution from consideration because it was past the point of maximum risk. Even the design-by-dependencies solution was borderline risk-wise: At 7.8

months, the risk was already 0.75, the maximum recommended value. The design-by-layers solution was at a comfortable 0.68 risk. The point of minimum risk was at 9.7 months with a risk value of 0.25.

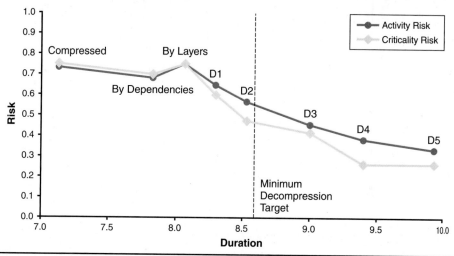

Figure 13-10 Discrete risk curves

Table 13-10 captures the risk value of these points, and Figure 13-11 visualizes them along the risk model curve.

Table 13-10 Risk model values and points of interest

Option	Duration (months)	Risk Model
Compressed	7.1	0.75
Maximum Risk	7.4	0.78
Design by Dependencies	7.8	0.74
Design by Layers	8.1	0.68
Minimum Direct Cost	8.46	0.56
D2	8.53	0.53
Minimum Decompression Target	8.6	0.52
D3	9.0	0.38
Minimum Risk	9.7	0.25

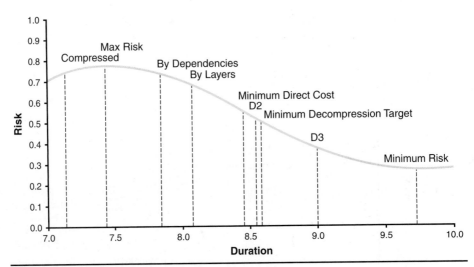

Figure 13-11 Risk model curve and points of interest

Finding the Decompression Target

Using the technique explained in Chapter 12, the design team calculated the minimum risk decompression target (where the risk curve's second derivative is zero) at 8.6 months, with a risk value of 0.52. This point lay between the D2 and D3 decompression points (see Figure 13-10), making the point to its right, D3, the recommended decompression target. The risk at the duration of D3 was 0.38 on the risk model, slightly less than the actual value of 0.42 for D3. While the risk value for the decompression target may seem low (significantly less than the ideal 0.5), it was in line with the recommendation in Chapter 12 to decompress design-by-layer projects to 0.4 to compensate for their inherent risk.

The last technique put to bear on finding the decompression target was calculating the point of minimum direct cost. However, the direct cost at the decompression points was unknown.

Examining Figure 13-8 and Table 13-7, the design team conservatively estimated that the decompression required three out of the four developers to keep working during the decompression. This allowed the team to calculate the direct cost for extending the project to the D5 decompression point. The design team added that extra direct cost to the known direct cost of the design-by-layers solution, which provided a direct cost curve and a well-fitted correlation model:

$$\text{Direct Cost} = 2.98t^2 - 50.42t + 244.53$$

Using the direct cost formula, the design team found the point of minimum direct cost at 8.46 months, right before D2. Substituting the 8.46-month duration into the risk formula provided a risk of 0.56. The duration difference between the minimum point of the direct cost model and the zero point of the second derivative of the risk model was 1%, confirming D3 as the decompression target. Incidentally, the minimum direct cost was 31.4 man-months, while the direct cost at D3 was 32.2 man-months, a difference of merely 3%.

RECALCULATING COST

Recommending D3 required the design team to provide the total cost at that point. While the direct cost was known from the prior formula, the indirect cost was unknown across the decompression range. The design team modeled the indirect cost for the three known solutions, obtaining a simple straight line described by the following formula:

$$\text{Indirect Cost} = 7.27t - 30.01$$

The design team added the direct and indirect cost equations together to come up with the formula for the total cost in the system:

$$\text{Total Cost} = 2.98t^2 - 50.42t + 244.53 + 7.27t - 30.01$$
$$= 2.98t^2 - 43.5t + 214.52$$

Using this formula, the total cost at D3 was 67.6 man-months.

> **Note**   Although they did not do so in real time with TradeMe's customer, the design team used the direct cost and risk models to find the project's risk crossover points. These came at 7.64 months and 0.77 risk (for the too-risky crossover point) and at 9.47 months and 0.27 risk (for the too-safe risk crossover point). These points coincided nicely with the guidelines of 0.75 and 0.3, respectively, and confirmed the validity of the project design points discussed previously.

PREPARING FOR THE SDP REVIEW

The best project design option so far was D3, the one-month decompression from the design-by-layers solution. It provided a simple, achievable project at reduced risk and virtually at minimum direct cost. The somewhat low indirect cost made this solution the optimal option for the project from duration, cost, and risk perspectives.

In addition to this optimal point, the design team presented the design-by-dependencies solution to the company's decision makers. It demonstrated that any attempt of decreasing the schedule would drastically increase the design risk and the execution risk due to high complexity and the unrealistic expected efficiency of the team.

Because of the potential resource shortage, the design team found it necessary to include the subcritical solution, but only with adequate decompression. Repeating similar steps as for the design-by-layers solution, the decompressed subcritical solution provided a risk of 0.47, a duration of 11.8 months, and a total cost of 79.5 man-months. The decompressed subcritical solution was presented both to show the consequences of understaffing the project and to show that the project was still feasible, if the need should arise.

Due to their higher risk, there was no point in considering the non-decompressed options of the design-by-layers and subcritical solutions. Table 13-11 summarizes the project design options that the design team presented at the SDP review.

Table 13-11 Viable project design options

Project Option	Duration (months)	Total Cost (man-months)	Risk	Complexity
Activity Driven	8	61	0.74	High
Architecture Driven	9	68	0.38	Low
Understaffed	12	80	0.47	Low

For the presentation, the design team renamed the design options to avoid project design jargon such as "normal," "decompression," "subcritical," and "by layers." In Table 13-11, the label "Activity Driven" stands for design by dependencies, "Architecture Driven" stands for design by layers, and "Understaffed" stands for subcritical.

The table used plain-language terms such as "High" and "Low" for complexity and rounded all numbers other than the risk values. The table gently prodded the decision makers toward the decompressed design-by-layers solution.

14

CONCLUDING THOUGHTS

The previous chapters focused on the technical aspects of designing a project. Certainly, you can view project design as a technical design task. After practicing project design for decades, I find that it is actually a mindset, not just an expertise. You should not simply calculate the risk or the cost and try to meet your commitments. You must strive for a complete superiority over every aspect of the project. You should prepare mitigations for everything the project can throw at you—which requires going beyond the mechanics and the numbers. You should adopt a holistic approach that involves your personality and attitude, how you interact with management and the developers, and the recognition of the effect that design has on the development process and the product life cycle. The ideas I have laid out for system and project design in both parts of this book open a portal to a parallel level of excellence in software engineering. It is up to you to keep that portal open, to keep improving, to refine these ideas, to develop your own style, and to adapt. This concluding chapter advises how you should approach these aspects, but more importantly shows you how to continue the journey.

WHEN TO DESIGN A PROJECT

There are several answers to the question of when to design a project. One straightforward response is "always." Compared with the dismal state of affairs for most software projects, what project design has to offer is understandably quite compelling.

As an engineer, I am wary of absolute answers like "never" and "always." You should answer the question of when to design a project from ROI perspective. Compare the time and cost of designing a project with the benefits of building the system in the fastest way, the least costly way, and the safest possible way. Since it takes just a few days to a week to design a project, from an ROI perspective it is easy to justify designing most projects. Furthermore, the larger the scope of the project, the more you should invest in project design that gives you the optimal solution. With a large and expensive project, even a minute change from the optimal point could be both huge in absolute terms and likely to surpass the cost of designing the project.

Another answer to the question of when to design a project is "whenever you have an aggressive deadline." Even without compression, merely having the most efficient team assigned along the critical path of a plain normal solution will beat any other approach, especially compared with projects that attempt to build the system iteratively.

THE REAL ANSWER

The final answer to the question of when to design a project is the most important section in this entire book. Imagine you have an idea for the next killer app, something that could be immensely successful. You need some capital to build it, to cover costs from hiring the people to paying for cloud compute time. You could seek venture capital in exchange for most of the equity and then work 60 hours a week for several years on something that is likely to fail. You could also self-fund the project: You could sell your house, liquidate your pension plan and life savings, and borrow from friends and family.

If you choose the self-funding route, would you invest in project design? Would this investment be a little investment in time and effort or a large one? Would you say that you do not have time for project design? Would you say that it is better to just start building something and figure things out later, or will you do whatever it takes to find out if the project is affordable before becoming broke and destitute? Would you skip any of the techniques or analysis of project design? Even if you can afford the project, would you not still design the project to identify the risk exclusion zones? Would you repeat all the calculations a second time for good measure? Would you first design the project to see if you should sell your house and quit your job? After all, if the project requires $3 million and you were able to muster only $2 million, you should keep the house, not the new startup. The same goes for the duration of the project. If you have only a one-year marketing window and the project is really a two-year project, then you should do nothing. When self-funded, would you also not prefer that your developers work against detailed assembly instructions of the project, as opposed to wasting your scant resources trying to figure it out on their own?

Next, imagine a project where the manager is held personally liable for any failure to meet the commitments. Instead of the manager earning a nice bonus when meeting the commitments, in the case of failure the manager has to pay out of pocket for the project cost overruns, if not the lost sales, as well as any contractual obligations. In such a situation, would the manager oppose project design or insist on it? Would the manager resist project design because "that is not how we do things here"? Would the manager invest a little or a lot in system and project design to ensure the commitments are aligned with what the team can produce? Would the manager avoid finding out where the death zone is? Would the manager give up on sound architecture that will ensure the project design itself will not change much? Would the manager say that since no one is working this way, that is a good enough reason not to design the project?

The dissonance is stark. Most people have a callous, cavalier, and complacent attitude when the company is paying. Most people avoid thinking for themselves because it is so much easier to dogmatically follow the common practices of a failing industry and use that as an excuse when squandering other people's money. Most just make excuses such as that they do not have the time, or that project design is the wrong process, or that project design is over-engineered. Yet when their head is on the chopping block, the same people become project design zealots. Such a difference in behavior is a direct result of lack of integrity, both personal and professional. The real answer to the question of when to design a project is *when you have integrity.*

Getting Ahead in Life

The best career advice I can give you is this:

Treat the company's money as your own.

Nothing else really matters. Most managers cannot tell the difference between a great design and a horrible design, so they will never promote or reward you based on architecture alone. However, if you treat the company's money as your own, if you thoroughly design the project to find the most affordable and safest way of building the system, and if you flat out refuse any other course of action, the higher-ups will notice. By showing the utmost respect for the company's money, you will earn their respect, because respect is always reciprocal. Conversely, people do not respect those who are disrespectful toward them. When you are accountable for your actions and decisions, your worth in the eyes of top management will drastically increase. If you repeatedly meet your commitments, you will earn the trust of the top brass. When the next opportunity comes, they will give it to the one person whom they trust to be respectful of their time and money: you.

This advice is drawn from my own career. Before I was 30 years old, I led the software architecture group of a Fortune 100 company in Silicon Valley, the most competitive place in the world for the software industry. My rise to the top had little to do with my architecture prowess (as discussed, that hardly ever amounts to much). I did, however, always bundle my system design with project design, and that made all the difference. In my mind, the company's money was my money.

FINANCIAL ANALYSIS

With most sizable projects, someone somehow must decide how to pay for the project. Project managers may even have to present the expected burn rate or cash flow of the project. This is especially important with large projects. For these projects, the customer is typically unable to pay a lump sum either at the beginning or the end of the project, requiring the developing organization to fund the effort via a payment schedule. In most cases, lacking any kind of knowledge about the project flow or its network design, financial planning is reduced to some amalgam of guesswork, wishful thinking, and functional decomposition of payments (e.g., a certain amount per feature). This often is a recipe for disaster. As it turns out, there is no need for guesswork about the financial side of the project. With very little extra work, you can extend your project design into a financial analysis of the project.

From your staffing distribution, you can calculate the cost of each time slice of the project. Next, present those costs as a running sum, either as absolute values or in relative terms (percentages). You can even present direct versus total cost over time, either numerically or graphically (for financial planning, you should use monetary units rather than effort units, so you need to know the cost of a man-month at your organization).

The reason for mentioning the financial planning aspect of the project in a book about software design has little to do with finance, as valuable as that is. In most software projects, the people who are trying to design the system and the project, to invest in best practices, and to meet their commitments face a grueling uphill struggle, as if everybody else is bent on doing everything the worst possible way.

Somewhere up in the organization is a financial planner or an officer, an executive, a VP, or a CIO who needs to make financial decisions. These people wield a great deal of power and authority, but are often flying blind. If you make these top people aware that you can design the financial details of the project to the degree shown here, then they will insist that you do so. Of course, being able to produce the cost and cash flow of the project hinges on a workable project design, which in turn stems from having the correct architecture. Suddenly, a senior person becomes your greatest ally for doing things properly.

GENERAL GUIDELINES

Do not design a clock.

After years of disappointments and disillusion from software projects, those exposed for the first time to the ideas of project design are captivated by its precision and fascinated by its engineering principles. They are tempted to go after every last digit in every calculation and to refine every last assumption and estimation, thereby missing the point of sound project design. The most important thing that project design enables is making educated decisions about the project: whether to proceed at all, and if so, under which option. The project design option you choose will always differ from reality, and the actual project execution will be similar, but not quite what you have designed. The project manager must follow up on the project design by frequently tracking the project against the plan and taking corrective actions (see Appendix A).

Even the best project design solution just gives you a fighting chance during execution—nothing more. Note that "best" in this context means a design that is the most calibrated to what your team can produce (in terms of time, cost, and risk), not necessarily the optimal design.

Think of project design as a sundial, rather than a clock. A sundial is an extremely simple device (a vertical stick in the ground), but it is good enough to tell the time down to the minute (if you know the date and the latitude). A clock can tell the time down to the second, but it is a far more intricate device in which every internal detail has to be perfectly tuned for it to work at all. By analogy, your project design effort needs to be only good enough to tell roughly to what it is possible to commit. Optimal precise solutions where every last detail is perfectly aligned are nice, but a normal, doable solution is a must.

ARCHITECTURE VERSUS ESTIMATIONS

Never design a project without a solid architecture that encapsulates the volatilities.

Without the correct system architecture, at some point the system design will change. Those changes mean that you will be building a different system which will void the project design. Once that happens, it does not matter if you had the best project design at the beginning of the project. As prescribed in the first part of the book, you need to invest the time to deal with the volatilities, whether or not you use the structure of *The Method* to do so.

Unlike architecture, estimations and specific resources are secondary to a good project design. The topology of the network (which derives from the architecture) dictates the duration of the project, not the capabilities of the developers or, to a point, the variation in individual estimations. Estimations that differ significantly from reality could affect the project drastically. However, as long as the estimation is more or less correct, then it does not matter if the real duration involved is somewhat larger or smaller. With a decent-size project you will have dozens of activities whose individual estimations may be off in either direction. Overall, these offsets will tend to cancel each other. The same is true with developers' capabilities. It makes a huge difference if you have the world's worst or best developer, but as long as you have decent developers, things will even out. It is more important to be creative in coming up with project design ideas, to recognize constraints, and to work around pitfalls than it is to get every estimation exactly right.

DESIGN STANCE

You should not apply the ideas in this book dogmatically.

You should adapt the project design tools to your particular circumstances without compromising on the end result. This book aims to show you what is possible, to trigger your natural curiosity, to encourage you be creative, and to lead.

When possible, do not design a project in secret. Design artifacts and a visible design process build trust with the decision makers. If stakeholders ask, educate them about what you are doing and why you are doing things this way.

OPTIONALITY

Communicate with management in Optionality.

When you engage with management, speak the language I call **Optionality**: succinctly describing the options from which management can choose, and enabling objective evaluation of these options. This is very much aligned with a core concept in project design: There is no "the" project. There are always multiple options for building and delivering any system. Each option is some viable combination of time, cost, and risk. You should therefore design several such options from which management may chose.

The essence of good management is choosing the right option. Moreover, giving people options empowers them. After all, if there is truly no other option, then there is also no need for the manager. Managers who lack options from which to choose will be forced to justify their existence by introducing arbitrary options.

Without a backing project design, such contrived options always have poor results. To avoid this danger, you must present management with a set of viable project design options, preselected by you. For example, Chapter 11 investigated a total of 15 project design options, but the corresponding SDP review had only 4 options.

That said, do not overdo Optionality. Giving too many options upsets people, a predicament known as the paradox of choice.[1] This paradox is rooted in the fear of missing out on some better option you did not choose, even if the option you did choose was good enough.

Here are my guidelines on how many options to present:

- Two options is too few—too close to no options at all.
- Three options is ideal; most people can easily choose between three options.
- Four options is fine as long as at least one of them (and maybe two) is an obvious mistake.
- Five options is too many options, even if they are all good options.

COMPRESSION

Do not exceed 30% compression.

Whichever way you choose to compress the project, a 30% reduction in schedule is the maximum compression you will likely see when starting from a sound normal solution. Such highly compressed projects will probably suffer from high execution and schedule risk. When you first begin using the project design tools and building competency within your team, avoid solutions with more than 25% compression.

Understanding the Project

Always compress the project, even if the likelihood of pursuing any of the compressed solutions is low.

Compression reveals the true nature and behavior of the project, and there is always something to gain by better understanding your own project. Compression allows you to model the project's time–cost curve, and obtaining formulas for cost and risk is helpful when you are required to assess the effect of schedule changes. It is immensely valuable to be able to quickly and decisively determine the likely consequence of a change request. The alternative is gut feel and conflict.

---

1. Barry Schwartz, *The Paradox of Choice: Why More Is Less* (Ecco, 2004).

Even if you suspect that an incoming request is unreasonable, saying "no"—especially to a person of authority and power—is not conducive to your career. The only way to say "no" is to get "them" to say "no." By showing the quantified effects on schedule, cost, and risk, you immediately bring to the surface what before you could only intuit, enabling an emotion-free, objective discussion. In the absence of numbers and measurements, anything goes. Ignorance of reality is not a sin, but malpractice is. If decision makers are aware of numbers that contradict their commitments to customers and still persist with those commitments, they are perpetrating fraud. Because such liability is unacceptable, in the presence of hard numbers, they will find ways of rescinding their commitments or changing previously "unchangeable" dates.

Compressing with Top Resources

Compress with top resources carefully and judiciously.

When relying on top resources, proper project design is essential to know where to apply them. As appealing as it may be, compressing with top resources may backfire. To begin with, top talent is typically scarce, so the top resources you require to meet your commitments may not be available. Waiting for them creates delays and defeats the purpose of the compression. Even when available, top resources may make things worse because leveraging them to compress the critical path could make a new critical path emerge. Since you assign your resources based on float and capabilities, you now run the risk that the worst developers will be working on that new critical path.

Even when assigned to formerly critical activities, the top resources often are idle, waiting for other activities and developers in the project to catch up. This reduces the project's efficiency. To avoid this situation, you may need a larger team that can compress other paths by working in parallel. Such an increase in team size will reduce efficiency and increase the cost. Finally, compressing using top resources often requires two or more such heroes to compress multiple critical or near-critical paths to see any benefit from the compression.

When assigning top resources, you should avoid doing so blindly (such as assigning the top resource to all current critical activities). Evaluate which network path would benefit the most from the resources, determine the effect on other paths, and even try combinations across chains. You may have to reassign the top resource several times based on the changes to the critical path. You should also look at activity size as well as the criticality. For example, you may have a large, noncritical activity with a high level of uncertainty that could easily derail the project. Assigning the top resources there will reduce that risk and ultimately help you meet your commitments.

Trimming the Fuzzy Front End

The easiest way of compressing the project is to trim the project's initial activities, the fuzzy front end.

While no project can be accelerated beyond its critical path, no such rule applies to the front end. Look for ways of working in parallel at the front end on preparatory or evaluation tasks. This would compress the front end (and thus the project) without any change to the rest of the project. For example, Figure 14-1 shows a project (the upper chart) with a long front end. The front end contains a few crucial technology and design choices that the architect had to settle before the rest of the project could proceed. By hiring a second architect as a contractor for two of these decisions, the front end duration was reduced by a third (the lower chart in Figure 14-1).

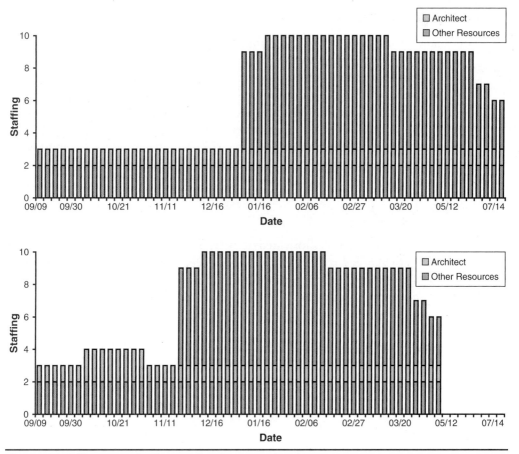

Figure 14-1 Trimming the front end with a second architect

PLANNING AND RISK

Preempt the unforeseen with float.

The risk index indicates whether the project will break down when it hits the first obstacle or whether the project can leverage that obstacle to introduce refinements, adapting to make the design a better approximation of reality. Having sufficient float (indicated by the low risk) gives you a chance to thrive in the face of the unforeseen.

I also find that the project's need for float is as much psychological as it is physical. The physical need is clear: You can consume float to handle changes and shift resources. The psychological need is the peace of mind of all involved. In projects with enough float, people are relaxed; they can focus and deliver.

Behavior, Not Values

Chapter 10 suggested 0.5 as the minimum decompression target and 0.3 as the minimum risk level. As valuable as these risk guidelines are, when examining the risk curve of the project you should be aware that behavior is more important than values. When decompressing the project, look for the risk tipping point rather than the 0.5 value. Something may be skewing the whole risk curve higher or lower, but there could still be a tipping point for risk. This is especially the case when the normal solution already has low risk. You may need to decompress the project, but you do that by using the tipping-point behavior.

DESIGN OF PROJECT DESIGN

Project design is a detailed-oriented activity. You should treat the act of project design as just another intricate effort that you need to map out and design. In other words, you need to design project design, and even use the tools of project design when doing so. You begin this design effort with the system design and proceed to designing the project as a single continuous design effort.

To help you get started, here is a list of common design activities:

1. Gather core use cases
2. Design the system and produce call chains and a list of components
3. List noncoding activities
4. Estimate the duration and required resources for all activities
5. Estimate the overall project using broadband and/or a tool

6. Design the normal solution

7. Explore the limited-resources solution

8. Find the subcritical solution

9. Compress using top resources

10. Compress using parallel work

11. Compress using activity changes

12. Compress to minimum duration

13. Perform throughput, efficiency, and complexity analysis

14. Produce the time–cost curve

15. Decompress the normal solution

16. Rebuild the time–cost curve

17. Compare the time–cost curve to the overall project estimation

18. Quantify and model risk

19. Find inclusion and exclusion and risk zones

20. Identify viable options

21. Prepare for SDP review

While some of these activities could take place in parallel to other activities, the activities in system design and project design do have interdependencies. The next logical step is to design your project design using a simple network diagram and even calculate the total duration of the effort. Figure 14-2 shows such a network diagram of the design of project design. You can identify the likely critical path using typical durations for the activities. If a single architect is designing the project, then the diagram will actually be a long string. If the architect has someone helping, or if the architect is waiting for some piece of information, the diagram suggests activities to do in parallel.

Activities 6, 7, 8, 9, 10, 11, and 12 in the list (shown in blue in Figure 14-2) are specific project design solutions. You can further break down each of those into this list of tasks:

1. Discover planning assumptions

2. Gather staffing requirements

3. Review and revise the list of activities, estimations, and resources

4. Decide on dependencies

5. Modify the network to accommodate constraints

6. Modify the network to reduce complexity

7. Assign resources to activities and rework the network

8. Draw the network diagram

9. Evaluate the shallow S curve

10. Evaluate the staffing distribution chart

11. Modify the planning assumptions and rework the network

12. Calculate cost elements

13. Analyze floats

14. Calculate risk

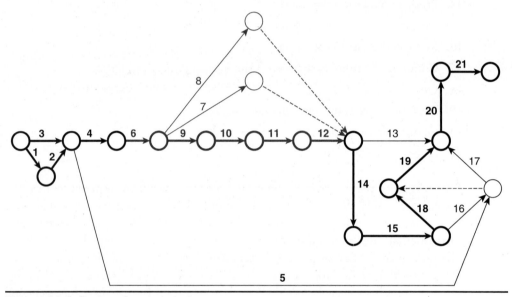

Figure 14-2 Design of project design

IN PERSPECTIVE

In any system it is important to distinguish between effort and scope. The architecture in a software system must be all-encompassing both in scope and in time. It must include all required components, and it must be correct at the present time and in the far future (as long as the nature of the business does not change). You must avoid the very expensive and destabilizing changes that are the result of a flawed design. When it comes to the effort, the architecture should be very limited. Part 1 of this book explained how you can come up with a solid, volatility-based decomposition in a few days to a week, even for a large system. Doing so requires knowing how to do things correctly, but it is certainly possible with practice and experience.

Compared to the architecture, design—especially the services detailed design or *Clients* user interface—is both more time-consuming and limited in scope. It may take several weeks to refine the detailed design of just a few interacting services.

Finally, coding is the most time-consuming and the most limited in scope. Developers should never code more than one service at a time, and they will spend considerable time testing and integrating each service as well.

Figure 14-3 illustrates in a qualitative manner the scope versus effort for a software project. You can see that scope and effort are literally inverses of each other. When something is wider in scope, it is narrow in effort, and vice versa.

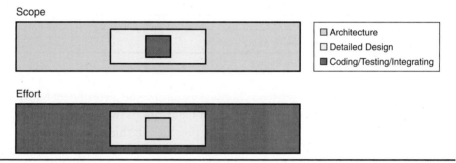

Figure 14-3 Scope versus effort in a software system

SUBSYSTEMS AND THE TIMELINE

Chapter 3 discusses the concept of mapping subsystems to vertical slices of the architecture. In a large project you may have several such subsystems. These subsystems should be fairly decoupled and independent from one another. Each subsystem has its own collection of activities, such as detailed design and construction. In a sequential project, the subsystems are consecutive, as shown in Figure 14-4.

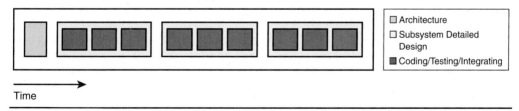

Figure 14-4 Sequential project life cycle

Note that the subsystems are always designed and constructed in the context of the existing architecture. The effort allocation in Figure 14-4 is still that of Figure 14-3.

You may be able to compress the project and start working in parallel. Figure 14-5 shows two views of concurrent subsystem development aligned against the timeline.

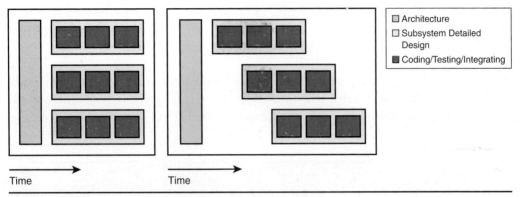

Figure 14-5 Parallel project life cycles

Which parallel life cycle you choose depends on the level of dependencies between the subsystems of the architecture. In Figure 14-5, the life cycle on the right staggers the subsystems to overlap on the timeline. In this case, you can start building a subsystem once the implementation of the interfaces of the subsystem on which it depends are complete. You can then work on the rest of the subsystem in parallel to the previous one. You can even create fully parallel pipelines like the layout on the left of Figure 14-5. In this case, you build each subsystem independently of and concurrently with the other subsystems with minimum integration.

THE HAND-OFF

The composition and makeup of the team has a significant effect on project design. Here, team composition refers specifically to the ratio of senior to junior developers. Most organizations (and even individuals) define seniority based on years of experience. The definition I use is that senior developers are those capable of designing the details of the services, whereas junior developers cannot. Detailed design takes place after the major architectural decomposition of the system into services. For each service, the detailed design contains the design of the service public interfaces or contracts, its messages and data contracts, and internal details such as class hierarchies or security.

Note the definition of senior developers is not developers who can or know how to do detailed design. Instead, senior developers are those capable of doing detailed design, once you show them how to do so correctly.

JUNIOR HAND-OFF

When all you have are junior developers, the architect must provide the detailed design of the services. This defines the **junior hand-off** between the architect and the developers. The junior hand-off disproportionally increases the architect's workload. For example, in a 12-month project, some 3 to 4 months of the overall duration could be spent simply on detailed design.

The architect's detailed design work can take place in the front end or while developers are constructing some of the services. Both of these options are bad.

Coming up with the correct details of all the services up front is very demanding, and seeing in advance how all the details across all services mesh together sets a very high bar. It is possible to design a few services up front, but not all of them. The real problem is that detailed design in the front end simply takes too long. Management is unlikely to understand the importance of detailed design and will cringe at the prospect of extending the front end to accommodate it. Consequently, management will force handing off the architecture to junior developers and doom the project.

Designing the services on the fly, in parallel to the developers who are constructing services that the architect has already designed, could work. However, overloading the architect with detailed design makes the architect a bottleneck and may considerably slow down the project.

SENIOR HAND-OFF

Senior developers are essential to address the detailed design challenge. If not already capable of doing so, with modest training and mentoring senior developers can perform the detailed design work, allowing for a **senior hand-off** between the architect and the developers.

With a senior hand-off, the architect can hand off the design soon after the SDP review, providing only a general outline of the services using gross terms for interfaces or just suggesting a design pattern. The detailed design now takes place as part of each individual service, and the architect just needs to review it and amend as needed. In fact, the only reason to pay for additional senior developers is to enable the senior hand-off. The senior hand-off is the safest way of accelerating any project because it compresses the schedule while avoiding changes to the critical path, increasing the execution risk, or introducing bottlenecks. Since shorter projects will cost less, it follows that senior developers actually cost less than junior developers.

SENIOR DEVELOPERS AS JUNIOR ARCHITECTS

The problem with the senior hand-off is the scant availability of senior developers. You may have one or two of them, and perhaps three, but not an entire team. If that is your situation, you should not use your one or two senior developers as developers. Instead, change the process to have these senior developers do mostly detailed design work. Figure 14-6 shows what that process flow looks like.

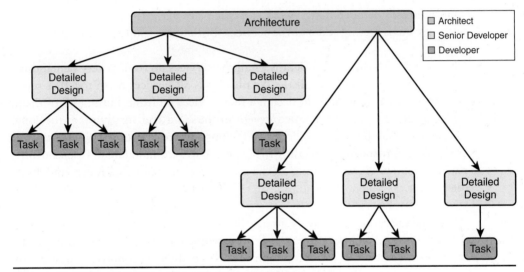

Figure 14-6 Working in parallel with junior architects

The architect must provide a comprehensive architecture, as discussed in Part 1 of this book. The architecture will not change during the life of the system, and the construction is always done in the context of that architecture. Producing the architecture still takes place at the project's front end. The front end may also contain the detailed design of the first handful of services. This detailed design is both done by the senior developers and used as a training and learning opportunity under the guidance of the architect. This, in effect, turns the senior developers into junior architects.

Once the detailed design of the services is complete, the junior developers can step in and construct the actual services. However, any design refinement, as trivial as it may be, requires the junior developers to consult with the senior developer who designed that service. Once finished with each service construction, the junior developers proceed to code review with the senior developers (not their junior peers), followed by integration and testing with other junior developers. Meanwhile, the senior developers remain busy with the detailed design of the next batch of services. Each design is reviewed with the architect before hand-off to the junior developers.

Working this way is the best and only way of mitigating the risks of the junior hand-off. Clearly, it also requires meticulous project design. You must know exactly how many services you can design in advance and how to synchronize the hand-offs with the construction. You must also add explicit service detailed design activities and even additional integration points to address the risk of extracting the detailed design out of the services.

In Practice

As with system design, when it comes to project design, you must practice. The basic expectation of professionals—from lawyers to doctors to pilots—is that they know their trade by heart and that they keep at it. Under fire, everybody sinks to their level of training. Unfortunately, unlike system design, hardly any software architect is even aware of project design or is trained in it, even though project design is both critical to success and, as discussed in Chapter 7, the software architect's responsibility.

Compounding the need for project design practice are two additional issues. First, project design is a vast topic. This book covers the core body of knowledge required of modern software architects, both system design and project design. In terms of its page count, project design outweighs system design by 2:1. You should now have a feeling that you are peering into a deep rabbit hole. You cannot internalize and correctly use the concepts of this book without training and practice. Figuring out project design by designing real projects on the job not only is asking for trouble, but also defies common sense. Would you like to be the first patient of a doctor fresh out of medical school? Would you like to fly with a new pilot? Are you proud of your first program?

Second, project design, in many cases, produces non-intuitive results. You will have to practice not just to master a massive body of knowledge, but also to develop a new intuition. The good news is that project design skills can be acquired, as is evident by the swift and marked improvement in the quality of the project designs and the success rate of those who do practice.

Chapter 2 emphasized the importance of system design practice. Always combine practice in designing a system and practice in designing the project to build it. Start with just a simple normal solution. Train until you are comfortable with normal solutions for your practice systems. Then, build from there to find the best solution as far as schedule, cost, and risk.

Examine your own past projects. With the advantage of hindsight, try to reconstruct the project design that took place and contrast it with what should have been done. Identify the planning assumptions, the classic mistakes, and the right decisions. Prepare for an SDP review by listing all the solutions you would have proposed if you could. Look at your current project. Can you list the activities, come up with the correct estimations based on what the team is presently doing, and calculate the true schedule and cost? What is the current risk level? What is required to decompress the project? What level of compression is feasible?

When you think you have got it right, raise the bar again and find ways of improving these designs. Never rest on your laurels. Develop new techniques, refine your own style, and become a passionate expert and advocate of project design.

DEBRIEFING PROJECT DESIGN

Debriefing is underutilized in the software industry, even though it is an effective technique with fantastic ROI. A debrief of your project design effort and results is important. It provides a way to share lessons learned across projects and roles so that each person can learn from the experience of others. All it takes is self-reflection, analysis, and the desire to improve. You should debrief each and every one of your projects and make the debriefing part of your software development life cycle. You should debrief each project as a whole and debrief each subsystem or milestone as well. The more you make debriefing part of your routine, the more likely you are to actually debrief and benefit from it.

The debrief topics depend on what you deem important and what needs improvement. They may include the following considerations:

- **Estimations and accuracy.** For each activity, ask yourself how accurate the initial estimation was when compared with the actual duration, and how many times you had to adjust the estimations and in which direction. Is there a noticeable pattern that you could incorporate in future projects to improve the estimations? Review the initial list of activities to see what you missed and what was superfluous. Calculate the extent to which the errors in the estimations canceled each other out.

- **Design efficacy and accuracy.** Compare the accuracy of the initial broad project estimation with the detailed project design and the actual duration and cost.

How accurate was your assessment of the throughput of the team? Was risk decompression necessary, and if so, was it too much or too little? Finally, was the compressed project doable, and how did the project manager and the team handle complexity?

- **Individual and team work.** How well did the team members work as a team or individually? Were there any bad apples? Can you make the team more productive in the future by using better tools or technology? Did the team communicate issues in a timely manner? How well did the team members understand the plan and their role in it?

- **What to avoid or improve next time.** Compile a prioritized list of all the mistakes or troubles encountered across people, process, design, and technology. For each item, identify how you could have detected it sooner or avoided it in the first place. List both actions that caused problems and actions that should have taken place. You should also include near-misses that did not end up causing harm.

- **Recurring issues from previous debriefs.** One of the best ways to improve is to avoid past mistakes and prevent known problems from happening. It is detrimental to everyone when the same mistakes appear in project after project. There is likely a very good reason why the same problem is recurrent. Nonetheless, you must eliminate recurring mistakes in spite of the challenges.

- **Commitment to quality.** What level of commitment to quality was missing or present? How intimately related was it to success?

It is important to debrief even successful projects that have met their commitments. You must know if you have succeeded just because you were lucky or because you had a viable system and project design. Even when the project is a success, could you have done a better job? What should you do to sustain the things you did right?

ABOUT QUALITY

In the abstract, everything in this book is about quality. The very purpose of having a sound architecture is to end up with the least complex system possible. This provides for a higher-quality system that will be easier to test and maintain. There is no denying it: Quality leads to productivity, and it is impossible to meet your schedule and budget commitments when the product is rife with defects. When the team spends less time hunting problems, the team spends more time adding value. Well-designed systems and projects are the only way to meet a deadline.

With any software system, quality hinges on having a project design that includes the crucial quality-control activities as an integral part of the project. Your project design must account for the quality control activities both in time and in resources. Do not cut corners if your project design goal is to build the system quickly and cleanly.

A side effect of project design is that well-designed projects are low-stress projects. When the project has the time and the resources it requires, people are confident in their own ability and in their project's leadership. They know the schedule is doable and that every activity is accounted for. When people are less stressed, they pay attention to details, and things do not fall between the cracks, resulting in better quality. In addition, well-designed projects maximize the team's efficiency. This contributes to quality by allowing the team to more readily identify, isolate, and fix defects in the least costly way.

Your system and project design effort should motivate the team to produce the highest-quality code possible. You will see that success is addictive: Once people are exposed to working correctly, they take pride in what they do and will never go back. No one likes high-stress environments afflicted by low quality, tension, and accusations.

QUALITY-CONTROL ACTIVITIES

Your project design should always account for quality-control elements or activities. These include the following:

- **Service-level testing.** When estimating the duration and effort of each service, make certain the estimation includes the time needed to write the test plan for the service, to run the unit test against the plan, and to perform integration testing. If relevant, add the time to roll the integration testing into your regression testing.
- **System test plan.** The project must have an explicit activity in which qualified test engineers write the test plan. This includes a list of all the ways to break the system and prove it does not work.
- **System test harness.** The project must have an explicit activity in which qualified test engineers develop a comprehensive test harness.
- **System testing.** The project must have an explicit activity in which the software quality-control testers execute the test plan while using the test harness.
- **Daily smoke tests.** As part of the indirect cost of the project, on a daily basis, you must do a clean build of the evolving system, power it up, and (figuratively) flush water down the pipes. This kind of smoke test will uncover issues in the plumbing of the system, such as defects in hosting, instantiation, serialization, connectivity, timeouts, security, and synchronization. By comparing the result with the previous day's smoke test, you can quickly isolate plumbing issues.

- **Indirect cost.** Quality is not free, but it does tend to pay for itself because defects are horrendously expensive. Make sure to account correctly for the required investments in quality, especially when it is in the form of indirect cost.

- **Test automation scripting.** Automating the tests should be an explicit activity in the project.

- **Regression testing design and implementation.** The project must have comprehensive regression testing that detects destabilizing changes the moment they happen across the system, subsystems, services, and all possible interactions. This will prevent a ripple effect of new defects introduced by fixing existing defects or simply making changes. While executing regression testing on an ongoing basis is often treated as an indirect cost, the project must contain activities for writing the regression testing and its automation.

- **System-level reviews.** Chapter 9 discussed the need to engage in extensive peer reviews at the service level. Since defects can occur anywhere, you should extend reviews to the system level. The core team and the developers must review the system requirements spec, the architecture, the system test plan, the system test harness code, and any additional system-level code artifacts. Both with service and system reviews, the most effective and efficient reviews are structured in nature[2] and have designated roles (moderator, owner, scribe, reviewers), as well as follow-ups to ensure the recommendations are applied across the system. At a minimum, the team should hold informal reviews that involve walking through these artifacts with one or more peers. Regardless of the method used, these reviews require a high degree of mutual involvement along with team spirit of commitment for quality. The reality is that delivering high-quality software is a team sport.

This list is only partial. The objective here is not to provide you with all the required quality-control activities, but rather to get you to think about all the things you must do in your project to control quality.

Quality-Assurance Activities

Your project design should always account for quality-assurance activities. Previous chapters (especially Chapter 9) have already discussed quality assurance, but you should add the following quality assurance activities to your process and your project design:

- **Training.** It costs significantly less (and is much better quality-wise) if your developers do not attempt to figure out new technologies on their own. By

---

2. https://en.wikipedia.org/wiki/Software_inspection

sending the developers to training (or bringing the training in-house), you instantly eliminate many defects due to learning curves or lack of experience.

- **Authoring key SOPs.** Software development is so complex and challenging that nothing should be left to chance. If you do not have standard operating procedures (SOPs) for all key activities, devote the time to researching and writing them.

- **Adopting standards.** Similar to SOPs, you must have a design standard (see Appendix C) and a coding standard. By following best practices, you will prevent problems and defects.

- **Engaging QA.** Actively engage a true quality-assurance person. Have that person review the development process, tune it to assure quality, and create a process that is both effective and easy to follow. This process should support investigation and elimination of the root cause of defects or, even better, should proactively prevent problems from happening in the first place.

- **Collecting and analyzing key metrics.** Metrics allow you to detect problems before they happen. They include development-related metrics such as estimation accuracy, efficiency, defects found in reviews, quality and complexity trends, as well as run-time metrics such as uptime and reliability. If required, devise the activities to build the tools that collect the metrics, and account for the indirect cost of collecting and analyzing them on a regular basis. Back it up with a SOP that mandates acting on abnormal metrics.

- **Debriefing.** As described in the previous section, debrief your work as you progress, and debrief the project as a whole once it is completed.

QUALITY AND CULTURE

Most managers do not trust their teams. Those managers have experienced too many disappointments, and they see little or no correlation between the effort the team expends and the desired results. Consequently, the managers resort to micromanaging everything. This is a direct result of a chronic deficit in trust. The developers respond to the micromanagement with frustration and apathy, and lose any remaining shred of accountability. This degrades trust even further, vindicating the sentiments of the managers.

The best way of turning this dynamic around is by infecting the team with a relentless obsession for quality. When totally committed to quality, the team will drive every activity from a perspective of quality, fixing the broken culture and creating an atmosphere of engineering excellence. To reach this state, you must provide the right context and environment. In practice, this means doing everything in this book—and more.

The result will be a transition from micromanagement to quality assurance. Allowing and trusting people to control the quality of their work is the essence of empowerment. Once this is in place, you will learn that quality is the ultimate project management technique, requiring very little management while maximizing the team's productivity. The managers now focus on facilitating the correct environment for the team, trusting the team to produce impeccable software systems, on time and on budget.

Appendices

A

PROJECT TRACKING

One of the most misunderstood quotes in history is attributed to Field Marshal Helmuth von Moltke, the Elder: "No battle plan survives contact with the enemy." Ever since, this statement has been taken out of context as a justification for no planning at all—the complete opposite of its original intent. Von Moltke, known as the architect of the Franco-Prussian War of 1870, was a military planning genius credited with a series of stunning military victories. Von Moltke realized that the key to success in the face of rapidly changing circumstances is to not rely on a single static plan. Instead, you must have the flexibility to pivot quickly between several meticulously laid-out options. The purpose of the initial plan is merely to provide a fighting chance by aligning the available resources with the objective as best as possible. From that point onward, one must constantly track against the plan and revise it as needed, often by coming up with variations of the current plan, switching to an alternative preplanned option, or devising new options altogether.

In the context of system and project design, von Moltke's insight is as relevant today as it was 150 years ago. The project design techniques in this book support two objectives. The first objective is to drive an educated decision during the SDP review, to ensure the decision makers choose a viable option. Such an option serves as a good-enough starting point coming into execution, allowing for a fighting chance. The second objective for project design is to adapt the plan during execution. The project manager must constantly correlate what is actually going on with the plan, and the architect needs to use the project design tools to redesign the project to respond to reality. This often takes the form of modest project redesign iterations. You want to avoid any gross corrections, and instead drive the project smoothly using numerous small corrections. Otherwise, the degree of correction required may be wrenching and cause the project to fail.

A good project plan is not something you sign off and file in a drawer, never again to see the light of day. A good project plan is a live document that you constantly revise to meet your commitments. This requires knowing where you are with respect to the plan, where you are heading, and what corrective actions to take in response to changing circumstances. This is what **project tracking** is all about.

Project tracking is part of project management and execution and is not the responsibility of the software architect. I therefore include project tracking in this book, but as an appendix to the main discussion of system and project design.

ACTIVITY LIFE CYCLE AND STATUS

Project tracking requires being able to tell where the project is across resources and activities. In the previous chapters, the discussion of project activities looked at activities mostly as atomic units, with a duration or cost estimation for each activity. This allows for designing the project regardless of what happens inside the activities. That approach is insufficient for project tracking. You can break each activity in the project—be it a service or a noncoding activity—into its own little life cycle, complete with internal tasks. Such tasks can be sequential, interleaved on the timeline, or iterative. For example, Figure A-1 shows a possible life cycle of a service.

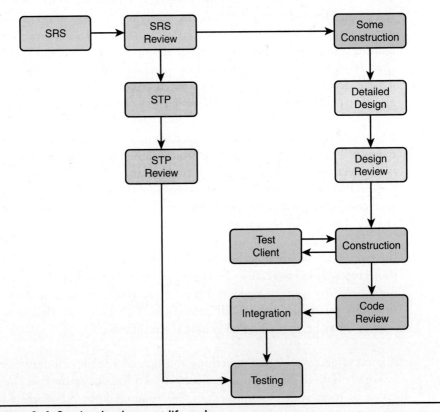

Figure A-1 Service development life cycle

Each service starts with a service requirement spec (SRS). This can be brief, as little as a few paragraphs or pages outlining what the service is required to do. The architect needs to review the SRS. With the SRS in place, the developer can proceed to write a service test plan (STP) listing all the ways the developer will later demonstrate the service does not work. Even with a senior hand-off, when the developer is capable of performing the detailed design of the service, the developer cannot always start the detailed design without gaining additional insight into the nature of the service. The best way of obtaining that insight is via some construction to get a first-hand understanding of what the technology can provide or what the available detailed design options are. Armed with that insight, the developer can proceed to design the details of the service, which the architect then reviews (perhaps with others). Once the detailed design is approved, the developer can construct the code for the service. In tandem with the construction of the service, the developer builds a white-box test client. This test client enables the developer to test every parameter, condition, and error-handling path by invoking the debugger on the evolving code. With the code complete, the developer reviews the code with the architect and the other developers, integrates the service with other services, and finally performs black-box unit testing against the test plan.

Note that each review task in the diagram must complete successfully. A failing review causes the developer to repeat the preceding internal task. For clarity, Figure A-1 does not show these retries.

Phase Exit Criteria

Regardless of the specific life-cycle flow, most activities will have **internal phases** such as `Requirements`, `Detailed Design`, or `Construction`. Each phase comprises one or more internal tasks, as shown in Figure A-2.

For example, the `Detailed Design` phase may include some construction, the detailed design itself, and the design review. The `Construction` phase may include the actual construction, the test client, and the code review.

To support tracking, it is important to define a **binary exit criterion** for each phase—that is, a single condition used to judge whether the phase is either done or not done. With the life cycle in Figure A-2 you can use the reviews and the testing as binary exit criteria for the phase. For example, the `Construction` phase is complete once you have had the code review, not simply when the code is checked in.

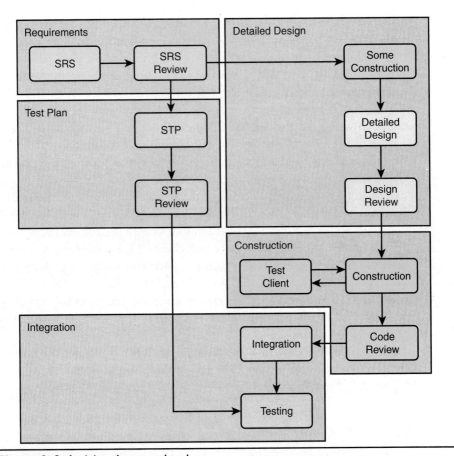

Figure A-2 Activity phases and tasks

PHASE WEIGHT

While each activity may have multiple phases, these phases may not contribute equally to the completion of the activity. You need to assess the contribution of a phase in the form of a weight—in this case, a percentage. For example, consider the activity with the phases listed in Table A-1. In this sample activity, the Requirements phase counts for 15% for the completion of the activity, while the Detailed Design phase counts for 20% of the completion.

You can allocate the weight of the phases in several ways. For example, you can estimate the importance of the phase, or you can estimate the duration in days for each phase and divide by the sum of all phases. Alternatively, you can just divide by the number of phases (e.g., with 5 phases, each phase counts as 20%), or you can even consider the type of the activity. For example, you may decide that the

Requirements phase will be weighted 40% for the UI activity and only 10% for the Logging activity.

Table A-1 Activity phases and weights

Activity Phase	Weight (%)
Requirements	15
Detailed Design	20
Test Plan	10
Construction	40
Integration	15
Total	100

For accurate tracking, it does not matter much which technique you use to allocate the weight of the phases as long as you apply the technique consistently across all activities. In most decent-size projects, you will end up with hundreds of phases across all activities. On average, any discrepancies in assigning weights will cancel each other.

ACTIVITY STATUS

Given the binary exit criterion and the weight of each phase, you can calculate the progress of each activity at any point in time. With tracking, **progress** is the completion status of an activity (or of the entire project) as a percentage.

The formula of the progress of an activity is:

$$A(t) = \sum_{j=1}^{m} W_j$$

where:

- W_j is the weight of phase j of the activity.
- m is the number of completed phases of the activity at time t.
- t is a point in time.

The progress of the activity at the time t is the sum of the weights of all the phases that are completed by the time t. For example, using Table A-1, if the first three phases (`Requirements`, `Detailed Design`, and `Test Plan`) are complete, then the activity is 45% complete (15 + 20 + 10).

Similarly to calculating the progress of an activity, you can and should keep track of the effort spent on each activity. With tracking, **effort** is the amount of direct cost spent on the activity (or on the entire project) as a percentage of the estimated direct cost for the activity (or for the entire project). The formula for the effort of an activity is:

$$C(t) = \frac{S(t)}{R}$$

where:

- `S(t)` is the cumulative direct cost spent on the activity at time `t`.
- `R` is the estimated direct cost for the activity.
- `t` is a point in time.

It is crucial to note that effort is unrelated to progress. For example, an activity estimated at 10 days duration with fixed resources could be only 60% complete 15 days after starting. This activity has already cost 150% of its planned direct cost.

> **Note**   Both progress and effort are unitless: They are percentages. This enables you to avoid specific values and compare them in the same analysis.

PROJECT STATUS

The formula for the progress of the project is:

$$P(t) = \frac{\sum_{i=1}^{N}\left(E_i {}^{*} A_i(t)\right)}{\sum_{i=1}^{N} E_i}$$

where:

- E_i is the estimated duration of activity `i`.
- $A_i(t)$ is the progress of activity `i` at time `t`.
- `t` is a point in time.
- `N` is the number of activities in the project.

The overall project progress at the time t is a ratio between two sums of estimations. The first is the sum of all the estimated duration of each individual activity multiplied by the activity's progress. The second is the sum of all activity estimations. Note that this simple formula provides the progress of the project across all activities, developers, life cycles, and phases.

PROGRESS AND EARNED VALUE

Chapter 7 discussed the concept of earned value. The formula for the planned earned value as a function of time and the formula for the progress of the project are very similar. If all activities complete exactly as planned, then the progress over time will match the planned earned value, the planned shallow S curve of the project. The progress of the project is simply the actual earned value to date.

To illustrate this point, consider the simple project in Table A-2. Suppose at the time t the UI activity is only 45% complete. Since 45% of 20% is 9%, the work done so far in the UI activity has earned 9% toward the completion of the project. In much the same way, you can calculate the actual earned value of all activities in the project at time t.

Table A-2 Example project current progress

Activity	Duration	Value (%)	Completed (%)	Actual Earned Value (%)
Front End	40	20	100	20
Access Service	30	15	75	11.25
UI	40	20	45	9
Manager Service	20	10	0	0
Utility Service	40	20	0	0
System Testing	30	15	0	0
Total	200	100	—	40.25

Summing up the actual earned value of all activities in Table A-2 reveals that the project is 40.25% complete at time t. This is the same value produced by the progress formula:

$$P(t) = \frac{40*1.0 + 30*0.75 + 40*0.45}{40 + 30 + 40 + 20 + 40 + 30} = 0.4025$$

ACCUMULATED EFFORT

The formula for the effort of the project is:

$$D(t) = \frac{\sum\limits_{i=1}^{N}(R_i * C_i(t))}{\sum\limits_{i=1}^{N}R_i} = \frac{\sum\limits_{i=1}^{N}\left(R_i * \dfrac{S_i(t)}{R_i}\right)}{\sum\limits_{i=1}^{N}R_i} = \frac{\sum\limits_{i=1}^{N}S_i(t)}{\sum\limits_{i=1}^{N}R_i}$$

where:

- R_i is the estimated direct cost of activity i.
- $C_i(t)$ is the effort of activity i at time t.
- $S_i(t)$ is the cumulative direct cost spent on activity i at time t.
- t is a point in time.
- N is the number of activities in the project.

The overall project effort is simply the sum of direct cost spent across all activities divided by the sum of all direct cost estimations of all activities. This provides effort as the overall direct cost expenditure as a percentage of the planned direct cost of the project.

Again note the similarity of the project effort to the planned earned value formula. If each activity is assigned to one resource, and the activities end up costing exactly as planned and complete on the planned dates, then the effort curve will match the planned earned value curve. If more (or less) than one resource is planned per activity, then you will have to track the effort against its own planned direct cost curve. However, in most projects the two curves should match closely. For simplicity's sake, the rest of this appendix assumes that each activity is planned for one resource.

ACCUMULATED INDIRECT COST

The indirect cost of the project is mostly a function of time and the structure of the team; it is independent of the effort or progress of individual activities. You can use a technique similar to those described so far to find the present status of the indirect cost. You need to identify the team members who contribute to indirect cost (such as the core team, DevOps, or testers) and keep track of the time they spend on the project minus their direct cost, if any.

Since indirect cost is independent of both the progress and effort of the project, tracking indirect cost is not terribly useful. All you are likely to see is a straight line going up, which does not help to suggest any corrective actions.

Tracking indirect cost is helpful, however, in one case: when reporting the total cost of the project to date, in which case you should add the indirect cost to the direct cost. The rest of this chapter looks at only the accumulated direct cost (the effort) when tracking the project and comparing it with the plan.

TRACKING PROGRESS AND EFFORT

Combining the actual progress of the project with the effort allows you to find the current status of the project. You should repeat these calculations at a recurring interval. This allows you to plot how the project's progress and effort fare with respect to the project's planned earned value. Figure A-3 demonstrates this form of tracking for an example project.

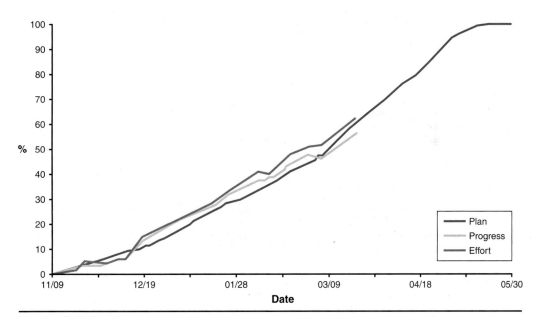

Figure A-3 Sample project tracking

The blue line in Figure A-3 shows the planned earned value of the project. The planned earned value should have been a shallow S curve; you will see shortly why it deviated from that form in this example. To the point in time shown on the graph, the green line shows the actual progress of the project (the actual earned value) and the red line illustrates the effort spent.

PROJECTIONS

Project tracking allows you to see exactly where the project is and where it has been. The real question, however, is not what the current status of the project is, but rather where the project is heading. To answer that question, you can project the progress and effort curves. Consider the generic project view of Figure A-4.

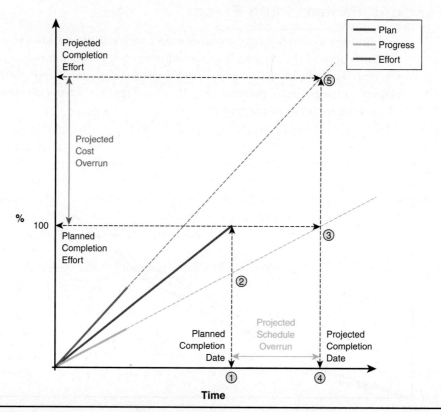

Figure A-4 Progress and effort projections

For simplicity, Figure A-4 replaces the shallow S curves with their linear regression trend lines, shown as solid lines in the figure. The blue line represents the planned earned value of the project. Ideally the green progress line and the red effort line should match the blue line. The project is expected to complete when the planned earned value reaches 100%, point 1 in Figure A-4. However, you can see that the green line (actual progress) is below the plan.

If you extrapolate the green progress line, you get the dashed green line in Figure A-4. You can see that by the time of point 1, the projected progress line reaches only about 65% of completion (point 2 in Figure A-4). The project will actually complete when the projected progress line reaches 100%, or point 3 in Figure A-4. The time of point 3 is point 4 in Figure A-4, and the difference between points 4 and 1 is the projected schedule overrun.

Much the same way, you can project the measured effort line and find point 5 in Figure A-4. The difference in effort between points 5 and 3 in Figure A-4 is the projected direct cost overrun (in percentage) of the project.

Note Since the indirect cost is usually linear with time, the projected schedule overrun in percentage also indicates the projected indirect cost overrun.

Suppose this is a year-long project, and you measure the project on a weekly interval. A month into the project you already have four reference points, enough to run a regression trend line that is well fitted to the measured progress and effort. Recall from Chapter 7 that the pitch or slope of the earned value curve represents the throughput of the team. Therefore, a month into a year-long project, you already have a good idea where the project is heading via a projection that is highly calibrated to the actual throughput of the team. The initial planned earned value was just that—initial. The projected progress and effort lines are what will likely happen.

Figure A-5 shows the actual projections for Figure A-3. Given the terms of the projection, the project is expected to have about a month schedule slip (or 13%) and some 8% effort overrun.

In Figure A-3 and Figure A-5, the planned earned value is a truncated shallow S curve because tracking started for this project after the SDP review. By deliberately dropping the very shallow start of the plan, the linear trend line projections become a better fit to the curves.

Note The files accompanying this book contain a template spreadsheet that allows you to easily track the project progress and effort and automatically project the trend lines.

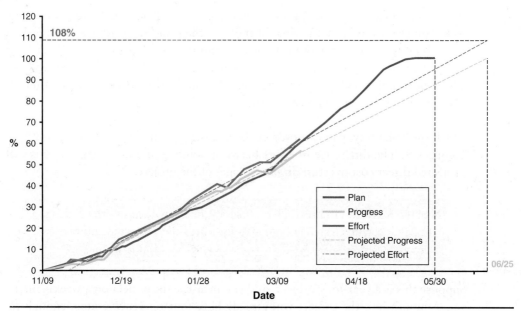

Figure A-5 Sample projected progress and effort

PROJECTIONS AND CORRECTIVE ACTIONS

Projecting the progress and the effort provides an unmatched ability to see where the project is and where it is heading. It then becomes possible to raise the bar again and discuss remedies. Note that when issues arise, it is important to treat the underlying problem, not the symptom of the problem. For example, missing the deadline or exceeding the planned effort are both symptoms of the problem, not the underlying problem itself. This section contains the common set of symptoms that you will encounter, the possible corrective actions to take, and even recommendations for the best course of action.

ALL IS WELL

Consider the progress and effort projections of Figure A-6. In the figure, the projected progress and effort lines coincide with the plan, and the project is poised to deliver on its commitments. You need do nothing about this state of affairs; there is no need to help or try to improve matters. Knowing when not to do something is as important as knowing when to do something.

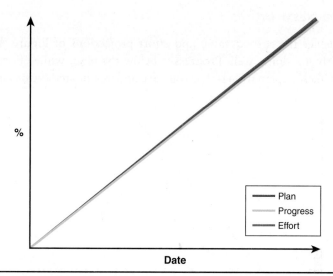

Figure A-6 All is well in this project.

Staying on the Plan

Having the progress and the effort align to such a degree with the plan should be the natural state of affairs in any project because that is the only way to meet your commitments. Most people have the wrong mental model for what it takes to meet the deadline. Many think that during the project they can drift away from the commitments and then, via heroic action and determination, they can meet the deadline at the end. While that could be the case, the chances of this happening are slim, and it is certainly not a repeatable expectation. Most projects do not have heroes, and the project cannot survive drastic gyrations.

The cardinal rule of project management is:

The only way to meet the deadline at the end is to be on time throughout the project.

Staying on the original plan (or on a revised plan) will never happen on its own and requires constant tracking by the project manager and numerous corrective actions throughout the project execution. You must respond to the information revealed by the trajectory of the projections and avoid opening a gap between the progress, the effort, and the plan.

UNDERESTIMATING

Consider the earned value and effort projections of Figure A-7. This project is clearly not doing well. Progress is below the plan, while effort is above the plan. The likely explanation is that you have underestimated the project and its activities.

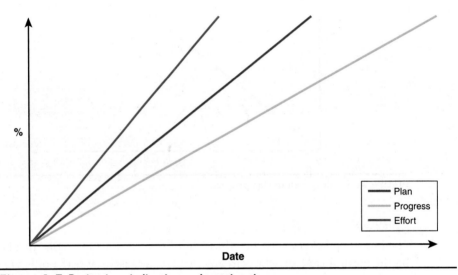

Figure A-7 Projections indicating underestimating

Corrective Actions

There are two obvious corrective actions when dealing with underestimation. The first is to revise the estimations upward based on the (now known) throughput of the team. In fact, you can see when the projected progress line reaches 100%, and that point in time becomes the new completion date of the project. Effectively, you will be pushing down the blue plan line until it meets the green progress line. This is a typical remedy in a feature-driven project, where you must achieve parity with a competing product or a legacy system, and there is no point in releasing the system while missing key aspects.

However, pushing the deadline out will not do in a date-driven project where you must release on a set date. In this case, you should take the second type of corrective action: reduce the scope of the project. By reducing the scope, the earned value of what the team has produced so far counts more, and the green progress line will come up to meet the blue plan line.

You can certainly apply a combination of pushing the deadline and reducing the scope, and the progress projection will tell you exactly how much or how little of each remedy is required. Whichever response you choose will require redesigning the project.

Sadly, the knee-jerk reaction of many who do not wish to compromise on the deadline or the scope is to throw more people on the project. As Dr. Fredrick Brooks observed, this is like trying to put out a fire by dousing it with gasoline.[1]

There are several reasons why adding people to a late project almost always makes matters much worse. First, even if adding people brings the green progress line closer to the blue plan, it will make the red effort line shoot up. It does not make sense to supposedly fix one aspect of the project by breaking another (especially if the project is already using more people than planned, as in Figure A-7). Second, you will have to onboard and train the new people. This requires interrupting the other team members, who often are the most qualified individuals and, importantly, are likely on the critical path; halting or slowing down their work will mean incurring a further delay to the project. You will end up paying both for the ramp-up time for the new people and for the time lost from the existing team who are assisting with the onboarding. Finally, even without the onboarding cost, the new team will be larger—and hence less efficient.

There is one exception to this rule, which is near the project's origin. At the beginning you can invest in wholesale onboarding of the team members. More importantly, you can get away with adding people at the origin because you can pivot to a more aggressive, compressed project design solution. Such a solution typically does require additional resources due to the parallel work. Note that compressing the project will introduce a higher level of risk and complexity, so you need to carefully weigh the full effect of the new solution.

RESOURCE LEAK

Consider the progress and effort projections of Figure A-8. In this project, both the progress and the effort are under the plan, and progress is even under the effort. This is often the result of resource leaks: People are assigned to your project but they are working on someone else's project. As a result, they cannot spend the required effort, and progress lags further. Resource leaks are endemic in the software industry, and I have observed leaks as high as 50% of the effort.

---

1. Frederick P. Brooks, *The Mythical Man-Month* (Addison-Wesley, 1975).

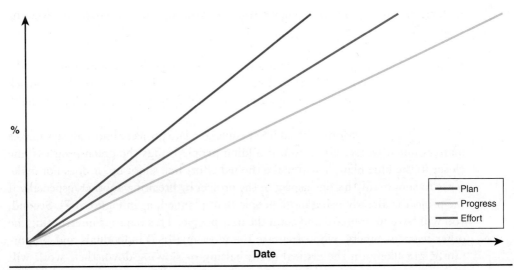

Figure A-8 Projections indicating resource leak

Corrective Actions

When identifying a resource leak, the natural instinct is to simply plug the leak. Plugging the leak, however, will tend to backfire: It could detonate the other project while making you the culprit. The best resolution is to call a meeting between the project manager of the project into which your team is leaking, yourself, and the lowest-level manager responsible for both. After showing the projections chart (such as Figure A-8), you present the overseeing manager with two options. If the other project is more important than your own project, then the green line in Figure A-8 represents what your team can produce under these new circumstances, and the deadline must move to accommodate that. But if your project is more important, then the project manager of the other team must immediately revoke all source control access to your team members and perhaps even assign a few of the other project's top resources to your project to compensate for the damage already done. By presenting the resolution options this way, whatever the manager decides, you win and regain the chance to meet your commitments.

OVERESTIMATING

Consider the progress and effort projections of Figure A-9. While it may look like this project is doing very well because progress is above plan, in reality the project is in danger due to overestimating. As discussed in Chapter 7, overestimating is just as deadly as underestimating. An additional problem with the project in

Figure A-9 is that the project is spending more effort than what the plan called for. This may be because too many people were assigned to the project or because the project is working in an unplanned parallel manner.

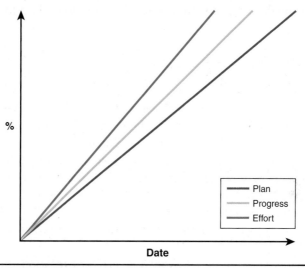

Figure A-9 Projections indicating overestimating

Corrective Actions

One simple corrective action for overestimating is to revise the estimations downward and bring the deadline in. The blue plan line in Figure A-9 will then come up to meet the green progress line, and you can calculate by how much to do just that. Unfortunately, bringing the deadline in likely has only downsides. Often delivering the system ahead of schedule has no benefits. For example, the customer may not pay until the agreed deadline, or the servers may not be ready, or the team might have nothing to do next. At the same time, reducing the duration will increase the pressure on the team. The way people respond to pressure is nonlinear. Some modest pressure may have positive results, whereas excessive pressure demotivates. If the team members respond to the pressure by giving up, the project implodes. It is usually hard to know where that thin line is.

Another corrective action is to keep the deadline where it is but revise the estimations downward and over-deliver by increasing the scope of the project. Adding things to do (perhaps starting work on the next subsystem) will reduce the actual earned value and the green progress line will come down to meet the blue plan line in Figure A-9. Adding value is always a good thing, but it does carry the over-pressure risk.

The best way of fixing overestimation is to release some of your resources. When you do so, the red effort line will go down since a smaller team costs less. The green progress line will come down because the smaller team has a reduced throughput. The smaller team should also be more efficient. If you detect the overestimation early enough, you can even choose a less compressed project solution.

MORE ON PROJECTIONS

The projections allow you to analyze where the project is heading long before an underlying problem becomes severe. Examine Figure A-4 again. Waiting until the project reaches point 2 in the figure and then correcting it up to the blue line requires a painful, if not devastating maneuver. Using projections, you can detect the trend much earlier, and perform a smaller correction before any significant gap appears between the lines. The earlier the action, the more time it has to take effect, the less disruptive it is to the rest of the project, the easier it is to run it past management, and the more likely it is to succeed. It is always better to be proactive than reactive, and an ounce of prevention is often worth a pound of cure.

Very much like driving a car, in your project execution you make frequent small corrections as opposed to a few drastic ones. Good projects are always smooth, whether in the planned earned value, the staffing distribution chart or, as in this case, the progress and effort lines.

Note that the technique shown here is analyzing the trend of the project, not the actual project. This is the correct way of driving the project. To use the car analogy again, you do not drive your car forward by looking down at the pavement or looking strictly in the rear-view mirror. Where the car is now or where it has been is largely irrelevant for driving it forward. You drive your car looking at where the car is going to be and taking corrective actions against that projection.

THE ESSENCE OF A PROJECT

Note that "project" can be both a noun (the project) and a verb (to project). This is not accidental. The essence of a project is the ability to project. It is called a project because you are supposed to project. Conversely, if you do not project, you do not have a project.

HANDLING SCOPE CREEP

Oddly, management may even try to change the scope of the project without modifying the duration and resources assigned to the project. This, in turn, creates a problem with you meeting your commitments.

Combining projections with project design is the ultimate way of handing unanticipated changes to the scope of the project. When anyone tries to increase (or decrease) the scope of the project and asks for your approval or consent, you should politely ask to get back to them with your answer. You now need to redesign the project to assess the consequences of the change. This redesign could be minor if the change does not affect the critical path or the cost and is within the capability of the team. Use the projections to judge your ability to deliver on the new plan from the perspective of the actual throughput and cost. Of course, the change could extend the duration of the project and increase the cost and demand for resources. You may have to choose another project design option, or even devise new project design options altogether.

When you get back to management, present the new duration and total cost that the change requires, including the new projections, and ask if they want to do it. If they cannot afford the new schedule and cost implications, then nothing really changed. If they accept them, then you have new schedule and cost commitments for the project. Either way, you will always meet your commitments. These commitments may not be the original ones the project started with, but then again, you are not the one who changed the plan.

BUILDING TRUST

Most software teams fail to meet their commitments. They have given management no reason to trust them and every reason to distrust them. As a result, management dictates impossible deadlines, while fully expecting them to slip. As discussed in Chapter 7, aggressive deadlines drastically reduce the probability of success, manifesting failure as a self-fulfilling prophecy.

Project tracking is a good way of breaking that vicious cycle. You should share the projections with every possible decision maker and manager. Constantly show the project's current benign status and the future trends. Demonstrate the ability to detect problems months before they raise their head. Insist on (or just take) corrective actions. All of these actions will establish you as a responsible, accountable, trustworthy professional. This will lead to respect and eventually trust. When you have gained the trust of those above you, they will tend to leave you alone to do your work, allowing you to succeed.

B

SERVICE CONTRACT DESIGN

The first part of this book addressed the system architecture: How to decompose the system into its components and services and how to compose the required behavior out of the services. This is not the end of the design and you must continue the process by designing the details of each service.

Detailed design is a vast topic, worthy of its own book. This appendix limits its discussion of detailed design to the most important aspect of the design of a service: the public contract that the service presents to its clients. Only after you have settled on the service contract can you fill in internal design details such as class hierarchies and related design patterns. These internal design details as well as data contracts and operation parameters are domain-specific and, therefore, outside the scope of this appendix. However, in the abstract, the same design principles outlined here for the service contract as a whole apply even at the data contract and parameter levels.

This appendix shows that even with a task as specific to your system as the design of contracts for your services, certain design guidelines and metrics transcend service technology, industry domains, or teams. While the ideas in this appendix are simple, they have profound implications for the way you go about developing your services and structuring the construction work.

IS THIS A GOOD DESIGN?

To understand how to design the services, you must first recognize the attributes of a good or a bad design. Consider the system architecture in Figure B-1. Is this a good design for your system? The system design in Figure B-1 uses a single large component to implement all the requirements of the system. In theory, you could build any system this way, by putting all the code in one monstrous function, with hundreds of arguments and millions of nested lines of conditional code. Yet no one in their right mind would suggest that a single large thing is a good design. It is literally the canonical example of what not to do. According to Chapter 4, you also cannot validate such a design.

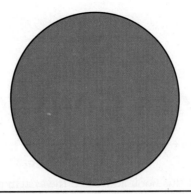

Figure B-1 Monolithic system design

Next, consider the design in Figure B-2. Is this a good design for your system? The system design in Figure B-2 uses a huge number of small components or services to implement the system (to reduce the visual clutter, the figure does not show cross-service interaction lines). In theory, you could build any system this way by placing every requirement in separate service. That, too, is not just a bad design, but another canonical example of what not to do. As with the previous case, you also cannot validate such a design.

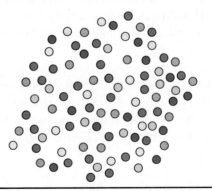

Figure B-2 Super-granular system design

Finally, examine the system design in Figure B-3. Is this a good design for your system? While you cannot state that Figure B-3 is a good design for your system, you could say that it is certainly a better design than a single large component or an explosion of small components.

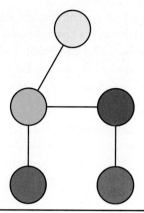

Figure B-3 Modular system design

MODULARITY AND COST

The ability to determine that the system design of Figure B-3 is better than the previous two is surprising. After all, you do not know anything about the nature of the system, the domain, the developers, or the technology—yet you intuitively know it is better. Whenever you evaluate a modular design, you are using a mental model described by Figure B-4.

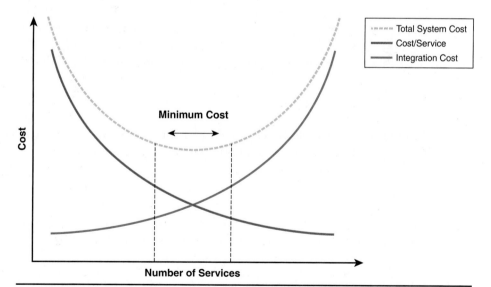

Figure B-4 Size and quantity effect on cost [Image adopted and modified from Juval Lowy, *Programming .NET Components*, 2nd ed. (O'Reilly Media, 2003); Juval Lowy, *Programming WCF Services*, 1st ed. (O'Reilly Media, 2007); and Edward Yourdon and Larry Constantine, *Structured Design* (Prentice-Hall, 1979).]

When you build a system out of smaller building blocks such as services, you have to pay for two elements of cost: the cost of building the services and the cost of putting it all together. You can build a system at any point on the spectrum between one large service and countless little services, and Figure B-4 captures the effect of that decomposition decision on the cost of building the system.

> **Note**   Part 2 of this book discussed system cost as a function of time and the design of the project. Figure B-4 shows another dimension—how the system cost is a function of the architecture of the system and the granularity of the services. Different architectures will have different time–cost–risk curves.

COST PER SERVICE

The implementation cost per service (the blue line in Figure B-4) represents some nonlinear behavior. As the number of services decreases, their size increases (up to one large monolith on the far-left side of the curve). The problem is that as the size of a service increases, its complexity increases in a nonlinear way. A service 2 times as big as another may be 4 times more complex, and a service 4 times as big may be 20 or 100 times more complex. Increased complexity, in turn, induces a nonlinear increase in cost. As a result, cost is a compounded, nonlinear, monotonically increasing function of size. Consequently, as the number of services decreases, service size increases, and with each size increase, the cost explodes in a nonlinear way. In contrast, with a system design that has a multitude of services (the far right side of Figure B-4), the cost per service is miniscule, approaching zero.

INTEGRATION COST

The integration cost of services increases in a nonlinear way with the number of services. This, too, is the result of complexity—in this case, the complexity of the possible interactions. More services imply more possible interactions, adding more complexity. As mentioned in Chapter 12, due to connectivity and ripple effects, as the number of services (n) increases, complexity grows in proportion to n^2 but can even be on the order of n^n. This interaction complexity directly affects the integration cost, which is why the integration cost (the red line in Figure B-4) is also a nonlinear curve. Consequently, at the far right side of Figure B-4, the integration cost shoots up ever higher as the number of services increases. In contrast, at the far left side of the curve where there is perhaps only single large service, the integration cost approaches zero since there is nothing to integrate.

AREA OF MINIMUM COST

With any given system you will always have to pay for both elements of cost (implementation cost and integration cost). The dashed green line in Figure B-4 represents the sum of these two cost elements, or the total system cost. As you can see, for any system there is an area of minimum cost, where the services are not too big and not too small, not too many and not too few. Whenever you design a system, you must bring it to the area of minimum cost (and keep it there). Note that you do not necessarily wish to be in the very minimum of the total cost curve, but merely in the area of minimum cost where the total system cost is relatively flat. Once the curve begins to level, the cost of finding the absolute minimum will exceed any savings in system cost. As mentioned in Chapter 4, every design effort always has a point of diminishing return where it is simply good enough.

What you must avoid are the edges of the chart, because these edges are nonlinearly worse and become many multiples (even dozens of times) more expensive. The challenge with building a nonlinearly more expensive system is that the tools all organizations have at their disposal are fundamentally linear tools. The organization can give you another developer and then another developer, or another month and then another month. But if the nature of the underlying problem is nonlinear, you will never catch up. Systems designed outside the area of minimum cost have already failed before anyone has written the first line of code.

> **Note** Functional decomposition designs always end up at the nonlinear edges of Figure B-4. As shown in Chapter 2, functional decomposition leads to either an explosion of small areas of functionally or a few massive accumulations of functionality, sometimes even side by side (see Figure 2-2).

As explained in Chapter 4, a good volatility-based decomposition provides the smallest set of building blocks that you can put together to satisfy all requirements—known and unknown, present and future. Such a decomposition yields a service count in the area of minimum cost, but it says nothing about their shape. Even when the decomposition follows *The Method* guidelines, keeping the services in the area of minimum cost requires you to design each service contract correctly.

SERVICES AND CONTRACTS

Each service in the system exposes a contract to its clients. The **contract** is merely a set of operations that the clients can call. As such, the contract is the public interface that the service presents to the world. Many programming languages even use the `interface` keyword to define the service contract. While the service contract is an interface, not all interfaces are service contracts. Service contracts are a formal interface that the service commits to support, unchanged.

To use an analogy from the human world, life is full of both formal and informal contracts. An employment contract defines (often using legal jargon) the obligations of both the employer and the employee to each other. A commercial contract between two companies defines their interactions as a service provider and a service consumer. These are formal forms of interfacing, and the parties to the contract often face severe implications if they violate the contract or change its terms. In contrast, when you hail a taxi, there is an implied informal contract: The driver will take you safely to your destination, and you will pay for this service. Neither of you signed a formal contract describing the nature of that interaction.

CONTRACTS AS FACETS

A contract goes beyond being just a formal interface: It represents a facet of the supporting entity to the outside world. For example, a person can sign an employment contract representing that person as an employee. That person could have other facets, but the employer only sees and cares about that particular facet. A person can sign additional contracts such as a land lease contract, a marriage contract, a mortgage contract, and so on. Each one of these contracts is a facet of the person: as an employee, as a landlord, as a spouse, or as a homeowner. Similarly, a service can support more than one contract.

FROM SERVICE DESIGN TO CONTRACT DESIGN

Well-designed services are in the area of minimum cost of Figure B-4. Unfortunately, it is difficult to answer the fundamental question of what makes a good service in this area. What you can do is go through a series of reasonable reductions until you find a question that you can answer. The first reduction assumes a one-to-one ratio between services and their contracts. Given this assumption, you could relabel Figure B-4, replacing the word "Service" with the word "Contract," and the behavior of the chart will remain unchanged.

In reality, a single service can support multiple contracts, and multiple services can support a specific contract. In these cases, the curves in Figure B-4 shift left to right or up and down, but their behavior remains the same.

ATTRIBUTES OF GOOD CONTRACTS

Under the assumption that services and contracts are mapped one-to-one, you have transformed the question "What is a good service?" into the question "What is a good contract?" Good contracts are logically consistent, cohesive, and independent facets of the service. These attributes are best explained using analogies from daily life.

Would you sign an employment contract that states you can only work at the company so long as you live at a specific address? You would reject such a contract because it is logically inconsistent to condition your employment status on your address. After all, if you do the agreed-upon work to the expected standard, where you live is irrelevant. Good contracts are always logically consistent.

Would you sign an employment contract that does not specify how much you are paid? Again, you would reject it. Good contracts are always cohesive and contain all the aspects required to describe the interaction—no more, no less.

Would you make your marriage contract dependent on your employment contract? You would reject this contract because the independence of the contract is just as important. Each contract or facet should stand alone and operate independently of the other contracts.

These attributes also guide the process of obtaining the contract. Would you pay a real estate lawyer to craft a contract just for you to rent your apartment? Or would you search the web for an apartment rental contract, print the first search result, fill in the blanks with the address and the rent, and be done with it? If an online contract is good enough for millions of other rentals without being specific to any apartment (which would truly be a nontrivial achievement), would it not be good enough for you? The contract must have evolved to include all the cohesive details such as rent and to avoid the inconsistent things like where the renters work. It must also be independent of other contracts—that is, a true stand-alone facet.

Note that you are not searching for a better contract than anyone else is using. You simply want to reuse the very same contract that everyone else is using. It is precisely because it is so reusable that it is a good contract. The final observation is that logically consistent, cohesive, and independent contracts are reusable contracts.

Note that reusability is not a binary trait of a contract. Every contract lies somewhere on the spectrum of reusability. The more reusable the contract, the more it is logically consistent, cohesive, and independent. Imagine the contract in front of the service in Figure B-1. That contract is massive, and it is extremely specific for that particular service. It is certainly logically inconsistent because it is a bloated dumping ground for everything that the system does. The likelihood that anyone else in the world will ever reuse that service contract is basically zero.

Next, imagine the contract on one of the tiny services in Figure B-2. That contract is miniscule and extremely specialized for its context. Something so small cannot possibly be cohesive. Again, the likelihood that anyone else will ever reuse that contract is zero.

The services in Figure B-3 offer at least some hope. Perhaps the contracts on the services in Figure B-3 have evolved to include everything pertaining to their interactions—no more, no less. The small number of interactions also indicates independent facets. The contracts could very well be reusable.

Contracts as Elements of Reuse

An important observation is that the basic element of reuse is the contract, not the service itself. For example, the computer mouse I use to write this book is unlike any other mouse. Each part of it is not reusable. The case of the mouse was designed for this particular mouse model, and I cannot mount it on any other mouse (except another instance of the same model) without costly modification. However, the interface "mouse–hand" is reusable; I can operate that mouse, and so can you. Your mouse supports exactly the same interface; put differently, it reuses the interface. Many thousands of different mouse models exist, yet it is precisely the fact that across all models each reuses the same interface which is the ultimate indication of a good interface. In fact, the interface "mouse–hand" should be called "tool–hand" (see Figure B-5).

Figure B-5 Reusing interfaces [Figure inspired by Matt Ridley, *The Rational Optimist: How Prosperity Evolves* (HarperCollins, 2010). Images: Mountainpix/Shutterstock; New Africa/Shutterstock.]

Our species has been reusing the "tool–hand" interface since prehistoric times. While no grain of stone from the stone axe is reusable in the mouse, and no piece of electronics from the mouse is useful in the stone axe, both reuse the same interface. Good interfaces are reusable, while the underlying services never are.

FACTORING CONTRACTS

When designing the contracts for your services, you must always think in terms of elements of reuse. That is the only way to assure that even after architecture and decomposition, your services will remain in the area of minimum cost. Note that the obligation to design reusable contracts has nothing to do with whether someone will actually end up reusing the contracts. The degree of actual reuse or demand for the contract by other parties is completely immaterial. You must design the contracts as if they will be reused countless times in perpetuity, across multiple systems including your current one and those of your competitors. A simple example will go a long way to demonstrate this point.

DESIGN EXAMPLE

Suppose you need to implement a software system for running a point-of-sale register. The requirements for the system likely have use cases for looking up an item's price, integrating with inventory, accepting payment, and tracking loyalty programs, among others. All of this can easily be done using *The Method* and the appropriate *Managers*, *Engines*, and so on. For illustration purposes, suppose the system needs to connect to a barcode scanner and read an item's identifier with it. The barcode scanner device is nothing more than a *Resource* to the system, so you need to design the service contract for the corresponding *ResourceAccess* service. The requirements for the barcode scanner access service are that it should be able to scan an item's code, adjust the width of the scanning beam, and manage the communication port to the scanner by opening and closing the port. You could define the `IScannerAccess` service contract like so:

```
interface IScannerAccess
{
   long ScanCode();
   void AdjustBeam();
   void OpenPort();
   void ClosePort();
}
```

The `IScannerAccess` service contract supports the required features of a scanner. This easily enables different types of service providers, such as the `BarcodeService` and the `QRCodeService` to implement the `IScannerAccess` contract:

```
class BarcodeScanner : IScannerAccess
{...}
class QRCodeScanner : IScannerAccess
{...}
```

You may feel content because you have reused the `IScannerAccess` service contract across multiple services.

FACTORING DOWN

Sometime later, the retailer contacts you with the following issue: In some cases it is better to use other devices, such as a numerical keypad, to enter item code. However, the `IScannerAccess` contract assumes the underlying device uses some kind of an optical scanner. As such, it is unable to manage non-optical devices such as numerical keypads or radio frequency identification (RFID) readers. From a reuse perspective, it is better to abstract the actual reading mechanism and rename the scanning operation to a reading operation. After all, which mechanism the hardware device uses to read the item code should be irrelevant to the system. You should also rename the contract to `IReaderAccess` and ensure there is nothing in the contract's design that precludes all types of code readers from reusing the contract. For example, the `AdjustBeam()` operation is meaningless for a keypad. It is better to break up the original the `IScannerAccess` into two contracts, and factor down the offending operation:

```
interface IReaderAccess
{
    long ReadCode();
    void OpenPort();
    void ClosePort();
}
interface IScannerAccess : IReaderAccess
{
    void AdjustBeam();
}
```

This enables now proper reuse of `IReaderAccess`:

```
class BarcodeScanner : IScannerAccess
{...}
class QRCodeScanner : IScannerAccess
{...}
class KeypadReader : IReaderAccess
{...}
class RFIDReader : IReaderAccess
{...}
```

FACTORING SIDEWAYS

With that change done, more time passes, and the retailer decides to have the software also control the conveyer belt attached to the point-of-sale workstation. This requires the software to start and stop the belt, as well as manage its communication port. While the conveyer belt uses the same kind of communication port as the reading devices, the belt cannot reuse `IReaderAccess` because the contract does not support a conveyer belt, and the belt cannot read codes. Furthermore, there is a long list of such peripheral devices, each with its own functionality, and the introduction of every one of them will duplicate parts of the other contracts.

Observe that every change in the business domain leads to a reflected change in the system's domain. This is the hallmark of a bad design. A good system design should be resilient to changes in the business domain.

The root problem is that `IReaderAccess` is a poorly designed contract. Even though all the operations are things a reader should support, `ReadCode()` is not logically related to `OpenPort()` and `ClosePort()`. The reading operation involves one facet of the device, as a provider of codes, something that is essential to the business of the retailer (it is an atomic business operation), while the port management involves a different facet relating to the entity as communication device. In this regard, `IReaderAccess` is not logically consistent: It is a mere grab-bag of every requirement for the service. `IReaderAccess` is more like the design in Figure B-1 than anything else.

A better approach is to factor sideways the `OpenPort()` and `ClosePort()` operations to a separate contract called `ICommunicationDevice`:

```
interface ICommunicationDevice
{
    void OpenPort();
    void ClosePort();
}
interface IReaderAccess
{
    long ReadCode();
}
```

The implementing services will have to support both contracts:

```
class BarcodeScanner : IScannerAccess,ICommunicationDevice
{...}
```

Note that the sum of work inside `BarcodeScanner` is exactly the same as with the original `IScannerAccess`. However, because the communication facet is independent of the reading facet, other entities (such as belts) can reuse the `ICommunicationDevice` service contract and support it:

```
interface IBeltAccess
{
    void Start();
    void Stop();
}
class ConveyerBelt : IBeltAccess,ICommunicationDevice
{...}
```

This design allows you to decouple the communication–management aspect of the devices from the actual device type (be it barcode readers or conveyer belts).

The real issue with the point-of-sale system was not the specifics of the reading devices, but rather the volatility of the type of devices connected to the system. Your architecture should rely on volatility-based decomposition. As this simple example shows, the principle extends to the contract design of individual services as well.

FACTORING UP

Factoring operations into separate contracts (like `ICommunicationDevice` out of `IReaderAccess`) is usually called for whenever there is a weak logical relation between the operations in the contract.

Sometimes identical operations are found in several unrelated contracts, and these operations are logically related to their respective contracts. Not including them would make the contract less cohesive. For example, suppose that for safety reasons, the system must immediately abort all devices. In addition, all devices must support some kind of diagnostics that assures they operate within safe limits. Logically, aborting is just as much a scanner operation as reading, and just as much a belt operation as starting or stopping.

In such cases, you can factor the service contracts up, into a hierarchy of contracts instead of separate contracts:

```
interface IDeviceControl
{
    void Abort();
    long RunDiagnostics();
}
interface IReaderAccess : IDeviceControl
{...}
interface IBeltAccess : IDeviceControl
{...}
```

CONTRACT DESIGN METRICS

The three contract design techniques (factoring down to a derived contract, factoring sideways to a new contract, or factoring up to a base contract) result in fine-tuned, smaller, and more reusable contracts. Having more reusable contracts is certainly a benefit, and the smaller contracts are necessary when starting with bloated contracts. But too much of a good thing is a bad thing. The risk is that you keep doing this until eventually you end up with contracts that are too granular and fragmented, as in Figure B-2. You therefore need to balance the two opposing forces: the cost of implementing the service contracts versus the cost of putting them together. The way to strike the balance is to use design metrics.

MEASURING CONTRACTS

It is possible to measure contracts and rank them from worst to best. For example, you could measure the cyclomatic complexly of the code. You are unlikely to have a simple implementation of a large complex contract, and the complexity of overly granular contracts would be horrendous. You could measure the defects associated with the underlying services: Low-quality services are likely the result of the complexity of poor contracts. You could measure how many times each contract is reused in the system, and how many times a contract was checked out and changed: Clearly a contract that is reused everywhere and has never changed is a good contract. You could assign weights to these measurements and rank the results. I have conducted such measurements for years across different technology stacks, systems, industries, and teams. Regardless of this diversity, some uniform metrics have emerged that are valuable in gauging the quality of contracts.

SIZE METRICS

Service contracts with just one operation are possible, but you should avoid them. A service contract is a facet of an entity, and that facet must be pretty dull if you can express it with just one operation. Examine that single operation and ask yourself some questions about it. Does it use too many parameters? Is it too coarse, so that you should factor the single operation into several operations? Should you factor this operation into an existing service contract? Is it something that should best reside in the next subsystem to be built? I cannot tell you which corrective action to take, but I can tell you that a contract with just one operation is a red flag, and you must investigate it further.

The optimal number of service contract operations is between 3 and 5. If you design a service contract with more operations, perhaps 6 to 9, you are still doing relatively well, but you have started to drift away from the area of minimum cost in Figure B-4. Take a look at the operations and determine whether any can be collapsed into other operations, since it is quite possible to over-factor operations. If the service contract has 12 or more operations, it is very likely a poor design. You should look for ways to factor the operations into either separate service contracts or a hierarchy of contracts. You must immediately reject contracts with 20 operations or more, as there are no possible circumstances where such contracts are benign. Such a contract is certain to plaster over some grave design mistake. You must have little tolerance for large contracts because of their nonlinear effects on development and maintenance costs.

Interestingly, in the human world you always use contract size metrics to assess the quality of a contract. For example, would you sign an employment contract that has just one sentence? You would decline this contract because there is no way that a single sentence (or even a single paragraph) could capture all the aspects of you as an employee. Such a contract is certain to leaves out crucial details such as liability or termination and may incorporate other contracts with which you are unfamiliar. On the other extreme, would you sign an employment contract containing 2000 pages? You would not even bother to read it, regardless of what it promises. Even a 20-page contract is cause for concern: If the nature of the employment requires so many pages, the contract is likely taxing and complex. But if the contract has 3–5 pages, you may not sign it, but you will read it carefully. From a reuse perspective, note that the employer will likely furnish you with the same contract as all other employees have. Anything other than total reuse would be alarming.

AVOID PROPERTIES

Many service development stacks deliberately do not have property semantics in contract definitions, but you can easily circumvent those by creating property-like operations, such as the following:

```
string GetName();
string SetName();
```

In the context of service contracts, avoid properties and property-like operations. Properties imply state and implementation details. When the service exposes properties, the client knows about such details, and when the service changes the client (or clients) would change along with it. You should not bother clients with the use of properties or even the knowledge of them. Good service contracts allow clients to invoke abstract operations without caring about the actual implementation. The clients simply invoke operations and let the service worry about how to manage its state.

A good interaction between a service provider and a service consumer is always behavioral. That interaction should be phrased in terms of `DoSomething()`, such as `Abort()`. How the service goes about doing that should be of no concern to the client. This, too, mimics real life: It is always better to tell than to ask.

Avoiding properties is also a good practice in any distributed system. It is always preferable to keep the data where the data is, and only invoke operations on it.

LIMIT THE NUMBER OF CONTRACTS

A service should not support more than one or two contracts. Since contracts are independent facets of the service, if the service supports three or more independent business aspects, it suggests the service may be too big.

Interestingly, you can derive the number of contracts per service using the estimation techniques of Chapter 7. Using only orders of magnitude, should the number of contracts per service be 1, 10, 100, or 1000? Clearly, 100 or 1000 contracts is a poor design, and even 10 contracts seems very large. So, in order of magnitude, the number of contracts per service is 1. Using the "factor of 2" technique, you can narrow the range further: Is the number of contracts more like 1, 2, or 4? It cannot be 8 because that is almost 10, which is already ruled out. So the number of contracts per service is between 1 and 4. This is still a wide range. To reduce the uncertainty, you can use the PERT technique, with 1 as the lowest estimation, 4 as the highest, and 2 as the likely number. The PERT calculation yields 2.2 as the number of contracts per service:

$$2.2 = \frac{1 + 4 * 2 + 4}{6}$$

In practice, in well-designed systems, the majority of services I have examined had only one or two contracts, with a single contract as the more common case. Of the services with two or more contracts, the additional contracts were almost always non-business-related contracts that captured aspects such as security, safety, persistence, or instrumentation, and those contracts were reused across other services.

> **Note** A good way of avoiding a proliferation of services is to add contracts to the services. For example, if your architecture calls for eight *Managers*, which exceeds the guideline from Chapter 3, perhaps you could represent some of these *Managers* as additional independent facets on other *Managers* and reduce the number of *Managers*.

USING METRICS

The service contract design metrics are evaluation tools, not validation tools. Complying with the metrics does not mean you have a good design—but violating the metric implies you have a bad design. As an example, consider the first version of `IScannerAccess`. That service contract has 4 operations, right in the middle of the range of the 3 to 5 operations metric, yet the contract was logically inconsistent.

Avoid trying to design to meet the metrics. Like any design task, service contract design is iterative in nature. Spend the time necessary to identify the reusable contract your service should expose, and do not worry about the metrics. If you violate the metrics, keep working until you have decent contracts. Keep examining the evolving contracts to see if they are reusable across systems and projects. Ask yourself if the contracts are logically consistent, cohesive, and independent facets. Once you have devised such contracts, you will see that they match the metrics.

THE CONTRACT DESIGN CHALLENGE

The ideas and techniques discussed in this appendix are straightforward, self-evident, and simple. Designing contracts is an acquired skill, and practice goes a long way toward getting it done quickly and correctly. However, there is a big difference between "simple" and "simplistic." While the ideas in this appendix are simple, they are far from simplistic. Indeed, life is full of ideas that are simple but not simplistic. For example, you may wish to be healthy. That is a simple idea that may involve changes to your diet, lifestyle, daily routine, and even work—none of which is simplistic.

Coming up with reusable service contracts is a time-consuming, highly contemplative task. It is absolutely paramount to get the contracts right, or you will face a nonlinearly worse problem (see Figure B-4). The real challenge is not designing the contracts (which is simple enough), but rather getting management's support to do so. Most managers are unaware of the consequences of incorrect contract design. By rushing to implementation, they will cause the project to fail. This is especially the case with a junior hand-off (see Chapter 14).

Even senior developers may require mentorship to be able to design contracts correctly, and you, as the architect, can guide and train them. This will enable you to make the contract design part of each service life cycle. With a junior team, you cannot trust the developers to come up with correct reusable contracts; most likely, they will come up with service contracts resembling Figure B-1 or Figure B-2. You must use the approach of Chapter 14 to either carve up the time to design the contracts before work begins or, preferably, use a few senior skilled developers to design the contracts of the next set of services in parallel to the construction activities for the current set of services (see Figure 14-6). You should use the concepts of this appendix and Figure B-4 to educate your manager on what it really takes to ship well-designed services.

C

DESIGN STANDARD

The ideas in this book are simple and consistent both internally and with every other engineering discipline. However, it can be overwhelming at first to come to terms with this new way of thinking about system and project design. Over time and with practice, applying these ideas becomes second nature. To facilitate absorbing them all, this appendix offers a concise design standard. The design standard captures all the design rules from this book in one place as a checklist. The list on its own will not mean much, because you still have to know the context for each item. Nevertheless, referring to the standard can ensure that you do not omit an important attribute or consideration. This makes the standard essential for successful system and project design by helping you enforce the best practices and avoid the pitfalls.

The standard contains two types of items: directives and guidelines. A **directive** is a rule that you should never violate, since doing so is certain to cause the project to fail. A **guideline** is a piece of advice that you should follow unless you have a strong and unusual justification for going against it. Violating a guideline alone is not certain to cause the project to fail, but too many violations will tip the project into failure. It is also unlikely that if you abide by the directives that you will have any reason to go against the guidelines.

THE PRIME DIRECTIVE

Never design against the requirements.

DIRECTIVES

1. Avoid functional decomposition.
2. Decompose based on volatility.
3. Provide a composable design.
4. Offer features as aspects of integration, not implementation.
5. Design iteratively, build incrementally.
6. Design the project to build the system.
7. Drive educated decisions with viable options that differ by schedule, cost, and risk.
8. Build the project along its critical path.
9. Be on time throughout the project.

SYSTEM DESIGN GUIDELINES

1. Requirements
   a. Capture required behavior, not required functionality.
   b. Describe required behavior with use cases.
   c. Document all use cases that contain nested conditions with activity diagrams.
   d. Eliminate solutions masquerading as requirements.
   e. Validate the system design by ensuring it supports all core use cases.

2. Cardinality
   a. Avoid more than five *Managers* in a system without subsystems.
   b. Avoid more than a handful of subsystems.
   c. Avoid more than three *Managers* per subsystem.
   d. Strive for a golden ratio of *Engines* to *Managers*.
   e. Allow *ResourceAccess* components to access more than one *Resource* if necessary.

3. Attributes
   a. Volatility should decrease top-down.
   b. Reuse should increase top-down.
   c. Do not encapsulate changes to the nature of the business.

    d. *Managers* should be almost expendable.

    e. Design should be symmetric.

    f. Never use a public communication channels for internal system interactions.

4. Layers

    a. Avoid open architecture.

    b. Avoid semi-closed/semi-open architecture.

    c. Prefer a closed architecture.

       i. Do not call up.

       ii. Do not call sideways (except queued calls between *Managers*).

       iii. Do not call more than one layer down.

       iv. Resolve attempts at opening the architecture by using queued calls or asynchronous event publishing.

    d. Extend the system by implementing subsystems.

5. Interaction rules

    a. All components can call *Utilities*.

    b. *Managers* and *Engines* can call *ResourceAccess*.

    c. *Managers* can call *Engines*.

    d. *Managers* can queue calls to another *Manager*.

6. Interaction don'ts

    a. *Clients* do not call multiple *Managers* in the same use case.

    b. *Managers* do not queue calls to more than one *Manager* in the same use case.

    c. *Engines* do not receive queued calls.

    d. *ResourceAccess* components do not receive queued calls.

    e. *Clients* do not publish events.

    f. *Engines* do not publish events.

    g. *ResourceAccess* components do not publish events.

    h. *Resources* do not publish events.

    i. *Engines*, *ResourceAccess*, and *Resources* do not subscribe to events.

PROJECT DESIGN GUIDELINES

1. General

    a. Do not design a clock.

    b. Never design a project without an architecture that encapsulates the volatilities.

    c. Capture and verify planning assumptions.

    d. Follow the design of project design.

    e. Design several options for the project; at a minimum, design normal, compressed, and subcritical solutions.

    f. Communicate with management in Optionality.

    g. Always go through SDP review before the main work starts.

2. Staffing

    a. Avoid multiple architects.

    b. Have a core team in place at the beginning.

    c. Ask for only the lowest level of staffing required to progress unimpeded along the critical path.

    d. Always assign resources based on float.

    e. Ensure correct staffing distribution.

    f. Ensure a shallow S curve for the planned earned value.

    g. Always assign components to developers in a 1:1 ratio.

    h. Strive for task continuity.

3. Integration

    a. Avoid mass integration points.

    b. Avoid integration at the end of the project.

4. Estimations

    a. Do not overestimate.

    b. Do not underestimate.

    c. Strive for accuracy, not precision.

    d. Always use a quantum of five days in any activity estimation.

    e. Estimate the project as a whole to validate or even initiate your project design.

    f. Reduce estimation uncertainty.

    g. When required, maintain correct estimation dialog.

5. Project network

    a. Treat resource dependencies as dependencies.

    b. Verify all activities reside on a chain that starts and ends on a critical path.

    c. Verify all activities have a resource assigned to them.

    d. Avoid node diagrams.

    e. Prefer arrow diagrams.

    f. Avoid god activities.

    g. Break large projects into a network of networks.

    h. Treat near-critical chains as critical chains.

    i. Strive for cyclomatic complexity as low as 10 to 12.

    j. Design by layers to reduce complexity.

6. Time and cost

    a. Accelerate the project first by quick and clean practices rather than compression.

    b. Never commit to a project in the death zone.

    c. Compress with parallel work rather than top resources.

    d. Compress with top resources carefully and judiciously.

    e. Avoid compression higher than 30%.

    f. Avoid projects with efficiency higher than 25%.

    g. Compress the project even if the likelihood of pursuing any of the compressed options is low.

7. Risk

    a. Customize the ranges of criticality risk to your project.

    b. Adjust floats outliers with activity risk.

    c. Decompress the normal solution past the tipping point on the risk curve.

       i. Target decompression to 0.5 risk.

       ii. Value the risk tipping point more than a specific risk number.

    d. Do not over-decompress.

    e. Decompress design-by-layers solutions, perhaps aggressively so.

    f. Keep normal solutions at less than 0.7 risk.

    g. Avoid risk lower than 0.3.

    h. Avoid risk higher than 0.75.

    i. Avoid project options risker or safer than the risk crossover points.

PROJECT TRACKING GUIDELINES

1. Adopt binary exit criteria for internal phases of an activity.

2. Assign consistent phase weights across all activities.

3. Track progress and effort on a weekly basis.

4. Never base your progress reports on features.

5. Always base your progress reports on integration points.
6. Track the float of near-critical chains.

SERVICE CONTRACT DESIGN GUIDELINES

1. Design reusable service contracts.
2. Comply with service contract design metrics
   a. Avoid contracts with a single operation.
   b. Strive to have 3 to 5 operations per service contract.
   c. Avoid service contracts with more than 12 operations.
   d. Reject service contracts with 20 or more operations.
3. Avoid property-like operations.
4. Limit the number of contracts per service to 1 or 2.
5. Avoid junior hand-offs.
6. Have only the architect or competent senior developers design the contracts.

INDEX